Struts 2 in Action

Struts 2 in Action

DONALD BROWN
CHAD MICHAEL DAVIS
SCOTT STANLICK

MANNING

Greenwich
(74° w. long.)

For online information and ordering of this and other Manning books, please visit
www.manning.com. The publisher offers discounts on this book when ordered in quantity.
For more information, please contact:

Special Sales Department
Manning Publications Co.
Sound View Court 3B   fax: (609) 877-8256
Greenwich, CT 06830   email: orders@manning.com

 Manning Publications Co.   Copyeditor: Benjamin Berg
Sound View Court 3B   Typesetter: Gordan Salinovic
Greenwich, CT 06830   Cover designer: Leslie Haimes

ISBN 1-933988-07-X
Printed in the United States of America
1 2 3 4 5 6 7 8 9 10 – MAL – 13 12 11 10 09 08

To world peace
and a global redistribution of prosperity

brief contents

contents

preface

In mid-2006, I started a new project. Since in this case I was developing for myself, under the banner of my own company, I had the pleasure of making all the technological choices myself. Most of my previous experience had been with Struts 1, a framework that proved to me that you wouldn't want to work without a framework, but no longer convinced me that I was working with the best option available. For my new project, I was going to choose one of the new, second-generation web application frameworks.

To be honest, I can no longer recall why I chose Struts 2. I know that I also considered using Spring's MVC framework, but something made me go with Struts 2. I probably chose Struts 2 because I figured it would be more widely in demand in my contract work. At any rate, the choice was not that impassioned. But once I started development, I almost couldn't believe the power of this new framework. It's the perfect blend of a dedication to software engineering, which yields high levels of architectural componentization and flexibility, and a willingness to be influenced by the innovations of others. While many people love to compare frameworks and quibble over which is best, we think that any of the serious contenders will quickly absorb the strengths of other technologies. The Struts 2 commitment to convention over configuration aptly demonstrates this.

So I was sold on Struts 2 by the time Manning contacted me later that year to see if I was interested in teaming up with Don Brown to write a Struts 2 book for their *In Action* series. I was looking at a busy upcoming year, but this was, as they say, an offer I couldn't refuse. It's been a pleasure working with Don, but mostly it's just nice to be able to pick his brain about the details of Struts 2. That alone is worth the price of admission.

Originally, the project was to rewrite Patrick Lightbody and Jason Carreira's *Web-Work in Action*. The core architecture of Struts 2, as you'll learn in this book, was taken directly from *WebWork in Action*. Before any Struts 2 books were available, many developers, myself included, used that book to learn Struts 2. As we started working on our book, it became clear that Struts 2, thanks to its large and highly active community, had moved far beyond that core. As it turns out, we wrote an entirely new book. Nonetheless, I learned Struts 2 from reading *WebWork in Action*, so my indebtedness to that book is nontrivial.

Things moved pretty fast, narratively speaking, from that time. We spent the better part of the next year writing, revising, gathering feedback from reviewers and Manning Early Access Program participants, and revising again. At some point, we realized the book would never get done if we didn't get some help. We were lucky to find Scott Stanlick, a metalhead drummer and Struts 2 activist, to make a contribution of several strong chapters that helped wrap the project up.

Now the book is done and you have it in your hot little hands. Enjoy. I hope the work we put in pays off by easing your entry into the world of Struts 2. Please visit the Manning Author Online forum to give us feedback and share with the community.

CHAD DAVIS

acknowledgments

We'd like to acknowledge all of the people who played important roles in the creation of this book. First of all, the project wouldn't have even started if not for Jackie Carter, Michael Stephens, and Marjan Bace of Manning Publications. After that, any coherence that the book may exhibit is largely to the credit of our developmental editor Cynthia Kane. We'd also like to thank Benjamin Berg, Dottie Marsico, Mary Piergies, Karen Tegtmeyer, Katie Tennant, Anna Welles, and any other folks at Manning whose efforts we're less aware of than we probably should be.

We'd also like to thank all of the developers who've spent time reading this manuscript and pointing out all of the problems. In particular, we'd like to thank our technical reviewer Wes Wannemacher, who went through the manuscript one last time shortly before it went to press. The following reviewers proved invaluable in the evolution of this book from manuscript to something worth a reader's investment of time and money: Christopher Schultz, Jeff Cunningham, Rick Evans, Joseph Hoover, Riccardo Audano, Matthew Payne, Bill Fly, Nhoel Sangalang, Matt Michalak, Jason Kolter, Patrick Steger, Kiryl Martsinkevich, Maggie Niemann, Patrick Dennis, Horaci Macias Viel, Tony Niemann, Peter Pavlovich, Andrew Shannon, Bas Vodde, and Wahid Sadik.

Finally, we'd like to extend a sincere thank you to the people who participated in the Manning Early Access Program. In particular, those who've left feedback in the Author Online forum have had a strong impact on the quality of the final printed product.

And for providing Spanish translations of the text resources, we'd like to thank Matthew Lindsey.

Thanks to all!

DON BROWN

This book started life as "Struts in Action, Second Edition," with new material building on the popular first edition by Ted Husted. The talented, now former, Manning editor Jackie Carter was at the helm, and my coauthor was the dependable Nick Heudecker. We were about two-thirds through writing the book when I timidly admitted to my editor that I had started work on Struts 2. Needless to say, the soon to be outdated material was set aside and this new project begun. Along with an updated topic came a highly recommended coauthor, Chad Davis, who has proven time and time again to be worth his weight in gold. To help us get the book out the door, the energetic Scott Stanlick joined the team and kept things moving along. Many thanks to our development editors and production team, who constantly impressed me with their thoroughness and dedication.

Struts 2 wouldn't be where it is today without the hard work of the Struts and Web-Work communities. It is the product of one of the few mergers in the open source world, and its success is a testament to the quality of both communities. In particular, thanks to the project founders Craig R. McClanahan (Struts), Rickard Öberg (Web-Work 1), and Jason Carreira and Patrick Lightbody (WebWork 2) for their vision and follow-through. When it came time to bring the WebWork 2 code into the Apache Struts project to jumpstart Struts 2, the core WebWork 2 developers Rene Gielen, Rainer Hermanns, Toby Jee, Alexandru Popescu, and Ian Roughley, in addition to Jason and Patrick, put in the hours to make Struts 2 a reality. Thanks to dependable Struts developers like Ted Husted, Martin Cooper, James Mitchell, Niall Pemberton, Laurie Harper, Paul Benedict, and Wendy Smoak for helping with the integration process. Since then, committers like Bob Lee, Musachy Barroso, Antonio Petrelli, Nils-Helge Garli, Philip Luppens, Tom Schneider, Matt Raible, Dave Newton, Brian Pontarelli, Wes Wannemacher, and Jeromy Evans have kept the fire going, developing key features like the plug-in system, portlet support, convention-based configuration, and many integration plug-ins.

Finally, my personal thanks to my best friend and wife Julie, and the constant source of distraction (in a good way) that is my son, Makoa. Thank you Mom and Dad for teaching me to constantly challenge myself, yet remain balanced. Thanks to Rudy Rania at BAE Systems and the Atlassian cofounders Mike Cannon-Brooks and Scott Farquhar for supporting open source and my involvement with Struts. Thanks to all the great volunteers at the Apache Software Foundation and thanks to you, the Struts community.

CHAD DAVIS

I would like to begin by thanking my wife Mary, who actually earned money during the past year, thus keeping the mortgage paid and food on the table. I'd also like to thank Dr. Coskun Bayrak, who insisted years ago that I apply my writing skills to my knowledge of computers, meager as both are. I am also thankful to my mother and father, who somehow convinced me I could do pretty much anything. Finally, I'd like to thank both Don Brown and Scott Stanlick for being such great guys, whom I hope to meet someday in person.

SCOTT STANLICK

I would like to thank the following for helping me procure, endure, and survive this writing gig:

The infamous Ted Husted for nominating me for the project and Manning's very own Michael Stephens for connecting the dots to make it happen.

Cynthia Kane and Chad Davis for helping me reach my Gmail free space threshold. It's amazing how well you can get to know people you couldn't even pick out of a police lineup! Of course, I have no firsthand knowledge of either one of them tangled up with the law.

Dave (d.), Laurie, Wes, and so many others on the mailing lists for helping me solve the coding problems when few others knew what the heck I was talking about.

My wife Jamie Kay for cheerleading me on and picking up the slack all those nights and weekends while this project had me holdup in my office writing, cursing, and coding. She quietly took care of everything and never complained once. Norah Jones, Neil Young, and Sheryl Crow for easing me back into sanity when I was about to jump. 54th Street Bar & Grill for providing the friendliest brews and BBQ during my late dinner breaks. Our heavenly father who brought the warm breeze through my office window so many evenings as I sat there writing. The wonderful Japanese oak Pro-Mark drumsticks that stood up during drum therapy. My understanding friends who didn't freak during the year I did not return their calls. The fine baristas at Starbucks and the makers of Red Bull for keeping me wired. Advil, Google and Pizza Hut. And you who are now reading our work as you begin your journey to Struts 2. I hope this book makes your travel safe and enjoyable.

about this book

Welcome to Struts 2! If you've picked up this book, we suspect you're a Java developer working with web applications who's somehow or other heard about Struts 2. Perhaps you've worked with the Struts 1 framework in the past, perhaps you've worked with another framework, or perhaps this is your first step into Java web application development. Whichever path has led you here, you're probably looking for a good introduction to the new Struts 2 framework. This book intends to give you that introduction and much more. If you've never heard of Struts 2, we cover the basics in enough depth to keep you in tow. If you know what Struts 2 does, but want a deeper understanding of how it does it, we'll provide that too.

Struts 2 is a Java web application framework. As you know, the Java world is vast and a Struts 2 application may travel far and wide in this world of Java. With that said, one of the biggest challenges faced by a Struts 2 book arises from trying to determine what content to include. This book could have been three times as long if we'd taken all of the good advice we received about what to include. We apologize to those whose course of normal development takes them outside the boundaries of our content. Please believe us when we say that we agonized over what to include and what not to include.

Struts 2 is much more than a revision of the Struts 1 framework. If you hadn't yet heard anything about Struts 2, you might expect, based upon the name, to find a new release of that proven framework. But this is not the case. Its relationship to that older framework is based in philosophy rather than in code base. Struts 1 was an action-oriented framework that implemented a Model-View-Controller (MVC) separation of concerns in its architecture. Struts 2 is a brand new implementation of those same MVC principles in an action-oriented framework. While the general lay of the land will seem familiar to Struts 1 developers, the new framework contains substantial architectural differences that serve to clean up the MVC lines and make the development process all that more efficient. We cover the new framework from the ground up, taking time to provide a true introduction to this new technology while also taking pains to give an inside view.

The organization of this book aims to walk you through Struts 2 in a sequence of increasing complexity. We start with a couple of preliminary chapters that introduce the technological context of the framework, give a high-level overview of the architecture, and present a bare-bones HelloWorld sample application to get your environment up and running. After this brief introduction, we set off into a series of chapters that cover the core concepts and components of the framework one by one. We take time to explain the functionality of each component in depth. We also provide real code examples as we begin the development of our full-featured sample application, the Struts 2 Portfolio. Finally, the later chapters provide some advanced techniques for tweaking a bit more out of the core components, as well as introducing some advanced features of the framework such as plug-ins and Spring integration. The following summarizes the contents chapter by chapter.

Roadmap

Chapter 1 gets us started gently. We begin with a quick survey of the context in which Struts 2 occurs, including short studies of web applications and frameworks. We then take the obligatory architectural look from 30,000 feet. Unless you're familiar with WebWork, the true code base ancestor of Struts 2, this high-level overview of the framework will be your first look at a fairly new and interesting way of doing things. Some advanced readers may feel comfortable skipping this first chapter.

Chapter 2 revisits the architectural principle of the first chapter as demonstrated in a HelloWorld sample application. We do two versions of HelloWorld. First, we show how to use XML to declare your Struts 2 architectural metadata; then we do it again using Java annotations for that same purpose. The HelloWorld application both reinforces architectural concepts and gives you a skeleton Struts 2 application.

Chapter 3 kicks off the core portion of the book by introducing and thoroughly covering the Struts 2 action component. Actions are at the heart of Struts 2, and it wouldn't make sense to start anywhere else. In addition to revealing the inner workings of this core component, we also begin to develop the full-featured Struts 2 Portfolio sample application in this chapter.

Chapter 4 continues the core topics by introducing one of the most important components of the framework, the interceptor. Struts 2 uses interceptors to implement almost all of the important functionality of the framework. We make sure you know what they are, how they work, and when you should consider implementing your own.

Chapter 5 finishes off the discussion of framework fundamentals by covering the data transfer mechanisms of the system. One of the most innovative features of Struts 2 is its automatic transfer and conversion of data between the HTTP and Java realms. Elusive but important players such as OGNL, the `ValueStack`, and the `ActionContext` are fully demystified and put to work for the average workingman developer.

Chapter 6 starts coverage of the view layer aspects of the framework. In particular, this chapter will introduce the Struts 2 Tag API. This introduction explains how to use the OGNL expression language to get your hands on the data in the `ValueStack` and `ActionContext`, which we met in the previous chapter. The chapter provides a reference to basic tags that you'll use to pull data into your rendering view pages, as well as tags to control the flow of your rendering view pages. Finally, we wrap up the chapter by providing a primer to the OGNL expression language, which will prove useful in your daily tag development.

Chapter 7 introduces the second major chunk of the Struts 2 tags, the Struts 2 UI components. The UI components are the tags that you use to build the user interfaces of your web application. As such, they include form components, text field components, and the like. But don't mistake the Struts 2 UI components for your father's HTML tags, if you know what I mean.

Chapter 8 rounds out treatment of the view layer of the framework by introducing the result component. This core component highlights the flexible nature of Struts 2. With Struts 2's highly decoupled result component, you can build results independent of the actions. After covering the basics, we show what we mean by building a JSON result that can return a JSON stream based on the data prepared by any action, regardless of whether that action knows anything about JSON. We use this example to implement some Ajax for the Struts 2 Portfolio.

Chapter 9 begins to show you how to bring your basic Struts 2 application up to industry standards. In particular, we take the opportunity to go off topic by showing you how to use Struts 2's Spring plug-in to bring dependency injection into your application. We then up the ante by showing you how to wield that Spring integration to upgrade your application to a JPA/Hibernate persistence layer that's managed by Spring's wonderful support for those technologies.

Chapter 10 continues the trend of making your application more refined by showing how to use Struts 2's validation framework to gain metadata-driven validation of your data.

Chapter 11 introduces the Struts 2 internationalization and localization support, and carefully walks you through all of the fine-grained details.

Chapter 12 introduces the Struts 2 plug-in architecture. Like any well-designed software, you should be able to extend the functionality without modifying existing code, and Struts 2 leverages the plug-in architecture for this very purpose. If you use Firefox or Eclipse, you already know how this works. The chapter explores the details and shows you how to write a plug-in from scratch.

Chapter 13 reveals best practices and tips from the trenches. This chapter presents topics that range from optimizing your development environment to registering your web features using a technique known as wildcard mappings. Of course, you will find a mishmash of useful tips in between.

Chapter 14 organizes a migration plan to help you transition from Struts 1.x to the exciting Struts Web 2.0 world. This chapter also points out similarities and differences between the two Struts versions.

Chapter 15 reveals techniques that let you leverage the true spirit of the framework. This chapter contains advanced concepts, and should be read several times before starting any large-scale Struts 2 project. It is chock-full of techniques that you'll be happy you leveraged as you look back over your code base.

Code conventions

The following typographical conventions are used throughout the book:

- Courier typeface is used in all code listings.
- Courier typeface is used within text for certain code words.
- *Italics* are used for emphasis and to introduce new terms.
- Code annotations are used in place of inline comments in the code. These highlight important concepts or areas of the code. Some annotations appear with numbered bullets like this ❶ that are referenced later in the text.

Code downloads

You can download the sample code for this book via a link found on the book's homepage on the Manning website, www.manning.com/Struts2inAction or www.manning.com/dbrown. This will get you the SampleApplication.zip archive file, which contains a couple of Java Servlet web application archive files-WAR files—as well as some documentation of the source. Instructions on how to install the application are contained in a README file in that download.

We should make a couple of points about the source code. First, all of the sample code for the book is contained in the Struts2InAction.war web application. Note that this web application uses a modularized structure to present a subapplication, if you will, for each of the chapters of the book. Throughout the book, we develop what we refer to as the Struts 2 Portfolio. This is our full-featured demonstration of a Struts 2 sample application. We develop the Struts 2 Portfolio incrementally throughout the chapters of the book. This means that the Struts2InAction.war web application contains many versions, in increasing power, of the Struts 2 Portfolio. The versions are modularized by chapter number.

Since we recognize that troubleshooting the deployment of a large application like the full Struts2InAction.war can be daunting to developers new to the platform, we've also provided a HelloWorld.war web application that contains only the HelloWorld portion of the larger sample application. This will help readers more quickly get a Struts 2 application up and running without the unwarranted complexity of such things as setting up a database.

Author Online

The purchase of *Struts 2 in Action* includes free access to a private forum run by Manning Publications where you can make comments about the book, ask technical questions, and receive help from the authors and other users. You can access and subscribe to the forum at www.manning.com/Struts2inAction. This page provides information on how to get on the forum once you are registered, what kind of help is available, and the rules of conduct in the forum.

Manning's commitment to our readers is to provide a venue where a meaningful dialogue among individual readers and between readers and authors can take place. It's not a commitment to any specific amount of participation on the part of the authors, whose contribution to the book's forum remains voluntary (and unpaid). We suggest you try asking the authors some challenging questions, lest their interest stray!

The Author Online forum and the archives of previous discussions will be accessible from the publisher's website as long as the book is in print.

about the title

By combining introductions, overviews, and how-to examples, the *In Action* books are designed to help learning *and* remembering. According to research in cognitive science, the things people remember are things they discover during self-motivated exploration.

Although no one at Manning is a cognitive scientist, we are convinced that for learning to become permanent it must pass through stages of exploration, play, and, interestingly, retelling of what is being learned. People understand and remember new things, which is to say they master them, only after actively exploring them. Humans learn *in action*. An essential part of an *In Action* book is that it is example-driven. It encourages the reader to try things out, to play with new code, and to explore new ideas.

There is another, more mundane, reason for the title of this book: our readers are busy. They use books to do a job or solve a problem. They need books that allow them to jump in and jump out easily and learn just what they want just when they want it. They need books that aid them *in action*. The books in this series are designed for such readers.

about the cover illustration

The figure on the cover of *Struts 2 in Action* is a shepherd from the moors of Bordeaux, "Berger des Landes de Bordeaux." The region of Bordeaux in southwestern France has sunny hills that are ideal for viniculture, as well as many open and marshy fields dotted with small farms and flocks of grazing sheep. Perched on his stilts, the shepherd was better able to navigate the boggy fields and tend to his charges.

The illustration is taken from a French travel book, *Encyclopedie des Voyages* by J. G. St. Saveur, published in 1796. Travel for pleasure was a relatively new phenomenon at the time and travel guides such as this one were popular, introducing both the tourist and the armchair traveler to the inhabitants of other regions of France and abroad.

The diversity of the drawings in the *Encyclopedie des Voyages* speaks vividly of the uniqueness and individuality of the world's towns and provinces just 200 years ago. This was a time when the dress codes of two regions separated by a few dozen miles identified people uniquely as belonging to one or the other. The travel guide brings to life a sense of isolation and distance of that period and of every other historic period except our own hyperkinetic present.

Dress codes have changed since then and the diversity by region, so rich at the time, has faded away. It is now often hard to tell the inhabitant of one continent from another. Perhaps, trying to view it optimistically, we have traded a cultural and visual diversity for a more varied personal life. Or a more varied and interesting intellectual and technical life.

We at Manning celebrate the inventiveness, the initiative, and the fun of the computer business with book covers based on the rich diversity of regional life two centuries ago brought back to life by the pictures from this travel guide.

Part 1

Struts 2:
a brand new framework

Struts 2 is indeed a brand new framework. We see it as one of the second-generation web application frameworks. In addition to including all the cutting-edge features one would expect from a new framework, Struts 2 introduces many architectural refinements that might not be familiar to some developers. All this means that we need to take the time to properly introduce this new framework to our readers. The first two chapters of this book serve that purpose.

In chapter 1, we provide a high-level introduction and overview. Before introducing the framework itself, we sketch the technological context in which a Java web application framework such as Struts 2 resides. This information may be old hat for some users, and it probably won't be adequate for full-on newbies. Our purpose is to provide a quick sketch of the technologies you should probably be familiar with if you're going to develop Struts 2 applications. We quickly get past the background stuff and provide a thorough high-level overview of the innovative architecture of Struts 2. This well-engineered architecture is definitely one of the framework's hallmarks.

Once the abstract preliminaries are out of the way, chapter 2 gets us on track to satisfying our *in Action* pedigree. Chapter 2 brings the concepts from the high-level overview down to earth with the HelloWorld sample application that gets a running Struts 2 application in your hands as early as possible. If you can't even wait until chapter 2, just skip chapter 1!

Struts 2:
the modern web
application framework

Modern web applications are situated in a complex technological context. Some books that you read might be about a single subject, such as the Java language, or a specific API or library. This book is about Struts 2, a full-featured web application framework for the Java EE platform. As such, this book must take into account the vast array of technologies that converge in the space of the Java EE.

In response to this complexity, we'll start by outlining some of the most important technologies that Struts 2 depends on. Struts 2 provides some powerful boosts to production through convention over configuration, and automates many tasks that were previously accomplished only by the sweat of the developer. But we think true efficiency comes through understanding the underlying technological context, particularly as these technologies become more and more obscured by the opacity of scaffolding and the like. That said, the first half of this chapter provides a primer on the Struts 2 environment. If you're comfortable with this stuff, feel free to skim or skip these sections entirely.

After sketching the important figures of the landscape, we'll move into a high-level overview of Struts 2 itself. We'll introduce how the Model-View-Controller (MVC) fits into the Struts 2 architecture. After that, we'll go through a more detailed account of what happens when the framework processes a request. When we finish up, you'll be fully ready for chapter 2's HelloWorld application.

Let's get going!

1.1   *Web applications: a quick study*

This section provides a rough primer on the technological context of a web application. We'll cover the technology stack upon which web applications sit, and take a quick survey of common tasks that all web applications must routinely accomplish as they service their requests. If you're quite familiar with this information, you could skip ahead to the Struts 2 architectural overview in section 1.3, but a quick study of the following sections would still provide an orientation on how we, the authors, view the web application domain.

1.1.1   *Using the Web to build applications*

While many Java developers today may have worked on web applications for most of their careers, it's always beneficial to revisit the foundations of the domain in which one is working. A solid understanding of the context in which a framework such as Struts 2 is situated provides an intuitive understanding of the architectural decisions made by the framework. Also, establishing a common vocabulary for our discussions will make everything easier throughout the book.

A web application is simply, or not so simply, an application that runs over the Web. With rapid improvements in Internet speed, connectivity, and client/server technologies, the Web has become an increasingly powerful platform for building all classes of applications, from standard business-oriented enterprise solutions to personal software. The latest iterations of web applications must be as full featured and easy to use as traditional desktop applications. Yet, in spite of the increasing variety in applications built on the web platform, the core workflow of these applications remains markedly consistent, a perfect opportunity for reuse. Frameworks such as Struts 2 strive to release the developer from the mundane concerns of the domain by providing a reusable architectural solution to the core web application workflows.

1.1.2   *Examining the technology stack*

We'll now take a quick look at two of the main components in the technology stack upon which a web application is built. In one sense, the Web is a simple affair: as with all good solutions, if it weren't simple, it probably wouldn't be successful. Figure 1.1 provides a simple depiction of the context in which Struts 2 is used.

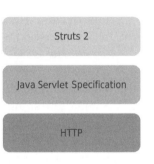

As depicted in figure 1.1, Struts 2 sits on top of two important technologies. At the heart of all Struts 2 applications lie the client/server exchanges of the HTTP protocol. The Java Servlet API exposes these low-level HTTP communications to the Java language. Although it's possible to write web applications by directly coding against the Servlet API, this is generally not considered a good practice. Basically, Struts 2 uses the Servlet API so that you don't have to. But while it's a good idea to keep the Servlet API out of your Struts 2

Figure 1.1 The Java Servlet API exposes the HTTP client/server protocol to the Java platform. Struts 2 is built on top of that.

code, it seems cavalier to enter into Struts 2 development without some idea of the underlying technologies. The next two sections provide concise descriptions of the more relevant aspects of HTTP and Java Servlets.

HYPERTEXT TRANSFER PROTOCOL (HTTP)

Most web applications run on top of HTTP. This protocol is a stateless series of client/server message exchanges. Normally, the client is a web browser and the server is a web or application server. The client initiates communication by sending a request for a specific resource. The resource can be a static HTML document that exists on the server's local file system, or it can be a dynamically generated document with untold complexity behind its creation.

Much could be said about the HTTP protocol and the variety of ways of doing things in this domain. We'll limit ourselves to the most important implications as seen from the perspective of a web application. We can start by noting that HTTP was not originally designed to serve in the capacity that web application developers demand of it. It was meant for requesting and serving static HTML documents. All web applications built on HTTP must address this discrepancy.

For web applications, HTTP has two hurdles to get over. It's stateless, and it's text based. Stateless protocols don't keep track of the relationships among the various requests they receive. Each request is handled as if it were the only request the server had ever received. The HTTP server keeps no records that would allow it to track and logically connect multiple requests from a given client. The server has the client's address, but it will only be used to return the currently requested document. If the client turns around and requests another document, the server will be unaware of this client's repeated visits.

But if we are trying to build more complex web applications with more complicated use cases, this won't work. Take the simplest, most common case of the secure web application. A secure application needs to authenticate its users. To do this, the request in which the client sends the user name and password must somehow be associated with all other requests coming from that client during that user session. Without the ability to keep track of relationships among various requests, even this introductory use case of modern web applications is impossible. This problem must be addressed by every modern web application.

Equally as troublesome, HTTP also is text based. Mating a text-based technology to a strongly typed technology such as Java creates a significant amount of data-binding work. While in the form of an HTTP request, all data must be represented as text. Somewhere along the way, this encoding of data must be mapped onto Java data types. Furthermore, this process must occur at both ends of the request-handling process. Incoming request parameters must be migrated into the Java environment, and outgoing responses must pull data from Java back into the text-based HTTP response. While this is not rocket science, it can create mounds of drudge work for a web application. These tasks are both error-prone and time-consuming.

JAVA SERVLET API

The Java Servlet API helps alleviate some of the pain. This important technology exposes HTTP to the Java platform. This means that Java developers can write HTTP server code against an intuitive object-oriented abstraction of the HTTP client/server communications. The central figures in the Servlet API are the servlet, request, and response objects. A servlet is a singleton Java object whose whole purpose is to receive requests and return responses after some arbitrary back-end processing. The request object encapsulates the various details of the request, including the all-important request parameters as submitted via form fields and querystring parameters. The response object includes such key items as the response headers and the output stream that will generate the text of the response. In short, a servlet receives a request object, examines its data, does the appropriate back-end magic, and then writes and returns the response to the client.

ESSENTIAL KNOWLEDGE   You should know Sun and the Servlet Specification. If you're unfamiliar with Sun's way of doing things, here's a short course. Sun provides a specification of a technology, such as the Servlet API. The specifications are generated through a community process that includes a variety of interested parties, not the least of which is Sun itself. The specification details the obligations and contracts that the API must honor; actual implementations are provided by various third-party vendors. In the case of the Servlet Specification, the implementations are *servlet containers*. These containers can be standalone implementations such as the popular Apache Tomcat, or they can be containers embedded in some larger application server. They also run the gamut from open source to fully proprietary. If you're unfamiliar with the Servlet Specification, we recommend reading it. It's short, to the point, and well written.

Before you deploy servlets, you must first package them according to the standards. The basic unit of servlet packaging is known as a *web application*. Though it sounds like a general term, a web application is a specific thing in servlet terminology. The Servlet Specification defines a web application as "a collection of servlets, HTML pages, classes, and other resources." Typically, a web application will require several servlets to service its clients' requests. A web application's servlets and resources are packaged together in a specific directory structure and zipped up in an archive file with a .war extension. A WAR file is a specialized version of the Java JAR file. The letters stand for *web application archive*. When we discuss chapter 2's HelloWorld application, we'll see exactly how to lay out a Struts 2 application to these standards.

Once you've packaged the web application, you need to deploy it. Web applications are deployed in *servlet containers*. A servlet is a special kind of application known as a *managed life cycle application*. This means that you don't directly execute a servlet. You deploy it in a container and that container manages its execution by invoking the various servlet life cycle methods. When a servlet container receives a request, it must first decide which of the servlets that it manages should handle the request. When the container determines which servlet should process a request, it invokes that servlet's service() method, handing it both a request and response object. There are other life cycle methods, but the service() method is responsible for the actual work.

Figure 1.2 shows the relationship between the key players of the Servlet API: servlets, web applications, and the servlet container.

As you can see, a servlet container can host one or more web applications. In figure 1.2, three web applications have been deployed to a single container. All requests, regardless of which web application they ultimately target, must first be handled by the container; it's the server. The servlet container typically listens on port 8080 for requests. When a request comes to that port, it must then parse the namespace of the request to discover which web application is targeted. From the namespace of the

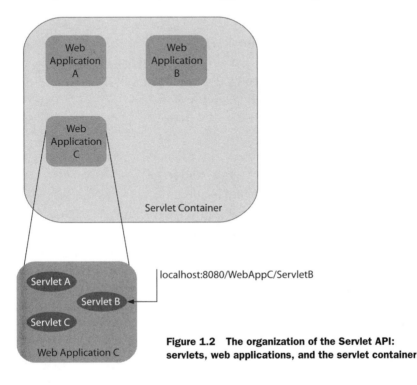

localhost:8080/WebAppC/ServletB

**Figure 1.2　The organization of the Servlet API:
servlets, web applications, and the servlet container**

URL, both the web application and the individual servlet targeted therein can be determined. The full details of this parsing process aren't in the scope of this overview, but figure 1.2 gives a rudimentary example of how a URL maps to a specific servlet, assuming the servlet container is listening for requests on the localhost network interface.

In addition to exposing HTTP to the Java language, the Servlet API provides other important high-level functions, such as a session mechanism that allows us to correlate groups of requests from a given client. As we explained earlier, HTTP doesn't provide a good sense of state across a set of requests, regardless of whether they all came from the same client. This is perhaps the most important benefit, in terms of higher-level functionality, that we receive from servlets. Without it, we'd be handling cookies and parsing embedded querystring session keys.

Apart from the session mechanism, the Servlet API doesn't provide a lot of higher-level functionality. It directly encapsulates the details of the client/sever exchange in a set of object-oriented abstractions. This means that we don't have to parse the incoming HTTP request ourselves. Instead, we receive a tidy request object, already wrapped in Java. We say this to make the point that, ultimately, the Servlet API is an infrastructure-level technology in the scope of modern web applications. As infrastructure, servlets provide the solid low-level foundation upon which robust web applications can be built. If you consider the routine needs of a web application, the Servlet API doesn't attempt to provide solutions for such things. Now that we know what servlets can do, let's look at what they leave undone. These common tasks of the domain are what a web application framework like Struts 2 will need to address.

1.1.3   *Surveying the domain*

With the Servlet API addressing the low-level client/server concerns, we can now focus on the application-level concerns. There are many tasks that all web applications must solve as they go about their daily routine of processing requests. Among these are

- Binding request parameters to Java types
- Validating data
- Making calls to business logic
- Making calls to the data layer
- Rendering presentation layer (HTML, and so on)
- Providing internationalization and localization

We'll examine each of the concerns briefly in the following paragraphs.

REQUEST PARAMETER BINDING AND DATA VALIDATION

Being a text-based protocol, HTTP must represent its request parameters in a text encoding. When these parameters enter our application, they must be converted to the appropriate native data type. The Servlet API doesn't do this for us. The parameters, as retrieved from the servlet request objects, are still represented as strings. Converting these strings to Java data types is easy enough but can be time-consuming and error-prone. Converting to simple types is tedious; converting to more complex types is both complex and tedious. And, of course, the data must also be validated before it can be allowed to enter the system. Note that there are two levels of validation. In the first case, the string must be a valid representation of the Java type to which you want to convert; for example, a ZIP code should not have any letters in it.

Then, after the value has been successfully bound to a Java type, the data must be validated against higher-level logic, such as whether a provided ZIP code is valid. An application must determine whether the value itself is within the acceptable range of values according to the business rules of the application. In addition to checking ZIP code validity, you might verify that an email address has the valid structure. Spending too many hours writing this kind of code can certainly make Java Jack a dull boy.

CALLS TO BUSINESS LOGIC AND THE DATA LAYER

Once inside the application, most requests involve calls to business logic and the data layer. While the specifics of these calls vary from application to application, a couple of generalizations can be drawn. First, despite variance in the details of these calls, they form a consistent pattern of workflow. At its core, the processing of each request consists of a sequence of work that must be done. This work is the *action* of an action-oriented framework. Second, the logic and function of this work represents a clear step outside of the web-related domain. If you look back to our list of the common tasks that a web application must do while processing its requests, you'll see that these calls to business logic and the data layer are the only ones that don't specifically pertain to the fact that this is a web application, as opposed to, say, a desktop application. If the application is well designed, the business logic and data layers would be completely oblivious to whether they were being invoked from a web application or a desktop application. So, while all web applications must make these calls, the notable thing about them is that they are outside the specific workflow concerns of a web application.

PRESENTATION RENDERING AND INTERNATIONALIZATION

It could be said that the presentation tier of a web application is just an HTML document. However, increasing amounts of complex JavaScript, fully realized CSS, and other embedded technologies make that no longer accurate. At the same time that front-end user interface technology is increasing in complexity, there's an increasing demand for internationalization. Internationalization allows us to build a single web application that can discover the locality of each user and provide locale-specific language and formatting of date, time, and currency. Whether an application returns a simple page of static text or a Gmail-esque super client, the rendering of the presentation layer is a core domain task of all web applications.

We've outlined the domain tasks that all web applications must address. What now? These tasks, by virtue of being common to the processing of nearly every request that comes to a web application, are perfect candidates for reuse. We'd hope that a web application framework would provide reusable solutions to such common tasks. Let's look at how frameworks can help.

1.2 *Frameworks for web applications*

Now that we've oriented ourselves to the domain in which web applications operate, we can talk about how a framework can alleviate the work of building them. To build powerful web applications, most developers need all the help they can get. Unless you want to spend hours upon hours solving the tasks outlined in the previous section by hand, you must use a framework, and there are a lot of them. Let's start with a fundamental question.

1.2.1   What's a framework?

A framework is a piece of structural software. We say *structural* because structure is perhaps a larger goal of the framework than any specific functional requirement. A framework tries to make generalizations about the common tasks and workflow of a specific domain. The framework then attempts to provide a platform upon which applications of that domain can be more quickly built. The framework does this primarily in two ways. First, the framework tries to automate all the tedious tasks of the domain. Second, the framework tries to introduce an elegant architectural solution to the common workflow of the domain in question.

DEFINITION   A *web application framework* is a piece of structural software that provides automation of common tasks of the domain as well as a built-in architectural solution that can be easily inherited by applications implemented on the framework.

A FRAMEWORK AUTOMATES COMMON TASKS

Don't reinvent the wheel. Any good framework will provide mechanisms for convenient and perhaps automatic solutions to the common tasks of the domain, saving developers the effort of reinventing the wheel. Reflecting back on our discussion of the common tasks of the web application domain, we can then infer that a web application framework will provide some sort of built-in mechanisms for tasks such as converting data from HTTP string representation to Java data types, data validation, separation of business and data layer calls from web-related work, internationalization, and presentation rendering. Good frameworks provide elegant, if not transparent, mechanisms for relieving the developer of these mundane tasks.

A FRAMEWORK PROVIDES AN ARCHITECTURAL SOLUTION

While everyone can appreciate automation of tedious tasks, the structural features of frameworks are perhaps more important in the big scheme of things. The framework's structure comes from the workflow abstractions made by the classes and interfaces of the framework itself. Being an action-oriented framework, one of the key abstractions at the heart of the Struts 2 architecture is the *action*. We'll see the others in a few pages. When you build an application on a framework, you are buying into that framework's architecture. Sometimes you can fight against the architectural imperative of the framework, but a framework should offer its architecture in a way that makes it hard to refuse. If the architecture of the framework is good, why not let your application gracefully inherit that architecture?

1.2.2   Why use a framework?

You don't have to use a framework. You have a few alternatives. For starters, you could forgo a framework altogether. But unless your application is quite simple, we suspect that the work involved in rolling your own versions of all the common domain tasks, not to mention solving all the architectural problems on your own, will quickly deter you. As the twenty-first century ramps up, various new web application platforms boast light-speed development times and agile interfaces. In the world of Java web applications, using a sleek new framework is the way to take advantage of these benefits.

If you want, you could roll your own framework. This is not a bad plan, but it assumes a couple of things. First, it assumes you have lots of smart developers. Second, it assumes they have the time and money to spend on a big project that might seem off topic from the perspective of the business requirements. Even if you have the rare trinity of smart people, time, and money, there are still drawbacks. I've worked for a company whose product is built on an in-house framework. The framework is not bad, but a couple of glaring points can't be overlooked. First, new developers will always have to learn the framework from the ground up. If you're using a mainstream framework, there's a trained work force waiting for you to hire them. Second, the in-house framework is unlikely to see elegant revisions that keep up with the pace of industry. In-house frameworks seem to be subject to architectural erosion as the years pass, and too many extensions are inelegantly tacked on.

Ultimately, it's hard to imagine creating twenty-first century web applications without using a framework of some kind. If you have X amount of hours to spend on a project, you might as well spend them on higher-level concerns than common workflow and infrastructural tasks. Perhaps it's not a question of whether to use a framework or not, but of which framework offers the solutions you need. With that in mind, it's time to look at Struts 2 and see what kinds of modern conveniences it offers.

1.3 The Struts 2 framework

Apache Struts 2 is a brand-new, state-of-the-art web application framework. As we said earlier, Struts 2 isn't just a new release of the older Struts 1 framework. It is a completely new framework, based on the esteemed OpenSymphony WebWork framework. By now, you should be tuned in to what a web application framework should offer. In terms of the common domain tasks, Struts 2 covers the domain well. It handles all the tasks we've identified and more. Over the course of the book, you'll learn how to work with the features that address each of those tasks in turn. At this introductory stage, it makes more sense to focus on the architectural aspects of the framework. In this section, we'll see how Struts 2 structures the web application workflow. In the next few sections, we'll look at the roots of Struts 2, see how those roots influence the high-level architecture, and take a slightly more detailed look at how the framework handles actual request processing.

1.3.1 A brief history

Struts 2 is a second-generation web application framework that implements the Model-View-Controller (MVC) design pattern. Struts 2 is built from the ground up on best practices and proven, community-accepted design patterns. This was also true for the first version of Struts. In fact, one of the primary goals of the first Struts was incorporating the MVC pattern from the desktop application world into a web application framework. The resulting pattern is occasionally called the *Model 2* pattern. This was a critical step in the evolution of well-designed web applications, as it provided the infrastructure for easily achieving the MVC separation of concerns. This allowed developers with few resources for such architectural niceties to tap into a ready-made best practice solution. Struts 1 can claim responsibility for many of the better-designed web applications of the last 10 years.

At some point, the Struts community became aware of the limitations in the first framework. With such an active community, identifying the weak and inflexible points in the framework wasn't hard to accomplish. Struts 2 takes advantage of the many lessons learned to present a cleaner implementation of MVC. At the same time, it introduces several new architectural features that make the framework cleaner and more flexible. These new features include interceptors for layering cross-cutting concerns away from action logic; annotation-based configuration to reduce or eliminate XML configuration; a powerful expression language, Object-Graph Navigation Language (OGNL), that transverses the entire framework; and a mini-MVC–based tag API that supports modifiable and reusable UI components. At this point, it's impossible to do more than name drop. We'll have plenty of time to fully explore each of these features. We need to start with a high-level overview of the framework. First, we'll look at how Struts 2 implements MVC. Then, we'll look at how the parts of the framework work together when processing a request.

NOTE   *Teaching old dogs new tricks, a.k.a. moving from Struts 1 to Struts 2*—Since we've stressed that Struts 2 is truly a new framework, you might be wondering how hard it will be to move from Struts 1 to Struts 2. There are some things to learn, interceptors and OGNL in particular. But while this is a new framework, it is still an action-oriented MVC framework. The whole point of design patterns such as MVC is the reuse of solutions to common problems. Reusing solutions at the architectural level provides an easy transferal of experience and knowledge. If you've worked with Struts 1, you already understand the MVC way of doing things and that knowledge will still be applicable to Struts 2. Since Struts 2 is an improved implementation of the MVC pattern, we believe that Struts 1 developers will not only find it easy to migrate to Struts 2, they'll find themselves saying, "That's how it always should've been done!"

1.3.2   *Struts 2 from 30,000 feet: the MVC pattern*

The high-level design of Struts 2 follows the well-established Model-View-Controller design pattern. In this section, we'll tell you which parts of the framework address the various concerns of the MVC pattern. The MVC pattern provides a separation of concerns that applies well to web applications. Separation of concerns allows us to manage the complexity of large software systems by dividing them into high-level components. The MVC design pattern identifies three distinct concerns: *model, view,* and *controller.* In Struts 2, these are implemented by the action, result, and `FilterDispatcher`, respectively. Figure 1.3 shows the Struts 2 implementation of the MVC pattern to handle the workflow of web applications.

Let's take a close look at each part of figure 1.3. We'll provide a brief description of the duties of each MVC concern and look at how the corresponding Struts 2 component fulfills those duties.

CONTROLLER—FILTERDISPATCHER

We'll start with the controller. It seems to make more sense to start there when talking about web applications. In fact, the MVC variant used in Struts is often referred to as a *front controller* MVC. This means that the controller is out front and is the first component to act in the processing. You can easily see this in figure 1.3. The controller's job is to map requests to

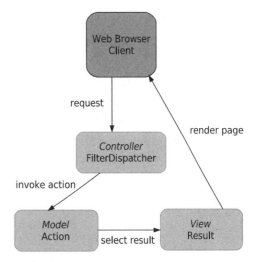

Figure 1.3   Struts 2 MVC is realized by three core framework components: actions, results, and the `FilterDispatcher`.

actions. In a web application, the incoming HTTP requests can be thought of as commands that the user issues to the application. One of the fundamental tasks of a web application is routing these requests to the appropriate set of actions that should be taken within the application itself. This controller's job is like that of a traffic cop or air traffic controller. In some ways, this work is administrative; it's certainly not part of your core business logic.

The role of the controller is played by the Struts 2 `FilterDispatcher`. This important object is a servlet filter that inspects each incoming request to determine which Struts 2 action should handle the request. The framework handles all of the controller work for you. You just need to inform the framework which request URLs map to which of your actions. You can do this with XML-based configuration files or Java annotations. We'll demonstrate both of these methods in the next chapter.

NOTE   Struts 2 goes a long way toward the goal of *zero-configuration* web applications. Zero-configuration aims at deriving all of an application's metadata, such as which URL maps to which action, from convention rather than configuration. The use of Java annotations plays an important role in this zero-configuration scheme. While zero-configuration has not quite been achieved, you can currently use annotations and conventions to drastically reduce XML-based configuration.

Chapter 2's HelloWorld application will demonstrate both the general architecture and deployment details of Struts 2 web applications.

MODEL—ACTION

Looking at figure 1.3, it's easy to see that the model is implemented by the Struts 2 action component. But what exactly is the model? I find the model the most nebulous of the MVC triad. In some ways, the model is a black box that contains the guts of the application. Everything else is just user interface and wiring. The model is the thing itself. In more technical terms, the model is the internal state of the application. This state is composed of both the data model and the business logic. From the high-level black box view, the data and the business logic merge together into the monolithic *state* of the application. For instance, if you are logging in to an application, both business logic and data from the database will be involved in the authentication process. Most likely, the business logic will provide an authentication method that will take the username and password and verify them against some persisted data from the database. In this case, the data and the business logic combine to form one of two states, "authenticated" or "unauthenticated." Neither the data on its own, nor the business logic on its own, can produce these states.

Bearing all of this in mind, a Struts 2 action serves two roles. First, an action is an encapsulation of the calls to business logic into a single unit of work. Second, the action serves as a locus of data transfer. It is too early to go into details, but we'll treat the topic in great depth during the course of this book. At this point, consider that an application has any number of actions to handle whatever set of commands it exposes to the client. As seen in figure 1.3, the controller, after receiving the request, must consult its mappings and determine which of these actions should handle the request. Once it finds the appropriate action, the controller hands over control of the request processing to the action by invoking it. This invocation process, conducted by the framework, will both prepare the necessary data and execute the action's business logic. When the action completes its work, it'll be time to render a view back to the user who submitted the request. Toward this end, an action, upon completing its work, will forward the result to the Struts 2 view component. Let's consider the result now.

VIEW—RESULT

The view is the presentation component of the MVC pattern. Looking back at figure 1.3, we see that the result returns the page to the web browser. This page is the user interface that presents a representation of the application's state to the user. These are commonly JSP pages, Velocity templates, or some other presentation-layer technology. While there are many choices for the view, the role of the view is clear-cut: it translates the state of the application into a visual presentation with which the user can interact. With rich clients and Ajax applications increasingly complicating the details of the view, it becomes even more important to have clean MVC separation of concerns. Good MVC lays the groundwork for easily managing the most complex front end.

NOTE   One of the interesting aspects of Struts 2 is how well its clean architecture paves the way for new technologies and techniques. The Struts 2 result component is a good demonstration of this. The result provides a clean encapsulation of handing off control of the processing to another object that will write the response to the client. This makes it easy for alternative responses, such as XML snippets or XSLT transformations, to be integrated into the framework.

If you look back to figure 1.3, you can see that the action is responsible for choosing which result will render the response. The action can choose from any number of results. Common choices are between results that represent the semantic outcomes of the action's processing, such as "success" and "error." Struts 2 provides out-of-the-box support for using most common view-layer technologies as results. These include JSP, Velocity, FreeMarker, and XSLT. Better yet, the clean structure of the architecture ensures that more result types can be built to handle new types of responses.

Since this favored MVC pattern has been around for decades, try visualizing what the MVC playing field would look like if the players were in fact nicely separated yet connectible. When I explain this to my students, I call it the Reese's peanut butter cup principle. Is this tasty treat chocolate or peanut butter? After your first bite, you discover it's both! How could you use this peanut butter if all you wanted was a PBJ sandwich? And so it goes with technology: how do you get all the richness you desire without actually "combining" the ingredients? Grab some sweets and continue reading to learn about Struts 2 and the framework request-processing factory.

1.3.3 How Struts 2 works

In this section, we'll detail processing a request within the framework. As you'll see, the framework has more than just its MVC components. We said that Struts 2 provides a cleaner implementation of MVC. These clean lines are only possible with the help of a few other key architectural components that participate in processing every request. Chief among these are the interceptors, OGNL, and the `ValueStack`. We'll learn what each of these does in the following walkthrough of Struts 2 request processing. Figure 1.4 shows the request processing workflow.

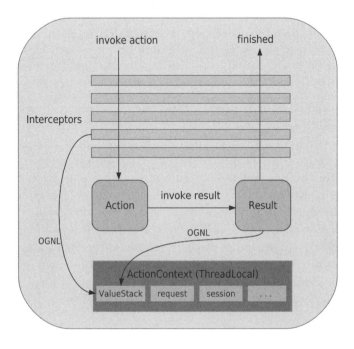

Figure 1.4 Struts 2 request processing uses interceptors that fire before and after the action and result.

The first thing we should consider is that the workflow of figure 1.4 still obeys the simpler MVC view of the framework that we saw earlier. In the figure, the `FilterDispatcher` has already done its controller work by selecting the appropriate action to handle the request. The figure demonstrates what really happens when the action is invoked by the controller. As you can see, a few extra parts are added to the MVC basics. We'll explain in the next paragraphs how the interceptors and the `ActionContext` aid the action and result in their processing of the request.

Figure 1.4 introduces the following new Struts 2 components: `ActionContext`, interceptors, the `ValueStack`, and OGNL. This diagram goes a long way toward showing what really happens in Struts 2. You could say that everything we'll discuss in this book is shown in this diagram. As interceptors come first in the request-processing cycle, we'll start with them. The name seems obvious, but what exactly do they intercept?

INTERCEPTORS

You may have noticed, while studying figure 1.4, that there is a stack of interceptors in front of the action. The invocation of the action must travel through this stack. This is a key part of the Struts 2 framework. We'll devote an entire chapter to this important component later in the book. At this time, it is enough to understand that most every action will have a stack of interceptors associated with it. These interceptors are invoked both before and after the action, though we should note that they actually fire after the result has executed. Interceptors don't necessarily have to do something both times they fire, but they do have the opportunity. Some interceptors only do work before the action has been executed, and others only do work afterward. The important thing is that the interceptor allows common, cross-cutting tasks to be defined in clean, reusable components that you can keep separate from your action code.

DEFINITION   Interceptors are Struts 2 components that execute both before and after the rest of the request processing. They provide an architectural component in which to define various workflow and cross-cutting tasks so that they can be easily reused as well as separated from other architectural concerns.

What kinds of work should be done in interceptors? Logging is a good example. Logging should be done with the invocation of every action, but it probably shouldn't be put in the action itself. Why? Because it's not part of the action's own unit of work. It's more administrative, overhead if you will. Earlier, we charged a framework with the responsibility of providing built-in functional solutions to common domain tasks such as data validation, type conversion, and file uploads. Struts 2 uses interceptors to do this type of work. While these tasks are important, they're not specifically related to the action logic of the request. Struts 2 uses interceptors to both separate and reuse these cross-cutting concerns. Interceptors play a huge role in the Struts 2 framework. And while you probably won't spend a large percentage of your time writing interceptors, most developers will find that many tasks are perfectly solved with custom interceptors. As we said, we'll devote all of chapter 4 to exploring this core component.

THE VALUESTACK AND OGNL

While interceptors may not absorb a lot of your daily development energies, the `ValueStack` and OGNL will be constantly on your mind. In a nutshell, the `ValueStack` is a storage area that holds all of the data associated with the processing of a request. You could think of it as a piece of scratch paper where the framework does its work while solving the problems of request processing. Rather than passing the data around, Struts 2 keeps it in a convenient, central location—the `ValueStack`.

OGNL is the tool that allows us to access the data we put in that central repository. More specifically, it is an expression language that allows you to reference and manipulate the data on the `ValueStack`. Developers new to Struts 2 probably ask more questions about the `ValueStack` and OGNL than anything else. If you're coming from Struts 1, you'll find that these are a couple of the more exotic features of the new framework. Due to this, and the sheer importance of this duo, we'll treat them carefully throughout the book. In particular, chapters 5 and 6 describe the detailed function of these two framework components.

DEFINITION   Struts 2 uses the `ValueStack` as a storage area for all application domain data that will be needed during the processing of a request. Data is moved to the `ValueStack` in preparation for request processing, it is manipulated there during action execution, and it is read from there when the results render their response pages.

The tricky, and powerful, thing about the `ValueStack` and OGNL is that they don't belong to any of the individual framework components. Looking back to figure 1.4, note that both interceptors and results can use OGNL to target values on the `ValueStack`. The data in the `ValueStack` follows the request processing through all phases; it slices through the whole length of the framework. It can do this because it is stored in a `ThreadLocal` context called the `ActionContext`.

DEFINITION   OGNL is a powerful expression language (and more) that is used to reference and manipulate properties on the `ValueStack`.

The `ActionContext` contains all of the data that makes up the context in which an action occurs. This includes the `ValueStack` but also includes stuff the framework itself will use internally, such as the request, session, and application maps from the Servlet API. You can access these objects yourself if you like; we'll see how later in the book. For now, we just want to focus on the `ActionContext` as the `ThreadLocal` home of the `ValueStack`. The use of `ThreadLocal` makes the `ActionContext`, and thus the `ValueStack`, accessible from anywhere in the same thread of execution. Since Struts 2's processing of each request occurs in a single thread, the `ValueStack` is available from any point in the framework's handling of a request.

Typically, it is considered bad form to obtain the contents of the `ActionContext` yourself. The framework provides many elegant ways to interact with that data without actually touching the `ActionContext`, or the `ValueStack`, yourself. Primarily, you'll use OGNL to do this. OGNL is used in many places in the framework to reference and manipulate data in the `ValueStack`. For instance, you'll use OGNL to bind HTML form fields to data objects on the `ValueStack` for data transfer, and you'll use OGNL to pull data into the rendering of your JSPs and other result types. At this point, you just need to understand that the `ValueStack` is where your data is stored while you work with it, and that OGNL is the expression language that you, and the framework, use to target this data from various parts of the request-processing cycle.

Now you've seen how Struts 2 implements MVC, and you've had a brief introduction to all the other important players in the processing of actual requests. The next thing we need to do, before getting down to the nuts and bolts of the framework's core components, is to make all of this concrete with a simple HelloWorld application in chapter 2. But first, a quick summary.

1.4   Summary

We started with a lot of abstract stuff about frameworks and design patterns, but you should now have a good understanding of the Struts 2 architecture. If abstraction is not to your taste, you'll be happy to know that we've officially completed the theoretical portion of the book. Starting immediately with chapter 2, the book will deal with only the concrete, practical matters of building web applications. But before we move on, let's take a moment to review what we've learned.

We should probably spend a moment to evaluate Struts 2 as a framework. Based upon our understanding of the technological context and the common domain tasks, we laid out two responsibilities for a web application framework at the outset of this chapter. The first responsibility of a framework is to provide an architectural foundation for web applications. We've seen how Struts 2 does this, and we discussed the design pattern roots that inform the Struts 2 architectural decisions. In particular, we have seen that Struts 2 takes the lessons learned from first-generation web application frameworks to implement a brand-new, cleaner, MVC-based framework. We have also seen the specific framework components that implement the MVC pattern: the action component, the result component, and the `FilterDispatcher`.

The other responsibility of frameworks is the automation of many common tasks of the web application domain. These tasks are sometimes referred to as cross-cutting concerns because they occur again and again across the execution of a disparate set of application-specific actions. Logging, data validation, and other common cross-cutting concerns should be separated from the concerns of the action and result. In Struts 2, the interceptor provides an architectural mechanism for removing cross-cutting concerns from the core MVC components. As we go further into the book, you'll see that the framework comes with many built-in interceptors to handle all the common tasks of the domain. You'll see that not only do they handle the bulk of the core framework functionality, they also can be just the thing to handle some of your own application-level needs. While you can probably avoid writing any interceptors yourself, we hope that the chapter on interceptors will inspire you to write your own.

We also took a high-level look at the actual request processing of the framework. We saw that each action has a stack of interceptors that fire both before and after the action and result have done their work. In addition to the MVC components and the interceptors, the `ValueStack` and the OGNL expression language play critical roles in the storage and manipulation of data within the framework. By now you should have a decent grasp of what the framework can do. In the next chapter's HelloWorld application, you'll see a concrete example of the framework components in action. Once we get that behind us, we'll move on to explore the core components of the framework, starting with chapter 3's coverage of the Struts 2 action.

Saying hello to Struts 2

This chapter covers

- Declaring your architecture
- Deploying a HelloWorld application
- Building an XML-based application
- Using Struts annotations

In the first chapter, we acquainted ourselves with the web application domain, learned how design patterns and frameworks help developers do their jobs, and conducted a quick survey of the Struts 2 architecture and request-processing pipeline. With that, we've now finished the abstract portion of the book. This chapter, which concludes the introductory section of the book, provides the practical and concrete details to bring the theoretical concepts from the first chapter down to earth. In particular, this chapter will demonstrate the basic Struts 2 architectural components with the HelloWorld sample application. This application isn't intended to demonstrate the full complexity of the framework. As we've said, we'll develop a full-featured sample application through the course of the book—the Struts 2 Portfolio application. The purpose of the HelloWorld application is just to get a Struts 2 application up and running.

But before we get to the HelloWorld application, we need to look at the fundamentals of configuring a Struts 2 application. In particular, we'll introduce at a type of configuration known as *declarative architecture*.

2.1 *Declarative architecture*

In this book, we use the phrase *declarative architecture* to refer to a type of configuration that allows developers to describe their application architecture at a higher level than direct programmatic manipulation. Similar to how an HTML document simply describes its components and leaves the creation of their runtime instances to the browser, Struts 2 allows you to describe your architectural components through its high-level declarative architecture facility and leave the runtime creation of your application to the framework. In this section, we'll see how this works.

2.1.1 *Two kinds of configuration*

First, we need to clarify some terminology. In the introduction to this chapter, we referred to the act of declaring your application's Struts 2 components as *configuration*. While there is nothing wrong with this nomenclature, it can be confusing. Hidden beneath the far-reaching concept of configuration, we can distinguish between two distinct sets of activity that occur in a Struts 2 project. One of these, the declarative architecture, is more central to actually building Struts 2 applications, while the other is more administrative in nature. Conceptually, it's important to distinguish between the two.

CONFIGURING THE FRAMEWORK ITSELF

First, we have configuration in the traditional sense of the word. These are the more administrative activities. Because the Struts 2 framework is flexible, it allows you to tweak its behavior in many areas. If you want to change the URL extension by which the framework recognizes which requests it should handle, you can configure the framework to recognize any extension that you like. By default, Struts 2 looks for URLs ending in `.action`, but you could configure the framework to look for `.do` (the Struts 1.x default extension) or even no extension at all. Other examples of configurable parameters include maximum file upload size and the development mode flag. Due to its administrative nature, we'll explain this type of configuration as we come to topics in the book that can be configured.

For now, we'll focus on how to build web applications.

DECLARING YOUR APPLICATION'S ARCHITECTURE

The more important type of configuration, which we'll refer to as declarative architecture, involves defining the Struts 2 components that your application will use and linking them together—or *wiring* them—to form your required workflow paths. By *workflow path*, we mean which action fires when a particular URL is hit, and which results might be chosen by that action to complete processing.

DEFINITION   Declarative architecture is a specialized type of configuration that allows developers to create an application's architecture through description rather than programmatic intervention. The developer describes the architectural components in high-level artifacts, such as XML files or Java annotations, from which the system will create the runtime instance of the application.

The developer needs only to declare which objects will serve as the actions, results, and interceptors of their application. This process of declaration primarily consists of specifying which Java class will implement the necessary interface. Almost all of the Struts 2 architectural components are defined as interfaces. In reality, the framework provides implementations for nearly all of the components you'll ever need to use. For instance, the framework comes with implementations of results to handle many types of view-layer technologies. Typically, a developer will only need to implement actions and wire them to built-in results and interceptors. Furthermore, the use of intelligent defaults and annotations can further reduce the manual tasks needed in this area.

2.1.2   Two mechanisms for declaring your architecture

Now we'll look at the nuts and bolts of declaring your architecture. There are two ways to do this: through XML-based configuration files or through Java annotations. Figure 2.1 demonstrates the dual interface to the declarative architecture.

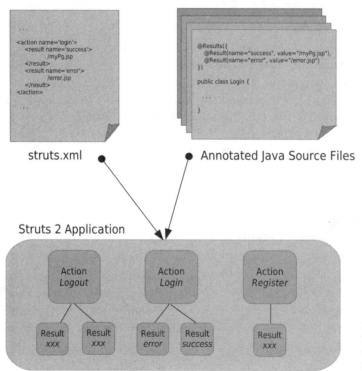

Figure 2.1   Declaring your Struts 2 application architecture with XML or annotations

As you can see, whether your application's Struts 2 components are declared in XML or in annotations, the framework translates them into the same runtime components. In the case of the XML, we have the familiar XML configuration document with elements describing your application's actions, results, and interceptors. With annotations, the XML is gone. Now, the metadata is collected in Java annotations that reside directly within the Java source for the classes that implement your actions. Regardless of which method you use, the framework produces the same runtime application. The two mechanisms are redundant in the sense that you can use whichever you like without functional consequence. The declarative architecture is the real concept here. Which style of declaration you choose is largely a matter of taste. For now, let's meet the candidates and see how each works.

XML-BASED DECLARATIVE ARCHITECTURE

Many of you are already familiar with the use of XML for declarative software development. Struts 2 allows you to use XML files to describe your application's desired Struts 2 architectural components. In general, the XML documents will consist of elements that represent the application's components. Listing 2.1 shows an example of XML elements that declare actions and results.

Listing 2.1 XML declarative architecture elements

```
<action name="Login" class="manning.Login">
   <result>/AccountPage.jsp</result>
   <result name="input">/Login.jsp</result>
</action>

<action name="Registration" >
   <result>/Registration.jsp</result>
</action>

<action name="Register" class="manning.Register">
   <result>/RegistrationSuccess.jsp</result>
   <result name="input">/Registration.jsp</result>
</action>
```

We won't go into the details of these elements now. We just show this as an example of what XML-style declarative architecture looks like. Typically, an application will have several XML files containing elements like these that describe all of the components of the application. Even though most applications will have more than one XML file, all of the files work together as one large description. The framework uses a specific file as the entry point into this large description. This entry point is the struts.xml file. This file, which resides on the Java classpath, must be created by the developer. While it's possible to declare all your components in struts.xml, developers more commonly use this file only to include secondary XML files in order to modularize their applications.

We'll see XML-based declarative architecture in action when we look at the Hello-World application in a few moments.

JAVA ANNOTATION–BASED DECLARATIVE ARCHITECTURE

A relatively new feature of the Java language, annotations allow you to add metadata directly to Java source files. One of the loftier goals of Java annotations is support for tools that can read metadata from a Java class and do something useful with that information. Struts 2 uses Java annotations in this way. If you don't want to use XML files, the declarative architecture mechanism can be configured to scan Java classes for Struts 2–related annotations. We'll explain how the framework finds the classes that it should scan for annotations when we demo the annotated version of HelloWorld, which we'll do shortly. Listing 2.2 shows what these annotations look like.

Listing 2.2   Using annotations for declarative architecture

```
@Results({
   @Result(name="input", value="/RegistrationSuccess.jsp" )
   @Result(value="/RegistrationSuccess.jsp" )
})

public class Login implements Action {

   public String execute() {

      //Business logic for login

   }
}
```

Note that the annotations are made on the Java classes that implement the actions. Listing 2.2 shows the code from the Login class, which itself will serve as the Login action. Just like their counterpart elements in the XML, these annotations contain metadata that the framework uses to create the runtime components of your application.

We'll fully explain this material throughout the course of the book, but it might be worthwhile to note the relationship between the Login action's XML element in listing 2.1 and the annotations of listing 2.2, which are made directly on the Login.java source itself. The annotation-based mechanism is considered by many to be a more elegant solution than the XML mechanism. For one thing, the annotation mechanism is heavily combined with convention-based deduction of information. In other words, some of the information that must be explicitly specified in the XML elements can be deduced automatically from the Java package structure to which the annotated classes belong. For instance, you don't need to specify the name of the Java class, as that is clearly implicit in the physical location of the annotations. Many developers also appreciate how annotations eliminate some of the XML file clutter that seems to increase year by year on the web application classpath. We'll demonstrate the fundamentals of annotation-based declarative architecture in the second version of the HelloWorld application provided later in this chapter.

WHICH METHOD SHOULD YOU USE?

Ultimately, choosing a mechanism for declaring architecture is up to the developer. The most important thing is to understand the concepts of the Struts 2 declarative architecture. If you understand those, moving between the XML or Java annotation–based mechanisms should be quite trivial. This book will use XML in its sample applications. We do this for a couple of reasons. First, we think the XML version is better suited to learning the framework. The XML file is probably more familiar to many of our readers, and, more importantly, it provides a more centralized notation of an application's components. This makes it easier to study the material when one is first learning the framework. Second, the annotations are a moving target at this point. The Struts 2 developers are ardently moving toward a zero-configuration system that uses convention over configuration, with annotations serving as an elegant override mechanism when conventions aren't followed. Many people are already using this system, but we think at this point it isn't the best approach to learning the framework. We do think that many of you will ultimately choose to use Java annotations to declare your application's components because of their elegance.

2.1.3   *Intelligent defaults*

Many commonly used Struts 2 components (or attributes of components) do not need to be declared by the developer. Regardless of which declaration style you choose, these components and attribute settings are already declared by the framework so that you can more quickly implement the most common portions of application functionality. Some framework components, such as interceptors and result types, may never need to be directly declared by the developer because those provided by the system handle the daily requirements of most developers. Other components, such as actions and results, will still need to be declared by the developer, but many common attribute settings can still be inherited from framework defaults.

DEFINITION   Intelligent defaults provide out-of-the-box components that solve common domain workflows without requiring further configuration by the developer, allowing the most common application tasks to be realized with minimum development.

These predefined components are part of the Struts 2 intelligent defaults. In case you're interested, many of these components are declared in struts-default.xml, found in the struts2-core.jar. This file uses XML to declare an entire package of intelligent default components, the `struts-default` package. Starting with the upcoming Hello-World application, and continuing through the rest of the book, we'll learn how to take advantage of the components offered in this default package.

2.2   *A quick hello*

Now we'll present two HelloWorld applications, one with XML and one with annotations, that will bring all this to life. First, we'll introduce the XML version of the application. We'll explore the use of the XML as well as discuss how the application demonstrates the Struts 2 architecture. We'll also introduce the basic layout of a Struts 2 application. Then we'll revisit the same application implemented with annotations, focusing on the annotations themselves. As we've said, the two styles of declaring your architecture are just two interfaces to the same declarative architecture. Which one you choose has no functional bearing on your Struts 2 application. The two HelloWorld applications, which differ only in the style of architectural declaration, will make this point concrete.

2.2.1 *Deploying the sample application*

To deploy an application, you need a servlet container. This sounds simple, but it's not. As authors of this book, we find this a troublesome question. Since servlet containers are built to the Servlet Specification, it doesn't matter which one you use. In short, you just need to deploy the sample applications on a servlet container. It's your choice. Some books attempt to walk you through the installation details for a specific container. The problem with this is that it's never as simple as they make it sound.

Furthermore, we think the benefits gained from learning to install a servlet container far outweigh any short-term gains to be had from any container-specific quick start we might try to provide. If you're experienced with Java web application development, you'll already have your own container preferences and know how to deploy a web application in your chosen container. If you're new to Java web application development, you can probably expect to spend a few hours reading some online documentation and working through the installation process. Deploying a web application on a running container is typically point-and-click simple. Choosing a servlet container can be overwhelming, but for newbies we recommend Apache Tomcat. It's arguably the most popular open source implementation of the Servlet Specification. It's both easy to obtain and certain to be as specified.

Though perhaps less fundamental than the choice of a servlet container, choosing an IDE and a build tool can be just as important. Our goal is to provide build- and IDE-agnostic sample applications. We recognize that we might save you some time by providing an Ant build file with Tomcat targets, for instance, but, if you don't use Ant and Tomcat, that doesn't help and may even hinder your progress. We should note that the Struts 2 community, along with much of the Java open source community, has strongly adopted Maven 2 as their build/project management tool. If you plan to have more than a fleeting relationship with the Struts 2 source code, a working knowledge of Maven practice would serve you well.

Provided you have a servlet container, the only thing left to do is deploy the sample application WAR file in accordance with the requirements of your container. You can obtain the sample application from the Manning web site. All of the sample code from this book is contained in a single Struts 2 web application. This application is packaged in the Struts2InAction.war file. Once you've deployed this web application to your container, point your browser to http://localhost:8080/ Struts2InAction/Menu.action to see the main menu for the sample application. Note that this assumes that the sample application has been deployed on your local machine and that the servlet container is listening on port 8080. Figure 2.2 shows the menu.

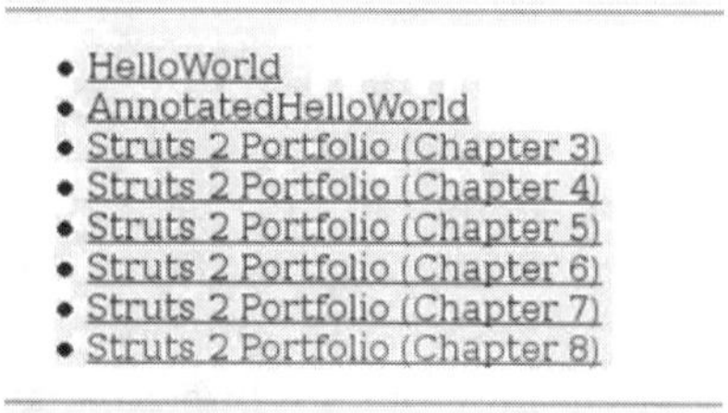

- HelloWorld
- AnnotatedHelloWorld
- Struts 2 Portfolio (Chapter 3)
- Struts 2 Portfolio (Chapter 4)
- Struts 2 Portfolio (Chapter 5)
- Struts 2 Portfolio (Chapter 6)
- Struts 2 Portfolio (Chapter 7)
- Struts 2 Portfolio (Chapter 8)

Figure 2.2 The sample application is organized into several mini-applications.

As you can see from figure 2.2, the sample application has been organized into a series of mini-applications. Basically, we have two versions of the HelloWorld application and many versions of the Struts 2 Portfolio application. Technically, all of these are just one big Struts 2 application. However, the flexibility of the framework allows us to cleanly modularize the sample code for all of the chapters so that we can present distinct versions of the application for each chapter. This allows us to, for instance, present a simple version of the Struts 2 Portfolio while covering the basics in early chapters, and then provide a full-featured version for later chapters.

> ### Extra! Extra! Independent HelloWorld WAR
>
> As we go to press, we've responded to feedback from our Manning Early Access Program (MEAP) readers by adding a separate WAR file version of the HelloWorld sample application. Many of our readers wanted to see HelloWorld in the simplest packaging possible. Other readers wanted to see a minimal Struts 2 web application. To fulfill both these requests, we've broken the XML-based HelloWorld out into a standalone web application. Accordingly, you'll find HelloWorld.war also bundled with the downloadable code on the Manning site. This allows you to deploy the HelloWorld application without configuring the database, or other resources, that the full application depends upon. Also, it provides you with a perfect skeleton application for jumpstarting your own projects.
>
> Note: We didn't remove HelloWorld from the main sample web application (Struts2InAction.war); we just created the bonus application for your convenience. You can work from either version as you read through this chapter, though we'll assume you're using the full Struts2InAction web application.

THE LAYOUT OF A STRUTS 2 WEB APPLICATION

The entire Struts2InAction.war file can be used as a template for understanding what's required of a Struts 2 web application. Most of the requirements for the application structure come from the requirements put on all web applications by the Servlet API. Figure 2.3 shows the exploded directory structure of the Struts2InAction.war file.

Again, if you aren't familiar with the Servlet Specification, a quick read might be worth your while. For our purposes, we'll outline the most important aspects. First, all of the top-level directories, except WEB-INF, are in the document root of the web application. Typically, this is where our JSP files will go. You can also put Velocity and FreeMarker templates here, as we'll do, but those resources can also load from JAR files on the classpath. In the sample application, we've organized our JSPs according to the chapter to which they belong. One important thing to note about the document root is that these resources can potentially be served as static resources by the servlet container. If not configured to prevent such access, a URL that directly points to resources in the document root can result in the servlet container spitting out that resource. Because of this, the document root is not considered a secure place for sensitive material.

All of the important stuff goes in WEB-INF. As you can see in figure 2.3, the top-level contents of WEB-INF include two directories, lib and classes, and the file web.xml. Note that there's also a directory called src, but that's our project source code. This is not a required part of the web application directory structure. We've put it here for convenience. You could put it anywhere, depending on the details of your build process. Ultimately, you'll most likely not want source code in a production-ready web application. We've done it this way as a convenient, build–agnostic alternative.

As for the other two directories, they're essential. The lib directory holds all of the JAR file dependencies that your application needs. In the sample application, we've placed all of the JARs commonly used by Struts 2 web applications. Note that Struts 2 is flexible. If you add some features that we don't use in this book, you might need to add additional JARs. Also note that, if you want to see the

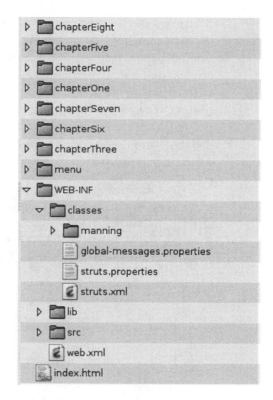

Figure 2.3   The exploded directory structure of our Struts 2 sample application

absolute minimum set of JARs, you should check out HelloWorld.war, referenced in an earlier sidebar. The classes directory holds all of the Java classes that your application will use. These are essentially no different than the resources in the lib directory, but the classes directory contains an exploded directory structure containing the class files, no JARs. In figure 2.3, you can see that the classes directory holds one directory, manning, which is the root of our applications Java package structure, and it holds several other classpath resource files, such as properties files and the struts.xml file we've already discussed.

In addition to the lib and classes directories, WEB-INF also contains the central configuration file of all web applications, web.xml. This file, formally known as the *deployment descriptor*, contains definitions of all of the servlets, servlet filters, and other Servlet API components contained in this web application. Listing 2.3 shows the web.xml file of our sample application.

Listing 2.3   The web.xml deployment descriptor of our sample application

```
<?xml version="1.0" encoding="UTF-8"?>
<web-app version="2.4" xmlns="http://java.sun.com/xml/ns/j2ee"
    xmlns:xsi="http://www.w3.org/2001/XMLSchema-instance"
    xsi:schemaLocation="http://java.sun.com/xml/ns/j2ee
```

```
         http://java.sun.com/xml/ns/j2ee/web-app_2_4.xsd">

    <display-name>S2 Example Application - Chapter 1 - Hello World
      </display-name>
                                                        FilterDispatcher:
                                                        Struts 2 begins here
    <filter>
       <filter-name>struts2</filter-name>        ←———┘
       <filter-class>org.apache.struts2.dispatcher.FilterDispatcher
         </filter-class>
       <init-param>                                   ←———┐
          <param-name>actionPackages</param-name>         Tell Struts
          <param-value>manning</param-value>              where to find
       </init-param>                                      annotations
    </filter>

    <filter-mapping>
       <filter-name>struts2</filter-name>
       <url-pattern>/*</url-pattern>                      A servlet
    </filter-mapping>                                     outside of
                                                          Struts
    <servlet>                                     ←———————┘
       <servlet-name>anotherServlet</servlet-name>
       <servlet-class>manning.servlet.AnotherServlet</servlet-class>
    </servlet>

    <servlet-mapping>
      <servlet-name>anotherServlet</servlet-name>
      <url-pattern>/anotherServlet</url-pattern>
    </servlet-mapping>

    <welcome-file-list>
       <welcome-file>index.html</welcome-file>
    </welcome-file-list>

</web-app>
```

For a Struts 2 application, the most important elements in this deployment descriptor are the filter and filter-mapping elements that set up the Struts 2 Filter-Dispatcher. This servlet filter is basically the Struts 2 framework. This filter will examine all the incoming requests looking for requests that target Struts 2 actions. Note the URL pattern to which this filter is mapped: "/*." This means the filter will inspect all requests. The other important thing about the configuration of the Filter-Dispatcher is the initialization parameter that we pass in. The actionPackages parameter is necessary if you're going to use annotations in your application. It tells the framework which packages to scan for annotations. We'll see more about this when we get to the annotated version of HelloWorld in a few pages.

One other interesting thing to note is that we've included a non-Struts 2 servlet in our web application. As we said earlier, a web application is defined as a group of servlets packaged together. Many Struts 2 web applications won't have any other servlets in them. In fact, since Struts 2 uses a servlet filter rather than a servlet, many Struts 2 applications won't have any servlets in them—unless you count compiled JSPs. Since it's not uncommon to integrate other servlets with the framework, we've included another servlet, as seen in listing 2.3, in our web application. We'll demonstrate using this servlet later in the book.

Now you should know how to set up a skeletal Struts 2 application. Everything in our sample application is by the book except for the presence of the source directory in WEB-INF. As we said, this has been done as a convenience. You'll probably want to structure your build according to industry best practices. We haven't provided such a build because we think it only complicates the learning curve. Now it's time to look at the HelloWorld application.

2.2.2   *Exploring the HelloWorld application*

The HelloWorld application aims to provide the simplest possible introduction to Struts 2. However, it also tries to exercise all of the core Struts 2 architectural components. The application has a simple workflow. It'll collect a user's name from a form, use that to build a custom greeting for the user, and then present the user with a web page that displays the customized greeting. This workflow, while ultrasimple, will clearly demonstrate the function and usage of all the Struts 2 components, such as actions, results, and interceptors. Additionally, it'll demonstrate the mechanics of how data flows through the framework, including the ValueStack and OGNL. As Struts 2 is a sophisticated framework, we'll be limited to a high-level view. Rest assured that the rest of the book will spend adequate time on each of these topics.

HELLOWORLD USER GUIDE

First, let's look at what the HelloWorld application actually does. Provided you've deployed the application to your servlet container, select the HelloWorld link from the menu we saw earlier. Note that we're starting with the XML version, not the annotated version. You'll be presented with a simple form, seen in figure 2.4, that asks for your name.

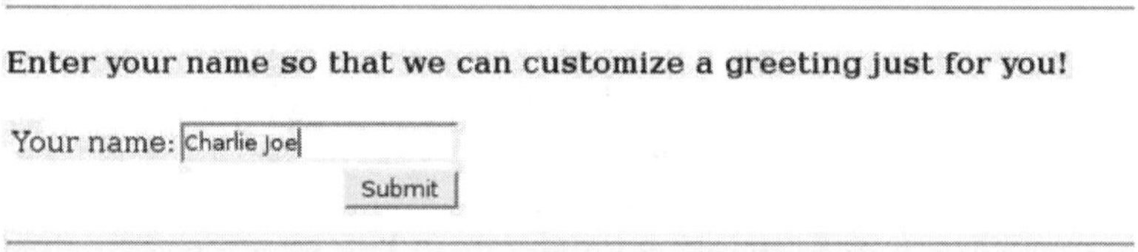

Enter your name so that we can customize a greeting just for you!

Your name: [Charlie Joe]

Submit

Figure 2.4   The first page collects the user's name.

Enter your name and click the Submit button. The application will prepare your customized greeting and return a new page for you, as seen in figure 2.5.

The figure shows the customized greeting message built by the action and displayed via a JSP page. That's it. Now, let's see what the Struts 2 architecture of this simple application looks like.

Custom Greeting Page

Hello Charlie Joe

Figure 2.5   The second page presents the customized greeting, built from the submitted name.

HELLOWORLD DETAILS

We'll begin by looking at the architectural components used by HelloWorld. This version of HelloWorld uses XML to declare its architecture. As we've said, the entry point into the XML declarative architecture is the struts.xml file. We've also said that many developers use this root document to include other XML documents, allowing for modularization. We've done this for the sample application, modularizing on the basis of chapters. Listing 2.4 shows WEB-INF/classes/struts.xml, the most important aspect of which are the `include` elements that pull in the modularized XML documents.

Listing 2.4 The entry point into XML-based declarative architecture

```
<?xml version="1.0" encoding="UTF-8" ?>
<!DOCTYPE struts PUBLIC
    "-//Apache Software Foundation//DTD Struts Configuration 2.0//EN"
    "http://struts.apache.org/dtds/struts-2.0.dtd">

<struts>

  <constant name="struts.devMode" value="true" />          ❶ Use constants
                                                              to tweak Struts
                                                              properties

    <package name="default" namespace="/" extends="struts-default">
      <action name="Menu">                     Menu action
        <result>/menu/Menu.jsp</result>        belongs to a
      </action>                                default package
    </package>
                                                              Include
                                                              modularized
      <include file="manning/chapterTwo/chapterTwo.xml"/>     XML docs
      <include file="manning/chapterThree/chapterThree.xml"/>

      . . .

      <include file="manning/chapterEight/chapterEight.xml"/>

</struts>
```

Though off topic, we should note that the constant element ❶ can be used to set framework properties; here we set the framework to run in development mode. You can also do this with property files, as we'll see later. Also off topic, we should note that struts.xml is a good place to define some global actions in a default package. Since our main menu doesn't belong to any of our modularized mini-applications, we place it here. Finally back on topic, we see the most important aspect of the struts.xml file, a long list of includes that pull all of our chapter-based XML documents into the declarative architecture. All of these files will be pulled into this main document, in line, to create a single large XML document.

The HelloWorld application belongs to the Chapter Two module of sample code. Listing 2.5 shows the contents of WEB-INF/classes/manning/chapterTwo/chapterTwo.xml.

Listing 2.5 Using XML for declarative architecture

```
<?xml version="1.0" encoding="UTF-8" ?>
<!DOCTYPE struts PUBLIC
    "-//Apache Software Foundation//DTD Struts Configuration 2.0//EN"
    "http://struts.apache.org/dtds/struts-2.0.dtd">

<struts>

  <package name="chapterTwo" namespace="/chapterTwo" extends="struts-
    default">
```

```
    <action name="Name">
      <result>/chapterTwo/NameCollector.jsp</result>
    </action>

    <action name="HelloWorld" class="manning.chapterTwo.HelloWorld">
      <result name="SUCCESS">/chapterTwo/HelloWorld.jsp</result>
    </action>

  </package>

</struts>
```

Note that the real file in the application contains detailed comments about the various elements. This is true for all the examples in this book, but when we print listings here we'll remove the comments for clarity. This simple application has only two actions, and one of them hardly does anything. Both the `Name` and the `HelloWorld` actions declare some results for their own use. Each result names a JSP page that it will use to render the result page. The only other elements here are the `struts` root element and the `package` element. The `struts` element is the mandatory document root of all Struts 2 XML files and the `package` element is an important container element for organizing your actions, results, and other component elements.

For now, the only thing we need to note about the `package` element is that it declares a namespace that'll be used when the framework maps URLs to these actions. Figure 2.6 shows how the namespace of the package is used to determine the URL that maps to our actions.

The mapping process is simple. The URL combines the servlet context with the package namespace and the action name. Note that the action name takes the .action extension. Chapter 3 will more fully cover the mechanics of namespaces. The first action, the `Name` action, doesn't do any real back-end processing. It merely forwards to the page that will present the user with a form to collect her name.

BEST PRACTICE   Use empty action components to forward to your results, even if they're simple JSPs that require no dynamic processing. This keeps the application's architecture consistent, prewires your workflow in anticipation of increases in complexity, and hides the real structure of your resources behind the logical namespace of the Struts 2 actions.

While we could technically use a URL that hits the form JSP directly, a well-accepted best practice is to route these requests through actions regardless of their lack of

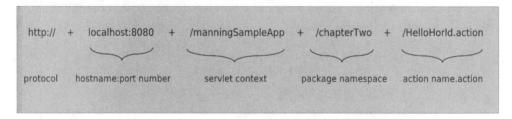

Figure 2.6   Anatomy of a URL: mapping a URL namespace to a Struts 2 action namespace

actual processing. As you can see, such pass-through actions do not specify an implementation class. They'll automatically forward to the result they declare. This action points directly at the NameCollector.jsp page, which renders the form that collects the name. Listing 2.6 shows the contents of /chapterTwo/NameCollector.jsp.

Listing 2.6   Using Struts 2 UI component tags to render the form

```
<%@ page contentType="text/html; charset=UTF-8" %>          Standard JSP
<%@ taglib prefix="s" uri="/struts-tags" %>                 directives

<html>

  <head>
    <title>Name Collector</title>
  </head>

  <body>                                                    Struts 2 UI
                                                            component
    <h4>Enter your name </h4>                               tags
    <s:form action="HelloWorld">
      <s:textfield name="name" label="Your name"/>
      <s:submit/>
    </s:form>

  </body>

</html>
```

At this point, we provide this listing only for the sake of full disclosure. We'll cover the Struts 2 UI component tags fully in chapter 6. For now, just note that a tag or two will render a complete HTML form. And, as you'll see, these tags also bind the form to the various features of the framework, such as automatic data transfer.

The second action, the `HelloWorld` action, receives and processes the submission of the name collection form, customizing a greeting with the user's name. While this business logic is still simple, it needs a real action. In its XML declaration, the `HelloWorld` action specifies `manning.chapterTwo.HelloWorld` as its implementation class. Listing 2.7 shows the simple code of this action implementation.

Listing 2.7   The `HelloWorld` action's `execute()` does the work

```
package manning.chapterTwo;

public class HelloWorld {

    private static final String GREETING = "Hello ";      The action's
                                                          business logic
    public String execute()  {

      setCustomGreeting( GREETING + getName() );
      return "SUCCESS";        Control string
    }                          will select result

    private String name;       JavaBeans properties
    private String customGreeting;   hold the data

    public String getName()  {
```

```
      return name;
    }

    public void setName(String name) {
      this.name = name;
    }

    public String getCustomGreeting()
    {
      return customGreeting;
    }

    public void setCustomGreeting( String customGreeting ){
      this.customGreeting = customGreeting;
    }
  }
}
```

As promised, there's not much to it. The execute() method contains the business logic, a simple concatenation of the submitted name with the greeting message. After this, the execute() method returns a control string that indicates which of its results should render the result page.

ACTION TIP   While many Struts 2 actions will implement the Action interface, which we'll cover in chapter 3, they're only obligated to meet an informal contract. The HelloWorld action satisfies that contract by providing an execute() method that returns a string. It doesn't need to actually implement the Action interface to informally satisfy the contract.

The only other important thing to note is the presence of JavaBeans properties to hold the application domain data. For now, recall that the action, as the MVC model component of the framework, both contains the business logic and serves as a locus of data transfer. Though there are other ways the action can hold the data, one common way is using JavaBeans properties. The framework will set incoming data onto these properties when preparing the action for execution. Then, during execution, the business logic in the action's execute() method can access and work with the data. Looking at the HelloWorld action, we see that the business logic both reads the name value from these properties and writes the custom greeting to these properties. In fact, it will be from these properties that the resulting JSP page will read the custom greeting.

Let's look at the JSP that renders the success result for the HelloWorld action. Listing 2.8 shows the HelloWorld.jsp file that does this rendering.

Listing 2.8   HelloWorld.jsp renders the result for the HelloWorld action

```
<%@ page contentType="text/html; charset=UTF-8" %>
<%@ taglib prefix="s" uri="/struts-tags" %>
<html>
    <head>
        <title>HelloWorld</title>
    </head>

    <body>

        <h3>Custom Greeting Page</h3>
```

```
<h4><s:property value="customGreeting"/></h4>
   </body>
</html>
```
⊲⎤ **Pulls data from**
　 ⎦ **ValueStack**

As you can see, this page is quite simple. The only thing to note is the Struts 2 `property` tag that displays the custom greeting message. Now you've seen all the code from front to back on a simple Struts 2 application.

　　You might still have questions about how the data gets from the front to the back of this process. Let's trace the path of data as it comes into, flows through, and ultimately exits the HelloWorld application. First, let's clear up some potential confusion regarding the location of data in the framework. In chapter 1, we learned that the framework provides something called the `ValueStack` for storing all of the domain data during the processing of a request. We also said that the framework uses a powerful expression language, OGNL, to reference and manipulate that data from various regions of the framework. But, as we've just learned, the action itself holds the domain data. In the case of the HelloWorld action, that data is held on JavaBeans properties exposed on the action itself. So, what gives?

　　In short, both are true. The data is both stored in the action and in the `ValueStack`. Here's how. First, domain data is always stored in the action. We'll see vari-

ants on this, but it's essentially true. This is great because it allows convenient access to data from the action's `execute()` method. So that the rest of the framework can access the data, the action object itself is placed on the `ValueStack`. The mechanics of the `ValueStack` are such that all properties of the action will then be exposed as top-level properties of the `ValueStack` itself and, thus, accessible via OGNL. Figure 2.7 demonstrates how this works with the `Hello-World` action as an example.

　　As figure 2.7 shows, the action holds the data, giving its own Java code convenient access. At the same time, the framework makes the properties of the action available on the `ValueStack` so that other regions of the framework can access the data as well. In terms of our HelloWorld application, the

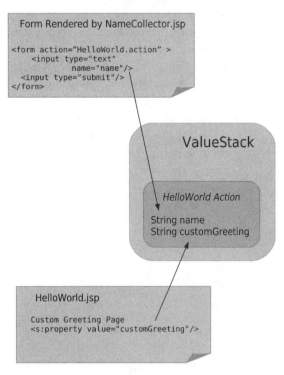

Figure 2.7　Every action is placed on the `ValueStack` so that its properties are exposed to framework-wide OGNL access.

two most important places this occurs are on the incoming form and the outgoing result page. In the case of the incoming request, the form field name attribute is interpreted as an OGNL expression. The expression is used to target a property on the ValueStack; in this case, the name property from our action. The value from the form field is automatically moved onto that property by the framework. On the other end, the result JSP pulls data off the customGreeting property by likewise using an OGNL expression, inside a tag, to reference a property on the ValueStack. Obviously, this complicated process needs more than a quick sketch. We'll cover it fully, particularly in chapters 5 and 6.

That gives us as much as we need to know at this point. We've seen how to declare actions and results. We've also learned a bit about how the data moves through the framework. You might've noticed that we didn't declare any interceptors. Despite the importance of interceptors, the HelloWorld application declares none of them. It avoids declaring interceptors itself by using the default interceptor stack provided by the framework. This is common practice.

One of the exciting new features of Struts 2 is the use of annotations instead of XML. What's the big deal? Let's see.

2.3   *HelloWorld using annotations*

Now we'll take a peek at the annotation-based version. We won't go back through how the application works. It's exactly the same. The only difference is in the declarative architecture mechanism used to describe our application's Struts 2 components. We've reimplemented the HelloWorld application and you can check it out by clicking the AnnotatedHelloWorld on the main menu page. It will work exactly the same. However, if you examine the source code, you'll see the difference.

As we've said, the annotations are placed directly in the source code of the actions. If we tell the framework where we keep our action classes, it will automatically scan them for annotations. The location of our actions is specified in an initialization parameter to the Struts 2 FilterDispatcher, defined in the web.xml deployment descriptor for the application. The following code snippet shows the relevant portions of that file.

```
<filter>
  <filter-name>struts2</filter-name>
  <filter-class>org.apache.struts2.dispatcher.FilterDispatcher
   </filter-class>

  <init-param>
    <param-name>actionPackages</param-name>
    <param-value>manning</param-value>     <--   Scan manning
  </init-param>                                   package for
</filter>                                         annotations
```

Note that the value of the parameter is a Java package name. But just telling the system where our action classes are isn't enough. In addition, we must somehow identify which classes are actions. To mark our classes as actions, we either make our actions implement the com.opensymphony.xwork2.Action interface or use a naming convention where our class names end with the word Action. We'll explain all about the Action interface in chapter 3. For now, all you need to know is that it's an interface that identifies the class as an action. In the annotation version of HelloWorld, one of our actions, the AnnotatedNameCollector, implements the Action interface to let the system know its true identity. The other action, AnnotatedHelloWorldAction, uses the naming convention.

Now that the framework knows how to find our annotations, let's see how they actually work. As we discuss annotations, we'll refer back to their counterparts in the XML version of HelloWorld. The most notable thing is that several of the elements disappear entirely. We don't have to provide any metadata for the package. If we accept the intelligent defaults of the annotation mechanism, the framework can create a package to hold our actions without our help. The framework makes some assumptions and generates the package for us. Most importantly, the framework assumes that our namespace for this package will be derived from the Java package namespace of the action class.

The entire Java package namespace isn't used. The framework only uses the portion of the package namespace beneath the package specified in the actionPackages parameter. In our case, we told the framework to look in the manning package, and our action classes reside in the manning.chapterOne Java package. The framework will give this package a namespace of chapterOne. In this fashion, all annotated actions in the same Java package will be added to the same Struts 2 package/namespace.

We also don't have to explicitly define the action, as we do with the XML method's action element. In fact, it's not possible to define the action ourselves. Since the annotations reside in the action class, the framework takes this as declaration of an action; this is convention over configuration at its finest. We don't need to inform Struts 2 about which class will provide the action implementation; it's obviously the class that contains the annotation. The name of the action is derived from the name of the Java class by a simple process. First, the Action portion of the class name, if present, is dropped. Second, the first letter is dropped to lowercase. For instance, this version of HelloWorld uses the AnnotatedHelloWorldAction class. After removing the ending and changing the case of the first letter, we end up with the following: http://localhost:8080/manningHelloWorld/chapterTwo/annotatedHelloWorld.action

We'll look at the annotations in the AnnotatedHelloWorldAction class first, since it's the core of our application. If you look at the source, you see that everything is the same as before. The only difference is the name and the presence of a class-level annotation. The most important part of the name is the use of the naming convention, where our class name ends with the word Action, to identify our class as an action. The annotation comes just before the class declaration:

```
@Result(name="SUCCESS", value="/chapterTwo/HelloWorld.jsp" )
```

Even if you're not familiar with Java annotations, it should be easy enough to see what's going on here. The information is exactly the same as in the XML elements.

While the package and action elements are gone, they've been derived from the Java class itself. Finally, the result annotation resides nested within the containing Java class and Java package, just as the result element was nested in the equivalent XML elements. The same wiring occurs; the same intelligent defaults are inherited.

We could leave off here, but we'd better say something about this other action. Do you recall that we wrapped NameCollector.jsp in an empty action element in the first example? We said that this use of a pass-through action, rather than hitting JSPs directly, was considered a best practice. We should try to do the same with our annotation version of the application. This is complicated by the fact that annotations occur within the action classes. This forces us to create an action class even though we don't really need one. But this isn't a problem.

If we look at AnnotatedNameCollector.java, we see that it is an empty class. This is shown in the following code snippet. It provides nothing but a container for the result annotation that points to our JSP page. This result annotation provides the same information as the corresponding `result` element from the XML version. Like the `result` XML element, it accepts the intelligent defaults for all attributes except the page it will render.

```
@Result( value="/chapterTwo/AnnotatedNameCollector.jsp" )

public class AnnotatedNameCollector extends ActionSupport {

    /* EMPTY */

}
```

There's more going on than we currently need to know, but we'll give the short version for now. This class extends `ActionSupport`. `ActionSupport` is a framework-provided implementation of the `Action` interface we mentioned earlier. In terms of action logic, it does nothing but render the result we've defined. It does provide some support to help some common tasks, which we'll learn about in chapter 3. For now, just note that it's a convenient helper class. Also, since it implements the `Action` interface for us, we can drop the class-naming convention and the framework will still pick this up while scanning for actions.

Now that we've covered the details of the two interfaces to Struts 2's declarative architecture, we should make sure you're not confused. Really, declarative architecture is what we're trying to learn, and it's cleanly designed. If the two styles of metadata make you dizzy, just breathe slowly and contemplate the clarity of the Struts 2 architecture that they both describe. Ultimately, the HelloWorld application, no matter how you describe it, consists of a pair of Struts 2 actions. The first one receives the request for the name collection form. The second one receives the name from the form, processes it, and returns the customized greeting.

2.4   *Summary*

There you go! We've broken the ice and gotten something up and running. Not only have we finished our HelloWorld, we've completed part 1 of this book. At this point, you should have a good grasp of the fundamentals of building a Struts 2 web application. Let's review what we've learned in this chapter before moving on.

In this chapter, we introduced the declarative architecture of Struts 2. While some refer to this as configuration, we like to distinguish between configuration of the framework itself and configuration of your application's architecture. The former, probably more correctly labeled configuration, involves tweaking or tuning the behavior and performance of the framework. The latter plays a much more central role in the development of our web applications; it involves the nuts and bolts of defining your application's structure. This is the declarative architecture of Struts 2.

The framework provides two interfaces for declaring the architectural components of which your application consists: XML and Java annotations. As we've seen, both are fairly simple. While annotations are considered by many to be more elegant than XML, we've opted to use XML because of its educational convenience. But we expect that many of you will ultimately choose annotations over XML. Once you've learned the framework, it'll be easy to start using annotations. As we've indicated, they're a part of a movement toward zero-configuration Struts 2 development. Please check the Struts 2 website for more information.

With the high-level overviews, architectural glosses, and the obligatory HelloWorld out of the way, we've officially completed the introductory portion of the book. Coming up is chapter 3, which kicks off part 2 by providing an in-depth discussion of Struts 2 actions. We'll also start developing our full-featured Struts 2 Portfolio sample application in chapter 3.

Part 2

Core concepts: actions, interceptors, and type conversion

Now that we've taken the general lay of the land, it's time to get down to business. The next few chapters introduce all the core components of the Struts 2 architecture. These components make up the functionality of your application as well as the framework itself. We'll provide in-depth discussions of the roles these components play in the framework, and back that up with real code samples as we start to build our Struts 2 Portfolio sample application.

In chapter 3, we jump right in and start working with the Struts 2 action. This component is the heart of the framework and is the component that a developer will spend the most time with on a daily basis. After that, chapter 4 introduces the interceptors. These critical components, while taking less of a developer's time, are where all of the framework's functionality is. Some developers will be unfamiliar with these components, but they're powerful and we take plenty of time to make sure everyone comes away with a firm grip on them. Chapter 5 finishes up the tour of the framework's core pieces by introducing the mechanisms that support the automatic data transfer and type conversion facilities. You can get by without knowing much about this stuff, but a solid footing will open new horizons of efficient and effective development.

By the time you finish this part, you'll be able to build your own Struts 2 application. If you're ready to start learning what Struts 2 is all about, these are the chapters for you.

3

Working with Struts 2 actions

This chapter covers

- Bundling actions into packages
- Implementing actions
- Introducing object-backed properties and `ModelDriven` actions
- Uploading files

With the overviews and introductions behind us, it's time to study the core components of Struts 2. First up, actions. As we've learned, actions do the core work for each request. They contain the business logic, hold the data, and then select the result that should render the result page. This is an action-oriented framework; actions are at its heart. In the end, you'll spend much of your time as a Struts 2 developer working with actions.

This chapter will give you everything you need to start building your application's actions. Using the XML-based mechanism for declarative architecture, we'll explore all of the options available to us when we declare our actions, see some convenience classes that aid development of actions, and cover the most common ways of carrying data in the action. The previous chapter used JavaBeans properties. We'll also see how interceptors work together with actions to provide much of the framework's functionality. In fact, we'll end with a useful case study of a file upload action. We will also start to develop our full-featured sample application, the Struts 2 Portfolio, to help demonstrate the concepts and techniques of this chapter.

As it turns out, we can't show you actions without introducing a fair amount of other material. We'll try to keep the focus on actions as much as possible. But you'll probably pick up enough of the other stuff to get your own simple Struts 2 application up and running. There's a lot to learn in this chapter. If you're ready, let's go.

3.1 *Introducing Struts 2 actions*

To set the stage, we'll start with a sketch of the role that actions play in the framework. We'll explain the purpose and various roles of the action component. We'll contrast the Struts 2 action with the similarly named component in Struts 1. And we'll study the obligations that an object serving in the role of an action has toward the framework in general. Struts 2 is an egalitarian enterprise. Any class can be an action as long as it satisfies its obligations to the framework. Let's find out what these important components do for the framework.

3.1.1 *What does an action do?*

Actions do three things. First, as you probably understand by now, an action's most important role, from the perspective of the framework's architecture, is encapsulating the actual work to be done for a given request. The second major role is to serve as a data carrier in the framework's automatic transfer of data from the request to the view. Finally, the action must assist the framework in determining which result should render the view that'll be returned in the request response. Let's see how the action component fulfills each of these various roles.

By the way, we're going to demonstrate our points in the coming paragraphs with examples from the HelloWorld application from chapter 2. But don't worry; we'll start building the real-world Struts 2 Portfolio in a few pages.

ACTIONS ENCAPSULATE THE UNIT OF WORK

Earlier in this book, we saw that the action fulfills the role of the MVC model for the framework. One of the central responsibilities of this role is the containment of business logic; actions use the execute() method for this purpose. The code inside this method should concern itself only with the logic of the work associated with the request. The following code snippet, from the previous chapter's HelloWorld application, shows the work done by the HelloWorldAction.

```
public String execute() {
    setCustomGreeting( GREETING + getName() );
    return "SUCCESS";
}
```

The action's work is to build a customized greeting for the user. As we can see, this action's execute() method does little else than build this greeting. In this case, the business logic amounts to little more than a concatenation. If it were much more complex, we'd probably have bumped that logic out to a business component and injected that component into the action. The use of dependency injection, which helps keep code such as actions clean and decoupled, is supported by the framework. We'll learn some techniques that utilize the framework's Spring integration for injecting these components later in the book. For now, just keep in mind that our actions hold the business logic, or at least the entry point to the business logic, and they should keep that logic as pure and brief as possible.

ACTIONS PROVIDE LOCUS FOR DATA TRANSFER

Being the model component of the framework also means that the action is expected to carry the data around. While you might think this would make actions more complicated, it actually makes them cleaner. Since the data is held local to the action, it's always conveniently available during the execution of the business logic. There might be a bunch of JavaBeans properties adding lines of code to the action, but when the `execute()` method references the data in those properties, the proximity of the data makes that code all the more succinct.

Listing 3.1, also from `HelloWorldAction`, shows the code that allows that action to carry request data.

Listing 3.1 Transferring request data to the action's JavaBeans properties

```
private String name;

public String getName() {
    return name;
}

public void setName(String name) {
    this.name = name;
}

private String customGreeting;

public String getCustomGreeting()
{
    return customGreeting;
}

public void setCustomGreeting( String customGreeting ){
    this.customGreeting = customGreeting;
}
```

The action merely implements JavaBeans properties for each piece of data that it wishes to carry. We saw this in action with the HelloWorld application. Request parameters from the form are moved to properties that have matching names. As we saw, the framework does this automatically. In this case, the `name` parameter from the name collection form will be set on the `name` property. In addition to receiving the incoming data from the request, these JavaBeans properties on the action will also expose the data to the result. The `HelloWorld` action's logic sets the custom greeting on the `customGreeting` property, which makes it available to the result as well.

In addition to these simple JavaBeans properties, there are a couple of other techniques for using the action as a data transfer object. We'll examine these alternatives later in this chapter, and will also examine the mechanisms by which the actual data transfer occurs. For now, we just want to recognize that the action serves as a centralized data transfer object that can be used to make the application data available in all tiers of the framework.

The use of actions as data transfer objects should probably ring some alarms in the minds of alert Struts 1 developers. In Struts 1, there's only one instance of a given action class. If this were still true, we couldn't use the action object itself as a data carrier for the request. In a multithreaded environment, such as a web application, it'd be problematic to store data in instance fields as we've seen. Struts 2 solves this problem by creating a new instance of an action for each request that maps to it. This fundamental difference allows Struts 2 objects to exist as dedicated data transfer objects for each request.

ACTIONS RETURN CONTROL STRING FOR RESULT ROUTING

The final duty of an action component is to return a control string that selects the result that should be rendered. Previous frameworks passed routing objects into the entry method of the action. Returning a control string eliminates the need for these objects, resulting in a cleaner signature and an action that is less coupled to specific routing code. The value of the return string must match the name of the desired result as configured in the declarative architecture. For instance, the `HelloWorldAction` returns the string `"SUCCESS"`. As you can see from our XML declaration, `SUCCESS` is the name of the one of the result components.

```
<action name="HelloWorld" class="manning.chapterOne.HelloWorld">
    <result name="SUCCESS">/chapterTwo/HelloWorld.jsp</result>
    <result name="ERROR">/chapterTwo/Error.jsp</result>
</action>
```

The HelloWorld application has a simple logic for determining which result it will choose. In fact, it'll always choose the `"SUCCESS"` result. Most real-world actions will have a more complex determination process, and the result choices will almost always include some sort of error result to handle problems that might occur during the action's interaction with the model. Regardless of the complexity, actions must ultimately return a string that maps to one of the result components available for rendering the view for that action.

You should now realize what an action does, but before we design one, we need to create the packages to contain them. In the next section, we'll see how to organize our actions into packages and take our first glimpse at the Struts 2 Portfolio application, the main sample application for this book.

3.2   *Packaging your actions*

Whether you declare your action components with XML or Java annotations, when the framework creates your application's architecture, it'll organize your actions and other components into logical containers called *packages*. Struts 2 packages are similar to Java packages. They provide a mechanism for grouping your actions based on commonality of function or domain. Many important operational attributes, such as the URL namespace to which actions will be mapped, are defined at the package level. And, importantly, packages provide a mechanism for inheritance, which among other things allows you to inherit the components already defined by the framework. In this section, we'll check out the details of Struts 2 packages by examining the Struts 2 Portfolio application's packaging.

First, we'll give a quick summary of our sample application's functionality and purpose in order to set the stage for factoring our actions into separate packages.

3.2.1 *The Struts 2 Portfolio application*

Throughout this book we'll develop and examine a sample application called the Struts 2 Portfolio. Artists can use the application to create an online portfolio of their work. The portfolio is a simple gallery of images. Artists must first register with the system to have a portfolio. It's free, but we'll collect some harmless personal information. Once the artist has an account, she can log in to the secure portion of the application to conduct such sensitive business as creating new portfolios, as well as adding and deleting images from those portfolios. The other side of the portfolio is the public side. A visitor to the public site can view the images in any of the portfolios. This public face of the portfolio won't be protected by security.

While this application is simple, it has enough complexity to demonstrate the core Struts 2 concepts, including packaging strategies. A quick analysis of our requirements tells us that we have two distinct regions in our web application. We have some functions that anyone can use, such as registering for accounts or viewing portfolios, and we have some secure functions, primarily account administration. Ultimately, these functionalities will be implemented with actions, and we can bet that the secure actions will have different requirements than nonsecure actions. Let's see how we can use Struts 2 packages to group our actions into secure and nonsecure packages.

3.2.2 *Organizing your packages*

It's up to you to decide on an organizational theme for your application's package space. We'll organize the Struts 2 Portfolio's packages based upon commonality of functionality, a common strategy. The important thing is to see how the packages can be declared and configured to achieve a given organizational structure. As noted earlier, you can declare your application's architectural components with XML files or with Java annotations located in your action class files. We also noted that we'll use XML files for our sample code. With that in mind, let's take a look at the chapterThree.xml file that declares the components for our first cut of the Struts 2 Portfolio application. You can find this file in /WEB-INF/classes/manning/chapterThree. This XML file contains declarations of two packages, one for public actions and one for secure actions. Listing 3.2 shows the declaration of the secure package.

Listing 3.2   Declaration of a package

```
<package name="chapterThreeSecure" namespace="/chapterThree/secure"
    extends="struts-default">
  <action name="AdminPortfolio" >
    <result>/chapterThree/AdminPortfolio.jsp</result>
  </action>

  <action name="AddImage" >
    <result>/chapterThree/ImageAdded.jsp</result>
  </action>

  <action name="RemoveImage" >
    <result>/chapterThree/ImageRemoved.jsp</result>
  </action>

</package>
```

The package declared in listing 3.2 contains all of the secure actions for the application. These actions require user authentication. A glance at the names of these actions should be sufficient to give a good idea of their functional purpose. Obviously, the actions that add and delete images from a portfolio should be secured behind authentication. We want to make sure that the user who's removing images from the portfolio actually owns that portfolio. Grouping these together allows us to share declarations of components that might be useful to our authentication mechanism. Additionally, we've chosen to give a special URL namespace to these secure actions. We want our users to notice from the URL that they have entered a secure region of the website.

Now, let's look at the package declaration itself. You can only set four attributes on a package: name, namespace, extends, and abstract. Table 3.1 summarizes these attributes.

Table 3.1   The attributes of the Struts 2 package

Attribute	Description
name (required)	Name of the package
namespace	Namespace for all actions in package
extends	Parent package to inherit from
abstract	If true, this package will only be used to define inheritable components, not actions

While it may be challenging to choose the strategy by which you divide your actions into packages, declaring them is simple. The only required attribute is the name. The name attribute is merely a logical name by which you can reference the package. In listing 3.2, we've named our package chapterThreeSecure. This, like all good names, indicates the purpose of this package: it contains the secure actions of the chapter 3 version of the Struts 2 Portfolio sample application.

Next, we set the `namespace` attribute to `"/chapterThree/secure"`. As we've seen, the `namespace` attribute is used to generate the URL namespace to which the actions of these packages are mapped. In the case of the `AddImage` action from listing 3.2, the URL will be built as follows: http://localhost:8080/manningHelloWorld/chapterThree/secure/AddImage.action

When a request to this URL arrives, the framework consults the `/chapterThree/secure` namespace for an action named `AddImage`. Note that you can give the same namespace to more than one package. If you do this, the actions from the two packages map to the same namespace. This isn't necessarily a problem. You might choose to separate your actions into separate packages for some functional reason that doesn't warrant a distinct namespace. In our case, we decide that we want the user to see a URL namespace change when he enters the secure region of the application.

NOTE *The Struts 2 Portfolio sample application*—We should make a few comments about the structure of the sample application. All of the sample code that we'll develop in this book comes in a single WAR file, Struts2InAction. war; it's one big web application in other words. (Recall that we also provided a skeletal repackaging of the HelloWorld example as a standalone web application, but that's just a bonus to help you see what a minimal Struts 2 web application looks like.) Inside the application are many "sub-applications," if you will. For instance, each chapter has its own version of the Struts 2 Portfolio. We've used the Struts 2 packaging mechanism to isolate these versions from one another. They all have their own namespaces and Struts 2 XML files. Not only does this allow us to offer versions of the Struts 2 Portfolio that focus on the specific goals of each chapter, thus decreasing the learning curve, it also serves to further demonstrate the usefulness of packages.

If you don't set the `namespace` attribute, your actions will go into the default namespace. The default namespace sits beneath all of the other namespaces waiting to resolve requests that don't match any explicit namespace. Consider the following: http://localhost:8080/manningHelloWorld/chapterSeventy/secure/AddImage.action

If this request arrives at our sample web application, the framework will attempt to locate the `/chapterSeventy/secure` namespace. As this namespace doesn't exist, the `AddImage` action won't be found in it. As a last resort, the framework will search the default namespace for the `AddImage` action. If it's found there, the URL resolves and the request is serviced. Note that the default namespace is actually the empty string `""`. You can also define a root namespace such as `"/"`. The root namespace is treated as all other explicit namespaces and must be matched. It's important to distinguish between the empty default namespace, which can catch all request patterns as long as the action name matches, and the root namespace, which is an actual namespace that must be matched.

The next attribute that we set in listing 3.2 is `extends`. This important attribute names another package whose components should be inherited by the current package. This is similar to the `extends` keyword in Java. If you think of the named package as being the superclass of your current package, you'll understand that the current package will inherit all the members of the superclass package. Furthermore, the current package can override members of the superclass package. Package inheritance plays a particularly important role in the use of the intelligent defaults we've been touting. Most of the intelligent defaults are defined in a built-in package called `struts-default`. You can inherit and use the components defined in that package by making your packages extend `struts-default`. But what exactly do you inherit?

3.2.3 *Using the components of the struts-default package*

Using the intelligent default components of the `struts-default` package is easy. You only need to extend that package when creating your own packages. Our `chapter-ThreeSecure` package does just this. By definition, an intelligent default shouldn't require that a developer do anything manually. Indeed, once you extend this package, many of the components automatically come into play. One good example is the default interceptor stack, which we've already used in the HelloWorld application. How did we use it?

DEFINITION   The `struts-default` package, defined in the system's struts-default.xml file, declares a huge set of commonly needed Struts 2 components ranging from complete interceptor stacks to all the common result types.

Here's the secret. Most of the interceptors that you'll ever need are found in the `struts-default` package that's declared in the struts-default.xml file. You can think of this important file as the framework's own declarative architecture artifact. The `struts-default` package that it defines contains common architectural components that all developers can reuse simply by having their own packages extend it. If you want to see the whole file, it can be found at the root level of the distribution's main JAR file, struts2-core.jar. Listing 3.3 shows the elements from this file that declare the default interceptor stack that will be used by most applications.

Listing 3.3 The `struts-default` package declares many commonly used components

```
<package name="struts-default">        ◁─┐  ❶ Package
                                             element
. . .

    <interceptor-stack name="defaultStack">  ◁─┐  Declares defaultStack
        <interceptor-ref name="exception"/>      ❷ interceptor stack
        <interceptor-ref name="alias"/>
        <interceptor-ref name="servlet-config"/>
        <interceptor-ref name="prepare"/>
        <interceptor-ref name="i18n"/>
        <interceptor-ref name="chain"/>
        <interceptor-ref name="debugging"/>
        <interceptor-ref name="profiling"/>
        <interceptor-ref name="scoped-model-driven"/>
        <interceptor-ref name="model-driven"/>
        <interceptor-ref name="fileUpload"/>
```

```
        <interceptor-ref name="checkbox"/>
        <interceptor-ref name="static-params"/>
        <interceptor-ref name="params">
            <param name="excludeParams">dojo\..*</param>
        </interceptor-ref>
        <interceptor-ref name="conversionError"/>
        <interceptor-ref name="validation">
            <param name="excludeMethods">input,back,cancel,browse</param>
        </interceptor-ref>
        <interceptor-ref name="workflow">
            <param name="excludeMethods">input,back,cancel,browse</param>
        </interceptor-ref>
    </interceptor-stack>

    . . .

    <default-interceptor-ref name="defaultStack"/>          ◁─┐  Sets the defaultStack
                                                              ❸  as default stack


    . . .

</package>
```

Inside the package element ❶, an interceptor stack is declared ❷. It's named, appropriately, defaultStack. Near the end of the listing, you can see that this stack is declared as the default interceptor stack for this package ❸, as well as any other packages that extend the struts-default package. Throughout the course of the book, we'll see and discuss all of the interceptors in the default stack. (We'll even learn how to write our own interceptors in chapter 4.) For now, we'll just point to one that you should be able to appreciate. Note the interceptor called params. If you've been wondering about the mysteriously automatic transfer of data from the request to the action, here's the answer. This important params interceptor has been the one moving data from the request parameters to our action's JavaBeans properties. There's no magic going on. The work is getting done with good old-fashioned lines of code. For the curious, these specific lines of code provide good insight into the inner workings of Struts 2; check out the source for com.opensymphony.xwork2.interceptor. ParametersInterceptor if you just can't help yourself.

As you can see from the params interceptor, much of the core functionality of the framework has been implemented as interceptors. While you're not *required* to extend the struts-default package when you create your own packages, omitting this bit of inheritance amounts to rejecting the core of the framework. Consider the package inheritance shown in Figure 3.1.

In this package, we see that the all-important defaultStack will be available to our chapterThreeSecure and chapterThreePublic packages. Figure 3.1 also shows someOtherPackage, which doesn't extend struts-default. This package starts from ground zero. Without the important interceptors defined in the defaultStack of the struts-default package, most of the framework's features are missing in action. Not the least of these would be the automatic data transfer we've discussed. Without these features, the framework is bare to say the least. You could always take the time

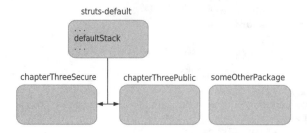

Figure 3.1   Much of the framework's functionality is obtained by extending the `struts-default` package.

to redeclare all of the components that the framework itself declares in the struts-default.xml file, but that would be tedious and pointless. Unless you have compelling reasons, you should always extend the `struts-default` package. And, as you'll see when we discuss interceptors in depth in chapter 4, the `struts-default` package declares its components in such a way as to make them flexible as well as reusable. All told, think twice before forgoing the extension of `struts-default`.

Now we have a pretty good idea of the mechanics of organizing our application into packages, as well as how to extend packages such as the built-in `struts-default` package. We've even seen one of the packages from the Struts 2 Portfolio sample application, the `chapterThreeSecure` package. In the end, packages will become something you don't think about much. In fact, once you have your application package structure in place, you won't even work with them much. We're now ready to build our Struts 2 Portfolio actions.

3.3   *Implementing actions*

Now it's time to start developing some actions. In this section, we'll cover all the basics of writing actions for your Struts 2 applications. As examples, we'll show you some of our actions from the chapter 3 version of the Struts 2 Portfolio application. While we'll provide thorough coverage of those actions, there's always more to investigate in the sample application than we have time to explore in the book. Don't hesitate to crack the source code; it's well commented!

Implementing Struts 2 actions is easy. Earlier in this chapter, we saw that the contract between the framework and the classes that back the actions provides a great deal of flexibility. Basically, any class can be an action if it wants. It simply must provide an entry method for the framework to invoke when the action is executed. Let's take a look at how the framework makes it even easier to implement your actions. As a case study, we'll continue our look at the Struts 2 Portfolio by digging into a couple of its own action classes.

> **NOTE**   Struts 2 actions don't have to implement the Action interface. Any object can informally honor the contract with the framework by simply implementing an execute() method that returns a control string.

3.3.1   *The optional Action interface*

Though the framework doesn't impose much in the way of formal requirements on your actions, it does provide an optional interface that you can implement. Implementing the Action interface costs little and comes with some convenient benefits. Let's see why most developers implement the Action interface when developing their actions, even though they don't have to.

WARNING Struts 2 gives developers both a fast development path built on intelligent defaults and an extremely high degree of flexibility to elegantly solve the most arcane use cases. When learning the framework, it can help to focus on the straightforward solutions supported by the intelligent defaults. Once comfortable with the normal way of handling things, the framework's flexibility will be natural and powerful. Without a good understanding of the straight and narrow, the framework's flexibility can admittedly leave one feeling concerned about which path to follow.

Most actions will implement the com.opensymphony.xwork2.Action interface. It defines just one method:

```
String execute() throws Exception
```

Since the framework doesn't make any type requirements, you could just put the method in your class without having your class implement this interface. This is fine. But the Action interface also provides some useful String constants that can be used as return values for selecting the appropriate result. The constants defined by the Action interface are

```
public static final String ERROR   "error"
public static final String INPUT   "input"
public static final String LOGIN   "login"
public static final String NONE    "none"
public static final String SUCCESS "success"
```

These constants can conveniently be used as the control string values returned by your execute() method. The true benefit is that these constants are also used internally by the framework. This means that using these predefined control strings allows you to tap into even more intelligent default behavior.

As an example, consider pass-through actions. Remember the pass-through action we used in the HelloWorld application? We said that it was a best practice to route even simple requests through actions. In the HelloWorld application, we used one of these empty actions to hit our JSP page that presents the form that collects the user's name. Here's the declaration of that action:

```
<action name="Name">
  <result>/chapterOne/NameCollector.jsp</result>
</action>
```

The Name action doesn't specify a class to provide the action implementation because there's nothing to do. We just want to go to the JSP page. Conveniently, the Struts 2 intelligent defaults provide a default action implementation that we inherit if we don't specify one. This default action has an empty execute() method that does nothing but automatically return the Action interface's SUCCESS constant as its control string. The framework must use this string to choose a result. Luckily, or maybe not so luckily, the default name attribute for the result element is also the SUCCESS constant. Since our sole result forgoes defining its own name, it inherits this default and is automatically selected by our action. This is the general pattern by which many of the intelligent defaults operate.

But wait; we don't need to implement the Action interface ourselves, because the framework provides an implementation we can borrow. Next we'll look at a convenience class that implements this and other helpful interfaces that help you further leverage the out-of-the-box features of the framework.

3.3.2   *The ActionSupport class*

In this section, we're going to introduce the ActionSupport class, a convenience class that provides default implementations of the Action interface and several other useful interfaces, giving us such things as data validation and localization of error messages. This convenience class is a perfect example of the Struts 2 straight and narrow we spoke of a bit earlier. The framework doesn't force you to use this, but it's a good idea to use it when learning the framework. In fact, it's pretty much always a good idea to use it unless you have reason not to.

Following in the tradition of "support" classes, ActionSupport provides default implementations of several important interfaces. If your actions extend this class, they automatically gain the use of these implementations. This alone makes this class worth learning. However, the implementations provided by this class also provide a great case study in how to make an action cooperate with interceptors to achieve powerfully reusable solutions to common tasks. In this case, validation and text localization services are provided via a combination of interceptors and interfaces. The interceptors control the execution of the services while the actions implement interfaces with methods that are invoked by the interceptors. This important pattern will become clearer as we work through the details of ActionSupport by examining its use in our Struts 2 Portfolio application, which we'll do a couple of pages from now.

BASIC VALIDATION

While Struts 2 provides a rich and highly configurable validation framework, which we'll fully examine in chapter 10, ActionSupport provides a quick form of basic validation that will serve well in many cases. Moreover, it's a great case study of how a cross-cutting task such as validation can be factored out of the action's execution logic through the use of interceptors and interfaces. The typical pattern is that the interceptor, while controlling the execution of a given task, may coordinate with the action by invoking methods that it exposes. Usually, these methods are part of a specific interface implemented by that action. In our case, ActionSupport implements two interfaces that coordinate with one of the interceptors from the default stack, the DefaultWorkflowInterceptor, to provide basic validation. If your package extends the struts-default package, thereby inheriting the default interceptor stack, and your action extends ActionSupport, thereby inheriting implementation of the two necessary interfaces, then you already have everything you need for clean validation of your data.

Just to make it clear where all of this built-in functionality comes from, we'll show you where these default interceptors are defined and how to ensure that you're inheriting them. Listing 3.4 shows the declaration of the `workflow` interceptor as it's found in the struts-default.xml file.

Listing 3.4   Declaration of `DefaultWorkflowInterceptor` from struts-default.xml

```
. . .

<interceptor name="workflow"       ❶
class="com.opensymphony.xwork2.interceptor.DefaultWorkflowInterceptor"/>

. . .

  <interceptor-stack name="defaultStack">        ❷

   . . .

   <interceptor-ref name="params"/>       ❸

   . . .

   <interceptor-ref name="workflow">
      <param name="excludeMethods">input,back,cancel,browse</param>      ❹
   </interceptor-ref>

   . . .

<interceptor-stack name="defaultStack">

   . . .
```

In listing 3.4, we first see the declaration element for the `workflow` interceptor ❶, specifying a name and an implementation class. Note that this is called the workflow interceptor because it will divert the workflow of the request back to the input page if a validation error is found. Next, we see the declaration of the default interceptor stack ❷. We haven't included all of the interceptors in this listing. Instead, we'll focus on the interceptors that participate in the validation process. Note that the `params` interceptor ❸ comes before the `workflow` interceptor ❹. The `params` interceptor will move the request data onto our action object. Then, the `workflow` interceptor will help us validate that data before accepting it into our model. The `workflow` interceptor must fire after the `params` interceptor has had a chance to move the data on to the action object. As with most interceptors, sequence is important.

Now, let's see how this validation actually works. We'll use one of our actions from this chapter's version of the Struts 2 Portfolio, the `Register` action, to demonstrate. As with the `params` interceptor, the `workflow` interceptor seeks to remove the logic of a cross-cutting task, validation in this case, from the action's execution logic. When the `workflow` interceptor fires, it'll first look for a `validate()` method on the action to invoke. You'll place your validation logic in `validate()`. This method is exposed via the `com.opensymphony.xwork2.Validateable` interface. Technically speaking, `Action-Support` implements the `validate()` method, but we have to override its empty implementation with our own specific validation logic.

As we've said, we're going to demonstrate the concepts and strategies of this book by developing the Struts 2 Portfolio application. In this section, we'll examine the Register action from the chapter 3 version of that application. Let's look at the entire source of that action class. Listing 3.5 shows the entire source of the Register action, found in the source directory of the sample application at manning/chapterThree/Register.java.

Listing 3.5   The Register action provides validation logic in the validate() method.

```java
public class Register extends ActionSupport {            ❶

    public String execute(){
        User user = new User();
        user.setPassword( getPassword() );
        user.setPortfolioName( getPortfolioName() );         ❷
        user.setUsername( getUsername() );

        getPortfolioService().createAccount( user );
        return SUCCESS;
    }
    private String username;
    private String password;
    private String portfolioName;

    public String getPortfolioName() {
        return portfolioName;
    }
    public void setPortfolioName(String portfolioName) {
        this.portfolioName = portfolioName;
    }
    public String getPassword() {                            ❸
        return password;
    }
    public void setPassword(String password) {
        this.password = password;
    }
    public String getUsername() {
        return username;
    }
    public void setUsername(String username) {
        this.username = username;
    }
    public void validate(){                                  ❹

        PortfolioService ps = getPortfolioService();     ❺     ❻
        if ( getPassword().length() == 0 ){
            addFieldError( "password", "Password is required.") );   ❼
        }
        if ( getUsername().length() == 0 ){
            addFieldError( "username", "Username is required." );
        }
```

```
if ( getPortfolioName().length() == 0  ){
   addFieldError( "portfolioName", "Portfolio name is required.");
}

if ( ps.userExists(getUsername() ) ){
   addFieldError("username", "This user already exists.");
}

}


public PortfolioService getPortfolioService( ) {

   return new PortfolioService();

}
```

While we show the entire source here, remember that we're somewhat focused on the validation mechanism offered by `ActionSupport`. With that in mind, we'll skim the nonvalidation parts and then focus on validation. We'll come back to treat the rest in detail over the next few pages. First, note that our action does indeed extend `Action-Support` ❶. Also, note that we provide an `execute()` ❷ method that contains the business logic, registering a user in this case. After that, we see a set of JavaBeans properties ❸. These are common features of actions; they serve to receive the data from the framework's automatic transfer and then carry that data throughout the framework's processing.

But now we're focused on examining the basic validation mechanism provided by `ActionSupport`. As you can see, our action provides a `validate()` method ❹ that contains all of our logic for checking the validity of the data received by our JavaBeans properties. This leaves this action's `execute()` method focused on business logic. The validation logic that we've provided is simple. We test each of the three fields to make sure they're not empty by testing the length of each `String` property ❻. If a piece of data doesn't validate, we create and store an error ❼ via methods provided by the `ActionSupport` superclass, such as `addFieldError()`.

We also test that the user doesn't already exist in the system ❽. This test requires a dip into our business logic and data tiers. At this point in the book, the Struts 2 Portfolio application uses a simple encapsulation of business logic and data persistence. The `PortfolioService` object is capable of conducting our simple business needs at this stage. In case you're interested, it contains all the business rules in its simple methods, and persists data only in memory. Even our current management techniques are crude; our action just instantiates a `PortfolioService` object ❺ when it needs one. Later in the book, we learn how to integrate with more sophisticated technologies for managing such important resources. For now, this keeps our study of the action component more clear.

What happens if validation fails? If any of the fields are empty, or if the username is already in the system, we call a method that adds an error message. After all the validation logic has executed, control returns to the `workflow` interceptor. Note that there is no return value on the `validate()` method. The secret, as we'll see, is in the error messages that our validation generates.

Even though control has returned to the workflow interceptor, it's not finished. What does the workflow interceptor do now? Now it's time to earn the "workflow" name. After calling the validate() method to allow the action's validation logic to execute, the workflow interceptor will check to see whether any error messages were generated by the validation logic. If it finds errors, then the workflow interceptor will alter the workflow of the request. It'll immediately abort the request processing and return the user back to the input form, where the appropriate error messages will be displayed on the form. Try it out! Fire up your application and open the chapter 3 version of the Struts 2 Portfolio at http://localhost:8080/Struts2InAction/chapterThree/PortfolioHomePage.action

Choose to create an account and fill out the form, but omit some data. For instance, we've omitted the password. When we submit the form, the validation fails and diverts the workflow back to the input form again, as seen in figure 3.2.

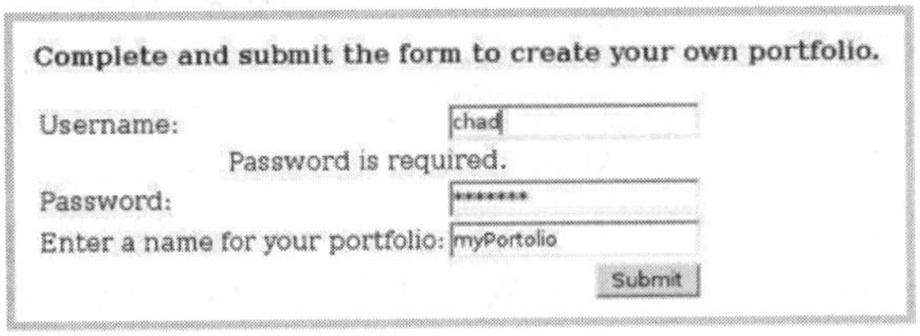

Figure 3.2 The default workflow interceptor returns us to the input form with validation error messages displayed on the appropriate fields.

Two obvious questions remain. Where were those error messages stored, and how did the workflow interceptor check to see whether any had been created? The com.opensymphony.xwork2.ValidationAware interface defines methods for storing and retrieving error messages. A class that implements this important interface must maintain a collection of error messages for each field that can be validated, as well as a collection of general error messages that pertain only to the action as a whole. Luckily for us, all of these methods and the collections that back them are already provided by the ActionSupport class. To use them, we invoke the following methods:

```
addFieldError ( String fieldName, String errorMessage )
addActionError ( String errorMessage )
```

To add a field error, we must pass the name of the field, as we do in listing 3.5, along with the message that we want displayed to the user. Adding an action-scoped error message is even easier, as you don't need to specify anything other than the message.

The ValidationAware interface also specifies methods for testing whether any errors exist. The workflow interceptor will use these to determine whether it should redirect the workflow back to the input page. If it finds that errors exist, it'll look for a result with the name input. The following snippet from chapterThree.xml shows that the Register action has declared such a result:

```
<action name="Register" class="manning.chapterThree.Register">

  <result>/chapterThree/RegistrationSuccess.jsp</result>
```

```
<result name="input">/chapterThree/Registration.jsp</result>

</action>
```

In this case, the `workflow` interceptor, if it finds errors, will automatically forward to the result that points to the Registration.jsp page because its name is `"input"`. And, of course, this JSP page is our input form.

Now we've seen how interceptors clean up the action's execution logic. But some of you might not be convinced. If you're tempted to complain, "But the validation method is still on the action object!" you're right. But this doesn't taint the most important separation of concerns; the validation logic is distinctly separate from the action's own execution logic. This is what keeps our action focused on its pure unit of work—registering a new user. Check out the `execute()` method's succinct phrasing of the business logic of this task:

```
public String execute(){

    User user = new User();
    user.setPassword( getPassword() );
    user.setPortfolioName( getPortfolioName() );
    user.setUsername( getUsername() );

    getPortfolioService().createAccount( user );
    return SUCCESS;
}
```

We just make the user object and create the account. No problem. If there were some exception that might be generated from our business object's account-creation process, we might have a bit of added complexity in our choice of which result we should display. For our purposes, we're just assuming success.

But it's not just about clean-looking code. A more subtle point is that the control flow of the validation process is also separated from the action. This isn't just a case of factoring the validation logic out of the `execute()` method and into a more readable helper method. The validation workflow is itself layered away from the action's workflow because the validation logic is invoked by the `workflow` interceptor. In other words, the `workflow` interceptor is really the one controlling the execution of the validation logic. The interceptors all fire before the action itself gets a chance to execute. This separation of control flow is what allows the `workflow` interceptor to abort the whole request processing and redirect back to the input page without ever entering the action's `execute()` method. This is exactly the kind of separation that interceptors are meant to provide.

Before moving on, some of you are probably wondering how the error message made its way onto the registration form when we sent the user back to try again. All of this is handled for you with the Struts 2 UI component tags. We won't cover these now, as we're staying focused on the action, but you'll learn all about them in chapter 7.

Now it's beginning to feel like we've really learned something. We can write actions that automatically receive and validate data. That's cool, but let's not get distracted from the real topic at hand. The real lesson to take out of this section is about how actions work together with interceptors to get common chores done without polluting the action's core logic. If you can wrap your mind around this action/interceptor teamwork, then you'll find the rest of the book merely an elaboration on that theme. Of course, there's a lot of cool stuff waiting for you in the remaining chapters, but this is the essence of the framework's approach to solving problems.

Before we move on, we need to look at the other problem that `ActionSupport` solves for you—localized message text.

USING RESOURCE BUNDLES FOR MESSAGE TEXT

In our `Register` action's validation logic, we set our error messages using `String` literals. If you look back at listing 3.5, you can see that we pass the `String` literal `Username is required` to the `addFieldError()` method. Using `String` literals like this creates a well-known maintenance nightmare. Furthermore, changing languages for different user locales is virtually impossible without some layer of separation between the source code and the messages themselves. The well-established best practice is to bundle these messages together into external and maintainable resource bundles, commonly implemented with simple properties files. `ActionSupport` provides built-in functionality for easily managing just that.

`ActionSupport` implements two interfaces that work together to provide this localized message text functionality. The first interface, `com.opensymphony. xwork2.TextProvider`, provides access to the messages themselves. This interface exposes a flexible set of methods by which you can retrieve a message text from a resource bundle. `ActionSupport` implements these methods to retrieve their messages from a properties file resource. No matter which method you use to retrieve your message, you'll refer to the message by a key. The `TextProvider` methods will return the message associated with that key from the properties file associated with your action class.

Getting started with a properties file resource bundle is easy. First, we need to create the properties file and give it a name that mirrors the action class for which it provides the messages. The following code snippet shows the contents from our `Register` action's associated properties file, Register.properties:

```
user.exists=This user already exists.
username.required=Username is required.
password.required=Password is required.
portfolioName.required=Portfolio Name is required.
```

In case you're unfamiliar with properties files, they're just simple text files. Each line contains a key and its value. In order to have the `ActionSupport` implementation of the `TextProvider` interface find this properties file, we just need to add it to the Java package that contains our `Register` class. In this case, you can find this file in the package structure at `manning.chapterThree`.

Once the properties file is in place, we can use one of the `TextProvider getText()` methods to retrieve our messages. Listing 3.6 shows our new version of the `Register` action's validate logic.

Listing 3.6 Using `ActionSupport` to get the validation error messages

```
public void validate(){

  PortfolioService ps = getPortfolioService();

  if ( getPassword().length() == 0 ){
    addFieldError( "password", getText("password.required") );      ❶
  }
  if ( getUsername().length() == 0 ){
    addFieldError( "username", getText("username.required") );
  }
  if ( getPortfolioName().length() == 0  ){
    addFieldError( "portfolioName", getText( "portfolioName.required" ));
  }
  if ( ps.userExists(getUsername() ) ){
    addFieldError("username", getText( "user.exists"));
  }
}
```

As you can see, instead of String literals, we now retrieve our message text from ActionSupport's implementation of TextProvider. We now use the getText() ❶ method to retrieve our messages from properties files based upon a key. This layer of separation makes our message text much more manageable. Changing messages means only editing the properties file; the source code's semantic keys never need to be changed.

ActionSupport also provides a basic internationalization solution for the localizing message text. The com.opensymphony.xwork2.LocaleProvider interface exposes a single method, getLocale(). ActionSupport implements this interface to retrieve the user's locale based upon the locale setting sent in by the browser. You could implement your own version of this interface to search somewhere else for the locale, such as in the database. But if the browser setting is good enough for your requirements, you don't have to do too much to achieve a basic level of internationalization.

You still retrieve your message texts as we did earlier. Even when we weren't taking advantage of it, ActionSupport's TextProvider implementation has been checking the locale every time it retrieves a message text for us. It does this by calling the getLocale() method of the LocaleProvider interface. With the locale in hand, the TextProvider, a.k.a. ActionSupport, tries to locate a properties file for that locale. Of course, you have to provide the properties file for the locale in question, or it will just serve up the standard English. But it's simple to provide properties files for all locales that you wish to support. In Struts 2 Portfolio, we're providing a Spanish properties file. The hard part is finding a translator. In order to see this in action, set your browser's language support to Spanish and submit the registration form again, omitting one of the fields to see the error message that it provides.

As with validation, the internationalization provided by ActionSupport is relatively primitive. If it suffices for your application, great. If you need more, we'll see how to get cutting-edge internationalization from the Struts 2 framework in chapter 11. For now, we've got a pretty decent start on building actions.

Next, we'll look at some alternative—advanced, some would say—methods of implementing our data transfer with complex objects instead of simple JavaBeans properties.

3.4   *Transferring data onto objects*

Up until now, our actions have all received data from the request on simple JavaBeans properties. While they are powerful and elegant, we can do even better. Rather than receiving each piece of data individually, and then creating an object on which to place these pieces of data, we can expose the complex object itself to the data transfer mechanisms of the platform. Not only does this save time by eliminating the need to create and populate the object that aggregates the individual pieces of data, it can also save work by allowing us to directly expose an already-existing domain object to the data transfer. While a couple of caveats must be kept in mind, the use of these complex objects as direct data transfer objects presents a powerful option to the developer.

NOTE   *Struts 1 to Struts 2 Perspective*—In case you're feeling homesick, we should note the departure of the familiar Struts 1 ActionForm. ActionForms played an important role in data validation and type conversion for the Struts 1 framework, but the cost was high. For each domain object, you typically had to create a mirroring form bean. To add insult to injury, you were then tasked with an additional manual data transfer when you finally moved the valid data from the form bean onto your domain object. For many, one of the biggest thrills of Struts 2 will be letting the framework transfer, validate, and bind data directly onto application domain objects, where it can stay!

If we want to use complex objects rather than simple JavaBeans properties to receive our data, we have a couple of options for implementing such deep transfers. Our first option is also JavaBeans-based. We can expose a complex object itself as a JavaBeans property and have the data moved onto the object directly. Another alternative is to use something called a ModelDriven action. This option involves a simple interface and another one of the default interceptors. Like the object-backed JavaBeans property, the ModelDriven action also allows us to use a complex Java object to receive our data. The differences between these two methods are slight, and there are no functional consequences to choosing one over the other. But you might prefer one over the other depending on your project requirements. We'll learn each technique and demonstrate with examples from the Struts 2 Portfolio.

3.4.1   *Object-backed JavaBeans properties*

We've already seen how the params interceptor, included in the defaultStack, automatically transfers data from the request to our action objects. To enable this transfer, the developer needs only to provide JavaBeans properties on her actions, using the same names as the form fields being submitted. This is easy, but despite this ease, we frequently find ourselves occupied with another tedious task. This tedious task consists of collecting these individually transferred data items and transferring them to an application domain object that we must instantiate ourselves. Listing 3.7 shows our previous version of the `Register` action's `execute()` method.

Listing 3.7 Collecting data and building the domain object by hand

```
public String execute(){

    User user = new User();
    user.setPassword( getPassword() );
    user.setPortfolioName( getPortfolioName() );     ❶
    user.setUsername( getUsername() );


    getPortfolioService().createAccount( user );

    return SUCCESS;
}
```

While we were impressed with the succinct quality of this method only a few pages ago, we can now see that five of the seven lines do nothing more than assemble the individual pieces of data ❶ that the framework has transferred onto our simple Java-Beans properties. We're still psyched that the data has been automatically transferred and bound to our Java data types, but why not ask for more?

Why not ask the framework to go ahead and transfer the data directly to our `User` object? Why not ask the framework to instantiate the user object for us? Since Struts 2 provides powerful data transfer and type conversion facilities, the true power of which we'll discover later in the book, we can ask for these things and get them. In this case, it's simple. Let's rewrite our `Register` action so that it replaces the individual JavaBeans properties with a single property backed by the `User` object itself. Listing 3.8 shows the new version of our new action as implemented in the `manning.chapterThree.objectBacked.ObjectBackedRegister` class.

Listing 3.8 Using an object-backed property to receive data transfers

```
public String execute(){

    getPortfolioService().createAccount( user );     ❶
    return SUCCESS;
}

private User user;

public User getUser() {
    return user;
}                                                    ❷
public void setUser(User user) {
    this.user = user;
}

public void validate(){

    . . .
```

```
if ( getUser().getPassword().length() == 0 ){        ③
    addFieldError( "user.password", getText("password.required") );
}

. . .

}
```

Listing 3.8 has now reduced our business logic to a one-liner. We hand an already instantiated and populated `User` object to our service object's account creation method ①. That's it. This logic is much cleaner because we let the framework handle instantiating our `User` object and populating its attributes with data from the request. Previously, we'd done this ourselves. In order to let the framework handle this tedious work, we simply replaced the individual JavaBeans properties with a single property backed by the `User` object itself ②. We don't even have to create the `User` object that backs the property because the framework's data transfer will handle this for us when it starts trying to move the data over. Note that our validation code now must use a deeper notation ③ to reach the data items, because they must go through the `user` property to get to the individual fields themselves.

Similarly, we also have to make a couple of changes in the way we reference our data from our results, JSPs in this case. First of all, we have to change the field names in the form that submits to our new action. The bottom line is that we now have another layer in our JavaBeans properties notation. The following code snippet shows the minor change to the `textfield` name in our form, found in our Registration_OB.jsp page.

```
<s:textfield name="user.username" label="Username"/>
```

As you can see, the reference now includes the user to reflect the depth of the property in the action. Previously, when we exposed each piece of user data as an individual JavaBeans property, our reference didn't require the user portion of this reference. The names of the other fields in this form are similarly transformed.

We make a similar alteration at the other end of the request. When we render our resulting success page, we must use the deeper property notation to access our data. The following code snippet from RegistrationSuccess_OB.jsp shows the new notation:

```
<h5>Congratulations! You have created </h5>
<h3>The <s:property value="user.portfolioName" /> Portfolio</h3>
```

As you can see, directly using an application domain object as a JavaBeans property allows us to let the framework do even more of our work for us. The minor consequences are that we have to go a dot deeper when we reference our data from the JSP pages. Now, we'll take a look at another method of exposing rich objects to the framework's data transfer facilities, one that gives us the same cleaner `execute()` method as the object-backed JavaBeans property, but doesn't introduce the extra dot in our view tier data access.

3.4.2   ModelDriven actions

`ModelDriven` actions depart from the use of JavaBeans properties for exposing domain data. Instead, they expose an application domain object via the `getModel()` method, which is declared by the com.opensymphony.xwork2.ModelDriven interface. While this method introduces a new interface, as well as another interceptor, it's simple in practice. The interceptor is already in the default stack; the data transfer is still automatic and even easier to work with than previous techniques. Let's see how it works.

Implementing the interface requires almost nothing. We have to declare that our action implements the interface, but there's only one method exposed by Model-Driven, the getModel() method. By *model*, we mean the model in the MVC sense. In this case, it's the data that comes in from the request and is altered by the execution of the business logic. That data is then made available to the view, JSP pages in the case of our Struts 2 Portfolio application. Listing 3.9 shows the new action code from the manning.chapterThree.modelDriven.ModelDrivenRegister class.

Listing 3.9 Automatically transferring request data to application domain objects

```
public class ModelDrivenRegister extends ActionSupport
            implements ModelDriven {          ❶

   public String execute(){
      getPortfolioService().createAccount( user );
      return SUCCESS;
   }

   private User user = new User();           ❷
   public Object getModel() {
      return user;
   }

   public void validate(){

   . . .

      if ( user.getPassword().length() == 0 ){
         addFieldError( "password", getText("password.required") );    ❸
      }

   . . .

   }

   . . .

}
```

First, we see that our new action implements the ModelDriven interface ❶. The only method required by this interface is getModel(), which returns our model object, the familiar User object. Note that with the ModelDriven method, we have to initialize the User object ourselves ❷. We'll see why in chapter 5 when we explore the details of the data transfer mechanisms, but for now just keep an eye on this slight but important detail.

We should note one pitfall to avoid. By the time the execute() method of your ModelDriven action has been invoked, the framework has obtained a reference to your model object, which it'll use throughout the request. Since the framework acquires its reference from your getter, it won't be aware if you change the model field internally in your action. This can cause some data inconsistency problems. If, during your execution code, you change the object to which your model field reference points, your action's model will then be out of sync with the one still held by the framework. The following code snippet demonstrates the problem:

```
public String execute(){
    user = new User();
    user.setSomething();
    getPortfolioService().createAccount( user );
    return SUCCESS;
}

private User user = new User();
public Object getModel() {
    return user;
}
```

In this action's execute() method, the developer has, for some reason, set the user reference to a new object. But the framework still has a reference to the original object as initialized in the instance field declaration for user. When the framework invokes the result, your JSP page data access will be resolved against the old object. Whatever this erroneous code has set, it'll be unavailable. You can, of course, manipulate that original model object to your heart's content. Just don't make a new one, or point the existing reference to another one!

As in the previous object-backed JavaBeans property method, using a domain object to receive all of the data allows us the luxury of a clean execute() method. Again we incur a slight penalty related to the depth of our references. As you can see in the validation code of listing 3.9, we now refer to the password by referencing the model object en route to the password field ❸.

However, we don't incur any depth of reference penalty in our view layer. All references in the JSP pages return to the simplicity of the original Register action that used the simple, individual JavaBeans properties for data transfer. The following code snippets, from Registration_MD.jsp

```
<s:textfield name="username" label="Username"/>
```

and RegistrationSuccess.jsp

```
<h5>Congratulations! You have created </h5>
<h3>The <s:property value="portfolioName" /> Portfolio</h3>
```

show the renewed simplicity of view-layer references to data carried in the Model-Driven action. This is considered one of the primary reasons for choosing the ModelDriven method over the object-backed JavaBeans property method of exposing domain objects to the data transfer.

Using domain objects for data transfer is great, but a word of caution is necessary. We'll explore a potential danger next.

3.4.3   *Last words on using domain objects for data transfer*

First, we want to point out a potential danger in using domain objects for data transfer. The problem comes when the data gets automatically transferred onto the object. As we've seen, if the request has parameters that match the attributes on your domain object, the data will be moved onto those attributes. Now, consider the case where your domain object has some sensitive data attributes that you don't really want to expose to this automatic data transfer, perhaps an ID. A malicious user could add an appropriately named querystring parameter to the request such that the value of that parameter would automatically be written to your exposed object's attribute. Of course, you can remove these attributes from the object, but then you start to lose the value of reusing existing objects rather than writing new ones. Unfortunately, there's no good solution to this issue yet. Usually, you won't have anything to worry about, but it's something to keep in mind when you're developing your actions.

Ultimately, it'll be up to you to choose a method of receiving the data from the framework. Each method has its purpose, and we believe that the requirements of your projects will typically determine which approach is most appropriate. Throughout the rest of this book, we'll see many examples of best practices and integration with other technologies that'll spell out some of the cases when one or another method serves best. Sometimes, its appropriate to use a little of each. Did we forget to mention that you can do all of them at the same time if you like? Again, the platform is flexible. Now it's time to look at a case study.

3.5   *File uploading: a case study*

At this point, you have the tools you need to write your application's action components and wire them into a rudimentary Struts 2 application. We suspect you've even deduced enough to get started implementing a view layer with JSP results. Later in the book, you'll see how much more the framework has to offer your view layer when we get to results, tags, UI components, and Ajax integration in part 3. For now, we want to round out our treatment of the action component by showing a useful case study that, while showing you how to do something practical, also serves to reiterate how actions and interceptors work together to solve the common problems of the web application domain.

Most of you will have to implement file upload at some point. Our sample application, the Struts 2 Portfolio, will need to upload some image files; otherwise the portfolio would be drab. One reason we're showing you how to upload files now, rather than later in the book, is that we believe it helps demonstrate the framework's persistent pattern of using interceptors to layer the logic of common tasks out of the action itself. So let's learn how our actions can work with an interceptor from the default stack to implement ultraclean and totally reusable file uploading.

3.5.1   *Getting built-in support via the struts-default package*

As with most tasks that you find yourself doing routinely, Struts 2 provides built-in help for file uploading. In this case, the default interceptor stack includes the `FileUpload-Interceptor`. As you might recall, struts-default.xml is the system file that defines all of the built-in components. Listing 3.10 shows the elements from that file that declare the `fileUpload` interceptor and make it a part of the default interceptor stack.

> **Listing 3.10   Declaring the `FileUploadInterceptor` and adding it to the stack**

```
<package name="struts-default">

   <interceptors>

   . . .

   <interceptor name="fileUpload"
     class="org.apache.struts2.interceptor.FileUploadInterceptor"/>

   . . .

   </interceptors>

   . . .

   <interceptor-stack name="defaultStack">

      . . .

      <interceptor-ref name="model-driven"/>
      <interceptor-ref name="fileUpload"/>
      <interceptor-ref name="params"/>

      . . .

   </interceptor-stack>

</package>
```

As you can see, the `struts-default` package contains a declaration of the file-Upload interceptor, backed by the `org.apache.struts2.interceptor.FileUpload-Interceptor` implementation class. This interceptor is then added to the default-Stack so that all packages extending the `struts-default` package will automatically have this interceptor acting on their actions. We make our Struts 2 Portfolio packages extend this package to take advantage of these built-in components.

3.5.2   *What does the fileUpload interceptor do?*

The `fileUpload` interceptor creates a special version of the automatic data transfer mechanisms we saw earlier. With the previous data transfers, we were dealing with the transfer of form field data from the request to matching JavaBeans properties on our action objects. The `params` interceptor, also part of the `defaultStack`, was responsible for moving all of the request parameters onto the action object wherever the action provided a JavaBeans property that matched the request parameter's name. In listing 3.10, you can see that the `defaultStack` places the `fileUpload` interceptor just before the `params` interceptor. When the `fileUpload` interceptor executes, it processes a multipart request and transforms the file itself, along with some metadata, into request parameters. It does this using a wrapper around the servlet request. Table 3.2 shows the request parameters that are added by this `fileUpload` interceptor.

Table 3.2   Request parameters exposed by the `FileUpload` interceptor

Parameter name	Parameter type and value
[file name from form]	`File`—the uploaded file itself
[file name from form]`ContentType`	`String`—the content type of the file
[file name from form]`FileName`	`String`—the name of the uploaded file, as stored on the server

After the `fileUpload` interceptor has exposed the parts of the multipart request as request parameters, it's time for the next interceptor in the stack to do its work. Conveniently, the next interceptor is the `params` interceptor. When the `params` interceptor fires, it moves all of the request parameters, including those listed in table 3.2, onto the action object. Thus, all a developer needs to do to conveniently receive the file upload is add JavaBeans properties to her action object that match the names in table 3.2.

FYI   We should note the elegant use of interceptors as demonstrated by the `fileUpload` interceptor. As we've said, the Struts 2 framework tries desperately to keep its action components as clean as possible. A large part of this effort consists of the use of interceptors to layer cross-cutting tasks away from the core processing tasks of the action itself. The `fileUpload` interceptor demonstrates this by encapsulating the processing of multipart requests and injecting the processed upload data into the action object's JavaBeans setter methods.

We've also referred to the role of interceptors in terms of preprocessing and postprocessing. In the case of the `fileUpload` interceptor, the preprocessing is the transformation of the multipart request into request parameters that the `params` interceptor will automatically move to our action. The postprocessing comes when the interceptor fires again after our action to dispose of the temporary version of the uploaded file.

How will all of this look in code? The Struts 2 Portfolio uses file uploading, so let's have a look.

3.5.3   *Looking at the Struts 2 Portfolio example code*

The Struts 2 Portfolio uses this file upload mechanism to upload new images to the portfolio. The first part of such a task is presenting a form through which users can upload files. You can visit the image upload page by first creating an account in the chapter 3 version of the Struts 2 Portfolio sample application. Our end-user workflow is incomplete right now, but we'll fix that in coming chapters. Once you've created an account, choose to work with your portfolio and choose to add a new picture. You'll see a page presenting you with a simple form to upload an image. The following code snippet, from chapterThree/ImageUploadForm.jsp, shows the markup that creates the form you see:

```
<h4>Complete and submit the form to create your own portfolio.</h4>

<s:form action="ImageUpload" method="post" enctype="multipart/form-data">

  <s:file name="pic" label="Picture"/>

  <s:submit/>
</s:form>
```

When we create this form, we have to take note of a couple of points. First, note that we're using Struts 2 tags to build the form. We'll cover the Struts 2 tag library in chapters 6 and 7. For now, just accept that this tag generates the HTML markup of a form that allows the user to upload a file. Next, note that we set the encoding type of the form to `multipart/form-data`. This important attribute signals to the framework that the request needs to be handled as an upload. Without this setting, it won't work. Finally, note that the file will be submitted by the form under the `name` attribute we provide to the `file` tag. This detail is important because you'll use this name to build the JavaBeans properties that will receive the upload data.

With our JSP ready to present the form, let's see the action that will receive and process the upload. First, make sure that the package to which your action belongs is extending the `struts-default` package so that it inherits the default interceptor stack, and the `fileUpload` interceptor. Listing 3.11, a snippet from our manning/ chapterThree/chapterThree.xml file, shows that we've done this.

Listing 3.11   Extending the `struts-default` package to inherit file upload processing

```
<package name="chapterThreeSecure" namespace="/chapterThree/secure"
  extends="struts-default">

  . . .

  <action name="AddImage" >
    <result>/chapterThree/ImageUploadForm.jsp</result>
  </action>

  <action name="ImageUpload" class="manning.chapterThree.ImageUpload">
    <result>/chapterThree/ImageAdded.jsp</result>
    <result name="input">/chapterThree/ImageUploadForm.jsp</result>
  </action>

  . . .

</package>
```

This is our package of secure actions for the Struts 2 Portfolio. We haven't added security yet, but we know that these actions will require security of some kind, so we've put them into a separate package. We'll add the security with a custom interceptor in chapter 4.

With the `defaultStack` and its file upload interceptor on our side, we just need to add properties to our action object that match the parameter names, as seen in table 3.2.

We've already seen that our file will be submitted under the name `pic`. Using the naming conventions in table 3.2, we can derive the JavaBeans property names that we need to implement. Listing 3.12 shows the JavaBeans properties implemented by the `manning.chapterThree.ImageUpload` class. (As always, check out the Struts 2 Portfolio source code if you want to see more of the sample code.)

Listing 3.12 The JavaBeans properties that'll receive the uploaded file and metadata

```
File pic;
String picContentType;
String picFileName;

public File getPic() {
   return pic;
}
   public void setPic(File pic) {
   this.pic = pic;
   }

public String getPicContentType() {
   return picContentType;
}
void setPicContentType(String picContentType) {
   this.picContentType = picContentType;
}

public void setPicFileName(String picFileName) {
   this.picFileName = picFileName;
}
public String getPicFileName() {
   return picFileName;
}
```

You're not obligated to implement all of these. If you choose not to implement some of them, you just won't receive the data. No harm, no foul. At any rate, using the `fileUpload` interceptor is about as easy as writing these JavaBeans properties. Thanks to the separation of the upload logic, the action's work itself is simple. As shown in the following code snippet from the `ImageUpload` action, the action can focus on the task at hand.

```
public String execute(){

   getPortfolioService().addImage( getPic() );
   return SUCCESS;

}
```

There's nothing here but the call to our business logic. The image file is conveniently just a getter away, just as all of the auto-transferred data has been. Thanks to the teamwork of the `fileUpload` interceptor and the `params` interceptor, uploading files is almost as easy as handling primitives. Incidentally, you can set the path to the directory where the action will save the image file with a parameter to the image upload action element in chapterThree.xml.

Now let's look at a couple of tweaks you can make to the `fileUpload` interceptor to handle such things as multiple file uploads.

MULTIPLE FILES AND OTHER SETTINGS

Uploading multiple files with the same parameter names is also supported. All you have to do is change your action's JavaBeans properties to arrays; that is, `File` becomes `File[]`, and the two strings become string arrays. The three arrays are always the same length, and their order is the same, meaning that index 0 for all three arrays represents the same file and file metadata. There are also many other configurable parameters regarding the `fileUpload` interceptor, ranging from the maximum file size to the implementation of the multipart request parser that'll be used to handle the request. In general, the extreme flexibility of the Struts 2 framework makes it impossible to provide complete coverage of all the details in a book such as this. This book strives to filter out as much of the extraneous detail as possible in order to make the concepts of the framework more visible. For such details and minutia, the Struts 2 website serves as a good reference.

3.6   *Summary*

In this chapter, we learned a lot about building Struts 2 actions. We began our tour of this important component by examining the role of actions within the framework. Actions have to do three things. First and foremost, they encapsulate the framework's interaction with the model. This means, ultimately, that the calls to the business logic and data tier will be found in the `execute()` method of the action class. The second job of the action is to serve as the data transfer object for the request processing. We suspect we've made this point particularly clear by now. Finally, the action also takes responsibility for returning a control string that'll be used by the framework to select the appropriate result component for rendering the view back to the user.

We also saw how to package our action components into Struts 2 packages. These packages help provide a logical organization to your application's framework components, actions in particular. Using the package structure, we can do several important things. We can map URL namespaces to groups of actions. We can also take advantage of the inheritance mechanisms of packages to define reusable groups of framework components. We've already used this feature by having our Struts 2 Portfolio packages extend the built-in `struts-default` package to take advantage of its default interceptor stack, among other things. Let this serve as a model for creating your own package hierarchies.

We then showcased a couple of key players provided by the framework to ease your work. First we saw the `Action` interface, which provides some important definitions of constants that the framework uses for commonly used control strings. After that, we took a long look at the functionality provided by the `ActionSupport` class. This helpful class implements several important interfaces and cooperates with key interceptors from the `defaultStack` to provide built-in implementations of such valuable domain tasks as validation and a basic form of internationalization. We demonstrated all of this with our Struts 2 Portfolio sample application.

One of the more important considerations when implementing your own Struts 2 actions will be the method of data transfer that you use. Several options are available. We covered two methods that both implement JavaBeans properties on the action object itself. The first of these matches simple properties to individual parameters on the incoming request. The next JavaBeans properties method provides properties that are backed by complex domain objects. Finally, we saw that you can use an entirely different method to expose your complex domain objects by implementing `ModelDriven` actions. The choice of which method to use will largely depend upon the requirements of your project and the action at hand. Flexibility is a recurring theme of the Struts 2 framework.

We rounded off the chapter with a case study. We looked at using one of the framework's built-in interceptors to add a file upload action to our sample application. While we saw that uploading files with Struts 2 can be easy, we also tried to point out some important lessons that this example demonstrates about the framework itself. In particular, we've shown what we mean when we say the framework tries to provide a clean implementation of MVC. In particular, the file upload example shows how proper cooperation between interceptors and actions can provide a web application with reusable and flexible encapsulations of cross-cutting tasks, as well as super-clean actions.

You know what an action is by now. Next up is a detailed look at interceptors, and we'll enhance the Struts 2 Portfolio by putting interceptors to good use.

Adding workflow with interceptors

This chapter covers
- Firing interceptors
- Exploring the built-in interceptors
- Declaring interceptors
- Building your own interceptors

In the previous chapter, we learned a great deal about the action component of the Struts 2 framework. From a developer's daily working perspective, the action component may well be the heart and soul of the framework. But working silently in the background are the true heroes of the hour, the interceptors. In truth, interceptors are responsible for most of the processing done by the framework. The built-in interceptors, declared in the `struts-default` package's `defaultStack`, handle most of the fundamental tasks, ranging from data transfer and validation to exception handling. Due to the rich set of the built-in interceptors, you might not need to develop your own interceptor for some time. Nonetheless, the importance of these core Struts 2 components cannot be underestimated. Without an understanding of how interceptors work, you'll never truly understand Struts 2.

After such a bold statement, we have no choice but to back it up with a detailed explanation of interceptors and the role they play in the framework. This chapter will begin by clarifying that architectural role with a brief conceptual discussion. We'll then dissect a couple of simple interceptors from the `defaultStack` (just so we can see what's inside), provide a reference section that covers the use of all the built-in interceptors, and end by creating a custom interceptor to provide an authentication service for our secure package's actions.

Incidentally, if you'd prefer to see a working code sample before hearing the explanation, feel free to skip ahead to the last section of this chapter, where we build a custom interceptor for the Struts 2 Portfolio application. After seeing one in action, you can always come back here for the theory. Just don't forget to come back!

4.1 Why intercept requests?

Earlier in this book, we described Struts 2 as a second-generation MVC framework. We said that this new framework leveraged the lessons learned by the first generation of MVC-based frameworks to implement a super-clean architecture. Interceptors play a crucial role in allowing the framework to achieve such a high level of separation of concerns. In this section, we'll take a closer look at how interceptors provide a powerful tool for encapsulating the kinds of tasks that have traditionally been an architectural thorn in the developer's side.

4.1.1 Cleaning up the MVC

From an architectural point of view, interceptors have immensely improved the level of separation we can achieve when trying to isolate the various concerns of our web applications. In particular, interceptors remove cross-cutting tasks from our action components. When we try to describe the kinds of tasks that interceptors implement, we usually say something like cross-cutting, or preprocessing and postprocessing. These terms may sound vague now, but they won't by the time we finish this chapter.

Logging is a typical cross-cutting concern. In the past, you might've had a logging statement in each of your actions. While this seemed a natural place for placing a logging statement, it's not a part of the action's interaction with the model. In reality, logging is administrative stuff that we want done for every request that the system processes. We call this *cross-cutting* because it's not specific to a single action. It cuts across a whole range of actions. As software engineers, we should instantly see this as an opportunity to raise the task to a higher layer that can sit above, or in front of, any number of requests that require logging. The bottom line is that we have the opportunity to remove the logging from the action, thus creating cleaner separation of our MVC concerns.

Some of the tasks undertaken by interceptors are more easily understood as being preprocessing or postprocessing tasks. These are still technically cross-cutting; we recommend not worrying about the semantics of these terms. We present these new terms mostly to give you some ideas about the specific types of tasks handled by interceptors. A good example of a preprocessing task would be data transfer, which we're already familiar with. This task is achieved with the `params` interceptor. Nearly every action will need to have some data transferred from the request parameters onto its domain-specific properties. This must be done before the action fires, and can be seen as mere preparation for the actual work of the action. From this aloof perspective, we can call it a preprocessing task. This is perfect for an interceptor. Again, this increases the purity of the action component by removing code that can't be strictly seen as part of a specific action's core work.

No matter whether we call the task cross-cutting or preprocessing, the conceptual mechanics of interceptors are clear. Instead of having a simple controller invoking an action directly, we now have a component that sits between the controller and the action. In Struts 2, no action is invoked in isolation. The invocation of an action is a layered process that always includes the execution of a stack of interceptors prior to and after the actual execution of the action itself. Rather than invoke the action's `execute()` method directly, the framework creates an object called an `ActionInvocation` that encapsulates the action and all of the interceptors that have been configured to fire before and after that action executes. Figure 4.1 illustrates the encapsulation of the entire action execution process in the `ActionInvocation` class.

As you can see in figure 4.1, the invocation of an action must first travel through the stack of interceptors associated with that action. Here we've presented a simplified version of the `defaultStack`. The `defaultStack` includes such tasks as file uploading and transferring request parameters onto our action. Figure 4.1 represents the normal workflow; none of the interceptors have diverted the invocation. This action will ultimately execute and return a control string that selects the appropriate result. After the result executes, each of the interceptors, in reverse order, gets a chance to do some postprocessing work. As we'll see, the interceptors have access to the action and other contextual values. This allows them to be aware of what's happening in the processing. For instance, they can examine the control string returned from the action to see what result was chosen.

One of the powerful functional aspects of interceptors is their ability to alter the workflow of the invocation. As we noted, figure 4.1 depicts an instance where none of the interceptors has intervened in the workflow, thus allowing the action to execute and determine which result should render the view. Sometimes, one of the interceptors will determine that the action shouldn't execute. In these cases, the interceptor can

ActionInvocation

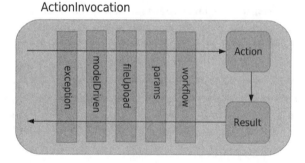

Figure 4.1 `ActionInvocation` encapsulates the execution of an action with its associated interceptors and results.

halt the workflow by itself returning a control string. Take the `workflow` interceptor, for example. As we've seen, this interceptor does two things. First, it invokes the `validate()` method on the action, if the action has implemented the `Validateable` interface. Next, it checks for the presence of error messages on the action. If errors are present, it returns a control string and, thus, stops further execution. The action will never fire. The next interceptor in the stack won't even be invoked. By returning the control string itself, the interceptor causes control to return back up the chain, giving each interceptor above the chance to do some postprocessing. Finally, the result that matches the returned control string will render the view. In the case of the `workflow` interceptor that has found error messages on the action, the control string is `"input"`, which typically maps back to the form page that submitted the invalid data.

As you might suspect, the details of this invocation process are thorny. In fact, they involve a bit of recursion. As with all recursion, it'll seem harmless once we look at the details, which we'll see shortly. But first we need to talk about the benefits we gain from using interceptors.

4.1.2 *Reaping the benefits*

Layering always makes our software cleaner, which helps with readability and testing and also provides flexibility. Once we've broken these cross-cutting, preprocessing, and postprocessing tasks into manageable units, we can do cool stuff with them. The two primary benefits we gain from this flexibility are reuse and configuration.

Everyone wants to reuse software. Perhaps this is the number-one goal of all software engineering. Reuse is a bottom-line issue from both business and engineering perspectives. Reuse means saving time, money, and maintainability. It makes everyone happy. And achieving it is simple. We just need to isolate the logic that we want to reuse in a cleanly separated unit. Once we've isolated the logic in an interceptor, we can drop it in anywhere we like, easily applying it to whole classes of actions. This is more exciting than clean architectural lines, but really it's the same thing. We've already been benefiting from code reuse by inheriting the `defaultStack`. Using the `defaultStack` allows us to reuse the data transfer code written by the Struts 2 developers, along with their validation code, their internationalization code, and so forth.

In addition to the benefits of code reuse, the layering power of interceptors gives us another important benefit. Once we have these tasks cleanly encapsulated in interceptors, we can, in addition to reusing them, easily reconfigure their order and number. While the `defaultStack` provides a common set of interceptors, arranged in a common sequence, to serve the common functional needs of most requests, we can rearrange them to meet varying requirements. We can even remove and add interceptors as we like. We can even do this on a per-action basis, but this is seldom necessary. In our Struts 2 Portfolio application, we'll develop an authentication interceptor and combine it with the `defaultStack` of interceptors that fires when the actions in our secure package are invoked. The flexible nature of interceptors allows us to easily customize request processing for the specific needs of certain requests, all while still taking advantage of code reuse.

WARNING   Struts 2 is extremely flexible. This strength is what separates it from many of its competitors. But, as we've mentioned, this can also be confusing when you first begin to use the framework. Thankfully, Struts 2 provides a strong set of intelligent defaults that allow developers to build most standard functionality without needing to think about the many ways in which they can modify the framework and its core components. In the case of interceptors, one of the framework's most flexible components, the `defaultStack` should serve in the vast majority of cases.

4.1.3 Developing interceptors

Despite their importance, many developers won't write many interceptors. In fact, most of the common tasks of the web application domain have already been written and bundled into the `struts-default` package. Even if you never write an interceptor yourself, it's still important to understand what they are and how they do what they do. If this chapter weren't core to understanding the framework, we would've placed it at the end of the book. We put this material here because we believe that understanding interceptors is absolutely necessary to successfully leveraging the power of the framework. First of all, you need to be familiar with the built-in interceptors, and you need to know how to arrange them to your liking. Second, debugging the framework can truly be confusing if you don't understand how the requests are processed. We think that interceptors ultimately provide a simpler architecture that can be more easily debugged and understood. However, many developers may find them counterintuitive at first.

With that said, when you do find yourself writing your own custom interceptors, you'll truly begin to enjoy the Struts 2 framework. As you develop your actions, keep your eyes out for any tasks that can be moved out to the interceptors. As soon as you do, you'll be hooked for life. But first, we should see how they actually work.

4.2   Interceptors in action

Now we'll look at how interceptors actually run. We'll look at the interceptor interface and learn the mysterious process by which an interceptor is fired. Along the way, we'll meet the boss man, the `ActionInvocation`; this important class orchestrates the entire execution of an action, including the sequential firing of the associated interceptor stack. We'll also take the time to look inside the code of two of the built-in Struts 2 interceptors, just to keep it real. But first let's start with the boss man.

4.2.1 The guy in charge: ActionInvocation

A few paragraphs back, we introduced the `ActionInvocation`. While you'll almost certainly never have to work directly with this class, a high-level understanding of it is key to understanding interceptors. In fact, knowing what `ActionInvocation` does is equivalent to knowing how Struts 2 handles requests; it's very important! As we said before, the `ActionInvocation` encapsulates all the processing details associated with the execution of a particular action. When the framework receives a request, it first must decide to which action the URL maps. An instance of this action is added to a newly created instance of `ActionInvocation`. Next, the framework consults the declarative architecture, as created by the application's XML or Java annotations, to discover which interceptors should fire, and in what sequence. References to these interceptors are added to the `ActionInvocation`. In addition to these central elements, the `ActionInvocation` also holds references to other important information like the servlet request objects and a map of the results available to the action. Now let's look at how the process of invoking an action occurs.

4.2.2 *How the interceptors fire*

Now that the `ActionInvocation` has been created and populated with all the objects and information it needs, we can start the invocation. The `ActionInvocation` exposes the `invoke()` method, which is called by the framework to start the execution of the action. When the framework calls this method, the `ActionInvocation` starts the invocation process by executing the first interceptor in the stack. Note that the `invoke()` method doesn't always map to the first interceptor; it's the responsibility of the `ActionInvocation` itself to keep track of what stage the invocation process has reached and pass control to the appropriate interceptor in the stack. It does this by calling that interceptor's `intercept()` method.

Interceptor firing order

When we say the first interceptor in the stack, we're referring to the first interceptor declared in the XML as reading from the top of the page down. Let's look at the declaration of the `basicStack` from struts-default.xml to see exactly what we mean.

```
<interceptor-stack name="basicStack">
    <interceptor-ref name="exception"/>
    <interceptor-ref name="servletConfig"/>
    <interceptor-ref name="prepare"/>
    <interceptor-ref name="checkbox"/>
    <interceptor-ref name="params"/>
    <interceptor-ref name="conversionError"/>
</interceptor-stack>
```

In the `basicStack`, the first interceptor to fire will be the `exception` interceptor. From here, each interceptor will fire in the same sequence as you would read down the page. So the last interceptor to fire will be the `conversionError` interceptor. After the result has rendered, the interceptors will each fire again, in reverse order, to give them the opportunity to do postprocessing.

Incidentally, the `basicStack`, not to be confused with the default `defaultStack`, is just a convenient chunk of common interceptors that the `struts-default` package makes available to you to ease the process of custom stack building in case you find that the `defaultStack` isn't quite what you need.

Now for the tricky part. Continued execution of the subsequent interceptors, and ultimately the action, occurs through recursive calls to the `ActionInvocation`'s invoke() method. Each time invoke() is called, ActionInvocation consults its state and executes whichever interceptor comes next. When all of the interceptors have been invoked, the invoke() method will cause the action itself to be executed. If this is cooking your noodle, hang in there. It'll clear up momentarily.

Why do we call it a recursive process? Let's have a look. The framework itself starts the process by making the first call to the ActionInvocation object's invoke() method . ActionInvocation hands control over to the first interceptor in the stack by calling that interceptor's intercept() method. Importantly, intercept() takes the ActionInvocation instance itself as a parameter. During its own processing, the interceptor will call invoke() on this object to continue the recursive process of invoking successive interceptors. Thus, in normal execution, the invocation process tunnels down through all of the interceptors until, finally, there are no more interceptors in the stack and the action fires. Again, the ActionInvocation itself maintains the state of this process internally so it always knows where it is in the stack.

Now let's look at what an interceptor can do when it fires. An interceptor has a three-stage, conditional execution cycle:

- Do some preprocessing.
- Pass control on to successive interceptors, and ultimately the action, by calling invoke(), or divert execution by itself returning a control string.
- Do some postprocessing.

Looking at some code will make these three stages more concrete. The following code snippet shows the intercept() method of the TimerInterceptor, one of the interceptors included in the struts-default package.

```
public String intercept(ActionInvocation invocation) throws Exception {
    long startTime = System.currentTimeMillis();        ❶
    String result = invocation.invoke();        ❷
    long executionTime = System.currentTimeMillis() - startTime;
        ... log the time ...        ❸
    return result;
}
```

The TimerInterceptor times the execution of an action. The code is simple. The intercept() method, defined by the Interceptor interface, is the entry point into an interceptor's execution. Note that the intercept method receives the ActionInvocation instance. When the intercept method is called, the interceptor's preprocessing phase consists of recording the start time ❶. Next, the interceptor must decide whether it'll pass control on to the rest of the interceptors and the action. Since this interceptor has no reason to halt the execution process, it always calls invoke(),passing control to whatever comes next in the chain ❷.

After calling invoke(), the interceptor waits for the return of this method. invoke() returns a result string that indicates what result was rendered. While this string tells the interceptor which result was rendered, it doesn't indicate whether the action itself fired or not. It's entirely possible that one of the deeper interceptors altered workflow by returning a control string itself without calling `invoke()`. Either way, when `invoke()` returns, a result has already been rendered. In other words, the response page has already been sent back to the client. An interceptor could implement some conditional postprocessing logic that uses the result string to make some decision, but it can't stop or alter the response at this point. In the case of the `TimerInterceptor`, we don't care what happened during processing, so we don't look at the string.

What kind of postprocessing does the `TimerInterceptor` do? It calculates the time that has passed during the execution of the action ❸. It does this simply by taking the current time and subtracting the previously recorded start time. When finished, it must finally return the control string that it received from `invoke()`. Doing this causes the recursion to travel back up the chain of interceptors. These outer interceptors will then have the opportunity to conduct any postprocessing they might be interested in.

Oh, my! Provided all of that sank in, your noodle should definitely be cooked by now. But we hope in a good way—by the vast possibilities that such an architecture allows! When contemplating the wide range of tasks that can be implemented in the reusable and modular interceptor, consider this short sampling of the available opportunities:

- During the *preprocessing* phase, the interceptor can be used to prepare, filter, alter, or otherwise manipulate any of the important data available to it. This data includes all of the key objects and data, including the action itself, that pertain to the current request.
- Call `invoke()` or divert workflow. If an interceptor determines that the request processing should not continue, it can return a control string rather than call the `invoke()` method on the `ActionInvocation`. In this manner, it can stop execution and determine itself which result will render.
- Even after the `invoke()` method returns a control string, any of the returning interceptors can arbitrarily decide to alter any of the objects or data available to them as part of their *postprocessing*. Note, however, that at this point the result has already been rendered.

As we've said, interceptors can be confusing at first. Furthermore, you can probably avoid implementing them yourself. However, we encourage you to reread these pages until you feel comfortable with interceptors. Even if you never make one yourself, a solid grasp of interceptors in action will ease all aspects of your development. Now let's move on to something simpler—the reference/user guide section of this chapter, wherein we will tell you all about the built-in interceptors that you can leverage when building your own applications.

4.3   *Surveying the built-in Struts 2 interceptors*

Struts 2 comes with a powerful set of built-in interceptors that provide most of the functionality you'll ever want from a web framework. In the introductory portion of this book, we said that a good framework should automate most of the routine tasks of the web application domain. The built-in interceptors provide this automation. We've already seen several of these and have used them in our Struts 2 Portfolio sample application. The ones we've used have all been from the `defaultStack` that we've inherited by extending the `struts-default` package. While this `defaultStack` is useful, the framework comes with more interceptors and preconfigured stacks than just that one. In this section, we'll introduce you to the most commonly used built-in interceptors. In the next section, we'll show you how to declare which of these interceptors should fire for your actions, and even how to arrange their order.

Now let's explore the offerings. If an interceptor is in the `defaultStack`, it'll be clearly noted as such.

4.3.1 *Utility interceptors*

First, we'll look at some utility interceptors. These interceptors provide simple utilities to aid in development, tuning, and troubleshooting.

TIMER

This simple interceptor merely records the duration of an execution. Position in the interceptor stack determines what this is actually timing. If you place this interceptor at the heart of your stack, just before the action, then it will time the action's execution itself. If you place it at the outermost layer of the stack, it'll time the execution of the entire stack, as well as the action. Here's the output:

```
INFO: Executed action [/chapterFour/secure/ImageUpload!execute] took 123 ms.
```

LOGGER

This interceptor provides a simple logging mechanism that logs an entry statement during preprocessing and an exit statement during postprocessing.

```
INFO: Starting execution stack for action /chapterFour/secure/ImageUpload

INFO: Finishing execution stack for action /chapterFour/secure/ImageUpload
```

This can be useful for debugging. Again, note that where you put this in the stack can change the nature of the information you learn from these simple statements. This interceptor serves as a good demonstration of an interceptor that does processing both before and after the action executes.

4.3.2 *Data transfer interceptors*

As we've already seen, interceptors can be used to handle data transfer. In particular, we've already seen that the `params` interceptor from the `defaultStack` moves the request parameters onto the JavaBeans properties we expose on our action objects. There are also several other interceptors that can move data onto our actions. These other interceptors can move data from other locations, such as from parameters defined in the XML configuration files.

PARAMS (DEFAULTSTACK)

This familiar interceptor provides one of the most integral functions of the framework. It transfers the request parameters to properties exposed by the `ValueStack`. We've also discussed how the framework uses OGNL expressions, embedded in the name attributes of your form's fields, to map this data transfer to those properties. In chapter 3, we explored techniques for using this to move data to properties exposed directly on our actions as well as on domain model objects with ModelDriven actions. The params interceptor doesn't know where the data is ultimately going; it just moves it to the first matching property it can find on the ValueStack. So how do the right objects get onto the ValueStack in time to receive the data transfer? As we learned in the previous chapter, the action is always put on the ValueStack at the start of a request-processing cycle. The model, as exposed by the ModelDriven interface, is moved onto the ValueStack by the modelDriven interceptor, discussed later in this chapter.

We'll fully cover the enigmatic ValueStack, and the equally enigmatic OGNL, in the next chapter when we delve into the details of data transfer and type conversion.

STATIC-PARAMS (DEFAULTSTACK)

This interceptor also moves parameters onto properties exposed on the ValueStack. The difference is the origin of the parameters. The parameters that this interceptor moves are defined in the action elements of the declarative architecture. For example, suppose you have an action defined like this in one of your declarative architecture XML files:

```
<action name="exampleAction" class="example.ExampleAction">
  <param name="firstName">John</param>
  <param name="lastName">Doe</param>
</action>
```

The static-params interceptor is called with these two name-value pairs. These parameters are moved onto the ValueStack properties just as with the params interceptor. Note that, again, order matters. In the defaultStack, the static-params interceptor fires before the params interceptor. This means that the request parameters will override values from the XML param element. You could, of course, change the order of these interceptors.

AUTOWIRING

This interceptor provides an integration point for using Spring to manage your application resources. We list it here because it is technically another way to set properties on your action. Since this use of Spring is such an important topic, we save it for a fuller treatment in chapter 10, which covers integration with such important technologies.

SERVLET-CONFIG (DEFAULTSTACK)

The servlet-config interceptor provides a clean way of injecting various objects from the Servlet API into your actions. This interceptor works by setting the various objects on setter methods exposed by interfaces that the action must implement. The following interfaces are available for retrieving various objects related to the servlet environment. Your action can implement any number of these.

- ServletContextAware—Sets the ServletContext
- ServletRequestAware—Sets the HttpServletRequest
- ServletResponseAware—Sets the HttpServletResponse

- `ParameterAware`—Sets a map of the request parameters
- `RequestAware`—Sets a map of the request attributes
- `SessionAware`—Sets a map of the session attributes
- `ApplicationAware`—Sets a map of application scope properties
- `PrincipalAware`—Sets the `Principal` object (security)

Each of these interfaces contains one method—a setter—for the resource in question. These interfaces are found in the Struts 2 distribution's `org.apache.struts2.interceptor` package. As with all of the data-injecting interceptors that we've seen, the `servlet-config` interceptor will put these objects on your action during the preprocessing phase. Thus, when your action executes, the resource will be available. We'll demonstrate using this injection later in this chapter, when we build our custom authentication interceptor; the `Login` action that'll work with the authentication interceptor will implement the `SessionAware` interface. We should note that best practices recommend avoiding use of these Servlet API objects, as they bind your action code to the Servlet API. After all the work the framework has done to separate you from the Servlet environment, you would probably be well served by this advice. Nonetheless, you'll sometimes want to get your hands on these important Servlet objects. Don't worry; it's a natural urge.

FILEUPLOAD (DEFAULTSTACK)

We covered the `fileUpload` interceptor in depth in the previous chapter. We note it briefly here for completeness. The `fileUpload` interceptor transforms the files and metadata from multipart requests into regular request parameters so that they can be set on the action just like normal parameters.

4.3.3   *Workflow interceptors*

The interceptors we've covered so far mostly realize some concrete task, such as measuring execution time or transferring some data. Workflow interceptors provide something else entirely. They provide the opportunity to conditionally alter the workflow of the request processing. By *workflow* we mean the path of the processing as it works its way down through the interceptors, through the action and result, and then back out the interceptors. In normal workflow, the processing will go all the way down to the action and result before climbing back out. Workflow interceptors are interceptors that inspect the state of the processing and conditionally intervene and alter this normal path, sometimes only slightly, and sometimes quite drastically.

WORKFLOW (DEFAULTSTACK)

One of the interceptors is actually named `workflow`. Consider this one to be the gold standard for what a workflow-oriented interceptor can do. We've already used and discussed this interceptor. As we've learned, it works with our actions to provide data validation and subsequent workflow alteration if a validation error occurs. Since we've already used this interceptor, we'll leverage our familiarity to learn more about how interceptors work by looking at the code that alters execution workflow. Listing 4.1 shows the code from this important interceptor.

Listing 4.1 Altering workflow from within an interceptor

```
public String intercept(ActionInvocation invocation)
  throws Exception {

  Action action = invocation.getAction();        ❶

  if (action instanceof Validateable) {
    Validateable validateable = (Validateable) action;    ❷
      validateable.validate();
  }
  if (action instanceof ValidationAware) {
    ValidationAware validationAwareAction =      ❸
    ValidationAware) action;

    if (validationAwareAction.hasErrors()) {     ❹
      return Action.INPUT;
    }
  }
  return invocation.invoke();
}
```

If you recall, the actions of our Struts 2 Portfolio use a form of validation implemented in a couple of interfaces that cooperate with the workflow interceptor. The action implements these interfaces to expose methods upon which the interceptor will work. First, the interceptor must obtain an instance of the action from the ActionInvocation ❶ so that it can check to see whether the action has implemented these interfaces. If the action has implemented the Validateable interface, the interceptor will invoke its validate() method ❷ to execute the action's validation logic.

Next, if the action implements the ValidationAware interface, the interceptor will check to see whether any errors were created by the validation logic by calling the hasErrors() method ❸. If some are present, the workflow interceptor takes the rather drastic step of completely halting execution of the action. It does this, as you can see, by returning its own INPUT control string ❹. Further execution stops immediately. The INPUT result is rendered, and postprocessing occurs as control climbs back out of the interceptor stack. Note that our Struts 2 Portfolio actions all inherit implementations of these interfaces by extending the ActionSupport convenience class.

The workflow interceptor also introduces another important interceptor concept: using params to tweak the execution of the interceptor. After we finish covering the built-in interceptors, we'll cover the syntax of declaring your interceptors and interceptor stacks in section 4.4.3. At that time, we'll learn all about setting and overriding parameters. For now, we'll just note the parameters that an interceptor can take. The workflow interceptor can take several parameters:

- alwaysInvokeValidate (true or false; defaults to true, which means that validate() will be invoked)
- inputResultName (name of the result to choose if validation fails; defaults to Action.INPUT)
- excludeMethods (names of methods for which the workflow interceptor shouldn't execute, thereby omitting validation checking for a specific entry point method on an action)

These should all be straightforward. Note that the workflow interceptor configured in the `defaultStack` is passed a list of `excludeMethods` parameters, as seen in the following snippet from struts-default.xml:

```
<interceptor-ref name="workflow">
  <param name="excludeMethods">input,back,cancel,browse</param>
</interceptor-ref>
```

This list of exclude methods is meant to support actions that expose methods other than `execute()` for various processing tasks related to the same data object. We haven't shown how to do this yet, but we will in chapter 15. For instance, imagine you want to use the same action to prepopulate as well as process a form. A common scenario is to combine the create, read, update, and delete (CRUD) functions pertaining to a single data object into a single action. For now, note that the main benefit of such a strategy is the consolidation of code that pertains to the same domain object. One difficulty with this strategy is that the process that prepopulates the form can't be validated because there is no data yet. To handle this problem, we can put the prepopulation code into an `input` method and list this method as one that should be excluded from the `workflow` interceptor's validation measurements.

Several other interceptors take `excludeMethods` and `includeMethods` parameters to achieve similar filtering of their processing. We'll note when these parameters are available for the interceptors that we cover in this book. In general, you should be on the lookout for such parameters any time you're dealing with an interceptor for which it seems logical that such a filtering would exist.

VALIDATION (DEFAULTSTACK)

We've already shown one basic form of validation offered by Struts 2. To recap that technique, the `Validateable` interface, as we've seen, provides a programmatic validation mechanism; you put the validation code into your action's `validate()` method and it'll be executed by the `workflow` interceptor. The `validation` interceptor, on the other hand, is part of the Struts 2 validation framework and provides a declarative means to validate your data. Rather than writing validation code, the validation framework allows you to use both XML files and Java annotations to describe the validation rules for your data. Since the validation framework is such a rich topic, chapter 10 is dedicated to it.

For now, we should note that the `validation` interceptor, like the `Validateable` interface, works in tandem with the `workflow` interceptor. Recall that the `workflow` interceptor calls the `validate()` method of the `Validateable` interface to execute validation code before it checks for validation errors. In the case of the validation framework, the `validation` interceptor itself executes the validation logic. The `validation` interceptor is the entry point into the validation framework's processing. When the validation framework does its work, it'll store validation errors using the same `Validation-Aware` methods that your handwritten `validate()` code does. When the `workflow` interceptor checks for error messages, it doesn't know whether they were created by the validation framework or the validation code invoked through the `Validateable` interface. In fact, it doesn't matter. The only thing that really matters is that the `validation` interceptor fires before the workflow interceptor, and this sequencing is handled by the defaultStack. You could even use both methods of validation if you liked. Either way, if errors are found, the workflow interceptor will divert workflow back to the input page.

PREPARE (DEFAULTSTACK)

The prepare interceptor provides a generic entry point for arbitrary workflow processing that you might want to add to your actions. The concept is simple. When the prepare interceptor executes, it looks for a prepare() method on your action. Actually, it checks whether your action implements the Preparable interface, which defines the prepare() method. If your action is Preparable, the prepare() method is invoked. This allows for any sort of preprocessing to occur. Note that while the prepare interceptor has a specific place in the defaultStack, you can define your own stack if you need to move the prepare code to a different location in the sequence.

The prepare interceptor is flexible as well. For instance, you can define special prepare methods for the different execution methods on a single action. As we said earlier, sometimes you'll want to define more than one execution entry point on your action. (See the CRUD example in chapter 15 for details.) In addition to the execute() method, you might define an input() method and an update() method. In this case, you might want to define specific preparation logic for each of these methods. If you've implemented the Preparable interface, you can also define preparation methods, named according to the conventions in table 4.1, for each of your action's execution methods.

Table 4.1 Parameters to the prepare interceptor

Action Method Name	Prepare Method 1	Prepare Method 2
input()	prepareInput()	prepareDoInput()
update()	prepareUpdate()	prepareDoUpdate()

Two naming conventions are provided. You can use either one. The use case is simple. If your input() method is being invoked, the prepareInput() method will be called by the prepare interceptor, giving you an opportunity to execute some preparation code specific to the input processing. The prepare() method itself will always be called by the prepare interceptor regardless of the action method being invoked. Its execution comes after the specialized prepare() method. If you like, you can turn off the prepare() method invocation with a parameter passed to the prepare interceptor:

```
alwaysInvokePrepare - Default to true.
```

The Preparable interface can be helpful for setting up resources or values before your action is executed. For instance, if you have a drop-down list of available values that you look up in the database, you may want to do this in the prepare() method. That way, the values will be populated for rendering to the page even if the action isn't executed because, for instance, the workflow interceptor found error messages.

MODELDRIVEN (DEFAULTSTACK)

We've probably already covered the modelDriven interceptor enough for one book. We'll just make a couple of brief notes here for the sake of consistency. The model-Driven interceptor is considered a workflow interceptor because it alters the workflow of the execution by invoking getModel(), if present, and setting the model object on the top of the ValueStack where it'll receive the parameters from the request. This alters workflow because the transfer of the parameters, by the params interceptor, would otherwise be directed onto the action object itself. By placing the model over the action in the ValueStack, the modelDriven interceptor thus alters workflow. This concept of creating an interceptor that can conditionally alter the effective functionality of another interceptor without direct programmatic intervention demonstrates the power of the layered interceptor architecture. When thinking of ways to add power to your own applications by writing custom interceptors, this is a good model to follow.

4.3.4 *Miscellaneous interceptors*

A few interceptors don't fit into any specific classification but are important or useful nonetheless. The following interceptors range from the core interceptors from the defaultStack to built-in interceptors that provide cool bells and whistles.

EXCEPTION (DEFAULTSTACK)

This important interceptor lays the foundation for rich exception handling in your applications. The exception interceptor comes first in the defaultStack, and should probably come first in any custom stacks you create yourself. The exception interceptor will catch exceptions and map them, by type, to user-defined error pages. Its position at the top of the stack guarantees that it'll be able to catch all exceptions that may be generated during all phases of action invocation. It can catch them because, as the top interceptor, it'll be the last to fire during postprocessing.

The Struts 2 Portfolio uses the exception interceptor to route all exceptions of type java.lang.Exception to a single, somewhat-unpolished error message page. We've implemented this in the chapterFourPublic package. The following snippet shows the code from the chapterFour.xml file that sets up the exception handling:

```
<global-results>
  <result name="error">/chapterFour/Error.jsp</result>
</global-results>

<global-exception-mappings>
  <exception-mapping exception="java.lang.Exception" result="error"/>
</global-exception-mappings>
```

First, we define a global result. We need to do this because this error page isn't specific to one action, and global results are available to all actions in the package. The exception-mapping element tells the exception interceptor which result to render for a given exception. When the exception interceptor executes during its postprocessing phase, it'll catch any exception that has been thrown and map it to a result. Before yielding control to the result, the exception interceptor will create an

ExceptionHolder object and place it on top of the ValueStack. The Exception-Holder is a wrapper around an exception that exposes the stack trace and the exception as JavaBeans properties that you can access from a tag in your error page. The following snippet shows our error JSP page:

```
<p><h4>Exception Name: </h4><s:property value="exception" /></p>
<p><h4>What you did wrong:</h4> <s:property value="exceptionStack" /></p>

<p><h5>Also, please confirm that your Internet is working before actually
   contacting us.</h4></p>
```

As you can see, our property tag, explained with the other Struts 2 tags in chapter 6, references the exceptionStack property that has been placed on the ValueStack. We've created an ErrorProne action, which automatically throws an exception, so we can see all this in action. For a guaranteed application failure, hit the error-prone link from the home page of the chapter 4 version of the application. Note that you don't need to have one page catch all exceptions; you can have as many exception mappings as you like, mapping specific exception types to a variety of specific results.

TOKEN AND TOKEN-SESSION

The token and token-session interceptors can be used as part of a system to prevent duplicate form submissions. Duplicate form posts can occur when users click the Back button to go back to a previously submitted form and then click the Submit button again, or when they click Submit more than once while waiting for a response. The token interceptors work by passing a token in with the request that is checked by the interceptor. If the unique token comes to the interceptor a second time, the request is considered a duplicate. These two interceptors both do the same thing, differing only in how richly they handle the duplicate request. You can either show an error page or save the original result to be rerendered for the user. We'll implement this functionality for the Struts 2 Portfolio application in chapter 15.

SCOPED-MODELDRIVEN (DEFAULTSTACK)

This nice interceptor supports wizard-like persistence across requests for your action's model object. This one adds to the functionality of the modelDriven interceptor by allowing you to store your model object in, for instance, session scope. This is great for implementing wizards that need to work with a data object across a series of requests.

EXECANDWAIT

When a request takes a long time to execute, it's nice to give the user some feedback. Impatient users, after all, are the ones who make all those duplicate requests. While the token interceptors discussed earlier can technically solve this problem, we should still do something for the user. The execAndWait interceptor helps prevent your users from getting antsy. We'll implement this functionality for the Struts 2 Portfolio application in chapter 15.

In addition to providing these useful interceptors, the struts-default package also provides several built-in stacks made of these interceptors. We've already seen the strutsDefault stack, but we should look at what else is available.

4.3.5   *Built-in stacks*

The Struts 2 framework comes with many built-in stacks that provide convenient arrangements of the built-in interceptors. We've been using one of these, the defaultStack, for all of our Struts 2 Portfolio packages. We inherit all of this, and other built-in stacks, just by having our packages extend the struts-default package defined in struts-default.xml. To make things simple, we recommend that you also use the defaultStack unless you have a clear imperative to do otherwise. Most of the other built-in stacks you could use are just pared-down versions of the defaultStack. This paring down is not done to make more efficient versions of the stacks by eliminating unnecessary interceptors. Rather, the smaller stacks are meant to be modular building blocks for building larger ones. If you find yourself building your own stacks, try to use these modular pieces to help simplify your task. Still, you might ask, why do we need the scoped-modelDriven interceptor in the stack if we aren't using it? Isn't this a performance hit? We think it isn't. So far, it seems that unused interceptors don't affect performance that much. Additionally, messing with the interceptors can be the fastest way to introduce debugging complexity. Ultimately, we always recommend using the built-in path of least resistance as long as possible—which means the defaultStack. While Struts 2 is flexible, it's also meant to perform well and be useful right out of the box.

4.4   *Declaring interceptors*

We can't go much further without learning how to set up our interceptors with the declarative architecture. In this section, we'll cover the details of declaring interceptors, building stacks, and passing parameters to interceptors. Since most of the interceptors that you'll typically need are provided by the struts-default package, we'll spend a fair bit of time perusing the interceptor declarations made in the struts-default.xml file. They serve as a perfect example of how to declare interceptors and stacks. After we look at the interceptors and stacks from the struts-default package, we'll also show how you can specify the interceptors that fire for a given action. You can do this at varying levels of granularity, starting with the broad scope of the framework's intelligent defaults and narrowing down to a per-action specification of interceptors.

We should also note that, at this point, XML is your only option for declaring your interceptors; the annotations mechanism doesn't yet support declaring interceptors.

4.4.1   *Declaring individual interceptors and interceptor stacks*

Basically, interceptor declarations consist of declaring the interceptors that are available and associating them with the actions for which they should fire. The only complication is the creation of stacks, which allow you to reference groups of interceptors all at once. Interceptor declarations, like declarations of all framework components, must be contained in a package element. Listing 4.2 shows the individual interceptor declarations from the struts-default package of the struts-default.xml file.

Listing 4.2   Interceptor declarations from the `struts-default` package

```
<package name="struts-default">

    . . .                              ❶ Interceptors
                                          element
    <interceptors>        <─┐
        <interceptor name="execAndWait" class="ExecuteAndWaitInterceptor"/>
        <interceptor name="exception" class="ExceptionMappingInterceptor"/>
        <interceptor name="fileUpload" class="FileUploadInterceptor"/>
        <interceptor name="i18n" class="I18nInterceptor"/>
        <interceptor name="logger" class="LoggingInterceptor"/>
        <interceptor name="modelDriven" class="ModelDrivenInterceptor"/>
        <interceptor name="scoped-modelDriven" class= . . ./>
        <interceptor name="params" class="ParametersInterceptor"/>
        <interceptor name="prepare" class="PrepareInterceptor"/>
        <interceptor name="static-params" class=. . ./>
        <interceptor name="servlet-config" class="ServletConfigInterceptor"/>
        <interceptor name="sessionAutowiring"
                       class="SessionContextAutowiringInterceptor"/>
        <interceptor name="timer" class="TimerInterceptor"/>          All   ❷
        <interceptor name="token" class="TokenInterceptor"/>      interceptor
        <interceptor name="token-session" class= . . . />          elements
        <interceptor name="validation" class= . . . />
        <interceptor name="workflow" class="DefaultWorkflowInterceptor"/>
        . . .
                                                              ❸ Declaring a stack
        <interceptor-stack name="defaultStack">       <─┐
            <interceptor-ref name="exception"/>
            <interceptor-ref name="alias"/>
            <interceptor-ref name="servlet-config"/>
            <interceptor-ref name="prepare"/>
            <interceptor-ref name="i18n"/>
            <interceptor-ref name="chain"/>
            <interceptor-ref name="debugging"/>
            <interceptor-ref name="profiling"/>
            <interceptor-ref name="scoped-modelDriven"/>
            <interceptor-ref name="modelDriven"/>
            <interceptor-ref name="fileUpload"/>               Interceptor   ❹
            <interceptor-ref name="checkbox"/>                  references
            <interceptor-ref name="static-params"/>
            <interceptor-ref name="params">
                <param name="excludeParams">dojo\..*</param>      <─┐
            </interceptor-ref>                               ❺ Parameters
            <interceptor-ref name="conversionError"/>
            <interceptor-ref name="validation">
                <param name="excludeMethods">input,back,cancel,browse</param>
            </interceptor-ref>
            <interceptor-ref name="workflow">
                <param name="excludeMethods">input,back,cancel,browse</param>
            </interceptor-ref>
        </interceptor-stack>

    </interceptors>
                                            ❻ Default
    <default-interceptor-ref name="defaultStack"/>    <─┐  reference

</package>
```

The interceptors element ❶ contains all the interceptor and interceptor-stack declarations of the package. Interceptor stacks are just a convenient way of referencing a sequenced chunk of interceptors by name. Each interceptor element ❷ declares an interceptor that can be used in the package. This just maps an interceptor implementation class to a logical name, such as mapping com.opensymphony. xwork2.interceptor.DefaultWorkflowInterceptor to the name workflow. (In listing 4.2, we've snipped the package names to make the listing more readable.) These declarations don't actually create an interceptor or associate that interceptor with any actions; they just map a name to a class.

Now we can define some stacks of interceptors ❸. Since most actions will use the same groups of interceptors, arranged in the same sequence, it's common practice to define these in small, building-block stacks. The struts-default package declares several stacks, most importantly the defaultStack.

The contents of the interceptor-stack element are a sequence of interceptor-ref elements. ❹ These references must all point to one of the logical names created by the interceptor elements. Creating your own stacks, as we'll see when we build a custom interceptor later in this chapter, is just as easy. The interceptor-ref elements can also pass in parameters to configure the instance of the interceptor that is created by the reference ❺.

Finally, a package can declare a default set of interceptors. ❻ This set will be associated with all actions in the package that don't explicitly declare their own interceptors. The default-interceptor-ref element simply points to a logical name, in this case the defaultStack. This important line is what allows our actions to inherit a default set of interceptors when we extend the struts-default package.

While this example is from the struts-default package, you can do the same in your own packages when you need to change the interceptors that fire for your actions. This can be dangerous for the uninitiated. Since most of the framework's core functionality exists in the default stack of interceptors defined in struts-default, you probably won't want to mess with those for a while. However, we'll show how to safely modify this stack when we build our custom authentication interceptor in a few pages.

XML DOCUMENT STRUCTURE

Before moving on to show how you specify the interceptors that'll fire for your specific actions, we should make a point about the sequence of elements within the XML documents we use for declarative architecture. These XML documents must conform to certain rules of ordering. For instance, each package element contains precisely one interceptors element, and that element must come in a specific position in the document. The complete DTD, struts-2.0.dtd, can be found on the Struts 2 website. For now, note the following snippet from the DTD, which pertains to the structure of listing 4.2:

```
<!ELEMENT struts (package|include|bean|constant)*>

<!ELEMENT package (result-types?, interceptors?, default-interceptor-ref?,
default-action-ref?, global-results?, global-exception-mappings?, action*)>
```

The first element definition specified the contents of the `struts` element. The `struts` element is the root element of an XML file used for the declarative architecture. As you can see in listing 4.2, struts-default.xml starts with the `struts` element. Moving on, this root element can contain zero or more instances each of four different element types. For now, we're only concerned with the `package` element. The contents of a `package` element, unlike the `struts` element, must follow a specific sequence. Furthermore, all of the elements contained in a `package` element, except for the actions, can occur only once. From this snippet, we glean the important information that our `interceptors` element must occur just once, or not at all, and must come after the `result-types` element and before the `default-interceptor-ref` element. The documents in the Struts 2 Portfolio application will demonstrate the correct ordering of elements, but, if you ever have questions, consult the DTD.

4.4.2 *Mapping interceptors to actions*

Much of the time, your actions will belong to packages that extend `struts-default`, and you'll be content to let them use the `defaultStack` of interceptors they inherit from that package. Eventually, you'll probably want to modify, change, or perhaps just augment that default set of interceptors. To do this, you have to know how to map interceptors to your actions. Associating an interceptor to an action is done with an `interceptor-ref` element. The following code snippet shows how to associate a set of interceptors with a specific action:

```
<action name="MyAction" class="org.actions.myactions.MyAction">
  <interceptor-ref name="timer"/>
  <interceptor-ref name="logger"/>
  <result>Success.jsp</result>
</action>
```

This snippet associates two interceptors with the action. They'll fire in the order they're listed. Of course, you already know enough about how Struts 2 applications work to know that this action, with just the `timer` and `logger` interceptors, wouldn't be able to accomplish much. It wouldn't have access to any request data because the `params` interceptor isn't there. Even if it could get the data from the request, it wouldn't have any validation. In reality, most of the functionality of the framework is provided by interceptors. You could define the whole set of them here, but that would be tedious, especially as you'd end up repeating the same definitions across most of your actions.

Stacks address this very situation. As it turns out, you can combine references to stacks and individual interceptors. The following snippet shows a revision of the previous `action` element that still uses the `defaultStack` while adding the other two interceptors it needs:

```
<action name="MyAction" class="org.actions.myactions.MyAction">
  <interceptor-ref name="timer"/>
  <interceptor-ref name="logger"/>
  <interceptor-ref name="defaultStack"/>
```

```
    <result>Success.jsp</result>
  </action>
```

We should note a couple of important things. First, this action names interceptors, not to mention the `defaultStack`, which are declared in the `struts-default` package. Because of this, it must be in a package that extends `struts-default`. Next, while actions that don't define any `interceptor-refs` themselves will inherit the default interceptors, as soon as an action declares its own interceptors, it loses that automatic default and must explicitly name the `defaultStack` in order to use it.

As we've seen, if an action doesn't declare its own interceptors, it inherits the default interceptor reference of the package. The following snippet shows the line from struts-default.xml that declares the default interceptor reference for the `struts-default` package:

```
  <default-interceptor-ref name="defaultStack"/>
```

When you create your own packages, you can make default references for those packages. We'll do this when we create the authentication interceptor in a few pages.

Now, let's see how to pass parameters into interceptors that permit such modifications of their behavior.

4.4.3   *Setting and overriding parameters*

Many interceptors can be parameterized. If an interceptor accepts parameters, the `interceptor-ref` element is the place to pass them in. We can see that the workflow interceptor in the `defaultStack` is parameterized to ignore requests to certain action method names, as specified in the `excludeMethods` parameter element.

```
  <interceptor-ref name="workflow">
    <param name="excludeMethods">input,back,cancel,browse</param>
  </interceptor-ref>
```

Passing parameters into interceptors is as simple as this. With the preceding method, you pass the parameters in when you create the `interceptor-ref`. This one is a part of a stack. What if we wanted to reuse the `defaultStack` from which this reference is taken, but we wanted to change the values of the `excludeMethods` parameter? This is easy enough, as demonstrated in the following snippet:

```
  <action name="YourAction" class="org.actions.youractions.YourAction">

    <interceptor-ref name="defaultStack">
      <param name="workflow.excludeMethods">doSomething</param>
    </interceptor-ref>
    <result>Success.jsp</result>
  </action>
```

First, we assume that this action belongs to a package that inherits the `defaultStack`. This action names the `defaultStack` as its interceptor reference but overrides the `workflow` interceptor's `excludeMethods` parameter. This allows you to conveniently reuse existing stacks while still being able to customize the parameters.

Next up, rolling your own authentication interceptor!

4.5   Building your own interceptor

We've said several times that you probably won't need to build your own interceptor. On the other hand, we hope that we've sold the power of interceptors well enough to get you itching to start rolling your own. Apart from the care needed when sequencing the stack and learning to account for this sequencing in your debugging, interceptors can be simple to write. We round out the chapter by creating an authentication interceptor that we can use to provide application-based security for our Struts 2 Portfolio application. This form of authentication is probably far too simple for most real applications, but it's a well-known use case and serves as a perfect example for interceptors.

We'll start by looking at the technical details of implementing an interceptor.

4.5.1   Implementing the Interceptor interface

When you write an interceptor, you'll implement the `com.opensymphony.xwork2.interceptor.Interceptor` interface:

```
public interface Interceptor extends Serializable {
  void destroy();
  void init();
  String intercept(ActionInvocation invocation) throws Exception;
}
```

As you can see, this simple interface defines only three methods. The first two are typical lifecycle methods that give you a chance to initialize and clean up resources as necessary. The real business occurs in the `intercept()` method. As we've already seen, this method is called by the recursive `ActionInvocation.invoke()` method. If you don't recall the details, you might want to reread section 4.2, which describes this interceptor execution process in detail.

We'll directly implement the `Interceptor` interface when we write our authentication interceptor. Sometimes you can take advantage of a convenience class provided with the distribution that provides support for method filtering. We saw parameter-based method filtering when we looked at the `workflow` interceptor. Such interceptors accept a parameter that defines methods for which the interceptor won't fire. This type of parameterized behavior is so common that an abstract implementation of the `Interceptor` interface has already taken care of the functionality involved in such method filtering. If you want to write an interceptor that has this type of parameterization, you can extend `com.opensymphony.xwork2.interceptor.MethodFilterInterceptor` rather than directly implementing the `Interceptor` interface. Since our authentication interceptor doesn't need to filter methods, we'll stick to the direct implementation.

4.5.2   Building the AuthenticationInterceptor

The authentication interceptor will be simple. If you recall the three phases of interceptor processing—preprocessing, calling `ActionInvocation.invoke()`, and postprocessing—you can anticipate how our `AuthenticationInterceptor` will function. When a request comes to one of our secure actions, we'll want to check whether the request is coming from an authenticated user. This check is made during preprocessing. If the user has been authenticated, the interceptor will call invoke(), thus allowing the action invocation to proceed. If the user hasn't been authenticated, the interceptor will return a control string itself, thus barring further execution. The control string will route the user to the login page.

You can see this in action by visiting the chapter 4 version of the Struts 2 Portfolio application. On the home page, there's a link to add an image without having logged in. The add image action is a secure action. Try clicking the link without having logged in. You'll be automatically taken to the login page. Now, log in and try the same link again. The application comes with a default user, username = "Arty" and password = "password". This time you're allowed to access the secure add image action. This is done by a custom interceptor that we've placed in front of all of our secure actions. Let's see how it works.

First, we should clear up some roles. The AuthenticationInterceptor doesn't do the authentication; it just bars access to secure actions by unauthenticated users. Authentication itself is done by the login action. The login action checks to see whether the username and password are valid. If they are, the user object is stored in a session-scoped map. When the AuthenticationInterceptor fires, it checks to see whether the user object is present in the session. If it is, it lets the action fire as usual. If it isn't, it diverts workflow by forwarding to the login page.

We should take a quick look at the manning.chapterFour.Login action on our way to inspecting the AuthenticationInterceptor. Listing 4.3 shows the execute code from the Login action. Note that we've trimmed extraneous code, such as validation and JavaBeans properties, from the listing.

Listing 4.3   The Login action authenticates the user and stores the user in session scope

```
public class Login extends ActionSupport implements SessionAware {        ❶

    public String execute(){

        User user = getPortfolioService().authenticateUser( getUsername(),
            getPassword() );                                                 ❷

        if ( user == null )
        {
            return INPUT;                            ❸
        }
        else{
            session.put( Struts2PortfolioConstants.USER, user );    ❹
        }

        return SUCCESS;
    }

    . . .

    public void setSession(Map session) {        ❺
        this.session = session;
    }
}
```

The first thing of interest is that our `Login` action uses the `SessionAware` interface ❶ to have the session-scoped map conveniently injected into a setter ❺. This is one of the services provided by the `ServletConfigInterceptor` provided in the `defaultStack`. (See the section on that interceptor earlier in this chapter to find out all the other objects you can have injected through similar interfaces.) As for the business logic of the login itself, first we use our service object to authenticate the username and password combination ❷. Our authentication method will return a valid `User` object if everything checks out, or null if it doesn't. If the user is null, we send her back to the `INPUT` result, which is the login form ❸ that she came from. If the user is not null, we'll store the user object in the session map ❹, officially marking her as an authenticated user.

With the `Login` action in place, we can look at how the `AuthenticationInterceptor` protects secure actions from unauthenticated access. Basically, the interceptor will check to see whether the user object has been placed in the session map. Let's check it out. Listing 4.4 shows the full code.

Listing 4.4   Inspecting the heart of the `AuthenticationInterceptor`

```
public class AuthenticationInterceptor implements Interceptor {         ⭠───┐

    public void destroy() {                                        Implements
    }                              Empty                            interceptor
                                   implementations
    public void init() {
    }

    public String intercept( ActionInvocation actionInvocation )       ❶
                             throws Exception{

      Map session = actionInvocation.getInvocationContext().getSession();
      User user = (User) session.get( Struts2PortfolioConstants.USER );   ❷

      if (user == null) {
         return Action.LOGIN;            ❸
      }
      else {

        Action action = ( Action ) actionInvocation.getAction();
                                                                          ❹
        if (action instanceof UserAware) {
           ((UserAware)action).setUser(user);
        }

        return actionInvocation.invoke();    ⭠──┐ Continue action
      }                                          ❺ invocation
    }

  }
```

The main part of the interceptor starts inside the `intercept()` method ❶. Here we can see that the interceptor uses the `ActionInvocation` object ❷ to obtain information pertaining to the request. In this case, we're getting the session map. With the session map in hand, we retrieve the user object stored under the known key.

If the user object is null ❸, then the user hasn't been authenticated through the login action. At this point, we return a result string, without allowing the action to continue. This result string, Action.LOGIN, points to our login page. If you consult the chapterFour.xml file, you'll see that the chapterFourSecure package defines the login result as a global result, available to all actions in the secure package. In chapter 8, we'll learn about configuring global results.

INSIDER TIP   If you consult the API, you'll see that the getInvocationContext() method returns the ActionContext object associated with the request. As we learned earlier, the ActionContext contains many important data objects for processing the request, including the ValueStack and key objects from the Servlet API such as the session map that we're using here. If you recall, we can also access objects in this ActionContext from our view layer pages (JSPs) via OGNL expressions. In this interceptor, we use programmatic access to those objects. Note that although it's always possible to get your hands on the ThreadLocal ActionContext, it's not a good idea. We recommend confining programmatic access to the ActionContext to interceptors, and using the ActionInvocation object as a path to that access. This keeps your APIs separated and lays the foundation for clean testing.

If the user object exists ❹, then the user has already logged in. At this point, we get a reference to the current action from the ActionInvocation and check whether it implements the UserAware interface. This interface allows actions to have the user object automatically injected into a setter method. This technique, which we copied from the framework's own interface-based injection, is a powerful way of making your action cleaner and more efficient. Most secure actions will want to work with the user object. With this interceptor in the stack, they just need to implement the UserAware interface to have the user conveniently injected. You can check out any of the secure actions in the Struts 2 Portfolio's chapterFour package to see how they do this. With the business of authentication out of the way, the interceptor calls invoke() on the ActionInvocation object ❺ to pass control on to the rest of the interceptors and the action. And that's that; it's pretty straightforward.

We need to point out one important detail before moving on. Interceptor instances are shared among actions. Though a new instance of an action is created for each request, interceptors are reused. This has one important implication. Interceptors are stateless. Don't try to store data related to the request being processed on the interceptor object. This isn't the role of the interceptor. An interceptor should just apply its processing logic to the data of the request, which is already conveniently stored in the various objects you can access through the ActionInvocation.

Now we'll apply this interceptor to our secure actions. Since we put all of our secure actions into a single package, we can build a custom stack that includes our AuthenticationInterceptor, and then declare that as the default interceptor reference for the secure package. This is the benefit of packaging actions according to shared functionality. Listing 4.5 shows the elements from chapterFour.xml that configure the `chapterFourSecure` package.

Listing 4.5   Declaring our interceptor and building a new default stack

```
<package name="chapterFourSecure" namespace="/chapterFour/secure"
 extends="struts-default">

  <interceptors>            ❶

    <interceptor name="authenticationInterceptor"          ❷
      class="manning.utils.AuthenticationInterceptor"/>

    <interceptor-stack name="secureStack">
      <interceptor-ref name="authenticationInterceptor"/>
      <interceptor-ref name="defaultStack"/>              ❸
    </interceptor-stack>

  </interceptors>

  <default-interceptor-ref name="secureStack"/>       ❹

  . . .
</package>
```

With all of our secure actions bundled in this package, we just need to make a stack that includes our `AuthenticationInterceptor` and then declare it as the default. You can see how easy this is. First, we must have an `interceptors` element ❶ to contain our `interceptor` and `interceptor-stack` declarations. We have to map our Java class to a logical name with an `interceptor` element ❷. We've chosen `authentication-Interceptor` as our name. Next, we build a new stack that takes the `defaultStack` and adds our new interceptor to the top of it ❸. We put it on top because we might as well stop an unauthenticated request as soon as possible. Finally, we declare our new `secure-Stack` as the default stack for the package ❹. Note that the `default-interceptor-ref` element isn't contained in the `interceptors` element; it doesn't declare any interceptors, it just declares the default value for the package. Every action in this package will now have authentication with automatic routing back to the login page, as well as injection of the user object for any action that implements the `UserAware` interface. It feels like we've accomplished something, no? The best part is that our interceptor is completely separate from our action code and completely reusable.

4.6   Summary

In this chapter we saw perhaps the most important component of the framework. Even though you can get away without developing interceptors for quite a while, a solid understanding of these important components is critical to understanding the framework in general. A grasp of interceptors will facilitate debugging and working with the framework. We hope we've given you a solid leg up on the road to interceptor mastery.

By now, you should have come to grips with the role of the interceptor in the framework. To reiterate, the interceptor component provides a nice place to separate the logic of various cross-cutting concerns into layered, reusable pieces. Tasks such as logging, exception handling, and dependency injection can all be encapsulated in interceptors. With the functionality of these common tasks thus modularized, we can easily use the declarative architecture to customize stacks of interceptors to meet the needs of our specific actions or packages of actions.

Perhaps the toughest thing to wrap your mind around, as far as interceptors go, is the recursive nature of their execution. Central to the entire execution model of the Struts 2 framework is the `ActionInvocation`. We learned how the `ActionInvocation` contains all the important data for processing the request, including everything from the action and its interceptors to the `ActionContext`. On top of this, it actually manages the execution process. As we've seen, it exposes a single, recursive `invoke()` method as an entry point into the execution process. `ActionInvocation` keeps track of the state of the execution process and invokes the next interceptor in the stack each time `invoke()` is called until, finally, the action is executed.

Interceptors themselves are invoked via their `intercept()` method. The execution of an interceptor can be broken into three phases: preprocessing, passing control on to the rest of the action invocation by calling `invoke()`, and postprocessing. Interceptors can also divert workflow by returning a control string instead of calling `invoke()`. They also have access to all key data via the `ActionInvocation` instance they receive. Ultimately, interceptors can do just about anything.

We also reviewed the functionality of many of the built-in interceptors that come with the `struts-default` package. Familiarity with these is critical to saving yourself from repeating work already done for you. We highly recommend staying up to date on the current set of interceptors available from the Struts 2 folks. They may have already built something you need by the time this book makes it onto your shelf. A quick visit to the Struts 2 website is always a good idea. Finally, we hope that our `AuthenticationInterceptor` has convinced you that it's easy to write your own interceptors. Again, we think the hardest part is understanding how interceptors work. Writing them is not so bad. We're confident that you'll soon find yourself with your own ideas for custom interceptors.

Now that we've covered actions and interceptors, we should be ready to move on to the view layer and start exploring the rich options that the framework offers for rendering result pages. Before we do that, we have one more stop on our tour of the core components of framework. Most likely, it's a stop you've been wondering about. Next up, chapter 5 will work on dispelling that mysterious OGNL cloud that surrounds the data transfer mechanisms of the framework.

Data transfer: OGNL
and type conversion

5

This chapter covers

- Transferring data
- Working with OGNL
- Using the built-in type converters
- Customizing type conversion

Now that we've covered the action and interceptor components, you should have a good idea of how the major chunks of server-side logic execute in the Struts 2 framework. We've avoided poking our noses into the details of two of the more important tasks that the framework helps us achieve: data transfer and type conversion. We've been able to avoid thinking about these important tasks because the framework automates them so well. This'll continue to be true for large portions of your development practice. However, if we give a small portion of our energy to learning how the data transfer and type conversion actually works, we can squeeze a whole lot more power out of the framework's automation of these crucial tasks.

We've already learned how to take advantage of the automatic data transfer for simple cases. In this chapter, we'll learn how to take advantage of more complex forms of automatic data transfer. Most of the increased complexity comes when transferring data onto more complex Java-side types, such as Maps and Lists. We haven't mentioned it much so far, but when the framework transfers data from string-based request parameters to strictly typed Java properties, it must also convert from string to Java type. The framework comes with a strong set of built-in type converters that support all common conversions, including complex types such as Maps and Lists. The central focus of this chapter will be explaining how to take advantage of the framework's ability to automatically transfer and convert all manner of data. At the end of the chapter, we'll also show you how to extend the type conversion mechanism by developing custom converters that can handle any types, including user-defined types.

This chapter also starts our two-part formal coverage of OGNL. OGNL is currently the default expression language used to reference data from the various regions of the framework in a consistent manner. We've already seen how to use OGNL expressions to point incoming form fields at the Java properties they should target when the framework transfers the request data. Accordingly, this chapter will cover OGNL from the point of view of incoming data transfer and type conversion. But OGNL is also going to be critical when we introduce the Struts 2 tag API in the next chapter. The tag is used to pull data out of the framework into the rendering response pages. We'll thus divide the coverage of OGNL between this chapter and the next. To be specific, this chapter will focus on how OGNL fits into the framework, and the role it plays in binding data throughout the various regions of the framework. The next chapter, which introduces tags, will cover the OGNL expression language from a more syntactic perspective, which you will need when using the tags.

Let's start by examining the data transfer and type conversion mechanisms at close range.

5.1   *Data transfer and type conversion: common tasks of the web application domain*

In chapter 1 of this book, we said that one of the common tasks of the web application domain was moving and converting data from string-based HTTP to the various data types of the Java language. If you've worked with web applications for many years, you'll be familiar with the tedious task of moving data from form beans to data beans. This boring task is complicated by the accompanying task of converting from strings to Java types. Parsing strings into doubles and floats, catching the exceptions that arise from bad data, and so on is no fun at all. Worse yet, these tasks amount to pure infrastructure. All you're doing is preparing for the real work.

Data transfer and type conversion actually happen on both ends of the request-processing cycle. We've already seen that the framework moves the data from the string-based HTTP requests to our JavaBeans properties, which are clearly Java types. Moreover, the same thing happens on the other end. When the result is rendered, we typically funnel some of the data from those JavaBeans properties back out into the resulting HTML page. Again, while we haven't given it much thought, this means that the data has been reconverted from the Java type back out to a string format.

This process occurs with nearly every request in a web application. It's an inherent part of the domain. No one will moan about handing this responsibility over to the framework. Nonetheless, there'll be times when you want to extend or configure this automated support. The Struts 2 type conversion mechanisms are powerful and quite easily extended. We think you'll be excited when you see the possibilities for writing your own custom converters. First, though, we need see who's responsible for all of this automated wizardry.

5.2 OGNL and Struts 2

We call it wizardry, but, as we all know, computers are rational machines. Perhaps unsolved mystery is a more accurate phrase. What exactly are these unsolved mysteries? To be specific, we haven't yet explained how all of that data makes it from the HTML request to the Java language and back out to HTML through the JSP tags. The next section will clarify this mysterious process.

5.2.1 What OGNL does

What OGNL does isn't mysterious at all. In fact, OGNL is quite ordinary. *OGNL* stands for the *Object-Graph Navigation Language*. Sounds perfectly harmless, right? No? Actually, I agree. It sounds horrifying, as if I should have studied harder in school. In an attempt to make it sound less academic, the makers of OGNL suggest pronouncing it like the last few syllables of "orthogonal."

OGNL is a powerful technology that's been integrated into the Struts 2 framework to help with data transfer and type conversion. OGNL is the glue between the framework's string-based HTTP input and output and the Java-based internal processing. It's quite powerful and, while it seems that you can use the framework without really knowing about OGNL, your development efforts will be made many times more efficient by spending a few moments with this oddly named power utility.

From the point of view of a developer building applications on the Struts 2 framework, OGNL consists of two things: an expression language and type converters.

EXPRESSION LANGUAGE

First, let's look at the expression language. We've been using OGNL's expression language in our form input field names and JSP tags. In both places, we've been using OGNL expressions to bind Java-side data properties to strings in the text-based view layers, commonly found in the name attributes of form input fields, or in various attributes of the Struts 2 tags. The simplicity of the expression language, in its common usage, makes for a ridiculously low learning curve. This has allowed us to get deep into Struts 2 without specifically covering it. Let's review what we've already been doing.

The following code snippet, from our Struts 2 Portfolio application's Registration-Success.jsp, shows a Struts 2 tag using the OGNL expression language:

```
<h5>Congratulations! You have created </h5>
<h3>The <s:property value="portfolioName" /> Portfolio</h3>
```

The OGNL expression language is the bit inside the double quotes of the value attribute. This Struts 2 property tag takes a value from a property on one of our Java objects and writes it into the HTML in place of the tag. This is the point of expression languages. They allow us to use a simplified syntax to reference objects that reside in the Java environment. The OGNL expression language can be much more complex than this single element expression; it even supports such advanced features as invoking method calls on the Java objects that it can access, but the whole idea of an expression language is to simplify access to data.

HEADS-UP   The integration of OGNL into the Struts 2 framework is tight. Pains have been taken to make the simplest use cases just that: simple. With this in mind, many instances of OGNL expressions require no special escaping. While there's an OGNL escape sequence, `%{expression}`, that signals to the framework when to process the expression as an expression rather than interpreting it as a string literal, this isn't often used. Using intelligent defaults, Struts 2 will automatically evaluate the string as an OGNL expression in all contexts that warrant such a default behavior. In contexts where strings are most likely going to be strings, the framework will require the OGNL escape sequence. As we move along, we'll specifically indicate which context is which.

Here's the other side of the coin. While the `property` tag, which resides in a result page, reaches back into the Java environment to pull a value from the `portfolioName` property, we've also seen that OGNL expressions are used in HTML forms to target properties in the Java environment as destinations for the data transfer. In both cases, the role of the OGNL expression is to provide a simple syntax for binding things like Struts 2 tags to specific Java-side properties, for moving data both into and out of the framework. OGNL creates the pathways for data to flow through the framework. It helps move data from the request parameters onto our action's JavaBeans properties, and it helps move data from those properties out into rendering HTML pages.

But we must investigate how the type conversion occurs when moving data between the string-based worlds of HTML and the native Java types of the framework.

TYPE CONVERTERS

In addition to the expression language, we've also been using OGNL type converters. Even in this simple case of the Struts 2 `property` tag, a conversion must be made from the Java type of the property referenced by the OGNL expression language to the string format of the HTML output. Of course, in the case of the `portfolioName`, the Java type is also a string. But this just means that the conversion is easy. Every time data moves to or from the Java environment, a translation must occur between the string version of that data that resides in the HTML and the appropriate Java data type. Thus far, we've been using simple data types for which the Struts 2 framework provides adequate built-in OGNL type converters. In fact, the framework provides built-in converters to handle much more than we've been asking of it. Shortly, we'll cover the built-in type converters and show you how to map your incoming form fields to a wide variety of Java data types, including all the primitives as well as a variety of collections. But, first, let's look at where OGNL fits into the framework, just to be clear about things.

5.2.2 *How OGNL fits into the framework*

Understanding OGNL's role in the framework, from an architectural perspective, will make working with it much easier. Figure 5.1 shows how OGNL has been incorporated into the Struts 2 framework.

Figure 5.1 shows the path of data into and out of the framework. Everything starts with the HTML form in the InputForm.html page, from which the user will submit a request. Everything ends with the response that comes back to the user, represented in figure 5.1 as ResultPage.html. Now, let's follow the data into and out of the framework and see how OGNL helps bind and convert the data as it moves from region to region.

DATA IN

Our data's journey starts at the InputForm.html page shown in figure 5.1. In this case, the form contains two text input fields. Note that, in the interest of space, we've created pseudo-HTML markup for these fields; this won't validate. The strings in the pseudo-text input tags are the name attributes of the fields. Again, it's important to realize that these names are valid OGNL expressions. All that we need now is a user to enter two values for the fields and submit the form to the framework.

When the request enters the framework, as we can see in figure 5.1, it's exposed to the Java language as an HttpServletRequest object. As we learned earlier, Struts 2 is built on the Servlet API. The request parameters are stored as name/value pairs, and

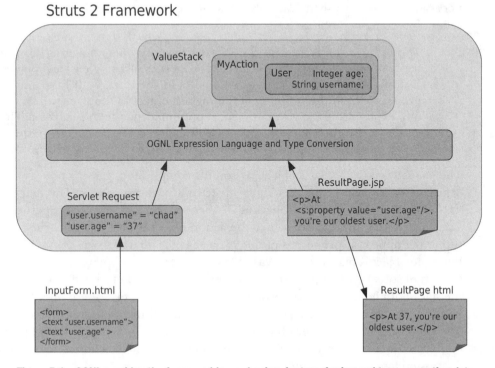

Figure 5.1 OGNL provides the framework's mechanism for transferring and type-converting data.

both name and value are Strings. As you can see in figure 5.1, the request object just has a couple of name/value pairs, where the names are the names of our form's text fields and the values are the values entered by the user when the form was submitted. Everything is still a string. This is where the framework and OGNL pick up the ball.

We know the framework is going to handle the transfer and type conversion of the data from these request parameters. The first question is where should the data go? OGNL will point the way. But, first, OGNL needs a context in which to search for its targets. In chapter 3, we saw that, when the framework automatically transfers parameters to our action object, the action is sitting on something called the ValueStack. In figure 5.1, we can see that our action object has been placed on the ValueStack. In the case represented by this figure, we're exposing our User object as a JavaBeans property on our action object. With our action object on the ValueStack, we're ready for OGNL to do its navigational work.

From our study of interceptors, we know that the params interceptor will move the data from the request object to the ValueStack. The tricky part of the job is mapping the name of the parameter to an actual property on the ValueStack. This is where OGNL comes in. The params interceptor interprets the request parameter name as an OGNL expression to locate the correct destination property on the ValueStack. If you look at this in figure 5.1, you might expect that the expression would need to be something more like myAction.user.username. To the contrary, only the user.username is necessary. This is because the ValueStack is a sort of virtual object that exposes the properties of its contained objects as its own.

DEFINITION   The ValueStack is a Struts 2 construct that presents an aggregation of the properties of a stack of objects as properties of a single virtual object. If duplicate properties exist—two objects in the stack both have a name property—then the property of the highest object in the stack will be the one exposed on the virtual object represented by the ValueStack. The ValueStack represents the data model exposed to the current request and is the default object against which all OGNL expressions are resolved.

The ValueStack is a virtual object? It sounds complicated, but it's not. The ValueStack holds a stack of objects. These objects all have properties. The magic of the ValueStack is that all the properties of these objects appear as properties of the ValueStack itself. In our case, since the action object is on the ValueStack, all of its properties appear as properties of the ValueStack. The tricky part comes when more than one object is placed on the ValueStack. When this happens, we can have a contention of sorts between properties of those two objects. Let's say that two objects on the stack both have a username property. How does this get resolved? Simply: the username exposed by the ValueStack will always be that of the highest object in the stack. The properties of the higher objects in the stack cover up similarly named properties of objects lower in the stack. We'll cover this in more detail when we discuss the OGNL expression language in chapter 6.

For now, this should be enough to see how the request parameters find the way to their correct homes. In figure 5.1, one of the request parameters is named user.age.

If we resolve this as an OGNL expression against the ValueStack, we first ask, "Does the ValueStack have a user property?" As we've just learned, the ValueStack exposes the properties of the objects it contains, so we know that the ValueStack does have a user property. Next, does this user property have an age property? Of course it does. Obviously, we've found the right property. Now what?

Once the OGNL expression has been used to locate the destination property, the data can be moved onto that property by calling the property's setter with the correct value. But, at this point, the original value is still the string "37". Here's where the type converters come into play. We need to convert the string to the Java type of the age property targeted by the OGNL expression, which is an int. OGNL will consult its set of available type converters to see if any of them can handle this particular conversion. Luckily, the Struts 2 framework provides a set of type converters to handle all the normal conversions of the web application domain. Conversion between strings and integers is provided for by the built-in type converters. The value is converted and set on the user object, just where we'll find it when we start our action logic after the rest of the interceptors have fired.

Now that we've seen how data makes it into the framework, let's work our way through the other half of figure 5.1 to see how it makes it back out.

DATA OUT

Now for the other half of the story. Actually, it's the same story, but in reverse. After the action has done its business, calling business logic, doing data operations, and so forth, we know that eventually a result will fire that'll render a new view of the application to the user. Importantly, during the processing of the request, our data objects will remain on the ValueStack. The ValueStack acts as a kind of place holder for viewing the data model throughout the various regions of the framework.

When the result starts its rendering process, it'll also have access to the Value-Stack, via the OGNL expression language in its tags. These tags will retrieve data from the ValueStack by referencing specific values with OGNL expressions. In figure 5.1, the result is rendered by ResultPage.jsp. In this page, the age of the user is retrieved with the Struts 2 property tag, a tag that takes an OGNL expression to guide it to the value it should render. But, once again, we must convert the value; this time we convert from the Java type of the property on the ValueStack to a string that can be written into the HTML page. In this case, the Integer object is converted back into a string for the depressing message that "At 37, you're our oldest user." Must be a social networking site.

Now you know what OGNL does. This chapter is going to focus on the framework's data transfer and type conversion. We won't say much more on the details of OGNL, such as its expression language syntax. We'll save that for the next chapter, which covers the Struts 2 tags. For now, you just need to understand the big picture of what OGNL does for the framework.

If you need a break before we go on to cover the built-in type converters, you could practice saying "OGNL."

5.3   *Built-in type converters*

Now that we've seen how OGNL has been integrated into the framework to provide automatic data transfer and type conversion, it's time to see the nuts and bolts of working with the built-in type converters. Here's where we'll learn how to safely guide a variety of data types into and out of the framework. As we saw in the previous section, type conversion plays an important role in that process. Out of the box, the Struts 2 framework can handle almost any type conversions that you might require. These conversions are done by the built-in type converters that come with the framework.

In this section, we'll show you what the framework will handle, give you plenty of examples, and show you how to write OGNL expressions for form field names that need to locate more complexly typed properties such as arrays, Maps, and Lists. In the coming pages, we'll provide a clear-cut how-to and reference for using OGNL to map incoming form fields to Java properties of all the types supported by the framework's built-in type converters. When you start developing the forms that'll submit data to your actions, this section will be a great reference.

5.3.1   *Out-of-the-box conversions*

The Struts 2 framework comes with built-in support for converting between the HTTP native strings and the following list of Java types:

- String—Sometimes a string is just a string.
- boolean/Boolean—true and false strings can be converted to both primitive and object versions of Boolean.
- char/Character—Primitive or object.
- int/Integer, float/Float, long/Long, double/Double—Primitives or objects.
- Date—String version will be in SHORT format of current Locale (for example, 12/10/97).
- array—Each string element must be convertible to the array's type.
- List—Populated with Strings by default.
- Map—Populated with Strings by default.

When the framework locates the Java property targeted by a given OGNL expression, it'll look for a converter for that type. If that type is in the preceding list, you don't need to do anything but sit back and receive the data.

In order to utilize the built-in type conversion, you just need to build an OGNL expression that targets a property on the ValueStack. The OGNL expression will either be the name of your form field, under which the parameter will be submitted in the HTTP request, or it'll be somewhere in your view-layer tags, such as one of the Struts 2 JSP tags. Again, our current discussion will focus on the data's entry into the framework as request parameters. Chapter 6 will focus on the tag point of view. However, this is mostly a matter of convenience; OGNL serves the same functional roles at both ends of the request processing—its expression language navigates our object graph to locate the specified property, and the type converters manage the data type translations between the string-based HTTP world and the strictly typed Java world. Data in, data out? It doesn't matter. The type conversion and OGNL will be the same.

5.3.2 *Mapping form field names to properties with OGNL expressions*

Hooking up your Java properties to your form field names to facilitate the automatic transfer and conversion of request parameters is a two-step process. First, you need to write the OGNL expressions for the name attributes of your form fields. Second, you need to create the properties that'll receive the data on the Java side. You could do these in reverse order; it doesn't matter. We'll go through each of the built-in conversions in the order from the preceding bulleted list, showing how to set up both sides of the equation.

PRIMITIVES AND WRAPPER CLASSES

Because the built-in conversions to Java primitives and wrapper classes, such as `Boolean` and `Double`, are simple, we provide a single example to demonstrate them. We won't show every primitive or wrapper type; they all work the same way. Let's start by examining the JSP-side OGNL. Listing 5.1 shows the chapter 5 version of our Struts 2 Portfolio's registration form, from Registration.jsp.

> **Listing 5.1 OGNL expressions that target specific properties on the `ValueStack`**

```
<h4>Complete and submit the form to create your own portfolio.</h4>
<s:form action="Register">
  <s:textfield name="user.username" label="Username"/>
  <s:password name="user.password" label="Password"/>
  <s:textfield name="user.portfolioName" label="Enter a name "/>
  <s:textfield name="user.age" label="Enter your age as a double "/>
  <s:textfield name="user.birthday" label="Enter birthday. (mm/dd/yy)"/>
  <s:submit/>
</s:form>]
```

This is nothing new. But now that you know that each input field name is actually an OGNL expression, you'll see a lot deeper into this seemingly simple form markup. Recall that our OGNL expressions resolve against the `ValueStack`, and that our action object will be automatically placed there when request processing starts. In this case, our `Register` action uses a JavaBeans property, `user`, backed directly with our `User` domain object. The following snippet, from our chapter 5 version of Register.java, shows the JavaBeans property that exposes our `User` object:

```
private User user;

public User getUser() {
  return user;
}
public void setUser(User user) {
  this.user = user;
}
```

If you want, you can see the full source for Register.java by looking at the sample application, but it's nothing new. The only thing important to our current discussion is the exposure of the user object as a JavaBeans property. Since the type of this property is our User class, let's look at that class to see what properties it exposes. Listing 5.2 shows the full listing of the User bean.

Listing 5.2   The JavaBeans properties targeted by the OGNL expressions in Listing 5.1

```
public class User {

  private String username;
  private String password;
  private String portfolioName;
  private Double age;
  private Date birthday;

  public String getPassword() {
    return password;
  }
  public void setPassword(String password) {
    this.password = password;
  }
  public String getPortfolioName() {
    return portfolioName;
  }
  public void setPortfolioName(String portfolioName) {
    this.portfolioName = portfolioName;
  }
  public String getUsername() {
    return username;
  }
  public void setUsername(String username) {
    this.username = username;
  }
  public Double getAge() {
    return age;
  }
  public void setAge(Double age) {
    this.age = age;
  }
  public Date getBirthday() {
    return birthday;
  }
  public void setBirthday(Date birthday) {
    this.birthday = birthday;
  }
}
```

As you can see, the action just exposes a bunch of JavaBeans properties to carry data. Let's put them to use. Go ahead and test the registration out. Click the Create an Account link from the chapter 5 version of the Struts 2 Portfolio application. The request comes into the framework with a map of name/value pairs that associate the name from the form input field with the string value entered. The name is an OGNL expression. This expression is used to locate the target property on the ValueStack. In the case of the Register action, the action itself is on top of the stack and an OGNL expression such as `user.birthday` finds the `user` property on the action, then finds the `birthday` property on that user object. In Java, this becomes the following snippet:

```
getUser().getBirthday();
```

OGNL sees that the birthday property is of Java type `Date`. It then locates the string-to-`Date` converter, converts the value, and sets it on the property. All of the simple object types and primitives are just this easy. If the incoming string value doesn't represent a valid instance of the primitive or type, then a conversion exception is thrown. Note the difference between type conversion and validation, and thus the difference between a type conversion error and a validation error. Validation code is about validating the data as valid instances of the data types from the perspective of the business logic of the action; this occurs via the `validation` interceptor or the `workflow` interceptor's invocation of the `validate()` method. Conversion problems occur when trying to bind the HTTP string values to their Java types; this occurs, for instance, when the `params` interceptor transfers the request data.

Conversion errors result in the user being returned to the input page, similar to validation errors. Normally, a default error message will inform the user that the string value he submitted cannot be converted to the Java type targeted by the OGNL. You can customize the error reporting done in the face of type conversion problems, but we'll save that for later in the book. In chapter 11, we'll learn how to customize the conversion exception handling and the error messages shown to the user when such conversion errors arise.

Now that we've seen how to map your incoming data to Java primitives and their wrapper classes, let's see what Struts 2 can do to automatically handle various multivalued request parameters.

HANDLING MULTIVALUED REQUEST PARAMETERS

As you probably know, multiple parameter values can be mapped to a single parameter name in the incoming request. There are a variety of ways for a form to submit multiple values under a single parameter name. There are also many ways to map these to Java-side types, implying a variety of ways to wield our OGNL. In the coming sections, we'll cover the ways you can handle this.

Struts 2 provides rich support for transferring multivalued request parameters to a variety of collection-oriented data types on the Java side, ranging from arrays to actual `Collections`. In the interest of being semi-exhaustive, we won't attempt to integrate the following examples into the functional soul of the Struts 2 Portfolio. Rather, you'll find that a portion of the chapter 5 version of the sample application has been specifically dedicated to demonstrating the various techniques shown in the coming pages.

For each of these examples, we'll reuse a single action object, the `DataTransferTest`. From the perspective of data transfer and type conversion, action objects need only expose the properties that'll receive the data. The `DataTransferTest` exposes all of the properties for the examples in this chapter. We did this to consolidate the various permutations of data transfer into a convenient point of reference. But each example is mapped in the chapterFive.xml file as a distinct Struts 2 action component, which is perfectly valid. Note the semantic difference between a Struts 2 action component and a Java class that provides an action implementation. We can, and do, reuse a single class for multiple actions.

These examples demonstrate how to set up the data transfer and type conversion. Our action will do little more than serve as a data holder for these examples. Forms will submit request data, the framework will transfer that data to the properties exposed on the action, the action will do nothing but forward to the success result, and that result will display the data by pulling it off of the action with Struts 2 tags. This should serve as a clean reference that'll make all the variations on data transfer and type conversion crystal clear. We encourage you to use this portion of the sample application as a reference for proper OGNL-to-Java property mapping.

Now, let's see how to have Struts 2 automatically transfer multiple values to array-backed properties.

ARRAYS

Struts 2 provides support for converting data to Java arrays. If you've worked with array-backed properties, also known as *indexed JavaBeans properties*, you'll appreciate the ease with which Struts 2 handles these properties. Most of these improvements come from the OGNL expression language's support for navigating to such properties. You can see the array data transfer in action by clicking the array data transfer link on the chapter 5 home page. Listing 5.3 shows the form from ArraysDataTransferTest.jsp that submits data targeted at array properties.

Listing 5.3 Targeting array properties for data transfer

```
<s:form action="ArraysDataTransferTest">
  <s:textfield name="ages" label="Ages"/>          ❶ These target
  <s:textfield name="ages" label="Ages"/>             the ages
  <s:textfield name="ages" label="Ages"/>             property

  <s:textfield name="names[0]" label="names"/>     ❷ These target
  <s:textfield name="names[1]" label="names"/>        the names
  <s:textfield name="names[2]" label="names"/>        property

  <s:submit/>
</s:form>
```

On the OGNL expression side, you just have to know how to write an expression that can navigate to an array property on a Java object. The form shown in listing 5.3 submits data to two different array properties. The first array property, named `ages`, will receive the data from the first three fields ❶. The second array property, `names`, will receive the data from the second three fields ❷. These properties, if the transfer is to work, must exist on the `ValueStack`. For this example, we'll expose the array properties on our action object, which we'll see momentarily.

This form demonstrates two syntaxes for targeting arrays with OGNL expressions. To understand what'll happen, we need to refresh our memories of the HTTP and Servlet API details that will occur as a result of this form being submitted. The first thing to remember is that the name of each input field, as far as HTTP and the Servlet

API are concerned, is just a string name. These layers know nothing about OGNL. With that in mind, it's time for a pop quiz. How many request parameters will be submitted by this form? The correct answer is four. The first three fields all have the same name; this'll result in a single request parameter with three values, perfectly valid in HTTP. On the other hand, the second set of fields will each come in as a distinct parameter with a single value mapped to it. When this request hits the framework, four request parameters will exist, as follows:

Parameter name	Parameter value(s)
ages	12, 33, 102
names[0]	Chad
names[1]	Don
names[2]	Beth

Now let's look at the implementation of the properties that'll receive this data. These properties will be exposed on our action object. Listing 5.4 shows the target properties, each of type Array, from DataTransferTest.java.

Listing 5.4 Array properties targeted by OGNL input field names

```
private Double[] ages ;
public Double[] getAges() {
   return ages;
}
public void setAges(Double[] ages) {
   this.ages = ages;
}
private String[] names = new String[10];
public String[] getNames() {
   return names;
}
public void setNames(String[] names) {
   this.names = names;
}
```

First, note that we don't need indexed getters and setters for these properties. OGNL handles all the indexing details. We just need to expose the array itself via a getter and setter pair. Now, consider what happens when the framework transfers the ages parameter. First, it resolves the property and finds the ages property on the action, as seen in listing 5.4. The value of the ages parameter in the request is an array of three strings. Since the ages property on the action is also an array, this makes the data transfer simple. OGNL creates a new array and sets it on the property. But OGNL does even more for us. In this case, the ages property is an array of element type Double. OGNL sees this and automatically runs its type conversion for each element of the array. Very nice! Also note that, since the framework is creating the array for us in these cases, we don't need to initialize the array ourselves. For this example, we used multiple text input fields with the same name to submit multiple values under the ages parameter. In real applications, parameters with multiple values mapped to them are frequently the result of input fields that allow selection of multiple values, such as a select box.

Now let's look at how the framework handles the three individual parameters with names that look like array indexing. As far as the Servlet API is concerned, these are just three unique names. We can see that they seem to refer to a single array, and provide indexing into that single array, but the Servlet API sees only unique strings. However, when the framework hands these names to OGNL, they're accurately interpreted as references to specific elements in a specific array. These parameters are set, one at a time, into the elements of the names array. We should make a couple of comments before moving on. First, using this method requires initializing the array. This is necessary because the OGNL expressions are targeting individual elements of an existing array; the previous method was setting the entire array, so it didn't require an existing array. Second, we still don't need indexed getters and setters!

With all of this in place, the framework will automatically transfer and convert the request parameters onto our action's properties. The action, in these examples, does nothing but forward to the result page, ArraysDataTransferSuccess.jsp. The following snippet shows the code from this page:

```
<h5>Congratulations! You have transferred and converted data to and from
    Arrays.</h5>
<h3>Age number 3 = <s:property value="ages[2]" /> </h3>
<h3>Name number 3 = <s:property value="names[2]" /> </h3>
```

We don't want to say too much about the Struts 2 tags now; that's the topic of the next chapter. But it should be easy enough to understand that this result page pulls some data off the action's array properties just to prove that everything's working. The rest of the examples in this chapter will follow a similar pattern of using a result page to pull the data off the action just to verify that the transfer and conversion is working. We may not show this code from the result pages every time though.

Many developers prefer to work with some of the more feature-rich classes from the Java Collections API. Next, we'll look at working with Lists.

LISTS

In a fashion similar to array properties, Struts 2 supports automatically converting sets of request parameters into properties of various Collection types, such as Lists. Using Lists is almost like using arrays. The only difference is that Lists, prior to Java 5, don't support type specification. This typeless nature of Lists has an important consequence for the type conversion mechanisms of Struts 2. When the framework works with arrays, the type conversion can easily find the element type by inspecting the property itself, as arrays are always typed in Java. With Lists, there's no way to automatically discover this.

We have two choices when working with `Lists`: either specify the type for our elements or accept the default type. By default, the framework will convert request parameters into `Strings` and populate the `List` property with those `Strings`. Our first example will accept this default behavior. The mechanics of using `Lists` are almost identical to using arrays. The following snippet shows the form field markup from ListsDataTransferTest.jsp that'll target some `List` properties.

```
<s:textfield name="middleNames[0]" label="middleNames"/>    These target the
<s:textfield name="middleNames[1]" label="middleNames"/>    middleNames
<s:textfield name="middleNames[2]" label="middleNames"/>    property

<s:textfield name="lastNames" label="lastNames"/>    These target
<s:textfield name="lastNames" label="lastNames"/>    the lastNames
<s:textfield name="lastNames" label="lastNames"/>    property
```

As you can see, we again show two different notations for referencing target properties with OGNL expressions. These are the same notations as used with arrays. The only difference is in the Java side. In Java, the `List` properties are much like the array properties except the type is different. Listing 5.5 shows the target `List` properties from DataTransferTest.java.

Listing 5.5   Using `List` properties to receive the data

```
private List lastNames ;

public List getLastNames()

{
   return lastNames;
}
public void setLastNames ( List lastNames ) {
   this.lastNames=lastNames;
}

private List middleNames ;

public List getMiddleNames()
{
   return middleNames;
}
public void setMiddleNames ( List middleNames ) {
   this.middleNames=middleNames;
}
```

These look much like the array properties, except the type is `List`. There are a couple of things to note. First, you don't have to preinitialize any of the `Lists`, even the ones that'll receive data from the indexed OGNL notation. Second, without type specification, the elements of these `Lists` will all be `String` objects. If that works for your requirements, great. In our case, our data is first and last names, so this is fine. But if you name your field `birthdays`, don't expect the framework to convert to `Dates`. It'll just make a `List` of `Strings` out of your incoming `birthday` strings. If you want to see this example in action, check out the List Data Transfer Test link on the chapter 5 home page. Again, the result page will pull some values out of the `List` properties on the action just to prove everything is working as advertised. If you want to look at the JSP to see the tags, check out ListsDataTransferSuccess.jsp.

Sometimes, you'll want to specify a type for your List elements rather than just working with Strings. No problem. We just need to inform OGNL of the element type we want for a given property. This is done with a simple properties file. The OGNL type conversion uses properties files for several things. Later in the chapter, when we write our own type converters, we'll see another use for these files. For now, we're just going to make a properties file that tells OGNL what type of element we want in our List property. In order to specify element types for properties on our action object, we create a file according to the naming convention shown in figure 5.2.

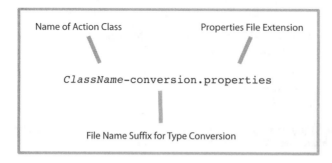

Figure 5.2   **Naming convention for type conversion properties files**

We then place this file next to the class in your Java package. We're going to create a file called DataTransferTest-conversion.properties and place it next to our DataTransferTest.java class in the manning.chapterFive package. If you check out the sample application, you'll see that this is the case. Figure 5.3 provides an anatomical dissection of the single property from that file.

This brief line, Element-weights=java.lang.Double, is all the type conversion process needs to add typed elements to our List. Now, our List property will work just like the array property; each individual element will be converted to a Double. Here's the markup from ListsDataTransferTest.jsp for our new weights property:

```
<s:textfield name="weights[0]" label="weights"/>
<s:textfield name="weights[1]" label="weights"/>
<s:textfield name="weights[2]" label="weights"/>
```

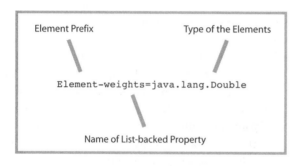

Figure 5.3   **Specifying the type for a List-backed property**

Note that we could've used the nonindexed OGNL notation. You may have a preference, but it doesn't matter to the framework. On the Java side, the property on the action object doesn't change. Here's the implementation of the List property from DataTransferTest.java.

```
private List weights;

public List getWeights() {
  return weights;
}

public void setWeights(List weight) {
  this.weights = weight;
}
```

You might've noticed that it's no different from the previous untyped version. This shouldn't be too surprising. Since the List is typeless from a Java point of view, we can't see that the elements are Doubles unless we try to cast them at runtime. Unless you want to modify the source code and test that the elements are actually Doubles, you'll have to take our word for it. Of course, when you use this technique in a real application, whose business logic will depend on those elements being Doubles, you'll know soon enough that they are, in fact, Doubles. Note that, if you want to see this in action, it's right there on the same page as the previous example.

NOTE *Java 5 generics and Type conversion*—If you have the pleasure of using Java 5 or higher, we highly recommend using generics to type your collections and maps. Besides being a recommended best practice, the Struts 2 type conversion mechanism can use generics-based typing to learn the correct target type for the conversions. If you do this, you don't have to use the properties file configuration. This is a big bonus for Java 5 users. Go Tiger!

Before moving on, we need to make one warning regarding this type specification process. When specifying the type for Lists and other Collections, take care not to preinitialize your List. If you do, you'll get an error. While untyped Lists will work whether you initialize your List or not, with type-specific List conversion, you can't preinitialize your List.

WARNING Don't preinitialize your List when using the typed element conversion mechanism supported by the ClassName-conversion.properties file.

Now we want to show a full-powered example. This example will use a List property that specifies the Struts 2 Portfolio's User class as its element type. This allows us to take advantage of the convenience of using Lists with the convenience of using our domain objects at the same time. Also, we want to prove to you that the type specification is actually working. Here's the markup, again from ListsDataTransferTest.jsp, that accesses our List of Users:

```
<s:textfield name="users[0].username" label="Usernames"/>
<s:textfield name="users[1].username" label="Usernames"/>
<s:textfield name="users[2].username" label="Usernames"/>
```

As you can see, these field names reference the username property on a User element in the users list, which is a property on our action. As before, from the property itself, which comes from DataTransferTest.java, we can discern nothing about the type of the elements it'll contain. Here's the property from our DataTransferTest action class:

```
private List users ;

public List getUsers()
{
   return users;
}
public void setUsers ( List users ) {
   this.users=users;
}
```

In order to make the framework populate our List with actual User objects, we once again employ the aid of the conversion properties file. The following line in DataTransferTest-conversion.properties specifies that our list-backed property will contain objects of type User.

```
Element_users=manning.utils.User
```

This is cool stuff. In case you want to verify the type-specific conversion, just check the tags in the ListsDataTransferSuccess.jsp page. They're reaching back into the List to retrieve usernames that simply wouldn't exist if the elements weren't of type User. If you've done much work with moving data around in older frameworks, we know you'll be able to appreciate the amount of work that something like this will save you.

Next, we'll point out a use case that you might not immediately infer from the previous examples. Let's assume that you have a List for which you specify a User element type. Now let's say that you expect an unpredictable amount of element data from the request. This could be due to something like a multiple select box. In this case, you simply combine the indexless naming convention with the deeper property reference. Note the following set of imaginary (they're not in the sample code) text fields:

```
<s:textfield name="users.username" label="Usernames"/>
<s:textfield name="users.username" label="Usernames"/>
<s:textfield name="users.username" label="Usernames"/>
```

This will submit a set of three username strings under the single parameter name of users.username. When OGNL resolves this expression, it'll first locate the users property. Let's assume this is the same users property as in the previous example. This means that users is a List for which the element type has been specified as User. This information allows OGNL to use this single parameter name, with its multiple values, to create a List and create User elements for it, setting the username property on each of those User objects.

That should be enough to keep you working with Lists for some time to come. Now we'll look at Maps, in case you need to use something other than a numeric index to reference your data.

MAPS

The last out-of-the-box conversion we'll cover is conversion to Maps. Similar to its support for Lists, Struts 2 also supports automatic conversion of a set of values from the HTTP request into a Map property. Maps associate their values with keys rather than indexes. This keyed nature has a couple of implications for the Struts 2 type conversion process. First, the OGNL expression syntax for referencing them is different than for Lists because it has to provide a key rather than a numeric index. The second implication involves specifying types for the Map properties. We've already seen that we can specify a type for our List elements. You can do this with Maps also. With Maps, however, you can also specify a type for the key object. As you might expect, both the Map element and key will default to a String if you don't specify a type. We'll explore all of this in the examples of this section. Again, the examples can be seen in action on the chapter 5 home page.

We'll start with a simple version of using a Map property to receive your data from the request. Here's the form markup from MapsDataTransferTest.jsp:

```
<s:textfield name="maidenNames.mary" label="Maiden Name"/>
<s:textfield name="maidenNames.jane" label="Maiden Name"/>
<s:textfield name="maidenNames.hellen" label="Maiden Name"/>

<s:textfield name="maidenNames['beth']" label="Maiden Name"/>
<s:textfield name="maidenNames['sharon']" label="Maiden Name"/>
<s:textfield name="maidenNames['martha']" label="Maiden Name"/>
```

These target the maiden-Names property

Again, the main difference between this and the List property version is that we now need to specify a key value, a string in this case. We're using first names as keys to the incoming maiden names. As you can see, OGNL provides a couple of syntax options for specifying the key. First, you can use a simple, if somewhat misleading, property notation. Second, you can use a bracketed syntax that makes the fact that the property is a Map more evident. It doesn't matter which you use, though you'll probably find one or the other more flexible in certain situations. Just to prove that the syntax doesn't matter, all of our fields in this example will submit to the same property, a Map going by the name of maidenNames. Since we haven't specified a type for this Map with a type conversion properties file, all of the values will be converted into elements of type String. Similarly, our keys will also be treated as Strings.

With the OGNL expressions in place in the form elements, we just need a property on the Java side to receive the data. In this case, we have a Map-backed property implemented on the DataTransferTest.java action. Here's the property that receives the data from the form:

```
private Map maidenNames ;

public Map getMaidenNames()
{
   return maidenNames;
}
```

```
public void setMaidenNames ( Map maidenNames ) {
   this.maidenNames=maidenNames;
}
```

Nothing special. If you want to see it in action, click Maps Data Transfer Test on the chapter 5 home page. You'll see that the MapsDataTransferTest.jsp page is successfully pulling some data out of the `maidenNames` property.

Now let's see an example where we specify the type for our `Map` elements. First, we just need to add a line to our DataTransferTest-conversion.properties file. Here's the line:

```
Element_myUsers=manning.utils.User
```

Again, this property simply specifies that the `myUsers` property, found on the `DataTransferTest` action, should be populated with elements of type `User`. How easy is that? Next, we need some form markup to submit our data to the `myUsers` property:

```
<s:textfield name="myUsers['chad'].username" label="Usernames"/>
<s:textfield name="myUsers['jimmy'].username" label="Usernames"/>
<s:textfield name="myUsers['elephant'].username" label="Usernames"/>

<s:textfield name="myUsers.chad.birthday" label="birthday"/>
<s:textfield name="myUsers.jimmy.birthday" label="birthday"/>
<s:textfield name="myUsers.elephant.birthday" label="birthday"/>
```

This form submits the data to a `Map` property named `myUsers`. Since we've specified a `User` element type for that map, we can use OGNL syntax to navigate down to properties, such as `birthday`, that we know will be present on the `Map` elements. Moreover, the conversion of our birthday string to a Java `Date` type will occur automatically even at this depth.

Just to make sure, we'll check the `myUsers` property on DataTransferTest.java to make sure it's still simple:

```
private Map myUsers ;

public Map getMyUsers()
{
   return myUsers;
}
public void setMyUsers ( Map myUsers ) {
   this.myUsers=myUsers;
}
```

That's pretty simple. Again, the Java code is still type unaware. You'll still have to cast those elements to `Users` if you access them in your action logic, but, as far as the OGNL references are concerned, both from the input-side form fields and from the result-side tags, you can take their type for granted. We should point out another cool feature while we're here. We've already noted that you don't have to initialize your `Maps` and `Lists`. The framework will create them for you. You might have also noticed, in this example, that the framework is creating the `User` objects for you as well. Basically, the framework will create all objects it needs as it tunnels down to the level of the birthday property on the `User`.

TIP The framework will automatically instantiate any intermediate properties in deep OGNL expressions if it finds them to be null when attempting to navigate to the target property. This ability to resolve null property access depends on the existence of a no-argument constructor for each property. So make sure that your classes have no-argument constructors.

In addition to specifying a type for the elements, you can specify a type for the key objects when using Map properties. Java Maps support all objects as keys. Just as with your values, OGNL will treat the name of your parameter as a string that it should attempt to convert to the type you specify. Let's say we want to use Integers as the keys for the entries in our Map property, perhaps so we can order the values. Let's make a version of myUsers that'll use Integers as keys. We'll call it myOrderedUsers. First, we add the following two lines to our DataTransferTest-conversion.properties file:

```
Key_myOrderedUsers=java.lang.Integer
Element_myOrderedUsers=manning.utils.User
```

These lines specify the key and element types for our myOrderedUsers Map property. As they say, we've been through most of this before, so we'll go fast. Here's the form markup that submits the data:

```
<s:textfield name="myOrderedUsers['1'].birthday" label="birthday"/>
<s:textfield name="myOrderedUsers['2'].birthday" label="birthday"/>
<s:textfield name="myOrderedUsers['3'].birthday" label="birthday"/>
```

Here we use a key value that is a valid Integer. If we didn't, we'd get a conversion error on the key when the framework tries to turn the string into the Integer type. This is no different from the myUsers example, except the keys are now Integer objects rather than Strings. Now let's look at the property that receives this data.

```
private Map myOrderedUsers ;

public Map getMyOrderedUsers()
{
   return myOrderedUsers;
}
public void setMyOrderedUsers ( Map myOrderedUsers ) {
   this.myOrderedUsers=myOrderedUsers;
}
```

As you can see, the Java property looks no different. It's still just a Map. The only important thing is that the name matches the name used in the OGNL expression. As we noted in the section on lists, if you're using Java 5 or higher, you can use generics to type your collections and maps, and Struts 2 will pick up on this during type conversion, making the properties file configuration unnecessary.

That does it for the built-in type conversions. We've seen a lot of ways to automatically transfer and convert your data. These methods provide a lot of flexibility. The variety of options can seem overwhelming at first. In the end, it's a simple process. You make a property to receive the data, then you write OGNL expressions that point to that property. Remember, you can consult the sample code for this chapter as a reference of the various OGNL-to-Java type mapping techniques.

The next section takes on an advanced topic. In case you want the framework to convert to some type that it doesn't support out of the box, you can write your own custom converters. It's a simple process, as you'll see.

5.4   *Customizing type conversion*

While the built-in type conversions are powerful and full featured, sometimes you might want to write your own type converter. You can, if you desire, specify a conversion logic for translating any string to any Java type. The only thing you need to do is create the string syntax and the Java class, then link them together with a converter. The possibilities are limitless. This is an advanced topic, but the implementation is simple and will provide insight that might help debugging even if you never need to write your own type converter.

In this section, we'll implement a trivial type converter that converts between strings and a simple `Circle` class. This means that we'll be able to specify a string syntax that represents a `Circle` object. The string syntax will represent the circle objects in the text-based HTTP world, and the `Circle` class will represent the same objects in the Java world.

Our converter will automatically convert between the two just as the built-in converters handle changing the string `"123.4"` into a Java `Double`. The syntax you choose for your strings is entirely arbitrary. For our demonstration we'll specify a string syntax as shown on the right.

Syntax	Example
`C:rinteger`	`C:r10`

If a request parameter comes in with this syntax, the framework will automatically convert it to a `Circle` object. In this section, we'll see how to implement the converter code and how to tell the framework to use our converter.

5.4.1   *Implementing a type converter*

As we've explained, type conversion is a part of OGNL. Due to this, all type converters must implement the `ognl.TypeConverter` interface. Generally, OGNL type converters can convert between any two data types. In the web application domain, we have a narrower set of requirements. All conversions are made between Java types and HTTP strings. For instance, we convert from `Strings` to `Doubles`, and from `Doubles` to `Strings`. Or, in our custom case, we'll convert from `Strings` to `Circles`, and from `Circles` to `Strings`.

Taking advantage of this narrowing of the conversion use case, Struts 2 provides a convenience base class for developers to use when writing their own type converters. The `org.apache.struts2.util.StrutsTypeConverter` class is provided by the framework as a convenient extension point for custom type conversion. The following snippet lists the abstract methods of this class that you must implement:

```
public abstract Object convertFromString(Map context, String[] values,
    Class toClass);

public abstract String convertToString(Map context, Object o);
```

When you write a custom converter, as we'll do shortly, you merely extend this base class and fill in these two methods with your own logic. This is a straightforward process, as we've noted. The only thing that might not be intuitive in the preceding signatures is the fact that the string that comes into your conversion is actually an array of strings. This is because all request parameter values are actually arrays of string values. It's possible to write converters that can work with multiple values, but, for the purposes of this book, we'll stick to a simple case of a single parameter value.

5.4.2 Converting between Strings and Circles

The logic that we put in the conversion methods will largely consist of string parsing and object creation. It's not rocket science. As with many of the Struts 2 advanced features, the stroke of genius will be when you decide that a given use case can be handled elegantly by something like a custom type converter. The implementation itself will take much less brainpower. Listing 5.6 shows our manning.utils.CircleTypeConverter. java file.

Listing 5.6 The `CircleTypeConverter` provides custom type conversion.

```
public class CircleTypeConverter extends StrutsTypeConverter {    ⟵──┐ Extends
                                                                        │ StrutsTypeConverter
    public Object convertFromString(Map context, String[] values,
                            Class toClass) {

        String userString = values[0];
        Circle newCircle = parseCircle ( userString );    ⟵ Convert String
        return newCircle;                                         to Circle

    }

    public String convertToString(Map context, Object o) {

        Circle circle = (Circle) o;
        String userString = "C:r" + circle.getRadius();    ⟵ Convert Circle
        return userString;                                        to String

    }

    private Circle parseCircle( String userString )
                        throws TypeConversionException
    {
        Circle circle = null;
        int radiusIndex = userString.indexOf('r') + 1;

        if (!userString.startsWith( "C:r")  )
            throw new TypeConversionException ( "Invalid Syntax");
        int radius;
        try {
            radius = Integer.parseInt( userString.substring( radiusIndex ) );
        }catch ( NumberFormatException e ) {
            throw new TypeConversionException ( "Invalid Value for Radius"); }

        circle = new Circle();
        circle.setRadius( radius );
        return circle;

    }
}
```

You should focus on the first two methods. We include the `parseCircle()` method here to make sure you realize nothing sneaky is going on. The first method, `convert-FromString()`, will be used to convert the request parameter into a `Circle` object. This is the same thing that has been happening behind the scenes when we've been taking advantage of the built-in type conversions that come with Struts 2 by default. All this method does is parse the string representation of a `Circle` and create an actual `Circle` object from it. So much for the mystique of data binding. Going back from a `Circle` object to a string is equally straightforward. We just take the bits of data from the `Circle` object and build the string according to the syntax we specified earlier.

5.4.3   *Configuring the framework to use our converter*

Now that we have our converter built, we have to let the framework know when and where it should be used. We have two choices here. We can configure our converter to be used local to a given action or globally. If we configure our converter local to an action, we just tell the framework to use the converter when handling a specific `Circle` property of a specific action. If we configure the converter to be used globally, it'll be used every time a `Circle` property is set or retrieved through OGNL anywhere in the application. Let's look at how each of these configurations is handled.

PROPERTY-SPECIFIC

The first choice is to specify that this converter should be used for converting a given property on a given action class. We've already worked with the configuration file used for configuring aspects of type conversion for a specific action. We used the ActionName-conversion.properties file when we specified types for our `Collection` property's elements in the earlier `Map` and `List` examples. Now we'll use the same file to specify our custom converter for a specific `Circle` property.

We've created a specific action to demonstrate the custom type conversion. This action is `manning.chapterFive.CustomConverterTest`. The action does little. Its most important characteristic for our purposes is that it exposes a JavaBeans property with type `Circle`, as seen in the following snippet:

```
private Circle circle;

public Circle getCircle() {
  return circle;
}
public void setCircle(Circle circle) {
  this.circle = circle;
}
```

This action has almost no execution logic. It functions almost exclusively as a carrier of our untransformed data. For our purposes, we're only interested in the type conversion that'll occur when a request parameter comes into the framework targeting this property. Here's the line from CustomConverterTest-conversion.properties that specifies our custom converter as the converter to use for this property:

```
circle=manning.utils.CircleTypeConverter
```

This simple line associates a property name, `Circle`, with a type converter. In this case, the type converter is our custom type converter. Now, when OGNL wants to set a value on our `Circle` property, it'll use our custom converter. Here's the form, from Custom-ConverterTest.jsp, that submits a request parameter targeting that property:

```
<s:form action="CustomConverterTest">
  <s:textfield name="circle" label='Circle'/>
  <s:submit/>
</s:form>
```

The name is an OGNL expression that'll target our property. Since the action object is on top of the `ValueStack` and the `Circle` property is a top-level property on that action, this OGNL expression is simple. Now let's try it out. Go to the Custom Converter Test link in the chapter 5 samples. Enter a valid `Circle` string in the form, as shown in figure 5.4.

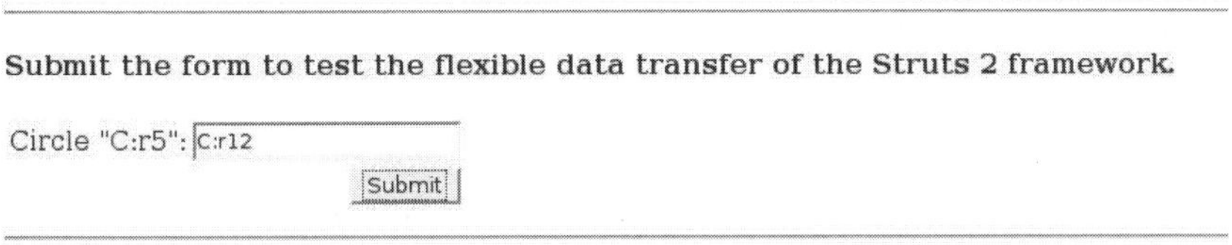

Submit the form to test the flexible data transfer of the Struts 2 framework.

Circle "C:r5": C:r12

Submit

Figure 5.4   Submitting a string that our custom `CircleTypeConverter` will convert into a Java `Circle` object

When this form is submitted, this string will go in as a request parameter targeted at our `Circle` property. Since this property has our custom converter specified as its converter, this string will automatically be converted into a `Circle` object and set on the `Circle` property targeted by the parameter name. Figure 5.5 shows the result page, Custom-ConverterSuccess.jsp, that confirms that everything has worked according to plan.

Our result page verifies that the conversion has occurred by retrieving the first and last name from the `Circle` property, which holds the `Circle` object created by the converter. And, just for fun, the result page also tests the reverse conversion by printing the `Circle` property as a string again.

While we're at it, try to enter a string that doesn't meet our syntax requirements. If you do, you'll be automatically returned to the form input page with an error message informing you that the string you entered was invalid. This useful and powerful mechanism is just a part of the framework's conversion facilities. Tapping into it for your

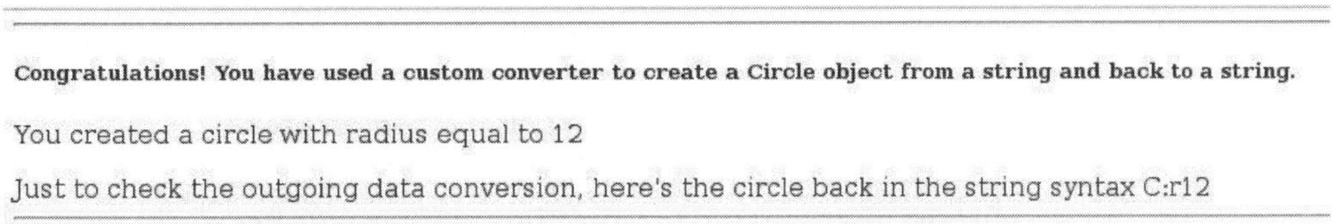

Congratulations! You have used a custom converter to create a Circle object from a string and back to a string.

You created a circle with radius equal to 12

Just to check the outgoing data conversion, here's the circle back in the string syntax C:r12

Figure 5.5   The result page from our custom conversion test pulls data from the `Circle` property to verify that the conversion worked.

custom type converters is easy. To access this functionality, we throw a `com. opensym-phony.xwork2.util.TypeConversionException` when there's a problem with the conversion. In our case, this exception is thrown by our `parseCircle()` method. When we receive the input string value, we do some testing to make sure the string meets our syntax requirements for a valid representation of a `Circle`. If it doesn't, we throw the exception.

GLOBAL TYPE CONVERTERS

We just saw how to set up a type converter for use with a specific property of a specific action. We can also specify that our converter be used for all properties of type `Circle`. This can be quite useful. The process differs little from our previous example, and we'll go through it quickly without an example. The differences are so minute, you can alter the sample code yourself if you want some first-hand proof. Instead of using the ActionClassName-conversion.properties file to configure your type converter, use xwork-conversion.properties. As you can probably tell, this is just a global version of the conversion properties. To this file, add a line such as follows:

```
manning.utils.Circle=manning.utils.CircleTypeConverter
```

Now, our custom type converter will run every time OGNL sets or gets a value from a property of the `Circle` type. By the way, the xwork-conversion.properties file goes on the classpath, such as in WEB-INF/classes/.

That wraps up custom type converters. As we promised, the implementation is easy. Now the challenge, as with custom interceptors, is finding something cool to do with them. One of the problems is that most of the converters you'll ever need have already been provided with the framework. Even if you never make a custom one, we're sure that knowing how they work will help in your daily development chores. If you do come up with a rad type converter, though, don't keep it a secret. Go to the Struts 2 community and let them know. We're all anxious to benefit from your labor!

5.5   *Summary*

That does it for our treatment of the Struts 2 data transfer and type conversion mechanisms. While you can get away with minimal awareness of much of the information in this chapter, trying to do so will only leave you frustrated and less productive in the long run, and even in the short run. Let's review some of the things we learned about how the framework moves data from one end of the request processing to the other, all while transparently managing a wide range of type conversions.

The Object-Graph Navigation Language (OGNL) is tightly integrated into Struts 2 to provide support for data transfer and type conversion. OGNL provides an expression language that allows developers to map form fields to Java-side properties, and it also provides type converters that automatically convert from the strings of the request parameters to the Java types of your properties. The expression language and type converters also work on the other end of the framework when Struts 2 tags in the view-layer pages, such as JSPs, pull data out of these Java properties to dynamically render the view.

We conducted an extensive review of the built-in type converters that come with the framework. We saw that they pretty much support all primitives and common wrapper types of the Java language. We also saw that they support a flexible and rich set of conversions to and from `Arrays` and `Collections`. And if that's not enough, you can always build your own custom type converters. Thanks to a convenient base class provided by the framework, implementing a custom converter is easy.

As we promised at the onset, this chapter started a two-part introduction to OGNL. This chapter's efforts focused more on the role that OGNL plays in the framework, providing a binding between string-based data of the HTTP realm and the strict type of the Java realm. We showed enough OGNL expression language details to make full use of the built-in type conversions to such complex property types as `Maps` and `Lists`.

Now, we're ready to head to the result side of the framework and see how data is pulled from the model, via tag libraries, and rendered in the view. The tags tend to take more advantage of the full expression language. Accordingly, in the next few chapters, which deal specifically with the tags, we'll spend a lot more time on the OGNL expression language. On to chapter 6!

Part 3

Building the view: tags and results

In part 2, we learned how the core of the framework processes each request. In particular, we learned how to write actions that contain the logic for each request, wrap that action logic with a stack of the appropriate interceptors, and take advantage of the framework's powerful data transfer and type conversion mechanisms. Though we've been using JSP pages to render simple views for our actions, we haven't gone into any of the details of the view layer. We now enter the part of the book that focuses on the view layer.

In Struts 2, the MVC view concerns are encapsulated in the result component. We've already become somewhat familiar with the result component even though we've said nothing regarding its details. In fact, actually developing results will be at least as rare as developing your own interceptors. Most of your development work will amount to little more than using built-in result types to hit JSP pages and Velocity templates. The built-in result types will handle the most common view-layer technologies, so you'll probably go through a lot of code before you find yourself writing your own. Nonetheless, we'll provide a detailed account of working directly with results in chapter 8.

For now, we're going to focus on the Struts 2 tag libraries because, while secondary to the result component itself, they're the tools you'll have in hand for most of your development efforts. The most common view-layer technologies are probably JSP, Velocity, and FreeMarker. While each of these has its own tags or macros, the Struts 2 framework provides a high-level tag API that you can use on all three rendering platforms. In addition to being a portable tag API, these

Struts 2 tags bring a lot to the table functionally. You'll find all of the features of any recently minted tag set, and more.

The Struts 2 tag libraries are divided into two groups: general-purpose tags and UI component tags. We'll start, in chapter 6, with the general-purpose tags. These tags provide all sorts of things from conditional logic to `ValueStack` manipulation to i18n help. We'll show you how the tags work, including an overview of their syntax and using OGNL to reference values on the `ValueStack`. We'll even include a primer on the most important parts of the OGNL expression language as used in the context of tags.

The UI component tags, which we'll introduce in chapter 7, are perhaps the most impressive part of the Struts 2 tags. These tags not only generate HTML form fields, but wrap those fields in layers of functionality that tap into all of the framework's various features. And if you need to customize the HTML output of a given UI-oriented tag, such as a form tag, you can change its HTML source template and thus change the way it renders across all uses, enabling reusable customization. The full richness of the UI components can't be captured in a couple of sentences, but we think you'll find them alluring after reading about them.

Building a view: tags

This chapter covers

- Working with data tags
- Controlling flow with control tags
- Surveying the miscellaneous tags
- Exploring the OGNL expression language

In this chapter, we'll start looking at the Struts 2 tag library in detail. We'll provide a good reference to the tags and clear examples of their usage. We'll also finish exploring the Object-Graph Navigation Language (OGNL). We've already seen how OGNL is used to bind form fields to Java properties, such as those exposed on our action, to guide the framework's automatic data transfer mechanism. In chapter 5, we learned about the type conversion aspects of OGNL in the context of data entering the framework.

Now, we'll focus on the OGNL expression language (EL) in the context of data exiting the framework through the Struts 2 tag API. While the previous chapter showed us how to map incoming request parameters to Java properties exposed on the `ValueStack`, this chapter will show you how to pull data off of those properties for the rendering of result pages. We'll explore the syntax of the OGNL EL and study the locations from which it can pull data. In particular, we'll look closely at the `ValueStack` and the `ActionContext`. These objects hold all of the data important to processing a given request, including your action object. While it may be possible to blissfully ignore their existence during much of your development, we think the benefits are too high not to spend a few minutes getting to know them.

But that won't take long, and we'll make the most of the remainder of the chapter. After we demystify these two obscure repositories, we'll provide a reference-style catalog of the general-use tags in the Struts 2 tag API. These powerful new tags allow you to wield the OGNL expression language to feed them with values. But tags are tags, and they also won't take long to cover. So, after covering the tags, we'll provide a concise primer to the advanced features of the OGNL expression language. In the end, you'll wield your OGNL expressions confidently as you navigate through the densest of object graphs to pull data into the dynamic rendering of your view pages. Bon appétit.

First, we need to take a moment to make sure you understand where the framework holds all the data you might want to access from the tags. This usage of globally accessible storage areas may not be familiar to developers coming from other frameworks, including Struts 1. In the next section, we'll take care of these crucial introductions.

6.1   *Getting started*

Before we talk about the details of how Struts 2 tags can help you dynamically pipe data into the rendering of your pages, let's talk about where that data comes from. While we focused on the data moving into the framework in the previous chapter, we'll now focus on the data leaving the framework. When a request hits the framework, one of the first things Struts 2 does is create the objects that'll store all the important data for the request. If we're talking about your application's domain-specific data, which is the data that you'll most frequently access with your tags, it'll be stored in the `ValueStack`. But processing a request requires more than just your application's domain data. Other, more infrastructural, data must be stored also. All of this data, along with the `ValueStack` itself, is stored in something called the `ActionContext`.

6.1.1   *The ActionContext and OGNL*

In the previous chapter, we used OGNL expressions to bind form field names to specific property locations on objects such as our action object. We already know that our action object is placed on something called the `ValueStack` and that the OGNL expressions target properties on that stack object. In reality, OGNL expressions can resolve against any of a set of objects. The `ValueStack` is just one of these objects, the default one. This wider set of objects against which OGNL expressions can choose to resolve is called the `ActionContext`. We'll now see how OGNL chooses which object to resolve against, as well as what other objects are available for accessing with OGNL.

TIP   The `ActionContext` contains all of the data available to the framework's processing of the request, including things ranging from application data to session- or application-scoped maps. All of your application-specific data, such as properties exposed on your action, will be held in the `ValueStack`, one of the objects in the `ActionContext`.

All OGNL expressions must resolve against one of the objects contained in the `ActionContext`. By default, the `ValueStack` will be the one chosen for OGNL resolution, but you can specifically name one of the others, such as the session map, if you like.

The `ActionContext` is a key behind-the-scenes player in the Struts 2 framework. If you've worked with other web application frameworks, particularly Struts 1, then you might be asking, "Why do I need an `ActionContext`? Why have you made my life more complicated?" We've been trying to emphasize that the Struts 2 framework strives toward a clean MVC implementation. The `ActionContext` helps clean things up by providing the notion of a context for the execution of an action. By *context* we mean a simple container for all the important data and resources that surround the execution of a given action. A good example of the type of data we're talking about is the map of parameters from the request, or a map of session attributes from the Servlet Container. In Struts 1, most of these resources were accessed via the Servlet stuff handed into the execution of every action. We've already seen how clean the Struts 2 action object has become; it has no parameters in its method signature to tie it to any APIs that might have little to do with its task. So, really, your life is much less complicated, though at first it might not seem so.

Before we show you all of the specific things that the `ActionContext` holds, we need to discuss OGNL integration. As we've seen, OGNL expressions target properties on specific objects. The resolution of each OGNL expression requires a root object against which resolution of references will begin. Consider the following OGNL expression:

```
user.account.balance
```

Here we're targeting the `balance` property on the `account` object on the `user` object. But where's the user object located? We must define an initial object upon which we'll locate the user object itself. Every time you use an OGNL expression, you need to indicate which object the expression should start its resolution against. In Struts 2, each OGNL expression must choose its initial object from those contained in the `Action-Context`. Figure 6.1 shows the `ActionContext` and the objects it contains, any of which you can point your OGNL resolution toward.

As you can see, the `ActionContext` is full of juicy treasures. The most important of these is the `ValueStack`. As we've said, the `ValueStack` holds your application's domain-specific data for a given action invocation. For instance, if you're updating a

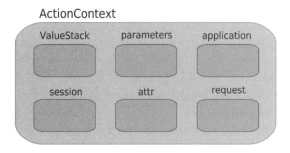

Figure 6.1 The `ActionContext` holds all the important data objects pertaining to a given action invocation; OGNL can target any of them.

student, you'll expect to find that student data on the ValueStack. We'll divulge more of the inner workings of the ValueStack in a moment. The other objects are all maps of important sets of data. Each of them has a name that indicates its purpose and should be familiar to seasoned Java web application developers, as they correspond to specific concepts from the Servlet API. For more information on where the data in these sets comes from, we recommend the Java Servlet Specification. The contents of each of these objects is summarized in table 6.1.

Table 6.1   The names and contents of the objects and maps in the ActionContext

Name	Description
parameters	Map of request parameters for this request
request	Map of request-scoped attributes
session	Map of session-scoped attributes
application	Map of application-scoped attributes
attr	Returns first occurrence of attribute occurring in page, request, session, or application scope, in that order
ValueStack	Contains all the application-domain–specific data for the request

The parameters object is a map of the request parameters associated with the request being processed—the parameters submitted by the form, in other words. The application object is a map of the application attributes. The request and session objects are also maps of request and session attributes. By *attribute* we mean the Servlet API concept of an attribute. Attributes allow you to store arbitrary objects, associated with a name, in these respective scopes. Objects stored in application scope are accessible to all requests coming to the application. Objects stored in session scope are accessible to all requests of a particular session, and so forth. Common usage includes storing a user object in the session to indicate a logged-in user across multiple requests. The attr object is a special map that looks for attributes in the following locations, in sequence: page, request, session, and application scope.

Now let's look at how we choose which object from the ActionContext our OGNL will resolve against.

SELECTING THE ROOT OBJECT FOR OGNL

Up until now, we've hidden the fact that an OGNL expression must choose one of the objects in the ActionContext to use as its root object. So how does the framework choose which object to resolve a given OGNL expression against? We did nothing about this while writing our simple input field names in the previous chapter. As with all Struts 2 mysteries, this comes down to a case of intelligent defaults. By default, the ValueStack will serve as the root object for resolving all OGNL expressions that don't explicitly name an initial object. You almost don't have to know that the ValueStack exists to use Struts 2. But, take our word, that's not a blissful ignorance.

Though you haven't seen it yet, OGNL expressions can start with a special syntax that names the object from the context against which they should resolve. The following OGNL expression demonstrates this syntax:

```
#session['user']
```

This OGNL expression actively names the session map from the `ActionContext` via the # operator of the expression language. The # operator tells OGNL to use the named object, located in its context, as the initial object for resolving the rest of the expression. With Struts 2, the OGNL context is the `ActionContext` and, thankfully, there's a session object in that context. This expression then points to whatever object has been stored under the key `user` in the session object, which happens to be the session scope from the Servlet API. This could be, for instance, the user object that our Struts 2 Portfolio login action stores in the session.

INSIDER SCOOP   As of version 2.1 of Struts 2, which will most likely be available by the time this book is printed, the expression language used by the framework will become pluggable. While this may sound unsettling, it's actually harmless. You can use OGNL, just as described in this book, or you can insert your own expression language into the framework. Any EL plugged into Struts 2 will have access to the same data and will serve the same purposes as we've described for OGNL. But don't panic: you can just use OGNL! Besides, it might be several versions before switching ELs becomes well established.

As far as the full syntax of OGNL goes, we'll wait a bit on that. In the previous chapter, we saw as much of the OGNL syntax as we needed for writing our input field names that would target our properties. At the most complex, this included expressions that could reference map entries via string and object keys. But OGNL is much more. The OGNL expression language contains many powerful features, including the ability to call methods on the objects you reference. While these advanced features give you a set of flexible and powerful tools with which to solve the thorn that you inevitably find stuck in your side late on a Friday afternoon, they aren't necessary in the normal course of things. We'll continue to delay full coverage of the OGNL expression language until the end of this chapter, preferring instead to only introduce as much as we need while demonstrating the tags. The main idea here is to understand the role that the expression language plays in the framework.

We'll start exploring that role by taking a long-delayed look at the default root object for all OGNL resolution, the `ValueStack`.

6.1.2   *The ValueStack: a virtual object*

Back to that default root object of the `ActionContext`. Understanding the `ValueStack` is critical to understanding the way data moves through the Struts 2 framework. By now, you've got most of what you need. We've seen the `ValueStack` in action. When Struts 2 receives a request, it immediately creates an `ActionContext`, a `ValueStack`, and an action object. As a carrier of application data, the action object is quickly placed on the ValueStack so that its properties will be accessible, via OGNL, to the far reaches of the framework.

First, these will receive the automatic data transfer from the incoming request parameters. As we saw in chapter 4, this occurs because the params interceptor sets those parameters on properties exposed on the ValueStack, upon which the action object sits. While other things, such as the model of the ModelDriven interface, may also be placed on the stack, what all data on the ValueStack has in common is that it's all specific to the application's domain. In MVC terms, the ValueStack is the request's view of the application's model data. There are no infrastructural objects, such as Servlet API or Struts 2 objects, on the ValueStack. The action is only there because of its role as domain data carrier; it's not there because of its action logic.

There's only one tricky bit about the ValueStack. The ValueStack pretends to be a single object when OGNL expressions are resolved against it. This virtual object contains all the properties of all the objects that've been placed on the stack. If multiple occurrences of the same property exist, those lowest down in the stack are hidden by the uppermost occurrence of a similarly named property. Figure 6.2 shows a ValueStack with several objects on it.

As you can see in figure 6.2, references to a given property resolve to the highest occurrence of that property in the stack. While this may seem complicated, it's actually not. As with most Struts 2 features, the flexibility and power to address complex use cases is there, but the common user can remain ignorant of such details.

Let's examine figure 6.2. As usual, the action object itself has been placed on the stack first. Then, a model object was added to the stack. This most likely has occurred because the action implements ModelDriven. Sometime after that, another object, apparently some sort of random-number-making bean, was added to the stack. By *bean* we simply mean a Java object that either serves as a data carrier or as a utility-providing

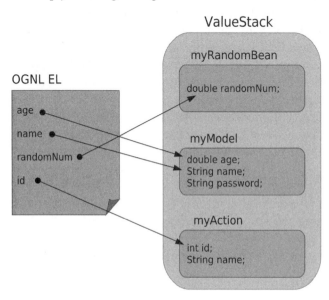

Figure 6.2 The ValueStack is the default object against which all OGNL expressions are resolved.

object. In other words, it's usually just some object whose properties you might want to access from your tags with OGNL expressions.

At present, we just want to see how the `ValueStack` appears as a single virtual object to the OGNL expressions resolving against it. In figure 6.2, we have four simple expressions. Each targets a top-level property. Behind the scenes, OGNL will resolve each of these expressions by asking the `ValueStack` if it has a property such as, for instance, name. The `ValueStack` will always return the highest-level occurrence of the name property in its stack of objects. In this case, the action object has a name property, but that property will never be accessed as long as the model object's name property sits on top of it.

> **Definition**
>
> When Java developers talk about beans in the context of view technologies, such as JSPs, they frequently mean something different than just a Java object that meets the JavaBeans standard. While these beans are most likely good JavaBeans as well, they don't have to be. The usage in this context more directly refers to the fact that the bean is a Java object that exposes data and/or utility methods for use in JSP tags and the like. Many developers call any object exposed like this a "bean."
>
> This nomenclature is a historical artifact. In the past, expression languages used in tags couldn't call methods. Thus, they could only retrieve data from an object if it were exposed as a JavaBean property. Since the OGNL expression language allows you to call methods directly, you could completely ignore JavaBeans conventions and still have data and utility methods exposed to your tags for use while rendering the page. However, in order to keep your JSP pages free of complexity, we strongly recommend following JavaBeans conventions and avoiding expression language method invocation as long as possible.

Just so you don't worry about it, we might as well discuss how that bean showed up on top of the stack. Prior to this point, we've just had stuff automatically placed on the `ValueStack` by the framework. So how did the bean get there? There are many ways to add a bean to the stack. Many of the most common ways occur within the tags that we'll soon cover. For instance, the push tag lets you push any bean you like onto the stack. You might do such a thing just before you wanted to reference that bean's data or methods from later tags. We'll demonstrate this with sample code when we cover those tags.

With a clear view of where the data is and how to get to it, it's time to get back to the Struts 2 tags that are the focus of this chapter, and are the means of pulling data from the `ActionContext` and `ValueStack` into the dynamic rendering of your view layer pages.

6.2 *An overview of Struts tags*

The Struts 2 tag API provides the functionality to dynamically create robust web pages by leveraging conditional rendering and integration of data from your application's domain model found on the `ValueStack`. Struts 2 comes with many different types of tags. For organizational purposes, they can be broken into four categories: *data tags, control-flow tags, UI tags,* and *miscellaneous tags.* Since they are a complex topic all to themselves, we'll leave the UI tags for chapter 7. This chapter examines the other three categories.

Data tags focus on ways to extract data from the ValueStack and/or set values in the ValueStack. Control-flow tags give you the tools to conditionally alter the flow of the rendering process; they can even test values on the ValueStack. The miscellaneous tags are a set of tags that don't quite fit into the other categories. These leftover tags include such useful functionality as managing URL rendering and internationalization of text. Before we get started, we need to make some general remarks about the conventions that are applied across the usage of all Struts 2 tag APIs.

6.2.1   *The Struts 2 tag API syntax*

The first issue to address is the multiple faces of the Struts 2 tag API. As we've mentioned earlier, Struts 2 tags are defined at a higher level than any specific view-layer technology. Using the tags is as simple as consulting the API. The tag API specifies the attributes and parameters exposed by the tag. Once you identify a tag that you want to use, you simply move on to your view technology of choice—JSP, Velocity, or FreeMarker. Interfaces to the tag API have been implemented in all three technologies. The differences in usage among the three are so trivial that we'll be able to cover them in the rest of this short subsection. After that, we present our functional reference of the tags, including a summary of their attributes and parameters. We also include examples of the tags in action. These examples are done in JSP, but we think you'll soon see that taking your knowledge of the Struts 2 tags API to one of the other technologies will take approximately zero effort. Let's start with JSPs.

JSP SYNTAX

The JSP versions of the Struts 2 tags are just like any other JSP tags. The following property tag demonstrates the simple syntax:

```
<s:property value="name"/>
```

The only other thing to note is that you must have the property taglib declaration at the top of your page before using the Struts 2 tags. This is standard JSP stuff, and the following snippet from one of our Struts 2 Portfolio application's JSPs should show you what you need:

```
<%@ page contentType="text/html; charset=UTF-8" %>
<%@ taglib prefix="s" uri="/struts-tags" %>
```

The second line, the taglib directive, declares the Struts 2 tag library and assigns them the "s" prefix by which they'll be identified.

VELOCITY SYNTAX

You can also use Velocity templates for your view technology. All you need to do is specify your result type to the built-in velocity result type. We'll see the details of declaring a result to use a Velocity result type in chapter 8. For now, rest assured that the framework supports using Velocity out of the box. Let's see how the Struts 2 tags are accessed from Velocity. In Velocity, the Struts 2 tag API is implemented as Velocity macros. This doesn't matter though; the API is the same. You just need to learn the macro syntax that specifies the same information. Here's the Velocity version of the property tag:

```
#sproperty( "value=name" )
```

Struts 2 tags that would require an end tag may require an #end statement in Velocity. Here's a JSP form tag from the Struts 2 Portfolio application that uses a closing tag:

```
<s:form action="Register">
  <s:textfield name="username" label="Username"/>
  <s:password name="password" label="Password"/>
  <s:textfield name="portfolioName" label="Enter a name"/>
  <s:submit value="Submit"/>
</s:form>
```

And here's the same tag as a Velocity macro:

```
#sform ("action=Register")
  #stextfield ("label=Username" "name=username")
  #spassword ( "label=Password" "name=password")
  #stextfield ( "label=Enter a name" "name=portfolioName")

  #ssubmit ("value=Submit")
#end
```

Again, it's the same tag, different syntax. Everything, as pertains to the API, is still the same.

FREEMARKER SYNTAX

The framework also provides out-of-the-box support for using FreeMarker templates as the view-layer technology. We'll see how to declare results that use FreeMarker in chapter 8. For now, here's the same property tag as it would appear in FreeMarker:

```
<@s.property value="name"/>
```

As you can see, it's more like the JSP tag syntax. In the end, it won't matter what view-layer technology you choose. You can easily access all the same Struts 2 functionality from each technology. While we'll demonstrate the tag API using JSP tags, we trust that you'll be able to painlessly migrate that knowledge to Velocity or FreeMarker according to the syntax conventions we've just covered.

Now we'll outline some important conventions regarding the values you pass into the attributes of your Struts 2 tags, regardless of which view technology you use.

6.2.2   *Using OGNL to set attributes on tags*

There are a couple of things you have to understand when setting values in tag attributes. The basic issue is whether the attribute expects a string literal value or some OGNL that'll point to a typed value on the ValueStack. We'll introduce this issue now, and revisit it as we cover the tags themselves.

First, we need to consider that an attribute on a tag is eventually going to be processed by the Java code that backs the tag implementation. But in the JSP page, for instance, everything is a string. Working with other technologies, you've become familiar with using some sort of escape sequence to force the attribute value to be parsed as an expression versus being interpreted as a string literal; this frequently leads to markup that borders on being hard to read, with its proliferation of ${*expression*} notation. In an effort to make the use of OGNL in tags more intuitive and readable, Struts 2 makes assumptions about what kind of data it expects for each attribute. In particular, a distinction is made in the handling of attributes whose type, in the underlying execution, will be String and those whose type will be non-String.

STRING AND NON-STRING ATTRIBUTES

If an attribute is of type String, then the value written into the attribute, in the actual JSP or Velocity page, is interpreted as a string literal. If an attribute is some non-String type, then the value written into the attribute is interpreted as an OGNL expression. This make sense because the OGNL expressions can point to typed Java properties on the ValueStack, thus making a perfect tool for passing in typed parameters. The following property tags demonstrate the difference between String and non-String attribute types:

```
nonExistingProperty on the ValueStack = <s:property
   value="nonExistingProperty" />

nonExistingProperty on the ValueStack = <s:property
   value="nonExistingProperty" default="doesNotExist" />
```

Here, we have two somewhat identical uses of the Struts 2 property tag. First of all, note that the property tag's value attribute is typed as Object, a non-String attribute. The use case of the property tag is to take a Java property, typically from the ValueStack, and write it as a string into the rendering page. As we know, the properties on the ValueStack might be of any Java type; the conversion to a string will be handled automatically by the OGNL type converters. The property tag's value attribute tells it the property to render to the page. In the case of these examples, both tags are looking for a property called nonExistingProperty.

The property tag will try to locate this property by resolving the value attribute's value as an OGNL expression. Since no specific object from the ActionContext is named with the # operator, it'll look on the ValueStack. As it turns out, nonExistingProperty doesn't exist on the ValueStack. What then? A null value will be converted to an empty string. In the case of the first tag, as you can see in figure 6.3, nothing will render.

But the second tag does write something: the string doesNotExist. The second property tag still tries to pull the nonExistingProperty from the ValueStack, which again comes up empty. However, it also specifies a default attribute that gives a value to use if the property doesn't exist. Since the purpose of the default attribute is to provide a default string for the tag to put in the page, its type is String. When the value given to an attribute is ultimately to be used as a string, it makes sense that the

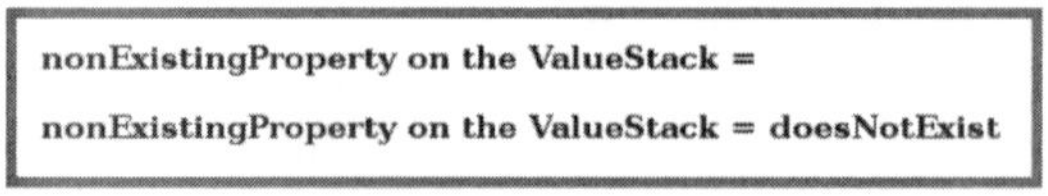

nonExistingProperty on the ValueStack =

nonExistingProperty on the ValueStack = doesNotExist

Figure 6.3   Output from property tags with no value: one specifies a default value while the other doesn't

default behavior is to interpret the attribute value as a string literal. Thus, the default value of doesNotExist isn't used as an OGNL expression. As you can see in figure 6.3, which shows the output of these two tags, the second tag uses doesNotExist as a string literal in its rendering.

HEADS-UP   Attributes passed to Struts 2 tags are divided into two categories. Attributes that'll be used by the tag as String values are referred to as *string attributes.* Attributes that point to some property on the ValueStack, or in the ActionContext are referred to as *nonstring attributes.* All nonstring attributes will be interpreted as OGNL expressions and used to locate the property that'll contain the value to be used in the tag processing. All string attributes will be taken literally as Strings and used as such in the tag processing. You can force a string attribute to be interpreted as an OGNL expression by using the %{*expression*} syntax.

If you've worked with other expression languages embedded into tags, you're probably wondering when and how you can use some sort of expression language escape sequence. Many of you are familiar with various markers, such as ${*expression*}, that indicate which text should be regarded as an expression and which as an actual string. The convention we've just described, where Struts 2 assumes that some attributes will be expressions and others will be strings, avoids many of the scenarios in which such escape sequences would be called for. However, we'll sometimes want to use an OGNL expression with a String attribute. What then?

FORCING OGNL RESOLUTION

Let's say, assuming the previous example of the nonExistingProperty, that you wanted to use a String property from the ValueStack as your default attribute value. In this case, you wouldn't want the default attribute to be interpreted as a string literal. You'd want it to be interpreted as an OGNL expression pointing to your String property on the ValueStack. If you want to force OGNL resolution of a String attribute, such as the default attribute of the property tag, then you need to use an OGNL escape sequence. This escape sequence is %{*expression*}. The following snippet revisits the scenario from the previous property tag example using the escape sequence to force the default attribute value to be interpreted as an OGNL expression:

```
nonExistingProperty on the ValueStack =
<s:property value="nonExistingProperty" default="%{myDefaultString}" />
```

Now the value of the default attribute will be interpreted as OGNL, and the actual string used as the default string will be pulled from the myDefaultString property on the ValueStack.

Note the similarity between the bracket syntax used to force the String attribute to evaluate as an OGNL expression and the JSTL Expression Language syntax.

Struts 2 OGNL Syntax	JSTL Expression Language
%{ *expression* }	${ *expression* }

OGNL uses % instead of $. While this may seem confusing to some JSP veterans, in reality you don't use the OGNL escape sequence very often. Due to the intelligent default behavior of the tags, you can almost always let the tags decide when to interpret your attributes as OGNL expressions and when to interpret them as string literals. This is another way that the framework eases the common tasks.

We recognize that some of this may be abstract at this point. Believe us, knowing string and nonstring attributes will make learning the tags much, much easier. Besides, we're now ready to look at the tags themselves, complete with plenty of sample code.

6.3   *Data tags*

The first tags we'll look at are the data tags. Data tags let you get data out of the `ValueStack` or place variables and objects onto the `ValueStack`. In this section, we'll discuss the `property`, `set`, `push`, `bean`, and `action` tags. In this reference, our goal is to demonstrate the common uses of these tags. Many of the tags have further functionality for special cases. To find out everything there is to know, consult the primary documentation on the Struts 2 website at http://struts.apache.org/2.x/.

> **ALERT** All of the tag usage examples found in the following reference section can be found in the chapter 6 version of the Struts 2 Portfolio sample application.

Most of these examples use the same action class implementation, `manning.chapterSix.TagDemo`. This simple action conducts no real business logic. It merely exposes and populates a couple of properties with data so the tags have something with which to work. In particular, two properties, `users` and `user`, are exposed; the first exposes a collection of all users in the system and the second exposes one user of your choice. For the purposes of a tag reference, we won't try to integrate these tag demonstrations into the core functionality of the Struts 2 Portfolio. We'll focus on making the usage clear.

6.3.1   *The property tag*

The `property` tag provides a quick, convenient way of writing a property into the rendering HTML. Typically, these properties will be on the `ValueStack` or on some other object in the `ActionContext`. As these properties can be of any Java type, they must be converted to strings for rendering in the result page. This conversion is handled by the framework's type converters, which we covered in chapter 5. If a specific type has no converter, it'll typically be treated as a string. In these cases, a sensible `toString()` method should be exposed on the class. Table 6.2 summarizes the most important attributes.

Table 6.2 `property` **tag attributes**

Attribute	Required	Default	Type	Description
value	No	\<top of stack\>	Object	Value to be displayed
default	No	null	String	Default value to be used if value is null
escape	No	True	Boolean	Whether to escape HTML

Now, let's look at a `property` tag in action. As with all the examples in this chapter, you can see this in action by clicking the `property` tag link on the chapter 6 home page of the sample application. The following tag accesses the `user` property exposed on the `ValueStack` via our `TagDemo` action:

```
<h4>Property Tag</h4>
The current user is <s:property value="user.username"/>.
```

The output is as you'd expect and is shown in figure 6.4.

In this case, the `user` property holds a user with the user-name of `mary`. When the `property` tag pulls the property out to render, it'll be converted to a string based on the appropriate type converters. While this property was a Java `String`, it still must be formally converted to a text string in the rendering page. See chapter 5 for more on the type conversion process.

Figure 6.4 Pulling the username into the page with the `property` tag

6.3.2 *The set tag*

In the context of this tag, *setting* means assigning a property to another name. Various reasons for doing this exist. An obvious use case would be taking a property that needs a deep, complicated OGNL expression to reference it, and reassigning, or setting, it to a top-level name for easier, faster access. This can make your JSPs faster and easier to read.

You can also specify the location of the new reference. By default, the property becomes a named object in the `ActionContext`, alongside the `ValueStack`, session map, and company. This means you can then reference it as a top-level named object with an OGNL expression such as `#myObject`. However, you can also specify that the new reference be kept in one of the scoped maps that are kept in the `ActionContext`. Table 6.3 provides the attributes for the `set` tag.

Table 6.3 `set` tag attributes

Attribute	Required	Type	Description
name	Yes	String	Reference name of the variable to be set in the specified scope.
scope	No	String	`application`, `session`, `request`, `page`, or `action`. Defaults to `action`.
value	No	Object	Expression of the value you wish to set.

Here's an example from the chapter 6 sample code:

```
<s:set name="username" value="user.username"/>
Hello, <s:property value="#username"/>. How are you?
```

In this case, we aren't saving much by making a new reference to the username property. However, it illustrates the point. In this sample, the `set` tag sets the value from the `user.username` expression to the new reference specified by the name property. Since we don't specify a scope, this new username reference exists in the default "action" scope—the ActionContext. As you can see, we then reference it with the # operator. Figure 6.5 shows the output.

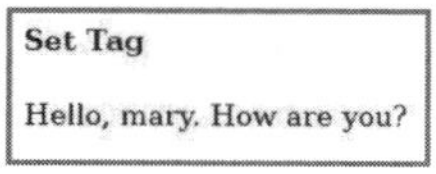

In case you're wondering what it looks like to set the new reference to a different scope, the following sets the new reference as an entry in the application scope map that is found in the ActionContext:

Figure 6.5   Using the set **tag to make data available throughout the page**

```
<s:set name="username" scope="application" value="user.username"/>
Hello, <s:property value="#application['username']"/>. How are you?
```

Note that we have to use the OGNL map syntax to get at the property in this case. We can't say we've made any readability gains here, but we have managed to persist the data across the lifetime of the application by moving it to this map. It's probably not a good idea to persist a user's username to the application scope, but it does serve to demonstrate the tag functionality.

6.3.3   *The push tag*

Whereas the set tag allows you to create new references to values, the push tag allows you to push properties onto the ValueStack. This is useful when you want to do a lot of work revolving around a single object. With the object on the top of the ValueStack, its properties become accessible with first-level OGNL expressions. Any time you access properties of an object more than a time or two, it'll probably save a lot of work if you push that object onto the stack. Table 6.4 provides the attribute for the push tag.

Table 6.4   push tag attributes

Attribute	Required	Type	Description
value	Yes	Object	Value to push onto the stack

Here's an example of the usage:

```
<s:push value="user">
  This is the "<s:property value="portfolioName"/>" portfolio,
  created by none other than <s:property value="username"/>
</s:push>
```

This push tag pushes a property named user, which is exposed by the TagDemo action as a JavaBeans property, onto the top of the ValueStack. With the user on top of the stack, we can access its properties as top-level properties of the ValueStack virtual object, thus making the OGNL much simpler. As you can see, the push tag has a start tag and close tag. Inside the body of the tag, we reference the properties of the user object as top-level properties on the ValueStack. The closing tag removes the user from the top of the ValueStack.

> **Tip**
>
> The `push` tag, and even the set tag to a limited extent, can be powerful when trying to reuse view-layer markup. Imagine you have a JSP template that you'd like to reuse across several JSP result pages. Consider the namespace of the OGNL references in that JSP template. For instance, maybe the template's tags use OGNL references that assume the existence of a `User` object exposed as a model object, as in `ModelDriven` actions. In this case, the template's tags would omit the `user` property and refer directly to properties of the user, for example `<s:property value="username"/>`.
>
> If you try to include this template in the rendering of a result whose action exposes a `User` object as a JavaBeans property, rather than a model object, then this reference would be invalid. It would need to be `<s: value="user.username"/>`. Luckily, the `push` tag gives us the ability to push the user object itself to the top of the `ValueStack`, thus making the top-level references of the template valid in the current action. In general, the `push` tag and the `set` tag can be used in this fashion.

If you want to see how this example actually renders, you can check out the sample code. But we think you'll find no surprises.

6.3.4 *The bean tag*

The `bean` tag is like a hybrid of the `set` and `push` tags. The main difference is that you don't need to work with an existing object. You can create an instance of an object and either push it onto the `ValueStack` or set a top-level reference to it in the `Action-Context`. By default, the object will be pushed onto the `ValueStack` and will remain there for the duration of the tag. In other words, the bean will be on the `ValueStack` for the execution of all tags that occur in between the opening and closing tags of the `bean` tag. If you want to persist the bean longer than the body of the tag, you can specify a reference name for the bean with the `var` attribute. This reference will then exist in the `ActionContext` as a named parameter accessible with the # operator for the duration of the request.

There are a few requirements on the object that can be used as a bean. As you might expect, the object must conform to JavaBeans standards by having a zero-argument constructor and JavaBeans properties for any instance fields that you intend to initialize with `param` tags. We'll demonstrate all of this, including the use of `param` tags, shortly. First, table 6.5 details the attributes for the `bean` tag.

Table 6.5 `bean` tag attributes

Attribute	Required	Type	Description
name	Yes	String	Package and class name of the bean that is to be created
var	No	String	Variable name used if you want to reference the bean outside the scope of the closing bean tag

Our first example demonstrates how to create and store the bean as a named parameter in the `ActionContext`. In this case, we'll create an instance of a utility bean that helps us simulate a `for` loop. This `counter` bean comes with Struts 2. For this example, we'll create the bean and use the `var` attribute to store it in the `ActionContext` as a named parameter. The following markup shows how this is done:

```
<s:bean name="org.apache.struts2.util.Counter" var="counter">
  <s:param name="last" value="7"/>
</s:bean>

<s:iterator value="#counter">
  <li><s:property/></li>
</s:iterator>
```

Figure 6.6 how this markup will render in the result page.

Now let's look at how it works. The bean tag's name attribute points to the class that should be instantiated. The var attribute, repeating a common Struts 2 tag API pattern, specifies the reference name under which the bean will be stored in the `ActionContext`. In this case, we call the bean `counter` and then refer to that bean instance in the iterator tag's value attribute with the appropriate OGNL. Since the bean is in the `ActionContext`, rather than on the `ValueStack`, we need to use the # operator to name it, resulting in the OGNL

Figure 6.6 Declaring a bean that you can use throughout a page

expression #counter. The bean tag is the first of a few tags we'll explore that are parameterized. In the case of the counter, we can pass in a parameter that sets the number of elements it will contain, in effect setting the number of times the iterator tag will execute its body markup.

TIP   The var attribute occurs in the usage of many Struts 2 tags. Any tag that creates an object, the bean tag being a good example, offers the var attribute as a way to store the object under a name in the `ActionContext`. The name comes from the value given to the var attribute. Most tags that offer the var attribute make it optional; if you don't want to store the created object in the `ActionContext`, it will simply be placed on the top of the `ValueStack`, where it'll remain during the body of the tag.

WARNING!   If you're using a version of Struts 2 that is older than 2.1, the var attribute should be replaced with the id attribute.

Now that the counter bean has been created and stored, we can use it from the Struts 2 iterator tag to create a simulation of `for` loop-style logic. The bean tag doesn't have to be used with the iterator tag; it's in this example because the counter bean is meant to be used with the iterator tag. The counter bean works in combination with the iterator tag, which we'll cover shortly, to provide a pseudo `for` loop functionality. Generally, the iterator tag iterates over a Collection, thus its number of iterations is based upon the number of elements in the Collection. For a `for` loop, we want to specify a number of iterations without necessarily providing a set of objects. We just want to iterate over our tag's body a certain number of times. The counter bean serves as a fake `Collection` of a specified number of dummy objects that allows us to control the number of iterations. In the case of our example, we do nothing more than print a number to the result stream during each iteration. Note that we use the `property` tag without any attributes; this idiom will simply write the top property on the `ValueStack` to the output.

NOTE The bean tag allows you to create any bean object that you might want to use in the page. If you want to make your own bean to use with this tag, just remember that it needs to follow JavaBeans conventions on several important points. It has to have no-argument constructor, and it must expose JavaBeans properties for any parameters it'll receive with the `param` tag, such as the counter bean's last parameter.

Now, let's look at how to use the `bean` tag to push a newly created bean onto the `ValueStack` rather than store it in the `ActionContext`. While we're at it, we'll further demonstrate the use of the `param` tag to pump parameters into our home-roasted bean. This is all simple. To use the `ValueStack` as the temporary storage location for our bean, we just use an opening-and-closing-style tag configuration. All tags inside the body of the `bean` tag will resolve against a `ValueStack` that has an instance of our `JokeBean` on top. Here's the example:

```
<s:bean name="manning.utils.JokeBean" >
  <s:param name="jokeType">knockknock</s:param>
  <s:property value="startAJoke()"/>
</s:bean>
```

In this example, also from the chapter 6 sample code, we create an instance of a utility bean that helps us create jokes. If you look at the sample application, you'll see that this outputs the first line of a joke—"knock knock." Though inane, this bean does demonstrate the sense of utility beans. If you want to provide a canned joke component to drop into numerous pages, something that unfortunately does exist in the real world, you could embed that functionality into a utility bean and grab it with the `bean` tag whenever you liked. This keeps the joke logic out of the core logic of the action logic.

This markup demonstrates using the `bean` tag to push the bean onto the `ValueStack` rather than place it as a named reference in the `ActionContext`. Note that we no longer need to use the `var` attribute to specify the reference under which the bean will be stored. When it's on top of the `ValueStack`, we can just refer to its properties and methods directly. This makes our code concise. The bean is automatically popped from the stack at the close tag.

Using the bean is easy. In this case, we use the OGNL method invocation syntax, `startAJoke()`. We do this just to demonstrate that the `bean` tag doesn't have to completely conform to JavaBeans standards—`startAJoke()` is clearly not a proper getter. Nonetheless, OGNL has the power to use it; we'll cover this and more in the primer at the end of this chapter.

Finally, note that we pass a parameter into our `JokeBean` that controls the type of joke told by the bean. This parameter is automatically received by our bean as long as the bean implements a JavaBeans property that matches the name of the parameter. If you look at the source code, you can see that we've done this. FYI: this joke bean also supports an `"adult"` joke mode, but you'll probably be disappointed; it's quite innocuous.

The `bean` tag is ultimately straightforward. What you want to be clear about is the difference between the use of the `var` attribute to create a named reference in the `ActionContext`, and the use of the opening and closing tags to work with the bean on the `ValueStack`. The real trick here is in understanding the `ValueStack`, `Action-Context`, and how OGNL gets to them. That's why we began this chapter with a thorough introduction to these concepts. If you're confused, you might want to refer back to those earlier sections.

With those fundamental concepts in place, the conventions of the `bean` tag, and other similar tags, should be straightforward enough. If you have all this straight, congratulate yourself on a mastery of what some consider to be the most Byzantine aspect of Struts 2.

6.3.5   *The action tag*

This tag allows us to invoke another action from our view layer. Use cases for this might not be obvious at first, but you'll probably find yourself wanting to invoke secondary actions from the result at some point. Such scenarios might range from integrating existing action components to wisely refactoring some action logic. The practical application of the `action` tag is simple: you specify another action that should be invoked. Some of the most important attributes of this tag include the `executeResult` attribute, which allows you to indicate whether the result for the secondary action should be written into the currently rendering page, and the `name` and `namespace` attributes, by which you identify the secondary action that should fire. By default, the namespace of the current action is used. Table 6.6 contains the details of the important attributes.

Table 6.6   `action` tag attributes

Attribute	Required	Type	Description
name	Yes	String	The action name
namespace	No	String	The action namespace; defaults to the current page namespace
var	No	String	Reference name of the action bean for use later in the page
executeResult	No	Boolean	When set to true, executes the result of the action (default value: false)

Table 6.6 `action` **tag attributes** *(continued)*

Attribute	Required	Type	Description
`flush`	No	`Boolean`	When set to true, the writer will be flushed upon end of action component tag (default value: true)
`ignoreContextParams`	No	`Boolean`	When set to true, the request parameters are not included when the action is invoked (default value: false)

Here's an example that chooses to include the secondary action's result:

```
<h3>Action Tag</h3>
<h4>This line is from the ActionTag action's result.</h4>
<s:action name="TargetAction" executeResult="true"/>
```

Note that the default is to not include the result, so we have to change this by setting the executeResult attribute to true. The output looks like figure 6.7.

One thing to note is that the result of the secondary action should probably be an HTML fragment if you want it to fit into the primary page.

Often, you might want the secondary action to fire, but not write a result. One common scenario is that the secondary action, instead of writing to the page, will produce side effects by stashing domain data somewhere in the ActionContext. After control returns, the primary action can access that data. The following markup shows how to target an action in this fashion:

```
<h4>This line is before the ActionTag invokes the secondary action.</h4>
<s:action name="TargetAction"/>
<h4>Secondary action has fired now.</h4>
<h5>Request attribute set by secondary action = </h5>
<pre> <s:property value="#request.dataFromSecondAction"/></pre>
```

The execution of the secondary action is a bit of a side effect unless we reach back to get something that it produced. We retrieve a property that was set by the secondary action into the request map, just to prove that the secondary action fired. You can check the output yourself by visiting the chapter 6 sample code. Many times, however, a side effect may be just what you want. Note also that the secondary action can receive, or not receive, the request parameters from the primary request, according to the ignoreContextParams attribute.

That finishes up our coverage of data tags. In the next section, we'll show how to introduce conditional logic to your page rendering with the control tags.

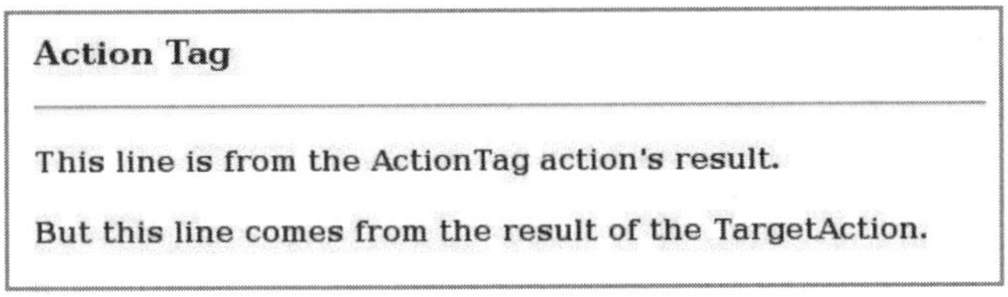

Action Tag

This line is from the ActionTag action's result.

But this line comes from the result of the TargetAction.

Figure 6.7 Using the `action` **tag to invoke another action from the context of a rendering page**

6.4   *Control tags*

Since most web pages are built on the fly, it's going to be valuable to learn how to manipulate, navigate over, and display data. Struts 2 has a set of tags that make it easy to control the flow of page execution. Using the `iterator` tag to loop over data and the `if/else/elseif` tags to make decisions, you can leverage the power of conditional rendering in your pages.

6.4.1   *The iterator tag*

Other than the `property` tag, the other most commonly used tag in Struts 2 is the `iterator` tag. The `iterator` tag allows you to loop over collections of objects easily. It's designed to know how to loop over any `Collection`, `Map`, `Enumeration`, `Iterator`, or array. It also provides the ability to define a variable in the `ActionContext`, the iterator status, that lets you determine certain basic information about the current loop state, such as whether you're looping over an odd or even row. Table 6.7 provides the attributes for the `iterator` tag.

Table 6.7   `iterator` **tag attributes**

Attribute	Required	Type	Description
`value`	Yes	`Object`	The object to be looped over.
`status`	No	`String`	If specified, an `IteratorStatus` object is placed in the action context under the name given as the value of this attribute.

We already saw the `iterator` tag in action when we looked at the `bean` tag. Now we'll take a closer look. The chapter 6 sample application includes an example that loops over a set of the `Users` of the Struts 2 Portfolio. Here's the markup from the result page:

```
<s:iterator value="users" status="itStatus">
  <li>
  <s:property value="#itStatus.count" />
  <s:property value="portfolioName"/>
  </li>
</s:iterator>
```

As you can see, it's straightforward. The action object exposes a set of users and the `iterator` tag iterates over those users. During the body of the tag, each user is in turn placed on the top of the `ValueStack`, thus allowing for convenient access to the user's properties. Note that our iterator also declares an `IteratorStatus` object by specifying the `status` attribute. Whatever name you give this attribute will be the key for retrieving the iterator status object from the `ActionContext`, with an OGNL expression such as `#itStatus`. In this example, we use the iterator status's `count` property to get a sequential list of our users. The output is shown in figure 6.8.

Existing User Portfolios:
- 1 Chad's Portfolio
- 2 Mary's Portfolio

Figure 6.8   Iterating over a set of data during page rendering

We should probably take a minute to see what else the `IteratorStatus` can provide for us.

USING ITERATORSTATUS

Sometimes it's desirable to know status information about the iteration that's taking place. This is where the `status` attribute steps in. The `status` attribute, when defined, provides an `IteratorStatus` object available in the `ActionContext` that can provide simple information such as the `size`, current index, and whether the current object is in the even or odd index in the list. The `IteratorStatus` object can be accessed through the name given to the `status` attribute. Table 6.8 summarizes the information that can be obtained from the `IteratorStatus` object.

As you can see, this list provides just the kind of data that can sometimes be hard to come by when trying to produce various effects within JSP page iterations. Happy iterating!

Table 6.8 Public methods of `IteratorStatus`

Method name	Return type
getCount	int
getIndex	int
isEven	boolean
isFirst	boolean
isLast	boolean
isOdd	boolean
modulus(int operand)	int

6.4.2 *The if and else tags*

Not many languages, of any sort, fail to provide the familiar `if` and `else` control logic. The `if` and `else` tags provide these familiar friends for the Struts 2 developer. Using them is as easy as you might suspect. As you can see in table 6.9, there's just one attribute, a Boolean `test`.

Table 6.9 `if` and `elseif` tag attribute

Attribute	Required	Type	Description
test	Yes	Boolean	Boolean expression that is evaluated and tested for true or false

Here's an example of using them. You can put any OGNL expression you like in the test.

```
<s:if test="user.age > 35">This user is too old.</s:if>
<s:elseif test="user.age < 35">This user is too young</s:elseif>
<s:else>This user is just right</s:else>
```

Here we conduct a couple of tests on a user object exposed by our action and, ultimately, found on the `ValueStack`. The tests are simple Boolean expressions; you can chain as many of the tests as you like.

That was easy enough. Indeed, the `if` and `else` tags are as simple as they seem, and remain that way in use. We still have a few useful tags to cover, and we'll hit them in the next section, which covers miscellaneous tags.

6.5   *Miscellaneous tags*

As we mentioned at the start of this chapter, Struts 2 includes a few different types of tags. You've already seen how the data tags and control tags work. Let's now look at the miscellaneous tags that, although useful, can't be easily classified. In this section, we'll discuss the Struts 2 `include` tag (a slight variation on the `<jsp:include>` tag), the `URL` tag, and the `i18n` and `text` tags (both used for internationalization). Finally, we'll take another look at the `param` tag, which you've already seen in the context of the `bean` tag, and show how it can be used to its full power.

6.5.1   *The include tag*

Whereas JSP has its own include tag, `<jsp:include>`, Struts 2 provides a version that integrates with Struts 2 better and provides more advanced features. In short, this tag allows you to execute a Servlet API–style include. This means you can include the output of another web resource in the currently rendering page. One good thing about the Struts 2 `include` tag is that it allows you to pass along request parameters to the included resource.

This differs from the previously seen `action` tag, in that the `include` tag can reference any servlet resource, while the `action` tag can include only another Struts 2 action within the same Struts 2 application. This inclusion of an action stays completely within the Struts 2 architecture. The `include` tag can go outside of the Struts 2 architecture to retrieve any resource available to the web application in which the Struts 2 application is deployed. This generally means grabbing other servlets or JSPs. The `include` tag may not make a lot of sense unless you're pretty familiar with the Servlet API. Again, the Servlet Specification is recommended reading: http://java.sun.com/products/servlet/download.html.

Table 6.10 lists the sole attribute for the `include` tag.

Table 6.10   `include` tag attribute

Attribute	Required	Type	Description
value	Yes	String	Name of the page, action, servlet, or any referenceable URL

We won't show a specific example of the `include` tag, as its use is straightforward. When using the `include` tag, you should keep in mind that you're including a JSP, servlet, or other web resource directly. The semantics of including another web resource come from the Servlet API. The `include` tag behaves similarly to the JSP include tag. However, it's more useful when you're developing with Struts 2, for two reasons: it integrates better with the framework, and it provides native access to the `ValueStack` and a more extensible parameter model. What does all of this mean?

Let's start with the framework integration. For example, your tag can dynamically define the resource to be included by pulling a value from the `ValueStack` using the `%{ ... }` notation. (You have to force OGNL evaluation here, as the value attribute is of type `String` and would normally be interpreted as a string literal.) Similarly, you can pass in querystring parameters to the included page with the `<s:param>` tag (discussed in a moment). This tag can also pull values from the `ValueStack`. This tight integration with the framework makes the Struts 2 `include` tag a powerful choice.

Another advantage to choosing the Struts 2 `include` tag over the native JSP version is plain-old user-friendliness. For example, it'll automatically rewrite relative URLs for you. If you want to include the URL `../index.jsp`, you're free to do so even though some application servers don't support that type of URL when using the JSP include tag. The Struts 2 `include` tag will rewrite `../index.jsp` as an absolute URL based on the current URL where the JSP is located.

6.5.2   *The URL tag*

When you're building web applications, URL management is a central task. Struts 2 provides a `URL` tag to help you do this. The tag supports everything you might want to do with a URL, from controlling parameters to automatically persisting sessions in the absence of cookies. Table 6.11 lists its attributes.

Table 6.11   `URL` tag attributes

Attribute	Required	Type	Description
`Value`	No	String	The base URL; defaults to the current URL the page is rendering from.
`action`	No	String	The name of an action to target with the generated URL; use the action name as configured in the declarative architecture (without the .action extension).
`var`	No	String	If specified, the URL isn't written out but rather is saved in the action context for future use.
`includeParams`	No	String	Selects parameters from `all`, `get`, or `none`; default is `get`.
`includeContext`	No	Boolean	If true, then the URL that is generated will be prepended with the application's context; default is `true`.
`encode`	No	Boolean	Adds the session ID to the URL if cookies aren't enabled for the visitor.
`scheme`	No	String	Allows you to specify the protocol; defaults to the current scheme (HTTP or HTTPS).

Here are a couple of examples. First we look at a simple case:

```
URL =   <s:url value="IteratorTag.action"/>

<a href='<s:url value="IteratorTag.action" />'> Click Me </a>
```

And here's the output markup:

```
URL = IteratorTag.action

<a href='IteratorTag.action'> Click Me </a>
```

The URL tag just outputs the generated URL as a string. First we display it for reference. Then we use the same markup to generate the href attribute of a standard anchor tag. Note that we set the target of the URL with the value attribute. This means we must include the .action extension ourselves. If we want to target an action, we should probably use the action attribute, as seen in the next example:

```
URL =     <s:url action="IteratorTag" var="myUrl">
            <s:param name="id" value="2"/>
          </s:url>
          <a href='<s:property value="#myUrl" />'> Click Me </a>
```

Now, let's see the markup generated by these tags:

```
URL =

<a href='/manningHelloWorld/chapterSix/IteratorTag.action?id=2'>
  Click Me
</a>
```

As you can see, the URL tag didn't generate any output in this example. This happened because we used the var attribute to assign the generated URL string to a reference in the ActionContext. This helps improve the readability of the code. In this example, our URL tag, with its param tags, has become unwieldy to embed directly in the anchor tag. Now we can just pull the URL from the ActionContext with a property tag and some OGNL. This is also useful when we need to put the URL in more than one place on the page.

The param tag used in this example specifies querystring parameters to be added to the generated URL. You can see generated querystring in the output. Note that you can use the includeParams attribute to specify whether parameters from the current request are carried over into the new URL. By default this attribute is set to get, which means only querystring params are carried over. You can also set it to post, which causes the posted form parameters to also be carried over. Or you can specify none.

6.5.3   *The i18n and text tags*

Many applications need to work in multiple languages. The process of making this happen is called *internationalization,* or *i18n* for short. (There are 18 letters between the I and the N in the word internationalization.) Chapter 11 discusses Struts 2's internationalization support in detail, but we'd like to take a moment to detail the two tags that are central to this functionality: the i18n tag and the text tag.

The text tag is used to display language-specific text, such as English or Spanish, based on a key lookup into a set of text resources. This tag retrieves a message value from the ResourceBundles exposed through the framework's own internationalization mechanisms. We'll explain this in greater detail in chapter 11. For now, we'll just note the usage of the tag; it takes a name attribute that specifies the key under which the message retrieval should occur. The framework's default Locale determination will determine the Locale under which the key will be resolved. Consult chapter 11 for full details on where to place properties files to make their resources available to this tag.

Table 6.12 lists the attributes that the text tag supports.

Table 6.12 text tag attributes

Attribute	Required	Type	Description
name	Yes	String	The key to look up in the ResourceBundle(s).
var	No	String	If specified, the text is stored in the action context under this name.

You can also name an ad hoc ResourceBundle for resolving your text tags. If you want to manually specify the ResourceBundle that should be used, you can use the i18n tag. Table 6.13 lists the attributes of the i18n tag.

Table 6.13 i18n tag attribute

Attribute	Required	Type	Description
name	Yes	String	The name of the ResourceBundle

Here's a quick example that shows how to set the ResourceBundle with the i18n tag and then extract a message text from it with the text tag:

```
<s:i18n name="manning.chapterSix.myResourceBundle_tr">

  In <s:text name="language"/>,
  <s:text name="girl" var="foreignWord"/>

</s:i18n>

"<s:property value="#foreignWord"/>" means girl.
```

Figure 6.9 shows the output.

The i18n tag simply specifies a resource bundle to use. The bundle is only used during the body of the tag. However, as our example demonstrates, you can "persist" a message from the bundle using the text tag's var attribute to set the message to the ActionContext as a named reference. This usage of the var attribute should be more familiar by now. The first text tag writes the message associated with

> Internationalization Tags
>
> In Turkish, "kiz" means girl.

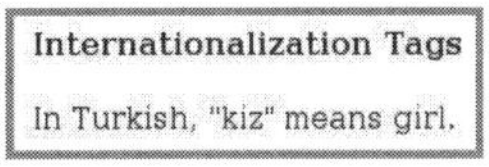

Figure 6.9 Using internationalization tags to pull text from ResourceBundles

the key "language" directly to the output. The second text tag stores the message associated with the key "girl" under the reference name "foreignWord".

These tags are simple, but seem out of context without full knowledge of the built-in internationalization features of Struts 2. In particular, you'll need to know how the framework locates, loads, and uses properties file ResourceBundles. We'll cover this in detail in chapter 11.

6.5.4   *The param tag*

The last tag we'll discuss has already been used throughout this chapter. The param tag does nothing by itself, but at the same time it's one of the more important tags. It not only serves an important role in using many of the tags covered in this chapter, it'll also play a role in many of the UI component tags, as you'll see in chapter 7. Table 6.14 lists the attributes you're now familiar with.

Table 6.14   param tag attributes

Attribute	Required	Type	Description
name	No	String	The name of the parameter
value	No	Object	The value of the parameter

Using the param tag has already been established in this chapter. In particular, our coverage of the bean tag showed a couple of use cases for the param tag, including as a means for passing parameters into your own custom utility objects. As long as you have the general idea, it's just a matter of perusing the APIs to see which tags can take parameters. Toward this end, it's always a good idea to consult the online documentation of the Struts 2 tags to see if a given tag can take a parameter of some sort. For one, this book doesn't attempt to be exhaustive in its coverage of the tags. Additionally, the tag API is always being improved and expanded. Struts 2 is a new framework and growth is rapid.

That's all of the general-use Struts 2 tags that we'll cover. Chapter 7 will cover the UI component tags, which allow you to quickly develop rich user interfaces in your pages. Before that, we'll touch on a couple of advanced topics that pertain to tag usage. First, we'll comment on the use of native tags from the various view technologies. After that, we'll provide a short OGNL expression language primer to empower your tag usage.

6.6   *Using JSTL and other native tags*

What if you want to use the native tags and expression languages of your chosen view-layer technology? That's fine, too. While the Struts 2 tags provide a high-level tag API that can be used across all three view technologies that the framework supports out of the box, you can use the tags and macros provided natively by each of those technologies if you wish. The JSTL, for instance, is still available in your JSP pages. We don't cover the JSTL in this book and assume that, if you have enough reason to use JSTL instead of the built-in Struts 2 tags, you probably already know quite a bit about the JSTL. We'll just note that the result types that prepare the environment for JSP, Velocity, and FreeMarker rendering do make the ValueStack and other key Struts 2 data objects available to the native tags of each technology. Bear in mind that the exposure of the Struts 2 objects to those native tags and ELs may not be consistent, due to the differences between those technologies.

Next up, the OGNL expression language details we've been promising for oh, so long.

6.7   *A brief primer for the OGNL expression language*

Throughout Struts 2 web applications, a need exists to link the Java runtime with the text-based world of HTML, HTTP, JSP, and other text-based view-rendering technologies. There must be a way for these text-based documents to reference runtime data objects in the Java environment. A common solution to this problem is the use of expression languages. As we've seen, Struts 2 uses OGNL for this purpose. We'll now take the opportunity to cover the features of this expression language that you'll most likely need to use in Struts 2 development.

Before we get too far, we should point out that this section could easily be skipped. For most use cases, you've probably already learned enough OGNL expression language to get by. You could treat this section as a rainy-day reference if you like. On the other hand, you'll probably find some stuff you can use immediately. It's your choice.

6.7.1   *What is OGNL?*

The Object-Graph Navigation Language exists as a mature technology completely distinct from Struts 2. As such, it has purposes and features much larger than its use within Struts 2. OGNL is an expression and binding language. In Struts 2, we use the OGNL expression language to reference data properties in the Java environment, and we use OGNL type converters to manage the type conversion between HTTP string values and the typed Java values.

In this last section, we'll try to summarize the syntax and some of the more useful features of the OGNL expression language. First we'll cover the syntax and features most commonly used in Struts 2 development. Then we'll cover some of the other OGNL features that you might find handy. OGNL has many of the features of a full programming language, so you'll find that most everything is possible. Also note that this section doesn't try to be a complete reference to OGNL. If you want more OGNL power, visit the website at www.ognl.org for more information.

WARNING   Keep those JSPs clean! While OGNL has much of the power of a full-featured language, you might want to think twice before squeezing the trigger. It's a well-established best practice that you should keep business logic out of your pages. If you find yourself reaching for the OGNL power tools, you might well be pulling business logic into your view layer. We're not saying you can't do it, but we recommend giving it a moment's thought before complicating your view pages with too much code-style logic. If you're getting complex in your OGNL, ask yourself if what you're doing should be done in the action or, at least, encapsulated in a helper bean that you can use in your page.

6.7.2   *Expression language features commonly used in Struts 2*

First, we should review the most common uses of the OGNL expression language in Struts 2 development. In this section, we'll look at how the expression language serves its purpose for most daily development. Basically, we use it to map the incoming data onto your `ValueStack` objects, and we use it in tags to pull the data off of the `ValueStack` while rendering the view. Let's look at the expression language features most commonly used in this work.

REFERENCING BEAN PROPERTIES

First of all, we need to define what makes an expression. The OGNL expression language refers to something called a *chain of properties*. This concept is simple. Take the following expression:

```
person.father.father.firstName
```

This property chain consists of a chain of four properties. We can say that this chain references, or targets, the `firstName` property of `person`'s grandfather. You can use this same reference both for setting and getting the value of this property, depending on your context.

SETTING OR GETTING?

When we use OGNL expressions to name our form input parameters, we're referring to a property that we'd like to have set for us. The following code snippet shows the form from our Struts 2 Portfolio application's Registration.jsp page:

```
<s:form action="Register">
  <s:textfield name="username" label="Username"/>
  <s:password name="password" label="Password"/>
  <s:textfield name="portfolioName" label="Enter a portfolio name."/>
  <s:submit/>
</s:form>
```

The name of each input field is an OGNL expression. These expressions refer to, for example, the `username` property exposed on the root OGNL object. As we've just learned, the root object is our `ValueStack`, which probably contains our action object and perhaps a model object. When the `params` interceptor fires, it'll take this expression and use it to locate the property onto which it should set the value associated with this name. It'll also use the OGNL type converters to convert the value from a string to the native type of the target property.

There is one common complication that arises when the framework moves data onto the properties targeted by the OGNL expressions. Take the deeper expression:

```
user.portfolio.name
```

If a request parameter targets this property, its value will be moved onto the `name` property of the `portfolio` object. One problem that can occur during runtime is a `null` value for one of the intermediate properties in the expression chain. For instance, what if the user hasn't been created yet? If you recall, we've been omitting initialization for many of our properties in our sample code. Luckily, the framework handles this.

When the framework finds a `null` property in a chain that it needs to navigate, it'll attempt to create a new instance of the appropriate type and set it onto the property. However, this requires two things on the developer's part. First, the type of the property must be a class that conforms to the JavaBeans specification, in that it provides a no-argument constructor. Without this, the framework can't instantiate an object of the type. Next, the property must also conform to the JavaBeans specification by providing a setter method. Without this setter, the framework would have no way of injecting the new object into the property. Keep these two points in mind and you'll be good to go.

In addition to targeting properties onto which the framework should move incoming data, we also use OGNL when the data leaves the framework. After the request is processed, we use the same OGNL expression to target the same property from a Struts 2 tag. Recall that the domain model data stays on the `ValueStack` from start to finish. Thus, tags can read from the same location that the interceptors write. The following snippet from the RegistrationSuccess.jsp page shows the property tag doing just this:

```
<h5>Congratulations! You have created </h5>
<h3>The <s:property value="portfolioName" /> Portfolio</h3>
```

In this snippet, we see that the Struts 2 property tag takes an OGNL expression as its `value` attribute. This expression targets the property from which the `property` tag will pull the data for its rendering process, a simple process where it merely converts the property to a string and writes it into the page.

As you can see, OGNL expressions, as commonly used in Struts 2, serve as pointers to properties. Whether the use case is writing to or reading from that property is up to the context. Though not nearly as common, you can also use the fuller features of the OGNL expression language, operators in particular, to write self-contained expressions that, for instance, set the data on a property themselves. But, as this is outside of the normal Struts 2 use case, we'll only discuss such features in the advanced section.

WORKING WITH JAVA COLLECTIONS

Java `Collections` are a mainstay of the Java web developer's daily workload. While the JavaBeans specification has always supported indexed properties, working with actual Java `Collections`, while convenient in the Java side, has always been a hassle in contexts such as JSP tags. One of the great things about the OGNL expression language is its simplified handling of `Collections`. We've already seen this in action when we demonstrated the automatic type conversion to and from complex `Collection` properties in the previous chapter. We'll now summarize the OGNL syntax used to reference these properties.

WORKING WITH LISTS AND ARRAYS

References to lists and arrays share the same syntax in OGNL. Table 6.15 summarizes the basic syntax to access list or array properties. To see these in action, refer back to the code samples from chapter 5 that demonstrated type conversion to and from lists and arrays.

As table 6.15 demonstrates, the syntax for referencing elements or properties of lists and arrays is intuitive. Basically, OGNL uses array index syntax for both. This makes perfect sense, due to the ordered, indexed nature of lists.

Table 6.15   OGNL expression language syntax for referencing elements of array and list properties

Java code	OGNL expression
`list.get(0)`	`list[0]`
`array[0]`	`array[0]`
`((User) list.get(0) ).getName()`	`list[0].name`
`array.length`	`array.length`
`list.size()`	`list.size`
`list.isEmpty()`	`list.isEmpty`

A couple of things warrant remarks. First, the reference to the `name` property of a list element assumes something important. As we know, Java `List`s are type-agnostic. In Java, we always have to cast the element to the appropriate type, in this case `User`, before we try to reference the `name` property. We can omit this in OGNL if we take the time to specify the `Collection` element type as we learned earlier in this chapter. This syntax assumes that has been done. We should also note that you can reference other properties, such as `length` and `size`, of arrays and lists. In particular, note that OGNL makes the `List` class's non-JavaBeans-conformant `size` method answer to a simple property reference. This is something nice that OGNL provides as free service to its valued customers!

OGNL also allows you to create `List` literals. This can be useful if you want to directly create a set of values to feed to something like a select box. Table 6.16 shows the syntax for creating these literals.

Table 6.16   Creating a list dynamically in OGNL

Java code	OGNL expression

`List list = new ArrayList(3);`
`list.add(new Integer(1) );`
`list.add(new Integer(3) );`
`list.add(new Integer(5) );`
`return list;`
	`{1,3,5}`

You probably only want to do this with trivial data, since creating complex data in the view layer would make a mess. Nonetheless, sometimes this will be the perfect tool for the job.

WORKING WITH MAPS

OGNL also makes referencing properties and elements of maps delightfully simple. Table 6.17 shows a variety of syntax idioms for referencing `Map` elements and properties.

Table 6.17 OGNL expression language syntax for referencing map properties

Java code	OGNL expression
`map.get("foo")`	`map['foo']`
`map.get( new Integer( 1) )`	`map[1]`
`User user = (User)map.get("userA");` `return user.getName();`	`map['userA'].name`
`map.size()`	`map.size`
`map.isEmpty()`	`map.isEmpty`
`map.get("foo")`	`map.foo`

As you can see, you can do a lot with maps. The main difference here is that, unlike `Lists`, the value in the index box must be an object. If the value in the box is some sort of numeric data that would map to a Java primitive, such as an `int`, then OGNL automatically converts that to an appropriate wrapper type object, such as an `Integer`, to use as the key. If a string literal is placed in the box, that becomes a string object which will be used for the key. The last row in the table shows a special syntax for maps with strings as keys. If the key is a string, you may use this simpler, JavaBeans-style property notation.

As for other object types that you might use as a key, you ultimately have the full power of OGNL to reference objects that might serve as the key. The possibilities are beyond the capacity of the table format. Note that, as with the `List` syntax, the direct reference to the `name` property on the uncast map element depends on the configuration of the OGNL type conversion to know the specific element type of the map, as we learned in chapter 6.

You can also create `Maps` on the fly with the OGNL literal syntax. Table 6.18 demonstrates this flexible feature.

Table 6.18 Creating maps dynamically in OGNL

Java code	OGNL expression

`Map map = new HashMap(2);`
`map.put("foo", "bar");`
`map.put("baz", "whazzit");`
`return map;`
	`#{ "foo" : "bar","baz" : "whazzit" }`

`Map map = new HashMap(3);`
`map.put(new Integer(1), "one");`
`map.put(new Integer(2), "two");`
`map.put(new Integer(3), "three");`
`return map;`
	`#{ 1 : "one",2 : "two", 3 : "three" }`

As you can see, the syntax for creating a `Map` literal is similar to that for creating a `List` literal. The main difference is the use of the # sign before the leading brace.

WARNING   OGNL uses the # sign in a few different ways. Each is distinct. The uses are completely orthogonal, so you shouldn't be confused as long as you're alert to the fact that they're different use cases. In particular, this isn't the same use of the # sign as we saw when specifying a nonroot object from the `ActionContext` for an expression to resolve against. We'll also see another use of the # sign in a few moments.

Dynamic maps are especially useful for radio groups and select tags. The Struts 2 tag libraries come with special tags for creating user interface components. These will be explored in chapter 7 . For now, just note that you can use literal maps to feed values into some of the UI components. If you wanted to offer a true/false selection that displays as a Yes/No choice, `#{true : 'Yes', false : 'No'}` would be the value for the `list` attribute. The value for the `value` attribute would evaluate to either true or false.

FILTERING AND PROJECTING COLLECTIONS

OGNL supports a couple of special operations that you can conduct on your collections. Filtering allows you to take a collection of objects and filter them according to some rule. For instance, you could take a set of users and filter them down to only those who're more than 20 years old. Projection, on the other hand, allows you to transform a collection of objects according to some rule. For instance, you could take a set of user objects, having both first and last name properties, and transform it into a set of `String` objects that combines the first and last name of each user into a single string. To clarify, filtering takes a `Collection` of size N and produces a new collection containing a subset of those elements ranging from size 0 to size N. On the other hand, projecting always produces a `Collection` with exactly the same number of elements as the original `Collection`; projecting produces a one-for-one result set.

The syntax for filtering is as follows:

```
collectionName.{? expression }
```

In the expression, you can use `#this` to refer to the object from the collection being evaluated. This is another distinct use of the # sign. The syntax for projection is as follows:

```
collectionName.{ expression }
```

Table 6.19 shows some examples of both of these useful operations in action.

Table 6.19   Producing new collections by filtering or projecting existing collections

OGNL expression	Description
`users.{?#this.age > 30}`	A filtering process that returns a new collection with only users who are older than 30
`users.{username}`	A projection process that returns a new collection of username strings, one for each user

Table 6.19 Producing new collections by filtering or projecting existing collections *(continued)*

OGNL expression	Description
`users.{firstName + ' ' + lastName}`	A projection process that returns a new collection of strings that represent the full name of each user
`users.{?#this.age > 30}.{username}`	A projection process that returns the usernames of a filtered collection of users older than 30

As you can see, each filtering or projection simply returns a new collection for your use. This convenient notation can be used to get the most out of a single set of data. Note that you can combine filtering and projection operations. That about covers it for aspects of OGNL that are commonly used in Struts 2. In the next section, we'll cover some of the advanced features that might help you out in a pinch, but, still, we recommend keeping it simple unless you have no choice.

6.7.3 *Advanced expression language features*

As we've indicated, OGNL is a full-featured expression language. In fact, its features rival that of some full-fledged programming languages. In this section, we give a brief summary of some of the advanced features that you might use in a pinch. Some of these things are basic features of OGNL, but advanced in the context of Struts 2 usage. Take our terminology with a grain of salt. Also, we'll make little effort to introduce use cases for these features. We consider their usage to be nonstandard practice. With that said, we also know that these power tools can save the day on those certain occasions that always seem to occur.

Table 6.20 Literals of the OGNL expression language

Literal type	Example
Char	`'a'`
String	`'hello'`
`"hello"`	Boolean
True	False
int	123
double	123.5
BigDecimal	123b
BigInteger	123h

LITERALS AND OPERATORS

Like most languages, the OGNL expression language supports a wide array of literals. Table 6.20 summarizes these literals.

The only thing out of the ordinary would be the usage of both single and double quotes for string literals. Note, however, that a string literal of a single character must use double quotes, or it'll be interpreted as a char literal. Table 6.21 shows the operators.

Table 6.21 Operators of the OGNL expression language

Operation	Example
add (+)	2 + 4 'hello' + 'world'
subtract (-)	5 - 3

Table 6.21   Operators of the OGNL expression language *(continued)*

Operation	Example
multiply (*)	8 * 2
divide (/)	9/3
modulus (%)	9 % 3
increment (++)	++foo foo++
decrement (--)	bar-- --bar
equality (==)	foo == bar
less than (<)	1 < 2
greater than (>)	2 > 1

As you can see, all the usual suspects are here. This would probably be a good time to note that the OGNL expression language also allows multiple comma-separated expressions to be linked in a single expression. The following snippet demonstrates this process:

```
user.age = 10, user.name = "chad", user.username
```

This relatively meaningless example demonstrates an expression that links three sub-expressions. As with many languages, each of the first two expressions executes and passes control on to the next expression. The value returned by the last expression is the value returned for the entire expression. Now we'll see how to invoke methods with OGNL.

CALLING METHODS

One power that many a JSP developer has wished for is the ability to call methods from the expression language. Until recently, this was rare. Actually, even the simplest property reference involves a method call. But those simple property references can invoke methods based on JavaBeans conventions. If the method you want to invoke doesn't conform to JavaBeans conventions, you'll probably need the OGNL method invocation syntax to get to it. This can sometimes get you out of a jam. It can also be useful in calling utility methods on helper beans. Table 6.22 shows how it works.

Table 6.22   Calling methods from the OGNL expression language

Java code	OGNL expression
utilityBean.makeRandomNumber()	makeRandomNumber()
utilityBean.getRandomNumberSeed()	getRandomNumberSeed() randomNumberSeed

Note that in this table we assume that a random number generator bean, named `utilityBean`, has been pushed onto the `ValueStack` prior to the evaluation of these OGNL expressions. With this bean in place, you can omit the object name in the OGNL expression, because it resolves to the `ValueStack` by default. First, we invoke the `makeRandomNumber()` method as you might expect. In the second example, we show that you can even use a full method invocation syntax to access JavaBeans properties, though you don't have to. The result is no different than when using the simpler property notation.

We should note that these method invocation features of the OGNL expression language are turned off during the incoming phase of Struts 2 data transfer. In other words, when the form input field names are evaluated by the `params` interceptor, method invocations, as well as some other security-compromising features of the expression language, are completely ignored. Basically, when the `params` interceptor evaluates OGNL expressions, it'll only allow them to point to properties onto which it should inject the parameter values. Nothing else is permitted.

ACCESSING STATIC METHODS AND FIELDS

In addition to accessing instance methods and properties, you can also access static methods and fields with the OGNL expression language. There are two ways of doing this. One requires specifying the fully qualified class name, while the other method resolves against the `ValueStack`. The syntax that takes the full class name is `@[fullClassName]@[property or methodCall]`. Here are examples of using full class names to access both a static property and a static method:

```
@manning.utils.Struts2PortfolioConstants@USER
@manning.utils.PortfolioUtilityBean@startImageWrapper()
```

Besides the @ signs, these are no different than normal property specification or method invocation. As we said, you can forgo specifying the class name if and only if your property or method will resolve on the `ValueStack`. Here we have the same two examples, but they assume that some object on the `ValueStack` exposes what they need. The syntax replaces the class name with the vs symbol, which stands for `ValueStack`:

```
@vs@USER
@vs@startImageWrapper()
```

That wraps up our coverage of some of the advanced features of OGNL. You'll probably find yourself coming back to this quick reference in the future as you butt heads with some odd wall or two. Again, we recommend taking it easy on the OGNL power tools. However, we're compelled to tell you that OGNL contains even more powerful features than we've felt comfortable divulging. For the full details, we refer you directly to the primary OGNL documentation found at www.ognl.org.

6.8   *Summary*

Well, that was a long chapter. That should be about as long as they'll get in this book. I'm worn out from writing it. To be fair, a large portion of the chapter was filled up with reference material, screen shots, tables, and the like. Let's take a moment to consider the range of information that this chapter covered.

This chapter started by trying to clarify where data is kept during request processing. This key concept may be one of the most challenging parts of learning Struts 2. It's not really that complicated; it's just different than some frameworks you might've worked with in the past. As we noted, with the cleaned-up action component—it has no heavy parameter list on the `execute()` method signature—there's a strong need for a location where we can centralize all the data important to the execution of the action. This data makes up the context in which the action executes. Thus, the location where most of the important data resides is known as the `ActionContext`.

The `ActionContext` contains all kinds of important data, ranging from request-, session-, and application-scoped maps to the all-important `ValueStack` itself. We saw that we can access all these data items via the OGNL expression language. In particular, we learned that, by default, OGNL will resolve against the `ValueStack`, but we can also specify a different object from the `ActionContext` for our OGNL expressions by using the # operator to name our initial object. The `ValueStack`, in addition to being the default object for OGNL, is also distinguished by its special qualities. The most important quality of the `ValueStack` is that it presents a synthesis of the properties in the stack as if they were all properties on a single virtual object, with duplicate properties resolving to the instance of the property highest in the stack.

This section has introduced brand-new concepts for our Struts 1 friends. These new capabilities allow complex websites to be built easily. This might be a good time to reward you with a break. For many, understanding these data repositories can be the biggest hurdle in learning Struts 2.

With all that out of the way, we ran through the Struts 2 tag API at a gallop. The most important things to remember about the tag API are that it's implemented at a layer higher than the specifics of a given view-layer technology. Everything we've learned about using the specific tags, though we demoed them in JSPs, can easily be transferred to Velocity or FreeMarker. Just consult the syntactical changes we specified in this chapter and go. The APIs are all the same.

Actually, we've just started our tour of the Struts 2 tag API. This chapter covered the general-use tags. In chapter 7, we'll look at the UI component tags. These powerful tags will help us build rich user interfaces for our view layer. We're now deep into the view layer of the Struts 2 framework. In many ways, it's just getting interesting. Wait till you see how easy it is to make powerful forms with the Struts 2 UI tags.

UI component tags 7

In the previous chapter, we introduced the Struts 2 tag API. As we saw, this high-level API provides a common set of tag functionality that you can access from any of three view-layer technologies: JSPs, Velocity, and FreeMarker templates. Learn the tag API once, and you'll start using it everywhere. We saw tags that helped us pull data from the ValueStack, iterate over collections of data, and even control the flow of page rendering with conditional logic of various sorts. Now it's time to start building a user interface with a special set of tags known as the UI component tags.

UI components take some introduction. Each UI component is a functional unit with which the user can interact and enter data. At the heart of each Struts 2 UI component is an HTML form control, such as a text field or select box. But don't be mistaken: these components are much more than just tags that output an HTML input element. They are a higher-level component, of which the HTML element is only the browser manifestation. They integrate all areas of the framework,

167

from data transfer and validation to internationalization and look and feel. Some of these components even combine more than one HTML form element to build new functional units for your pages.

In addition to all their functional capacity, the UI components are built on a layered, mini-MVC architecture that isolates the HTML markup output of a given component into an underlying FreeMarker template. This empowers the developer to modify the components themselves simply by modifying these underlying templates. This flexibility can provide developers with a powerful tool for meeting the finicky demands of user-interface requirements while still leveraging the reusability of a component-based architecture. This chapter will familiarize you with the UI component architecture, as well as provide a hands-on tour of the various component tags and demonstrate their use with sample code from the Struts 2 Portfolio.

This chapter might seem long, but the UI components have a lot to offer, and much of this chapter's later parts are reference-oriented. You probably won't need to read about the more advanced UI components until you need to use them.

7.1   Why we need UI component tags

I used to say that I'd never be a front-end developer. All of those hackish browser workarounds and convoluted JavaScript tangles, a million different ways to solve common problems, a dozen ways to solve each eccentric browser-specific problem—this is no place for anyone with an inclination toward order. Now things are clearing up as browsers begin to reach a higher level of standards compliance. You can now count on a large share of browsers behaving as you'd expect most of the time.

But this increasing compliance to standards hasn't made life simpler. Instead of taking a moment to appreciate the calm, developers have taken advantage of the stabilizing front-end platform to pile on a whole new wave of front-end complexity. Each day, dynamic front ends, powered by Ajax and other rich-client technologies, get closer to becoming commonplace requirements. A new web application framework, such as Struts 2, would be in grave error if it didn't lay the architectural foundations for managing the increasing complexity of the front end. The Struts 2 UI components pull this off quite well. In this chapter, we'll see how.

7.1.1   More than just form elements

As most of the work of an HTML user interface is accomplished by forms and form elements, many of the UI component tags correlate to HTML elements. There's a Struts 2 UI component for all of the commonly used HTML form elements. Moving past this one-to-one relationship, the more complex UI components wrap a couple of HTML elements into a single unit to create a new form widget. If you like, you can think of the rendering of the corresponding HTML element(s) as the foundation of the UI component. But, ultimately, the UI components are more than the sum of their underlying HTML elements. The following list summarizes some of the things that a UI component can do for you:

- Generate HTML markup
- Bind HTML form fields to Java-side properties
- Tie into framework type conversion
- Tie into framework validation
- Tie into framework internationalization

In this section, we'll explain each of these functional roles. We'll start with generating the markup.

GENERATING THE HTML MARKUP

First of all, each UI component tag does indeed generate a wad of HTML markup. This markup defines the corresponding HTML element and frequently some additional layout markup. This is the simplest aspect of the component tags. For instance, the Struts 2 `textfield` tag creates an HTML text input element. To parameterize the output of the component, the Struts 2 tag exposes various attributes to the developer. Many of these attributes mirror those found on the HTML element itself, frequently in a one-to-one fashion. However, as is typical for Struts 2, you won't usually need to define many of the attributes by hand. Their values will be deduced by the framework based on convention and intelligent defaults. This makes your page code much cleaner, faster, and more reusable.

As a simple example, let's look at the Struts 2 `textfield` component. Consider the following Struts 2 `textfield` tag:

```
<s:textfield name="username" label="Username"/>
```

As you can see, the only attributes that we set are `name` and `label`, but the output, shown in the following snippet, deduces a lot of information from these two attributes:

```
<td class="tdLabel">
  <label for="Register_username" class="label">Username:</label>
</td>
<td>
  <input type="text" name="username" value="" id="Register_username"/>
</td>
```

First of all, don't be confused by the table markup. This is done by the XHTML theme, one of the themes you can choose to determine the layout style used when rendering the UI component. We'll cover it in detail in section 7.2. For now, it's enough to know that the XHTML theme uses a table to control the layout of form elements. It also adds some class attributes for CSS control, and it can even generate a simple default stylesheet for these styles, if you like. Later, when we cover themes, you'll see that you can choose other themes for rendering your tags, including a theme that will use pure CSS for form layout.

For now, let's not think about the layout. If we look at the HTML elements themselves, we can see that the `textfield` component tag produced two: a `label` and an `input`. As you'd expect, it generates the HTML input field, with `type` set to `text`. It also creates an `id` by concatenating the enclosing form's `name` with the input field's `name`; note that we haven't shown the enclosing form in this example. Since CSS and JavaScript both depend so heavily on the existence of ids, this has become a foundational feature of the component tags. Additionally, the textfield tag, following HTML best practices, creates a label element to be used for displaying the name of the field to the user.

While this markup generation eases your development, it's not enough to warrant the use of the term *component*. Don't get misled into equating the UI component with a tag that just generates the markup for an HTML element. The textfield tag does much more than create the markup shown.

WARNING   Don't freak out! Many developers start to twitch when we tell them that the UI component tags will generate the HTML markup for them. If you're getting jittery, just focus on your breathing and hear us out. The Struts 2 UI component tags were carefully designed as a mini-MVC UI component framework of their own. The HTML view of each component is isolated into a single FreeMarker template that can easily be edited. Thus, you can tweak the Struts 2 UI components to generate HTML that meets your own idiosyncratic requirements. Now, rather than being a one-off hack, your quirky HTML will be a quirky component. You will, if you like, be able to share your quirky markup across many pages and projects.

You probably expected that the component tags would generate the markup for the corresponding HTML elements. We'll now move on to the other services provided by the UI components that integrate them with the whole framework and truly set them apart.

BINDING FORM FIELDS TO VALUESTACK PROPERTIES

Creating the HTML elements is just the beginning. Once the HTML elements are in place, the UI components wire these elements into all the rich functionality of the Struts 2 framework. For starters, they bind the form input fields to the properties on the ValueStack. This binding lays the foundation for a bidirectional flow of data between UI components and the domain model objects on the ValueStack. We've already explored this in some depth, but we'll now reiterate the role that the UI components play in this.

When you're looking at a form generated by Struts 2 UI component tags, the form fields you see are tied to the back-end Java properties in two directions. First, ValueStack data can flow into your form for prepopulation, if you desire. Then, when the form is posted, the data from those form fields will flow back into the framework and be automatically transferred onto the ValueStack. When we covered actions in chapter 3, we discussed the incoming data at length. We'll now go through an example to show how the full binding of UI components to the ValueStack also works in the outgoing mode to power easy prepopulation of your forms.

As we've already learned, the name of a UI component is what binds the component to a ValueStack property. The name, as it's interpreted as an OGNL expression, is used to locate a property on the stack. During rendering, a UI component will pull the value from the stack, if it exists, to prepopulate the form. On submission, that same name will be used to locate the target of the framework's automatic data transfer. Let's look at an example of how this works.

In order to show both the form pre-population and submission phases, we've added an Update Account feature to the Struts 2 Portfolio application. Go to the chapter 7 section of the sample application and log in to an account. From there, choose to update your account details. When you do, you'll be presented with an account update form that's prepopulated with your existing account details, shown in figure 7.1.

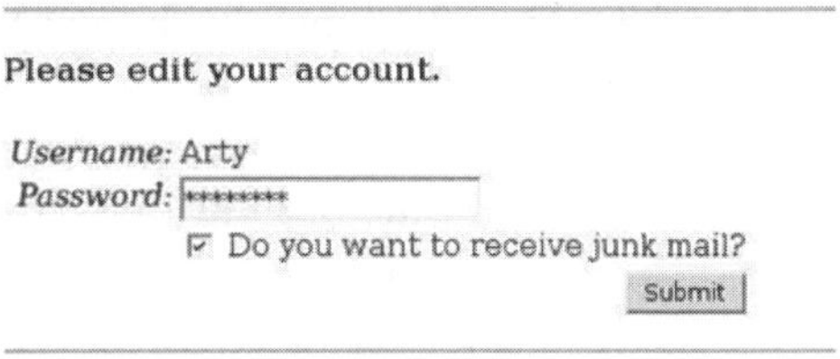

Please edit your account.

Username: Arty
Password: ********
☑ Do you want to receive junk mail?
Submit

Figure 7.1 The account form is prepopulated with data from properties on the `ValueStack`.

As you can see, the form has been prepopulated. Clearly, the UI components have already been bound to Java-side properties. Before we edit anything, let's look at how we've built the actions and JSP result pages to drive this account update example.

First of all, we've broken the process of updating the account into two actions. The first action retrieves the current account data and builds a prepopulated form. The second action, which the form will submit to, will accept the revised account information, validate it, and persist it. The use of two actions is perhaps inelegant, but it serves as a better illustration of the prepopulation and submission phases of the component. In chapter 15, we explore a common technique of combining these phases into a single action that can handle all aspects of data manipulation for a given data object, a.k.a. the Create-Read-Update-Delete (CRUD) action.

The first action, `UpdateAccountForm`, will build a prepopulated form. All this action needs to do is expose the appropriate `User` object. We'll do this by exposing the `User` object as a domain model object, à la `ModelDriven` actions. Listing 7.1 shows the `UpdateAccountForm` action in full.

Listing 7.1 The `UpdateAccountForm` exposes a `User` to prepopulate the form

```
public class UpdateAccountForm extends ActionSupport
  implements UserAware, ModelDriven {           ❶

  public String execute(){          ❷
    return SUCCESS;
  }

  private User user;

  public void setUser(User user) {         ❸
    this.user = user;
  }

  public Object getModel() {    ❹
    return user;
  }
}
```

This action implements the `UserAware` interface ❶, developed in conjunction with the `AuthenticationInterceptor` we built in chapter 4, to receive an injection of the current `User` object into a setter method ❸. This action is in the secure package that has that interceptor in its stack. This is great, because it saves the work of having to manually retrieve the `User` object that'll be used to prepopulate our form. We also implement the `ModelDriven` interface ❶, because we'll expose our `User` object as a domain model object rather than as a local JavaBeans property. This, in combination with the automatic injection of the `User` as described previously, allows us to use an extremely elegant syntax where we implement our `getModel()` to just return the already-injected user ❹.

Since all this action needs to do is retrieve and expose the `User` object for the purpose of form prepopulation, we're done! But we haven't even hit the `execute()` method yet! No problem; if we've made it this far, we can assume success ❷. Any problems would've been intercepted at the levels of data conversion or validation. What's our result?

As you would see if you consulted manning/chapterSeven/chapterSeven.xml, the `SUCCESS` result points to the UpdateAccountForm.jsp page. This page presents a prepopluated and editable form of user account information. This page contains the UI component tags that'll build our account update form. The essential markup from the UpdateAccountForm.jsp page is shown in the following snippet:

```
<s:form action="UpdateAccount">
  <s:textfield name="username" label="Username" readonly="true"/>      ❶
  <s:password name="password" label="Password"/>
  <s:textfield name="portfolioName" label="Enter a name."/>
  <s:submit/>
</s:form>
```

The most important aspect of these tags is the `name` attribute. The `name` attribute is what binds each component to the properties exposed on the `ValueStack`, thus allowing data from the current stack to flow into the form fields during the page rendering prepopulation stage, and also allowing data from this form's eventual submission to flow from that request onto the receiving action's `ValueStack` properties. This is what we mean when we say that a UI component binds the form field to Java-side properties on the `ValueStack`. And this works, ultimately, because the name of an input field is interpreted by the framework as an OGNL expression that ties everything together.

Since our `UpdateAccountForm` action exposes the `User` object via the `ModelDriven` interface's `getModel()` method, our `name` attribute OGNL can be simple, top-level references. For example, we can bind to the username of our model object with a simple username ❶. With this binding in place, this `textfield` component will pull the value off of the `ValueStack`'s username property, which is actually our user's username property, and use that value in the creation of the actual form field. In other words, it'll write that value into the input field's `value` attribute. The rest of the form components are handled similarly. Here's the resulting HTML source:

```
<input type="text" name="username" value="Arty" readonly="readonly"
    id="UpdateAccount_username"/>
```

```
<input type="password" name="password" id="UpdateAccount_password"/>

<input type="hidden" name="__checkbox_receiveJunkMail" value="true" />
```

Voilà, these are our prepopulated form fields. For ease of reading, we've stripped out all of the markup except the form input elements themselves. As you can see, the input elements have had their `value` attribute set with the data from the bound property on the `ValueStack`. Refer back to figure 7.1 to see how this looks on the page. As you can see, UI components, in addition to just generating the HTML element, make easy work of form prepopulation.

HEADS-UP   Though we've made it sound like the `name` attribute is responsible for the prepopulation, it's actually the `value` attribute at work. We've glossed over this a bit thanks to the intelligent default behavior of the framework. In truth, the UI components expose a `value` attribute, which takes an OGNL expression pointing to a Java property that should be used to fill in the value of the form field during prepopulation. You can do it this way if you like. However, since you'll almost always prepopulate from a property with the same name as the property that'll be the target of the posted data, the framework will simply propagate the `name` attribute's OGNL over to the `value` attribute. If ever need to prepopulate from a different property than you'll submit to, feel free to set the `value` attribute independently from the `name` attribute.

The other side of the UI component data binding is the incoming request parameters from the submitted form. We've spent a lot of time on that already, so we won't rehash how the automatic data transfer works. We'll summarize this section by noting that the UI component does indeed bind itself, via the `name` attribute as an OGNL expression, to both outgoing and incoming properties on the `ValueStack` to achieve both prepopulation of forms and automatic data transfer when a form is posted.

In addition to providing built-in binding to `ValueStack` properties, UI components also provide integration with several framework features, including type conversion, validation, and internationalization.

INTEGRATION WITH TYPE CONVERSION, VALIDATION, AND INTERNATIONALIZATION

We've already seen how the UI components can bind a form field to a property on the `ValueStack` to make the data flow effortlessly from the user interface to the back-end Java code. There are several other functions encapsulated in the UI components. In this section, we'll discuss how the components tie into the framework's type conversion, validation, and internationalization mechanisms.

For type conversion and validation, the UI components automatically handle error messages when there's a problem. As you've seen, problems with type conversion or validation cause the request to return the user back to the input form. When this happens, the UI components will automatically detect the presence of errors associated with themselves, and display error messages accordingly. You can customize these error messages and even tie them into the internationalization features to provide localized error messages to your users. For a full discussion of these functionalities, please consult chapters 5 and 10.

As we've indicated, UI components can tap into the internationalization mechanism to provide localized error messages. They can also tap into the internationalization to provide localized label names for your UI components. This feature uses the key attribute provided by all UI components. When using the key attribute, you can simplify your form field markup to a high level. You can set just this attribute and it'll pull a localized label from a framework ResourceBundle and intelligently deduce the name and value attributes to fully complete the component's bindings. This is fully explored in chapter 11.

Now that we've convinced you that the Struts 2 UI components provide much more than just an HTML element on the page, let's learn how to use them. The first thing we need to do is explain that mini-MVC architecture in a bit more depth.

7.2   *Tags, templates, and themes*

We've covered the functional aspects of the UI components. Now we need to say something about their unique architecture. You might be thinking that an architecture for tags is a bit much. We understand that response. But once you see what the tag architecture provides, we think you'll fully appreciate the effort. The most important benefit of the mini-MVC architecture of the UI components is reusable customization.

Let's start with a high-level introduction. Figure 7.2 shows the architecture of the UI component framework.

The UI components are built on a layered architecture. As a developer, you need to be clear about three things: *tags*, *templates*, and *themes*. At the top of figure 7.2, the component API is exposed as a JSP tag in a page. This tag is first processed in its native environment—the JSP tag is processed as a JSP tag. As we learned in the previous chapter,

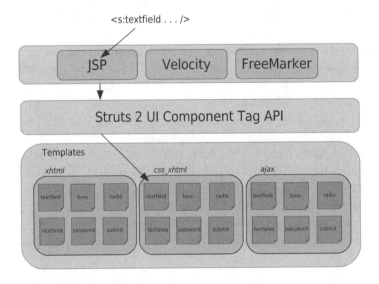

Figure 7.2   Tags, templates, and themes work together to provide feature-rich, flexible, extensible UI components.

the tag API can be utilized from several view-layer technologies. The native tag, such as a JSP Struts 2 `textfield` tag, is just a wrapper around the framework's corresponding UI component API, such as the `org.apache.struts2.components.TextField` component class. As you can see in figure 7.2, the native tag quickly hands control over to this component API for actual processing. The UI component layer processes the logic of the tag and prepares the data. It then hands off the rendering task to the underlying FreeMarker templates.

WARNING   Don't be confused by the fact that the UI components use FreeMarker templates for their own rendering. This is an internal detail of the mini-MVC component framework itself; it has no bearing on your choice of JSP, Velocity, or FreeMarker for your view-layer pages. The internal FreeMarker templates are used to generate the output of the tag itself, which'll show up in whatever kind of page you put the tag. If you want to customize the tag output, you'll have to work with the underlying FreeMarker templates. But your view layer isn't bound to FreeMarker just because the framework uses it internally. Incidentally, we'll show you how to customize those templates in chapter 13.

In this way, the markup output of the tag API is layered away from the Java classes that conduct the logic; thus we have a mini-MVC. As with all MVCs, the main benefit is the ability to easily change the "view" of the tag without needing to touch the business logic embedded in the tag's component class. We'll show you how to customize the view of the tags yourself in chapter 13. For now, we'll focus on explaining how to work with the several view options that are bundled with the framework. Several *themes* of templates are available for rendering the tags. The `css_xhtml` theme, for instance, renders the tags with pure CSS-based layout markup.

All of this will be explained in the following sections, which go into more detail about the layers shown in figure 7.2: tags, templates, and themes.

7.2.1   *Tags*

Tags are quite simple. As we explained in chapter 6, the Struts 2 tag API is high-level API. In other words, the functionality and use of the tags is defined outside the details of a given view-layer technology. The tag API could be implemented in any technology. By default, the framework provides implementations of the tag API for JSP, Velocity, and FreeMarker. In chapter 6, we explained how to use the tags with each of these technologies. Regardless of which you use, the native tag will delegate the processing to the UI component framework. The framework manages the logic and data model for the tag, processing the logic associated with the tag as well as collecting the relative data. The data might come from tag attributes or parameters, as well as from the `ActionContext` and `ValueStack`. This data is all made available to the template that'll render the HTML view of the UI component. The framework uses FreeMarker templates for rendering the UI components.

7.2.2   *Templates*

As we've said, every tag has a FreeMarker template that'll render its markup. As with most templating technologies, a FreeMarker template looks like a normal text file. Inside the plain text, special FreeMarker directives are included that can dynamically pull in data and render the resulting output. In the case of the UI component tags, a template takes the data model, as collected by the tag logic, and blends that data with the static parts of the template to create the final markup that'll be in your HTML page. Note that regardless of whether the tag was invoked from a JSP or a Velocity template, the same template will receive the same set of parameters and render the resulting markup in exactly the same way.

If you never customize or create your own templates, you don't need to concern yourself with these details in any greater detail than this. However, we think that customizing the tags will appeal to many users. If you want to customize the templates, they are readily accessible in the Struts 2 JAR, or you can override them by inserting your own in the classpath. In chapter 13, we'll provide a demonstration of some techniques for customizing these templates. If you never customize them, you should be fine as long as you understand that the UI components use FreeMarker templates to handle their rendering.

7.2.3   *Themes*

It's easy to understand that an underlying template generates the markup for a given tag. However, it's more complicated than that. In fact, each tag has several versions of the underlying template at its disposal. Each of these versions belongs to a different theme. A theme, as shown in figure 7.2, is a group of templates, one for each tag more or less, that'll render the tags in some consistent fashion or manner. For instance, one theme renders the tags to work with HTML table layout, while another renders them to work with CSS. Several themes are bundled with the framework, and you can choose which one you want your tags to use.

There are several ways to specify the theme. By default, all tags will render under the xhtml theme. You can change this default theme for the whole application, or you can specify a different theme on a per-page or per-tag basis. In the rendering scenario of figure 7.2, we can see that the css_xhtml theme, which uses pure CSS to lay out the elements of a form, has been selected. Right now, Struts 2 comes with four themes for rendering your UI components: simple, xhtml, css_xhtml, and ajax. Table 7.1 summarizes the characteristics of these themes.

Table 7.1   The built-in UI component themes

Theme	Description
simple	Renders the basic HTML element.
xhtml	Renders the UI component using a table to provide the layout.

Table 7.1   The built-in UI component themes *(continued)*

Theme	Description
`css_xhtml`	Renders the UI component using pure CSS to provide the layout.
`ajax`	Extends `xhtml` and provides rich Ajax components. This theme is not quite finished as of this writing… but is a good starting point for building Ajax applications nonetheless. Check the Struts 2 website for more details.

These themes are straightforward. The `simple` theme is rarely used on its own. The `simple` theme does little more than build the basic HTML element itself. While this isn't too useful on its own, it provides a good core for creating more complicated themes. In fact, the other themes that come with Struts 2 all take advantage of this and use the `simple` theme to render the basic HTML element at the core of their more complex markup. They do this by extending the `simple` theme. Extending a theme is a technique you can use to create new themes; again, we'll explore this topic in chapter 13. While the `simple` theme may rarely be used on its own, the other three themes presented in table 7.1 all provide full-featured UI components that integrate fully with the Struts 2 framework.

CHANGING THE THEME

Before moving on to discuss the use of the UI components themselves, we should show how to change the theme under which they render. By default, the components will render under the `xhtml` theme, which uses HTML tables for layout of the forms. Many developers are moving away from the use of HTML tables for layout. If you want to do this, you'll probably want to change the default rendering theme to `css_xhtml`. The default theme is changed by overriding the `default` property. All of the framework's default properties are defined in `default.properties`, found in the Struts 2 core JAR file at `org.apache.struts2`. To override any of the framework's default properties, you only need to create your own properties file, named struts.properties, and place it in the classpath. To change the default theme, just create a struts.properties file with the following property definition:

```
struts.ui.theme=css_xhtml
```

Then just make sure it's on the classpath. Most people put it in the web application at WEB-INF/classes/struts.properties. With this in place, all UI components will render under the `css_xhtml` theme. Now your application will use CSS and `div`s instead of HTML tables for its layout.

You can also change the theme on a more fine-grained level by specifying the `theme` attribute of the components themselves. You can, for instance, specify that a certain `textfield` should be rendered under a certain theme. Or you can specify the theme for a given `form` component, thus causing all components in that form to render with that theme.

That's about all there is to setting themes. And that finishes up our general introduction to tag usage; it's time for specifics. We understand that the UI components can seem complex at first glance. Admittedly, they're more complex than the tags of previous frameworks, but, on the other hand, they do a whole lot more. There's more to learn, but it's worth it. In particular, keep the mini-MVC in mind. When it comes time to customize your tag output to meet some rather particular requirements, we think you'll find the added sophistication pays off in triple. Now let's meet the UI components and start demonstrating their use with the Struts 2 Portfolio. Any lingering confusion will dissolve with a bit of practical experience.

7.3   UI Component tag reference

Now that we've done a high-level overview of the UI component architecture, it's time to learn to use the UI component tags themselves. In this section, we provide both a reference and a demonstration of the most common UI component tags. For each tag, we'll provide a description and a list of attributes and parameters, and demonstrate usage.

REFERENCE   The components in this reference are covered in order of most com-
USER TIP   monly used to more, shall we say, specialized. Since usage of the compo-
                  nents follows certain patterns, our coverage of the first tags in the
                  reference includes much more detailed explanation of these usage pat-
                  terns. We recommend reading everything through section 7.3.4 in order
                  to learn how the tags work in general. Almost every developer will need
                  all of these tags anyway; we're not wasting your time here. After that, you
                  don't need to read unless you see a tag you want to use.

We'll start by summarizing the attributes and usage common to all of the UI components.

7.3.1   Common attributes

The list of attributes common to all the Struts 2 UI component tags is large. This is mostly a reflection of the numerous attributes exposed by the underlying HTML elements. If you're like me, a huge table of attributes can be a bit of a brain freeze. We'll focus on the core usage of the Struts 2 tags themselves, and leave the details of various HTML- and JavaScript-related attributes, such as event handlers, to you. While the following tables are long, they aren't exhaustive. If you want the definitive list of all attributes supported by the tags, visit the Struts 2 website. In general, you can assume that all attributes of the underlying HTML elements are supported in at least a pass-through manner.

When browsing the following tables, a few things should be kept in mind. First of all, we need to recall what we learned in the previous chapter about attribute data types and the use of OGNL expressions in attribute values. If the data type is `String`, then the attribute value will be interpreted as a string literal. This means that it won't be evaluated as an OGNL expression unless you force that evaluation with the `%{ expression }` notation. On the other hand, all non-`String` data types will be automatically evaluated as OGNL expressions. Generally, this means that you won't have to use the formal OGNL expression brackets often because you'll typically feed literal strings to the `String` attributes and OGNL expressions to the non-`String` data types.

Table 7.2 shows the common attributes of the UI components.

All of the components that we'll cover in this chapter support the attributes listed in table 7.2. We'll cover the usage of these attributes in more detail as we work our way through the components in the next sections. Most components also use a few specialized attributes. These will be presented with the component itself.

Table 7.2 Common attributes for all UI tags

Attribute	Theme	Data type	Description
name	simple	String	Sets `name` attribute of the `form` input element. Also propagates to the `value` attribute of the component, if that attribute isn't set manually. The name itself is used by the component to target a property on the `ValueStack` as destination for the posted request parameter value.
value	simple	Object	OGNL expression pointing to `ValueStack` property used to set the value of the form input element for pre-population. Defaults to the `name` attribute.
key	simple	String	Pulls localized label from `ResourceBundle`, and can propagate to `name` attribute, and thus to `value` attribute. See chapter 11.
label	XHTML	String	Creates an HTML label for the component. Not needed if setting using the `key` attribute and localized text.
labelPosition	XHTML	String	Location of the element label: left or top.
required	XHTML	Boolean	If `true`, an asterisk appears next to the label indicating the field is required. By default, the value is `true` if a field-level validator is mapped to the field indicated in the `name` attribute.
id	simple	String	HTML `id` attribute. Components will create a unique ID if one isn't specified. IDs are useful for both JavaScript and CSS.
cssClass	simple	String	HTML `class` attribute, for CSS.
cssStyle	simple	String	HTML `style` attribute, for CSS.
disabled	simple	Boolean	HTML `disabled` attribute.
tabindex	simple	String	HTML `tabindex` attribute.
theme	N/A	String	Theme under which component should be rendered, such as `xhtml`, `css_xhtml`, `ajax`, `simple`. Default value is `xhtml`, set in default.properties.
templateDir	N/A	String	Used to override the default directory name from which templates will be retrieved.
template	N/A	String	Template to look up to render the UI tag. All UI tags have a default template (except the component tag), but the template can be overridden.

In addition to these attributes, the components also support the common JavaScript event handler attributes, such as `onclick` and `onchange`. Basically, the components support any HTML attribute you'll want to set. In common tag usage, you'll typically only use a few of these attributes, such as `name`, `key`, `label`, and `value`. Rather than trying to explain these attributes in a vacuum, we'll explain them in the context of actual UI component tag examples.

7.3.2   Simple components

In this section, we'll introduce the most commonly used UI components. We'll start with the infrastructural components, including the important `form` component, which acts as a container for all the other components. With the preliminaries out of the way, we'll meet many of the simpler components such as `textfield`, `password`, and `checkbox`. After that, we'll hit the collection-backed components.

READERS'   The organization of this reference section has been designed to require
COURTESY   the least amount of reading. Basically, we'll cover all the stuff you'll use
first. We'll also use our coverage of these essentials, such as text fields and select boxes, to demonstrate the fundamental patterns of usage common to all components. This structure means you can safely stop reading as soon as you have what you need. Later sections will point you toward richer components, but if you're not interested you won't need to keep reading.

THE HEAD COMPONENT

We will start with the `head` component. This tag doesn't do anything by itself, but it plays an important role in supporting the other tags. The `head` tag must be placed within the HTML `head` element, where it generates information generally found in that location. This information includes HTML link elements that can reference CSS stylesheets, as well as script elements that can define JavaScript functions or reference files of such functions. Since many of the UI component tags come with rich functionality, this `head` tag can link to commonly used JavaScript libraries that help implement that functionality.

Note that if a tag depends upon the resources pulled in by the `head` tag, it'll appear to not work if you omit the `head` tag. This is a common source of "bugs." If you're using the xhtml theme, this tag also loads a default CSS stylesheet that defines some basic styles for the form elements rendered under the xhtml theme. If your requirements aren't that rigid, this basic styling may be all you need. As you can see from the following snippet from one of our Struts 2 Portfolio application's JSP pages, adding this tag to your page is easy:

```
<head>
  <title>Portfolio Registration</title>
  <s:head/>
</head>
```

No attributes are required. This tag can discover all of the information it needs. What does it create? Here's the markup, assuming it renders under the default xhtml theme. Note that we've abbreviated this a bit. We just want to show you that the head tag generates links to stylesheets and JavaScript libraries:

```
<link rel="stylesheet" href=" . . . styles.css" type="text/css"/>

<script language="JavaScript" type="text/javascript" src=". . .dojo.js"/>

<script language="JavaScript" type="text/javascript" src="dojoRequire.js"/>
```

Obviously, this tag doesn't do much by itself. It's more of a helper tag that lays the foundation for other, more concretely productive tags that'll come later in the page. When we cover tags that depend on its presence, we'll explicitly indicate their reliance on the head tag.

THE FORM COMPONENT

The form component is probably the most important of all. This critical UI component provides the central tie-in point to your Struts 2 application. It's the form, after all, that targets your Struts 2 actions. In addition to the common attributes defined at the beginning of this section, the form component also uses the attributes summarized in table 7.3.

Table 7.3 provides concise descriptions of the attributes. In practice, it's easy. Let's jump right in by looking at an example. The following snippet shows the form from chapter 7's Login.jsp page:

```
<s:form action="Login">
  <s:textfield name="username" label="Username"/>
  <s:password name="password" label="Password"/>
  <s:submit/>
</s:form>
```

The markup up is simple. The action attribute is the most important. We simply specify the action name, sans .action extension, to which we want to submit the form. The name given here is the logical name given to the action in the declarative architecture, in our chapterSeven.xml file in this case. Note that if we specify the action attribute without specifying the namespace attribute, it'll assume the current namespace. Since we frequently target actions within the same namespace as the current request, this

Table 7.3　Frequently used form tag attributes

Attribute	Data type	Description
action	String	Target of form submission—can be name of Struts 2 action or a URL.
namespace	String	Struts 2 namespace under which to search for named action (above), or from which to build the URL. Defaults to current namespace.
method	String	Same as HTML form attribute. Defaults to POST.
target	String	Same as HTML form attribute.
enctype	String	Set to multipart/form-data if doing file uploads.
validate	Boolean	Turns on client-side JavaScript validation, works with Validation Framework.

allows for clean markup. Indeed, we've specified only one attribute. For everything else, we let the framework provide intelligent defaults.

Listing 7.2 shows the output generated by this `form` tag.

Listing 7.2   HTML Output from a form UI component

```
<form id="Login" name="Login" onsubmit="return true;"
  action="/manningSampleApp/chapterSeven/Login.action" method="POST">

  <label for="Login_username" class="label">Username:</label>
  <input type="text" name="username" value="" id="Login_username"/>

  <label for="Login_password" class="label">Password:</label></td>
  <input type="password" name="password" id="Login_password"/>

  <input type="submit" id="Login_0" value="Submit"/>

</form>
```

Remember when we said that the UI components generate layout-related markup? We've suppressed that from this listing; we don't want to confuse things while we're trying to understand the functional parts of the tag. Functionally, the most important attribute is the `action` attribute. In this case, the `action` attribute has become a fully qualified path even though our tag only specified a logical action name. Struts 2 lets us specify a simple logical name for our `action` attribute, and it then generates the full URL for that action.

TIP   When your form targets another Struts 2 action, you only need to specify the logical name of the action. You don't need to add the .action extension. And if it's in the same namespace as the current action—the one whose result is rendering the page—you don't even need to specify the namespace. Intelligent defaults like this allow for cleaner, faster coding.

The `form` component tag also creates sensible values for several other attributes, notably the `id` and `method` attributes. The generated ID is unique and built on the name of the action itself. Interior fields of the form will also build upon this naming convention so that you can count on these IDs when applying relevant JavaScript techniques.

NOTE   Most of the Struts 2 UI components will automatically generate IDs and names for components even if you don't specify those attributes yourself. This important step lays the foundation for JavaScript and CSS functionality that depends upon being able to specify elements in the HTML DOM by their unique ID. If you don't need these, it's nonintrusive. However, if you ever find yourself needing to go back and use IDs, you can rest assured that all of your pages have been prepared for just such an occasion.

In this example, we followed the most common use case of aiming our form submission at another Struts 2 action. The tag's default behavior supports this, but, as always, the framework is flexible and allows you to easily target any web resource. To be complete, we'll outline the process by which the form tag generates the final action URL for the HTML form. The following list shows the steps followed when determining how to create the URL:

1　If no `action` attribute is specified, the current Struts 2 action is targeted again.

2　If the `action` attribute is specified, it's first interpreted as the name of a Struts 2 action. If no `namespace` attribute is specified, then the action is resolved against the namespace of the current request. If a `namespace` attribute is specified, the action will be searched for in that namespace. Note that actions are specified without the .action extension.

3　If the value set in the `action` attribute doesn't resolve to a Struts 2 action declared in your declarative architecture, then it'll be used to build a URL directly. If the string begins with a slash (`/`), then this is assumed to be relative to the `ServletContext` and a URL is made by appending this to the `Servlet-Context` path. If the value doesn't start with a slash, then the value is used directly as the URL. Note that the `namespace` attribute, even if specified, is not used in these cases.

The first option is relatively self-explanatory. A URL is generated that'll submit to the same action again. The second option, which involves targeting named Struts 2 actions, is also simple. Mostly you'll do as we did in the example; you'll target an action in the same namespace as the current action. You can also specify an alternate namespace under which the framework should search for the named action. The following snippet shows how to make our chapter 7 version of the login form submit to the chapter 4 `Login` action:

```
<s:form action="Login" namespace="/chapterFour">
```

This tag will generate the following HTML code, building a URL for the `action` attribute that targets the `Login` action in the `chapterFour` namespace. Here's the output:

```
<form id="Login" name="Login" onsubmit="return true;"
action="/manningSampleApp/chapterFour/Login.action" >
```

As you can see, this'll hit the `Login` action in the `chapterFour` namespace. Not exactly what we want, but it serves to demonstrate the syntax for specifying a different namespace.

If the value of the `action` attribute doesn't map to an action name, then the value will be used directly to build a URL. Typically, the process shouldn't get to option three unless you're intentionally specifying a URL rather than an action name. If you want to specify a URL, you have a couple of choices. First, you can specify a path that starts with a slash, such as

```
<s:form action="/chapterSeven/PortfolioHomePage.jsp">
```

Note that we have to specify the .jsp extension. This is because we're specifying an actual URL here. In the previous cases, we were naming an action by its logical name and letting the framework generate the URL for us. The following snippet shows how the framework uses the previous tag to build a URL by appending the action value directly onto the `ServletContext` path:

```
<form id="PortfolioHomePage" onsubmit="return true;"
action="/manningSampleApp/chapterSeven/PortfolioHomePage.jsp">
```

If you want to specify a full URL yourself, to target an external resource, just do so. The framework will know what you're doing because the value doesn't resolve to an action and it doesn't start with a slash. So we can specify a full URL as follows:

```
<s:form action="http://www.google.com">
```

This form tag will generate a form that submits to Google. Again, probably not what you want, but this demonstrates how to specify a full URL in case you need to link to target an external resource.

Finally, if you specify a value that doesn't start with a leading slash, doesn't resolve to a action, and doesn't represent a full URL, then the value will be printed as-is into the HTML action attribute. For instance:

```
<s:form action="MyResource">
```

This tag will generate a form like the following:

```
<form id="MyResource" onsubmit="return true;" action="MyResource">
```

When a browser sees a URL like this, it'll interpret it as relative to the URL of the current page. If this form is in our chapterSeven/LoginForm.action page, the browser will start from chapterSeven and build a URL like this: http://localhost:8080/manningSampleApp/chapterSeven/MyResource

If you do this, be sure that the resource exists. Typically, relative paths are used to hit static resources, such as images, rather than the application server's dynamic resources. It's unlikely that your form will want to target a static resource. And best practices warn against targeting a dynamic resource, such as a JSP, directly. Accepted best practice is to use a pass-through action to target JSPs and other dynamic resources.

Now that you know how the form sets up the HTML form element itself, we should take a look at the layout-related markup that's also generated by the component. As we've indicated, the UI component tags generate additional markup to handle layout. By default, the components render under the xhmtl theme. This theme generates an HTML table to format the form elements. Listing 7.3 shows the full markup generated by the form tag in the example, rendered under the default xhtml theme.

Listing 7.3   The full markup generated by the form component

```
<form id="Login" name="Login" onsubmit="return true;"
  action="/manningSampleApp/chapterSeven/Login.action" method="POST">

    <table class="wwFormTable">
      <tr>
        <td class="tdLabel">
          <label for="Login_username"class="label">Username:</label>
        </td>
        <td>
          <input type="text" name="username" value=""
              id="Login_username"/>
        </td>
      </tr>

      <tr>
        <td class="tdLabel">
```
❶

❷

```
        <label for="Login_password" class="label">Password:</label>
      </td>
      <td>
        <input type="password" name="password" id="Login_password"/>
      </td>
    </tr>

    <tr>
      <td colspan="2">
        <div align="right">
          <input type="submit" id="Login_0" value="Submit"/>
        </div>
      </td>
    </tr>
  </table>
</form>
```

We don't need to examine this too much. After all, the whole point of the component is to keep you from having to think about this kind of stuff. We just wanted to show it once so that you know what to expect. The main bit here is that the xhtml theme generates an HTML table that handles the layout of the form and the form elements. The username text field, for instance, is situated in a single row of the table ❶. You should also note that the elements have class attributes defined for CSS tie-in ❷.

Admittedly, this is a big wad of HTML goo. But remember that this markup is all generated from the underlying FreeMarker templates. This means that you can easily alter the template if you need to make some changes to the markup. Again, we'll learn how to modify these templates in chapter 13.

Now that we've seen how to deploy the form component, we need to add some input fields to that form.

THE TEXTFIELD COMPONENT

This is one tag you can't avoid using. This component generates the ubiquitous text input field. And, as usual, the most common things are easy in Struts 2. The main thing you need to understand about the textfield tag is how the name attribute and the value attribute tie into the framework. If you don't recall how this works, refer back to our explanation in section 7.1.1. If you're clear on how the name and value attributes function as OGNL expressions that bind the component to a property on the ValueStack, you're good to go.

In addition to the common UI component attributes summarized previously, textfield makes frequent use of a few more attributes of its own. Table 7.4 summarizes these attributes.

Table 7.4 Important textfield attributes

Attribute	Data type	Description
maxlength	String	Maximum length for field data.
readonly	Boolean	If true, field is uneditable.
size	String	Visible size of the textfield.

Now, let's a look at an example from the Struts 2 Portfolio application. The following snippet shows the login form from the chapter 7 sample code, Login.jsp:

```
<s:form action="Login">
  <s:textfield key="username"/>
  <s:password name="password" label="Password"/>
  <s:submit/>
</s:form>
```

Since we've already demonstrated, in section 7.1.1, the use of the `name` and `value` attributes to configure a `textfield` component, we'll now show how it works with the `key` attribute. The `key` attribute can be used to pull a localized label value from a `ResoureBundle`; the global-resources.properties file found in the root of the classpath in this case. When you do this, you don't have to set the `label` attribute manually. But, if you're using the `key` attribute, you might as well let the framework handle a couple of other things for you as well.

As we've seen, you can omit setting the `value` attribute by letting the framework use the `name` value as an OGNL expression that points to the property that'll provide the value for the `value` attribute. The framework is inferring the `value` from the `name`. The `key` attribute ups the ante. In addition to allowing you to pull a localized message in for your label, the framework can infer the `name` attribute from the `key` attribute, thereby inferring the `value` attribute as well. The end result, as seen in the previous snippet, is a clean tag that specifies only the `key` attribute.

CONVENTIONAL WISDOM   When the framework does work for you, as when using the `key` attribute to infer the other attributes of a UI component, the magic is all about convention. In general, Struts 2 can save you loads of time if you can follow conventions that it understands. In this case, the framework expects that the value you give for the `key` attribute can locate a localized message in a `ResourceBundle` *and* locate a property on the `ValueStack`. You must follow this synergy when creating your `ResourceBundle` properties files and naming the properties of your data model. If you follow this convention, the framework will do the work for you. If you scoff at convention, no tool is smart enough to divine your logic.

Here's the markup generated by the `textfield` portion of this JSP snippet:

```
<tr>
  <td class="tdLabel">
    <label for="Login_username" class="label">Username:</label>
  </td>
  <td>
    <input type="text" name="username" value="" id="Login_username"/>
  </td>
</tr>
```

Since this is the first form field we've discussed, we decided to show you the layout-related markup generated by the tag as well. We do this just so you see that, under the xhtml theme, each input field tag generates its own row and table data markup to position itself within the table created by the form tag. This is true for all UI components that generate a form field under the xhtml theme. As you might expect, if you use the css_xhtml theme, a CSS-based version of layout markup will be generated instead.

In addition to the table markup, the most striking thing about this example is how specifying a single attribute, key, was able to do so much. In addition to getting a localized message for our label, the key created the input field's name attribute, which of course is an OGNL expression binding the field to a property on the ValueStack. Through this binding, the value might also be set, but not in this case. In this case, our value attribute is empty because the matching property on the ValueStack was empty, or nonexistent, when this form rendered; we're not prepopulating the login form.

Using the key property is elegant, but you need to be using ResourceBundles to provide the text messages for the label. When the component renders, it'll attempt to find a text message using the key attribute value for the ResourceBundle lookup key. This is a highly recommended practice, as it allows you to externalize your text messages in a manageable location. For the Struts 2 Portfolio application, we've followed a common web application practice of putting our text resources in properties files.

The framework makes it particularly easy to use properties files. Two convenient options are to externalize your messages in a global properties file or in individual properties files local to a specific class. In this case, we've added a global properties file to the application. This file, global-messages.properties, resides in the classpath at WEB-INF/classes/, and contains the following property:

```
username=Username
```

Again, note that the key of this property matches the OGNL expression that we use to target the username property on the ValueStack. This works great because the same hierarchical namespace works well in both places. In this example, our key/OGNL is simple, but deeper expressions will work fine.

In order to use global properties files, you need to tell Struts 2 where to find them. As always, such configuration details can be controlled through system properties in the struts.properties file. This file, which the user must create, goes on the classpath, typically at /WEB-INF/classes/struts.properties. Here's the property we set to specify a properties file that should be picked up by the framework:

```
struts.custom.i18n.resources=global-messages
```

The framework's built-in support for managing localized text in ResourceBundles goes quite a bit further than this. For a complete discussion, see chapter 11.

THE PASSWORD COMPONENT

The password tag is essentially like the textfield tag, but in this case the input value is masked. As with all input fields, the name, value, and key attributes are the most important. Table 7.5 summarizes the additional attributes frequently used with the password tag.

Table 7.5 Important `password` attributes

Attribute	Data type	Description
maxlength	String	Maximum length for field data.
readonly	Boolean	If `true`, field is uneditable.
size	String	Visible size of the text field.
showPassword	Boolean	If set to `true`, the password will be prepopulated from the `ValueStack` if the corresponding property has a value. Defaults to false. Populated value will still be masked in proper password fashion.

While there are no surprises, we'll look at a sample just to make it real. The following snippet, again from this chapter's Login.jsp page, defines a password field:

```
<s:form action="Login">
  <s:textfield key="username"/>
  <s:password name="password" label="Password"/>
  <s:submit/>
</s:form>
```

In this case, we specify the `name` attribute and the `label` attribute. (You could use the `key` attribute if you have set up some `ResourceBundles`.) Again, the `name` value is understood as an OGNL expression that binds the component to a specific property on the `ValueStack`:

```
<label for="Login_password" class="label">Password:</label>
<input type="password" name="password" value="" id="Login_password"/>
```

As you can see, the output is just like `textfield`. The `password` tag generates a label and a password field. Note that, in this example, the tag is actually rendered under the `xhtml` theme, but we've stripped out the table markup to clarify what's going on with the HTML elements.

THE TEXTAREA COMPONENT

The `textarea` tag generates a component built around the HTML `textarea` element. As with all form fields, the `name`, `value`, and `key` attributes are the most important. Table 7.6 summarizes the additional attributes frequently used with the `textarea` tag.

Table 7.6 Important `textarea` attributes

Attribute	Data type	Description
cols	Integer	Number of columns.
rows	Integer	Number of rows.
readonly	Boolean	If `true`, field is uneditable.
wrap	String	Specifies whether the content in the `textarea` should wrap.

From the development point of view, there's no difference between this and the text-field. Because of this, we'll spare you the example.

THE CHECKBOX COMPONENT

The checkbox component uses a single HTML checkbox to create a Boolean component. Take heed, this component isn't equivalent to an HTML checkbox. It's specialized for Boolean values only. The property you bind it to on the Java side should be a Boolean property. Don't worry; there's another component, the checkboxlist, that solves the other checkbox use case—a list of checkboxes, all with the same name, that allow the user to submit multiple values under that single name. The checkbox component is focused on a true or false choice. We'll see the checkboxlist component in a few pages when we cover the collection-backed components.

In addition to the commonly used attributes we've already defined, the checkbox component also uses the attributes defined in table 7.7.

Table 7.7 Important checkbox attributes

Attribute	Data type	Description
fieldValue	String	The actual value that'll be submitted by the checkbox. May be true or false; true by default.
value	String	In combination with fieldValue, determines whether the checkbox will be checked. If the fieldValue = true, and the value = true, then the box will be checked.

To demonstrate the usage of the checkbox, we've modified our Struts 2 Portfolio data model to include a Boolean value. We'll now track whether a user wants to receive junk mail. We've added a Boolean field to the User object and we'll give the user an opportunity to express their junk mail preference during registration. The Registration action is where the User object is first created and persisted. Here's the form from Registration.jsp that collects the account information, including the new junk mail preference Boolean value.

```
<s:form action="Register">
  <s:textfield name="username" label="Username"/>
  <s:password name="password" label="Password"/>
  <s:textfield name="portfolioName" label="Enter a portfolio name"/>
  <s:checkbox name="receiveJunkMail" fieldValue="true" label="Check to
    receive junk mail"/>
  <s:submit/>
</s:form>
```

The checkbox component is deceptively easy to define. In fact, we didn't even need to set the fieldValue because true is the default value. We've done this just for clarity. This means that the checkbox, if checked, will submit a true value to the framework. The following code shows the actual HTML checkbox element output by this component:

```
<input type="checkbox" name="receiveJunkMail" value="true"
  id="Register_receiveJunkMail"/>
```

As we specified in the `fieldValue` attribute, the `value` attribute of the checkbox is true. To receive this Boolean value, we implemented a JavaBeans property on our `Register` action. This property is shown in the following snippet:

```
private boolean receiveJunkMail;

public boolean isReceiveJunkMail() {
  return receiveJunkMail;
}
public void setReceiveJunkMail(boolean receiveJunkMail) {
  this.receiveJunkMail = receiveJunkMail;
}
```

We haven't been showing the Java code for most of the UI components. We only do so here to drive home the point that the `checkbox` component works with Boolean values. If the junk mail checkbox is checked, then its `true` value will be submitted to this Boolean property, in concordance with the OGNL of the `name` attribute. Fairly simple. But what about prepopulation?

Prepopulation is usually accomplished with the `value` attribute of the UI component. It's more complex with the `checkbox`. We now have to specify the value that the field will input as well as the current value of the Java-side property. These aren't equivalent values in the context of the `checkbox`, as they would be with a `textfield`. Reflecting the independence of these two values, the `checkbox` component exposes two attributes, `value` and `fieldValue`. The `fieldValue` attribute determines the actual `value` attribute of the HTML element—the value that'll be submitted if the box is checked. Meanwhile, the `value` attribute, as with the other UI components, points to the actual Java-side property to which the component is bound, a Boolean in this case. The `checkbox` component will handle the translation of the Java-side Boolean into the semantics of whether the `checkbox` should be checked. In our simple example, our `checkbox` `fieldValue` is true. Thus, if our Java-side property, pointed to by the `value` attribute, is false, then the box should be unchecked. If our Java-side property is true, then the box should be checked. Of course, in all of this, recall that our `name` attribute will be reused for the `value` attribute if we don't set it manually.

All of this matters most when prepopulating the form. The registration form is not prepopulated because there is no existing user data at that point. If you want to see how the `checkbox` prepopulates, check out the account update process available when you log into an existing account. We won't detail this update action here, as the prepopulation process was covered earlier in the chapter.

We've now covered the simple UI components. The next set of UI components are those that present a set of options to the user. These options are typically backed by collections of data on the Java side. We'll explore these collection-backed components in the next section.

7.3.3   *Collection-backed components*

This section will introduce a set of components that allow a user to select a choice from a set of options. In some ways, this is a simple and familiar task to most web developers. One of the most common scenarios involves a user being presented with a list of states or countries. The user selects one of the options and that value is sent under the name of the select box itself.

As this plays out in a Java web application, we typically have a Java-side property that is some sort of collection of data. This might be an array, a `Map`, or a `List`. A full complement of types is supported by the Struts 2 tags. The basic logic of the collection-backed components is that the Java-side data set is presented to the user as a set of options. The user then selects one of the options, such as `Colorado`, and that value is submitted with the request.

Some of the complications encountered with these components involve whether the Java-side data set consists of simple types, such as `Strings` or `ints`, that can be themselves used as the option values, or of complex types, such as our `User` object, which don't map so easily to an option value. As you'll see, the Struts 2 collection-backed components provide a mechanism for indicating which of the `User` object's properties should be used as the option value. We'll start by demonstrating the simpler case of using a data set of simple types, then move on to the more complex use case of complex types.

We'll explain all of this in the context of our first, and most ubiquitous, component—the `select` component.

THE SELECT COMPONENT

The `select` component is perhaps the most common collection-based UI component. This component is built on the HTML select box, which allows the user to select a value from a list of options. In a Java web application, it's common to build these lists of options from `Collections`, `Maps`, or arrays of data. The `select` component offers a rich, flexible interface for generating select boxes from a wide assortment of back-end data sets. Just to make this easy, we'll start with a trivial but illustrative sample of using a `List` to build a `select` component. In this first example, the `List` will be of `Strings`; we'll show how to use sets of complex types in a minute. The following snippet shows the simplest use case of the `select` UI component:

```
<s:select name="user.name" list="{'Mike','Payal','Silas'}" />
```

The `list` attribute of the `select` component points to the data set that will back the component. We've supplied an OGNL list literal for this value. You'll typically be using an OGNL expression to point to a list of data on the `ValueStack` rather than generate a list literally. Here, we're striving to simplify the usage while introducing the tag. As usual, the `name` attribute is an OGNL expression that'll target a destination property on the `ValueStack`. One of the strings in the list will be selected, submitted, and transferred by the framework onto the property referenced by our `name` attribute. We've seen this many times by now.

Here's how the preceding tag renders into HTML to present the user with the choice:

```
<select name="user.name" id="ViewPortfolio_user_name">
  <option value="Mike">Mike</option>
  <option value="Payal">Payal</option>
  <option value="Silas">Silas</option>
</select>
```

Again, we've removed the layout-related markup from the HTML output of this component. As you can see, each of the values in the list was used to create an `option` element. But what about prepopulation? Since we didn't specify a value attribute ourselves, the `name` attribute will be used to infer the value. If the `ValueStack` had contained a value in the property `user.name` when this tag rendered, that value would've been matched against the values of the option elements to preselect one of them. In this case, none have been preselected; the `ValueStack` must not have contained a value for the `user.name` property. That's about as simple as it gets. But if you understand the principle, the rest should make sense. Let's move on to the richer use cases of the `select` component.

Now we'll see how the `select` component supports using a wide range of data sets and offers flexible control over the various attributes of the generated HTML select box. Table 7.8 summarizes the attributes specific to using the `select` UI component.

Table 7.8   Important `select` attributes

Attribute	Data type	Description
list	Collection, Map, Array, or Iterator	A set of data used to generate the options for the select box.
listKey	String	The property of the `List`'s elements to be used for the value submitted when those elements are complex types; `key` by default.
listValue	String	The property of the `List`'s elements to be used for the content of the option when those elements are complex types—in other words, the string seen by the user; `value` by default.
headerKey	String	Used with the header. Specifies the value to submit if the user selects the header.
headerValue	String	Shown to the user as a header for the `List`, for example "States", "Countries".
emptyOption	Boolean	Used with the header. Places an empty spacer option between the header and the real options.
multiple	Boolean	User can select more than one value.
size	String	Number of choices shown at one time.

We'll now demonstrate a `Collection`-backed `select` component with an example from the Struts 2 Portfolio application. We've added a couple of functions to our home page that allow a user to select a portfolio for viewing. At this point, our sample application doesn't have a database and, hence, doesn't use numeric keys to identify such things as portfolios or artists. At this point, artist usernames must be unique. Furthermore, a portfolio name must be unique in the context of the artist who owns it. We can then assume that a username and portfolio name pair serves as a unique key for retrieving a given portfolio. The following examples use these requirements.

If you check the chapter 7 home page, you'll see some additions to our user interface. The first of these is a select component that asks the user to choose an artist. A screen capture of this component is shown in figure 7.3.

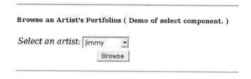

The user can now select an artist and browse that artist's work. After the artist has

Figure 7.3 **The** select **component presents a** Collection **of data as a set of choices.**

been selected, the user will be taken to a page that presents her with a similar box presenting a selection of the portfolios associated with the chosen artist. Feel free to explore the full workflow of the application at your convenience. For now, we'll focus on how selecting an artist works. The following snippet from this chapter's Portfolio-HomePage.jsp file shows how the select box in figure 7.3 is created:

```
<h5>Browse an Artist's Portfolios ( Demo of select component. )</h5>
  <s:form action="SelectPortfolio" >
  <s:select name="username" list='users' listKey="username"
     listValue="username" label="Select an artist" />
  <s:submit value="Browse"/>
</s:form>
```

This example seems more complicated than the first example we gave. It's not really though. First, we point the list attribute at a Collection of User objects exposed by our action class; check out manning.chapterSeven.PortfoioHomePage if you want to see this property. Next, we have two new attributes: listKey and listValue. These attributes are required, since the collection backing this select, unlike the first example we showed, holds complex types, Users, rather than simple strings. These new attributes allow us to select the specific properties from our User objects to use in building the component. The tag will iterate over the collection of Users and build an option element from each one. There will be one option element for each artist in the system then.

Two questions remain. First, how should we derive the value of each option element, the value that'll be submitted when that option is selected? Easy. The listKey attribute binds one of the properties of your object to the value attribute of the generated option element, which determines the request parameter value that'll be submitted if that option is selected. This key nomenclature comes from the idea that the value attribute of the select box is frequently set to the key value of the data object. Sometimes this is a numeric key from the database, but it doesn't have to be. It just needs to be a unique identifier. As we've said, usernames work for us at this point. Thus, we've set the listKey attribute to the username property.

Next question. How should we represent that choice to the user—what'll the body of the option element be? Again, an easy answer. The listValue attribute determines what the user will see in the UI select box. In other words, this determines the text visually displayed by each option. Don't be confused. This isn't the HTML option element's value attribute; that attribute is set by the previously explained listKey. In this case, we've set both listKey and listValue to the same property, username. This is only because the username is both a unique identifier and a good string for visually representing the options to the user.

Now, let's see how the `select` tag renders. The following snippet shows the markup generated by that tag as it iteratively renders over the set of Users in the list:

```
<form id="SelectPortfolio" name="SelectPortfolio"
    action="/manningSampleApp/chapterSeven/SelectPortfolio.action" >
  <select name="username" id="SelectPortfolio_username">
    <option value="Jimmy">Jimmy</option>
    <option value="Chad">Chad</option>
    <option value="Mary">Mary</option>
  </select>
  <input type="submit" id="SelectPortfolio_0" value="Browse"/>
</form>
```

As you can see, there is an `option` element for each of the elements in the collection of Users. Each option uses the username both to depict the option to the user and to set the `value` attribute. Remember that the `value` attribute of the `option` element is set by the `listKey`, whereas the display string is set by the `listValue`. And that's how you wire a `select` component to a Java-side `Collection` property. As we've said, you can use a variety of Java-side types to back your components. Let's do the same thing again, with a `Map` on the Java side.

The following snippet shows the same component from the home page implemented with a `Map` of users instead of a `Collection`.:

```
<h5>Browse an Artist's Portfolios ( Demo of select component. )</h5>
<s:form action="SelectPortfolio" >
  <s:select name="username" list='users'  listValue="value.username"
    label="Select an artist" />
  <s:submit value="Browse"/>
</s:form>
```

As the `Map` that backs this holds the same Users as the previous example's `Collection`, this tag will generate exactly the same output as before. There are some slight differences in how the data is accessed, though. When the tag iterates over the `Map` of users, it doesn't iterate directly over the `User` objects themselves. This is just a detail of the Java `Map` API. Instead, it iterates over `Entry` objects. The `Entry` object has two properties, the `key` and the `value`. In our case, the `key` is the username and the `value` is the User object itself.

By default, the `select` component's `listKey` attribute will be set to key and, thus, point to the username. Also by default, the `listValue` attribute will be set to value and, thus, point to the `User` object. If you're using `Maps`, you can sometimes accept these defaults. In this example, we use the default `listKey` because our keys are our usernames, which is what we want. As for the `listValue`, we can't just use the entire value from the entry, because that would be the entire `User` object. If our `User` object implemented a suitable `toString()` method, we could allow the `select` component to use it for representing the choices to the user. But it doesn't. So, as you can see, we use a concise OGNL expression to target the `portfolioName` as the `listValue`. The bottom-line difference between using maps and using collections is that maps may require a longer OGNL expression, such as value.username instead of just username. Here's the markup generated from rendering our select component tag:

```
<form id="SelectPortfolio" name="SelectPortfolio"
    action="/manningSampleApp/chapterSeven/SelectPortfolio.action" >
  <select name="username" id="SelectPortfolio_username">
    <option value="Jimmy">Jimmy</option>
    <option value="Chad">Chad</option>
    <option value="Mary">Mary</option>
  </select>
  <input type="submit" id="SelectPortfolio_0" value="Browse"/>
</form>
```

As you can see, everything is the same as when we rendered the tag using a Collection of users. The Map we use for this example contains the same set of User objects as the Collection. The notation for reaching the data is different, but functionally it doesn't matter whether you use Maps or Collections.

The bottom line is that you can easily build a select component from any group of data. You can even pass arrays and iterators to the tag. We won't detail these uses, but they work pretty much as you would expect.

Tip

If you understand the ValueStack and the use of OGNL expressions in the tag attributes, you'll have no trouble exploring all the rich functionality offered by the Struts2 UI component tags. We can't begin to cover every bit of functionality they offer in the space of this book. Even if we could, our laborious efforts would be undermined by the constant flow of new components. A rich set of Ajax tags is in the foundry as we write.

Just keep in mind that all of the tags use the ValueStack. Some even push objects temporarily onto the ValueStack so that they can conveniently access the properties of those tags during their brief rendering cycle. For instance, when the select tag iterates over the set of objects handed to its list attribute, it pushes each object, temporarily, onto the ValueStack. The OGNL expressions in the tag's attributes can then resolve against this state of the ValueStack. When the iteration cycle ends, the object is popped and a new one is pushed when the next iteration cycle begins. This is the power of the ValueStack.

THE RADIO COMPONENT

The radio component offers much the same functionality as the select component, but presented in a different manner. Figure 7.4 shows what the radio component looks like on the page.

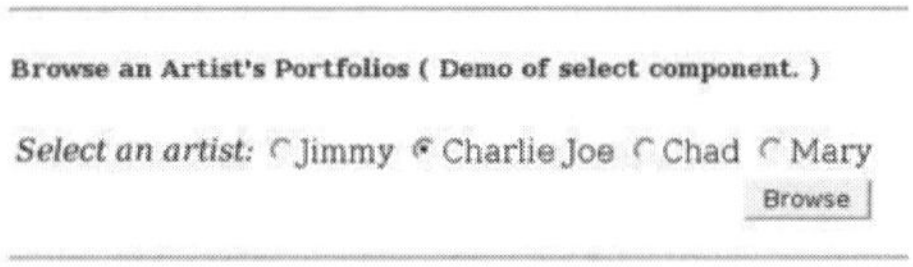

The usage of the radio component is the same as the select component, except

Browse an Artist's Portfolios (Demo of select component.)

Select an artist: ○ Jimmy ● Charlie Joe ○ Chad ○ Mary

Browse

Figure 7.4 The radio component presents a collection of data as a set of choices.

that it has a few less attributes. For instance, the radio component doesn't allow multiple selections. You can use Collections, Maps, arrays, and Iterators, just as before. Again, the radio component tag uses the common UI component attributes. In addition to the common attributes, the radio component uses the attributes summarized in table 7.9.

Table 7.9   Important radio attributes

Attribute	Data type	Description
list	Collection, Map, Array, or Iterator	A set of data used to generate the radio selections.
listKey	String	The property of the collection's elements to be used for the value submitted; key by default.
listValue	String	The property of the collection's elements to be used for the content of the option; in other words, the string seen by the user; value by default.

As we said, the usage is nearly identical to the select component. In fact, to generate the screen shot of the radio component, we merely changed the name of the tag in PortfolioHomePage.jsp from select to radio. That's it. Because of this, we won't go into details on this component.

THE CHECKBOXLIST COMPONENT

The checkboxlist component is also similar to the select component. As you can see in figure 7.5, it presents the same selection choices, but using checkboxes, so it allows for multiple selections.

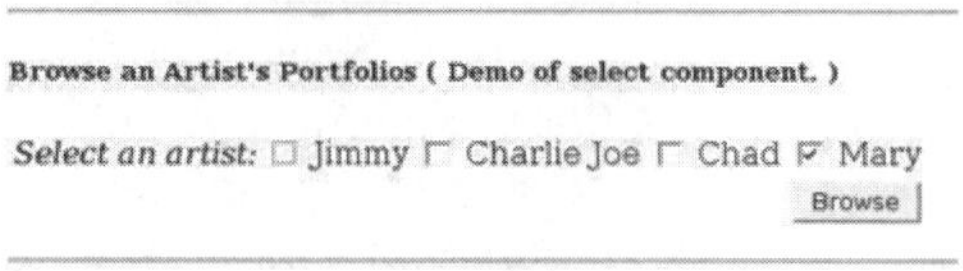

Using the checkboxlist is just like using the select component with the multiple selection option chosen. Again,

Figure 7.5   The checkboxlist component presents a collection of data as a set of choices from which the user can select several.

for our screenshot, we just changed the name of the tag in PortofolioHomePage.jsp from select to checkboxlist. In addition to the common UI component attributes, the checkboxlist also frequently uses the attributes summarized in table 7.10.

Table 7.10   Important checkboxlist attributes

Attribute	Data type	Description
list	Collection, Map, Array, or Iterator	A set of data used to generate the checkboxlist selections.
listKey	String	The property of the collection's elements to be used for the value submitted; key by default.
listValue	String	The property of the collection's elements to be used for the content of the option, in other words, the string seen by the user; value by default.

Note that these attributes are used in the same manner as for the other collection-driven UI components, such as the select component.

PREPOPULATION WITH COLLECTION-BACKED COMPONENTS

Prepopulation of the collection-backed components may not seem straightforward at first glance. For starters, we'll call it preselection, as that more accurately describes what'll happen. It works just as the prepopulation of the simple component tags; the value attribute points to a property on the ValueStack that'll be used as the current value when preselecting one of the options. Remember, you'll frequently leave the value attribute unset, allowing the framework to infer it from the name attribute, as we've seen.

With simpler components, like the textfield, the value will directly populate the input field. With collection-backed components, we don't have a simple input field; we have a selection of options. Each of these HTML options has a value attribute that represents the value of the component if that option is selected. The trick, then, is to use the value attribute of the Struts 2 tag to match one of those option values. When a match occurs, that option is preselected. Let's demonstrate how this preselection works.

To do so, we'll modify the PortfolioHomePage to automatically select one of the artists as the default choice. Let's imagine that, each week, the Struts 2 Portfolio will feature the work of one artist by making that artist the default choice. In order to have one of the options preselected, we must provide a property on the ValueStack that holds the username, our key, of the default artist. We've implemented a method on our PortfolioService that returns the username of the currently featured artist. We'll retrieve this and set it on a defaultUsername property on the action. To make things clearer, we'll specify the component's value attribute separately from the name attribute, rather than letting the framework infer it. The following snippet shows the code from the PortfolioHomePage action's execute() method, which does the necessary work:

```
public String execute(){
  Collection users = getPortfolioService().getUsers();        ❶
  setUsers( users );

  String selectedUsername = getPortfolioService().getDefaultUser();   ❷
  setDefaultUsername( selectedUsername );

  return SUCCESS;
}
```

First, we set the collection of users that'll be used to create the collection-backed component ❶. Then, we retrieve the username of the featured artist, and we set this on the defaultUsername JavaBeans property ❷ on the action itself. This'll make it available on the ValueStack. Now, let's see how this works with our radio component.

```
<s:form action="SelectPortfolio" >
  <s:radio name="username" list='users' value="defaultUsername"
    listKey="username" listValue="username" label="Select an artist" />
  <s:submit value="Browse"/>
</s:form>
```

Just as in the previous examples, we point the component to our collection of Users and tell it to use each User's username as both the listKey and listValue. Then, we preselect our artist of the week by pointing the value attribute at our defaultUser-name property. At the moment, our featured artist is the user Chad. So the following markup is generated by our tag and action logic:

```
<input type="radio" name="username"  value="Jimmy"/>
<input type="radio" name="username"  value="Charlie Joe"/>
<input type="radio" name="username"  checked="checked" value="Chad"/>
<input type="radio" name="username"  value="Mary"/>
```

As you can see, the username of the featured user was Chad, so the radio button with that value was checked. Note that you can easily go back and reimplement this to stash the featured artist's username in a property on the action called username. Then you wouldn't have to manually specify the value attribute separately from the name attribute. This would've been confusing in our example, since our listKey and listValue attributes are also usernames. How can this be? Consider that the listKey and listValue are used during the iterative cycle of the collection-backed components. During this cycle, each of the Users in the collection is pushed onto the ValueStack. Thus, the listKey and listValue hit the property as found on the current User object. But when the name attribute resolves, the iteration hasn't started; the top object on the ValueStack is the action, not one of the Users. This subtlety explains how the same OGNL, username, can mean different things depending upon the state of the ValueStack. This is admittedly tricky. But once you master the ValueStack, it'll all seem elegant and powerful.

This same preselection process works for all of the collection-backed components. We should make a point about multiple selection before moving on. If you're working with a multiple-selection component, such as the select component with the multiple attribute set to true, your value attribute can point to a property that contains more than one choice, such as an array of usernames in our case. The component will select each of those values.

That does it for the components that we expect all developers will need to use on a regular basis. We'll round out the chapter by pointing you toward some rich components that would enhance any page.

7.3.4   *Bonus components*

We call this the bonus components section because these components are useful but, for one reason or another, not quite as much as the previous components. For this reason, we'll be slightly less exhaustive in our explanations. We'll provide enough to make sure you can use them, but we won't explore advanced cases. As always, we recommend visiting the Struts 2 site to get the details on the full set and functionality of UI component tags.

THE LABEL COMPONENT

The label component shouldn't be confused with the label generated by the other UI components we've covered previously. The label component has a special and simple use case. Figure 7.6 shows how a label component is used.

In the form shown in the figure, the user-name property of a User is written onto the form in a read-only form. This is the purpose of a label component. Usage is straightforward, as you can see from the following snippet, which shows the tag that created the label shown in figure 7.6:

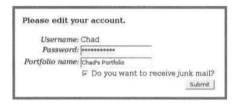

Please edit your account.

Username: Chad
Password: ***********
Portfolio name: Chad's Portfolio
☑ Do you want to receive junk mail?
Submit

Figure 7.6 A `label` **component can be used to display read-only data on a form.**

```
<s:label name="username" label="Username" />
```

Basically, it's just like a read-only textfield.

THE HIDDEN COMPONENT

The hidden component also satisfies a specific use case. Frequently, we need to embed hidden request parameters into a form without showing them to the user. Sometimes you set the values of these hidden fields with values from the server. Sometimes you use JavaScript functionality to calculate the values for these hidden fields. This book won't show you how to write JavaScript, but it'll show you how to use the hidden component. Here's the markup:

```
<s:hidden name="username" />
```

And here's the hidden input field as written into the HTML:

```
<input type="hidden" name="username" value="Chad"
   id="UpdateAccount_username"/>
```

Note that this example obviously rendered with a username property on the Value-Stack that contained the value of Chad. As you might guess, this can't be seen on the page in the browser, but it'll be submitted with the other request parameters.

Now, we'll move on to a more complex component of the bells-and-whistles class.

THE DOUBLESELECT COMPONENT

The doubleselect component addresses the common need to link two select boxes together so that selecting one value from the first box changes the set of choices available in the second box. Such a component might link a first select box of state names to a second box of city names. If you select California in the first box, you get a list of California cities in the second box. When you change to another state, the second box automatically changes to reflect this choice.

To use the doubleselect component, you first have to tell the component which data set it should use to generate the first select box. This works just like setting up a normal select component. The same attributes are used and they function in the same fashion as before. Next, you have to specify a property that'll refer to another data set that can be used as the second list. This property will effectively need to refer to multiple sets of data, most likely one for each item in the first list—for example, a set of cities for each state in the first list. While this can begin to sound tricky, you need to recall that all these things resolve against the ValueStack. With this in mind, everything should make perfect sense. Well, let's hope so anyway.

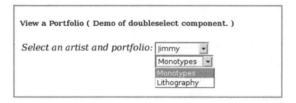

Figure 7.7 The `doubleselect` component dynamically populates a secondary select box based on the primary select box's choice.

Let's start by looking at a screen shot to see what we're doing. Figure 7.7 shows a `doubleselect` component that we've put on our `PortfolioHomePage`.

To select a portfolio to view, you must first select an artist from the primary select box. The `doubleselect` component will then dynamically populate the second box with the names of all of that artist's portfolios. After browsing for a few minutes, the user will select one of the portfolios and that portfolio will be displayed.

The following snippet shows how this `doubleselect` was set up:

```
<h4>Select a portfolio to view.</h4>
  <s:form action="ViewPortfolio">
  <s:doubleselect name="username" list='users' listKey="username"
    listValue="username" doubleName="portfolioName"
    doubleList="portfolios" doubleListValue="name" />
  <s:submit value="View"/>
</s:form>
```

The attributes are just like the normal select box, except there's a second set of attributes that refers to the secondary select box with names such as `doubleXXX`. As we indicated before, the first set of attributes works just like the standard `select` component.

Notably, the `list` attribute refers to a property that holds a set of data from which the first select box will be generated. In this case, it's a set of `User` objects exposed as the `users` property on our `PortfolioHomePage` action. While this tag renders, it'll iterate over each user in the collection, pushing that user onto the `ValueStack` while it renders the markup related to that particular user. In the case of the `doubleselect` component, the markup related to each user will be some JavaScript for dynamically repopulating the secondary select box with the portfolios for that user.

The `doubleList` attribute, like the `list` attribute, is an OGNL expression that points to a property on the `ValueStack`. In logical terms, it points to a set of data that'll be used to build the secondary select box. As we've said, while the `doubleselect` component iterates over the `users`, it pushes each user onto the `ValueStack`. We've implemented our `User` class so that it exposes each user's set of portfolios as a property named `portfolios`. Thus, when a specific user object is on the `ValueStack`, the OGNL expression `portfolios` will evaluate to that user's collection of portfolios. This use of the `ValueStack` as a mini-execution context for each iterative cycle of a tag's rendering is powerful. Try to keep this in mind when you get ready to build your own components, which we'll learn how to do in chapter 13.

As this is a bonus component, and as JavaScript can eat up some book space in a hurry, we won't show you the HTML source generated by this `doubleselect`. But you can always look at it yourself. Ultimately, the `doubleselect` component is a convenient and powerful component that also, incidentally, illustrates elegant use of the ValueStack that drives dynamic generation of HTML with minimal lines of code count.

7.4 Summary

This chapter introduced the powerful Struts 2 UI component tags. With these components in hand, you should be able to quickly assemble rich interfaces that easily wire all your application domain data to the keystrokes and mouse clicks of your end users. If we've done our job, you now understand that the component tags are much more than just tags. In reality, the Struts 2 UI component tags are a mini-MVC framework unto themselves. Let's recap the highlights of this lengthy chapter.

We started the chapter off by detailing how these component tags differ from plain, ordinary tags. First of all, these components do a whole lot more than just render an HTML element. Based on which theme you choose, they can render additional markup to support everything from rich layout to the structural foundations for advanced JavaScript and Ajax support. Perhaps more importantly, the UI components, with a helping hand from OGNL, bind your user interface to all the framework's internal components, including the Validation Framework and the ValueStack. This powerful binding allows you to accomplish such things as automatic validation error reporting and form prepopulation with minimum coding.

We also took pains to assure you that the autogeneration of markup wasn't going to tie your hands as a developer. In fact, the opposite is true. Instead of making it harder to handle special cases and quirky requirements, the UI component architecture has been carefully designed to allow the developer to modify the underlying templates as little or as much as necessary to bend the components to their own needs. Most importantly, your modifications will still fit into the component structure, so you'll be able to reuse and manage your new components as elegantly as the next Struts 2 guru. We'll learn all about modifying the components in chapter 13.

While we don't need to take time to rehash the specifics of the various tags we introduced in this chapter, we want to make a couple of points about them. First of all, we've tried to provide you with a solid understanding of how the UI component tags work. We've also tried to provide you with examples and demonstrations of the most commonly used components and their most common use cases. As always, the Struts 2 framework provides easy paths to the most common tasks, and then leaves the door open for nearly anything else. With this in mind, there's much we left unsaid about even the most common tags. If you need something that doesn't seem to be here, please refer to the Struts 2 website for a comprehensive listing of all the details of each tag. There are even more components than we've shown. In particular, there are additional tags of the rich functionality variety. The website is your best resource for an up-to-date list of the full set of tags.

Now it's time to wrap up the view part of the book. We noted in the introductory section of the book that the view component of the framework was something called the *result*. Working with results is so easy that we haven't said much about them. But we will now. The next chapter discusses the result in detail.

Results in detail

This chapter covers

- Working with results
- Dispatching and redirecting requests
- Building custom results
- Using results with Velocity or FreeMarker

This chapter wraps up part 3. If you recall from the early chapters, the *result* is the MVC view component of the Struts 2 framework. As the central figure of the view, you might be wondering why we started with two chapters on the Struts 2 tag API and left the result for last. Easy. For common development practice, you don't need to know much about the result component itself. In fact, if you use JSP pages for your results, you don't even need to know that the framework supports many different types of results, because the default result type supports JSPs. But the framework comes with support for many different kinds of results, and you can write your own results as well. This chapter explores the details of this important Struts 2 component.

In order to make sure you know what they are and how they work, we start by building a custom result that demonstrates a technique for developing Ajax applications on the Struts 2 platform. Seeing how the framework can easily be adapted to return nontraditional results, such as those required by Ajax clients, serves as a perfect demonstration of the flexibility of the result component. It both teaches you the internals of results and gives you an example of Struts 2 Ajax development. After that, we go on to tour the built-in results that the framework provides for your convenience. These include the default result that supports JSP pages, as well as alternative page-rendering options such as Velocity or FreeMarker templates.

Let's start by refreshing ourselves on the Struts 2 architecture and the role played by results in that architecture.

8.1   Life after the action

To quickly refresh ourselves, a Struts 2 action conducts the work associated with a given request from the client. This work generally consists of a set of calls to business logic and the data tier. We've seen how actions expose JavaBeans properties or model objects for carrying domain data. And we've seen how they provide an `execute()` method as the entry point into their business logic. When the framework determines that a given request should be handled by a given action, the action receives the request data, runs its business logic, and leaves the resulting state of domain data exposed on the `ValueStack`. The last thing the action does is return a control string that tells the framework which of the available results should render the view. Typically, the chosen result uses the data on the `ValueStack` to render some sort of dynamic response to the client.

We've seen this in action throughout the book—in chapter 3 in particular—but we still don't know much about results. So what exactly is a result? In the introductory section of this book, we described the result as the encapsulation of the MVC view concerns of the framework.

DEFINITION   A *classic web application architecture* uses the HTTP request and response cycle to submit requests to the server, and receive dynamically created HTML page responses back from that server. This architecture can most notably be distinguished from Ajax web applications that generally receive HTML fragments, XML, or JSON responses from the server, rather than full HTML pages.

In a classic web application, these view concerns are generally equivalent to creating an HTML page that's sent back to the client. The intelligent defaults of the framework are in perfect tune with this usage. By default, the framework uses a result type that works with JSPs to render these response pages. This result, the `dispatcher` result, makes all the `ValueStack` data available to the executing JSP page. With access to that data, the JSP can render a dynamic HTML page.

Thanks to the intelligent defaults, we've been happily using JSPs from our earliest HelloWorld example, all the while oblivious to the existence of a variety of result types. The following snippet shows how easy it is to use JSPs under the default settings of the framework:

```
<action name="PortfolioHomePage" class=". . . PortfolioHomePage">
  <result>/chapterEight/PortfolioHomePage.jsp</result>
</action>
```

As the snippet demonstrates, you can get your JSPs up and running without knowing anything about what a result is. All you need to know is that a result is the element into which you stuff the location of your JSP page. And that's about all you need to know as long as your project stays the JSP course.

But what if you want to use Velocity or FreeMarker templates to render your HTML pages? Or what if you want to redirect to another URL rather than rendering a page for the client? These alternatives, which also follow the general request and response patterns of a classic web application, are completely supported by the built-in result types that come with the framework. Starting in section 8.2, we'll provide a tour of these commonly used results. If all you want to do is switch from JSPs to FreeMarker or Velocity, or redirect to another URL instead of rendering the HTML page yourself, you can skip ahead to the reference portion of this chapter.

If you want, however, to see how you can adapt results to nonstandard patterns of usage, such as the nonclassic patterns of Ajax applications, then stick around.

8.1.1 Beyond the page: how to use custom results to build Ajax applications with Struts 2

In the rest of this section, we're going to build a custom result that can return a response suitable for consumption by an Ajax client. This example, while focusing on an Ajax use case, is meant, first and foremost, to serve as a thorough introduction to results. But we've chosen Ajax as our example because we know that all new web application frameworks will have to support Ajax. In short, we feel that Struts 2 provides a strong platform for building Ajax applications, and we believe that the flexibility of the result component is a cornerstone of this strength. Thus, it's only natural to use an Ajax example as our case study of a custom result.

As we mentioned, a classic web application returns full HTML page responses to the client. Figure 8.1 illustrates this pattern.

In figure 8.1, the client makes a request that maps to some action. This action, most likely, takes some piece of request data, conducts some business logic, then exposes the subsequent domain data on the ValueStack. The action then passes control to a result that renders a full HTML page, using the prepared data, to build the new HTML page. The key thing here is that the response is a full HTML page, which the client browser uses to rerender its entire window. The response sent back to the client in figure 8.1 is probably rendered by a JSP under the default dispatcher result type. As we've seen, the framework makes this classic pattern of usage easy.

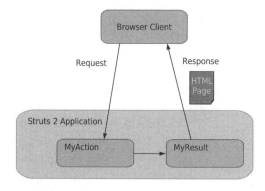

Figure 8.1   Classic web applications return full HTML page responses to the client.

On the other hand, Ajax applications do something entirely different. Instead of requesting full HTML pages, they only want data. This data can come in many forms. Some Ajax applications want HTML fragments as their responses. Some want XML or JSON responses. In short, the content of an Ajax response can be in a variety of formats. Regardless of their differences, they do share one distinct commonality: none of them want a full HTML page. Figure 8.2 illustrates a typical Ajax request and response cycle.

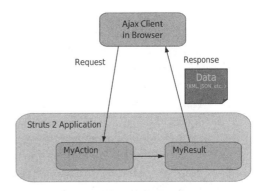

Figure 8.2 Ajax applications expect only data, such as JSON or XML, in the response.

When the Ajax client receives the response, it won't cause the browser to rerender the entire HTML page. On the contrary, it carefully examines the data serialized in the XML or JSON and uses that data to make targeted updates to the affected regions of the current browser page. This is a different kind of response. Luckily, Struts 2 can easily handle this with the flexibility of its result component.

8.1.2 *Implementing a JSON result type*

One of the most challenging things about developing a modern Ajax-based web application is that most of the web application frameworks weren't exactly designed for the innovative patterns of HTTP communication used by them. As we've indicated, the Struts 2 result component provides the adaptive power to make a variety of Ajax techniques fit the framework like a glove. In this section, we're going to develop a result type that can return JSON responses to an Ajax client.

JavaScript Object Notation (JSON) provides a succinct text-based serialization of data objects. JSON can be a powerfully succinct and lightweight means of communication between a web application server and an Ajax client. By using JSON, we can serialize our Java-side data objects and send that serialization in a response to the client. On the client side, we can easily deserialize this JSON into runtime JavaScript objects and make targeted updates to our client-side view without requiring a page refresh. Sounds pretty clean in theory, and it's even cleaner in practice.

HOT LINK   If you want to learn more about JSON, visit the website at http://www. json.org/.

AN AJAX CLIENT TO DEMO OUR RESULT

If we're going to demonstrate a JSON result, we need to actually put some Ajax into our web app. For these purposes, we add an Ajax artist browser to the Struts 2 Portfolio page. This browser provides the visitor with a means of browsing the various artists who're currently hosting portfolios on the site. The visitor can peruse the list of artists and see such details as each artist's full name and the set of portfolios that artist has on the site. From the chapter 8 home page of the sample application, enter the site as a visitor and follow the link to the artist browser. Figure 8.3 shows the Ajax artist browser.

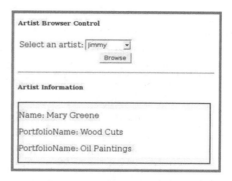

The artist browser is simple. The visitor can peruse some basic information about the selected artist. This information is displayed in the blue box and is updated when the visitor selects a different artist in the select box control. This selection causes an Ajax request to be sent to our Struts 2 application. The response to this request is a JSON serialization of the artist in question. When this response arrives, our JavaScript client code

Figure 8.3   Our artist browser submits Ajax requests to the web application and receives JSON responses via our custom `JSONResult`.

instantiates a JavaScript object from that JSON and uses it to dynamically update the information in the blue window. Nothing else in the window is changed. While simple, this demonstrates a solid Ajax strategy where the page in the browser is an application unto itself. Requests to the server are for JSON-based data, not new pages.

CODING THE JSONRESULT

First things first. If we plan to have Ajax clients demanding JSON responses, we need to build a result that can do that. This leads us to our custom `JSONResult`. Making a custom result is, in some ways, just as easy as writing an action. The only requirement imposed on a result implementation is that it implement the `com.opensymphony.xwork2.Result` interface, as shown:

```
public interface Result extends Serializable {
    public void execute(ActionInvocation invocation) throws Exception;
}
```

As with most framework components, a simple interface defines a highly decoupled and nonrestrictive contract for the component implementation. In this case, we need only provide an `execute()` method for an entry point. This method receives the `ActionInvocation`, which gives it access to all the relevant information for the current request. As we've learned, this `ActionInvocation` provides access to such things as the action itself, the `ActionContext`, and the `ValueStack`. This is how results get their hands on the data.

Let's dive in and have a look at our `JSONResult`. Listing 8.1 shows the full code of our custom result.

Listing 8.1   Serializing objects from the `ValueStack` into JSON responses

```
public class JSONResult implements Result {                    ❶

    public static final String DEFAULT_PARAM = "classAlias";   ❷

    String classAlias;                                         ❸

    public String getClassAlias() {
```

```
      return classAlias;
   }
public void setClassAlias(String classAlias) {          ❸
   this.classAlias = classAlias;
}
public void execute(ActionInvocation invocation)        ❹
   throws Exception {

   ServletActionContext.getResponse().setContentType("text/plain");   ❺
   PrintWriter responseStream =
     ServletActionContext.getResponse().getWriter();    ❻

   ValueStack valueStack = invocation.getStack();
   Object jsonModel = valueStack.findValue("jsonModel");   ❼

   XStream xstream = new XStream(new JettisonMappedXmlDriver());   ❽

   if ( classAlias == null ){
     classAlias = "object";
   }
   xstream.alias(classAlias, jsonModel.getClass() );    ❾

   responseStream.println(xstream.toXML( jsonModel ));   ❿

   }

}
```

Admittedly, there might be a few unfamiliar things in this code. But it's short and simple, as you'll soon see. Basically, this result just takes data from the ValueStack and writes it to the response stream as JSON. Let's go line by line.

First, we implement the result interface ❶. Before getting to the execute() method ❹, which we must implement to fulfill the responsibilities of that interface, we do some stuff to parameterize our result. With a little code, we can allow our results to accept parameters from their XML declarations via the param tag. For this result, we want to accept a parameter than gives us a logical name under which our root data object will be serialized to the JSON. We'll explain why in a moment, but for now just observe that we implement a JavaBeans property classAlias ❸ and then provide a constant called DEFAULT_PARAM ❷ that names our classAlias as the default parameter. Each result can define a default parameter, which can be passed in without being named.

Now, to the heart of the matter. Once inside the execute() method, we get down to work. Since we're going to return an HTTP response to the client, we use the ServletActionContext, a servlet-specific subclass of the ActionContext, to set the content type ❺ on the servlet response object and get the output stream ❻ from that same object. This is standard fare for all results that write a response for the client. Next, we use the ActionInvocation to retrieve the ValueStack and programmatically pull the domain object we want to serialize from it ❼. Note that in this naive, but easy-to-follow, result implementation, we're requiring that the action place the object that it wants to send to the client in a property called jsonModel. We could perhaps parameterize this also, but we'll save that for later refactoring.

Point of interest

Default parameters provide another mechanism for supporting intelligent defaults. The result type we've been using with JSPs, the `RequestDispatcher`, takes the location of the JSP page as a default parameter. If you were to consult the source code for the `RequestDispatcher` result, you'd find that it defines location as its default parameter in the same fashion as the `JSONResult` defines the `classAlias` parameter as its default. The benefit of defining a default parameter is that you don't have to name that parameter when you pass it in.

In the following result definition, you can see that we just put the location of the JSP in the body of the `result` element, rather than submitting it via a `param` tag.

```
<result>/chapterEight/VisitorHomePage.jsp</result>
```

This path value is automatically set to the location property of the `RequestDispatcher` result object. It would be valid, but unnecessary, to specify the location property with an explicit `param` tag as follows:

```
<result type="dispatcher">
   <param name="location">/chapterEight/VisitorHomePage.jsp</
   param>
</result>
```

Much more verbose. Thanks to the framework's dedication to intelligent defaults, we can usually avoid such lengthy elements in our declarative architecture documents. Note that we also added the unnecessary `type` attribute here. It's unnecessary because the `RequestDispatcher` is the default result type as long as you inherit from the `struts-default` package.

Now it's time to serialize that object. We're using a couple of open source packages to do this: XStream (http://xstream.codehaus.org) and Jettision (http://jettison.codehaus.org). XStream allows us to serialize Java objects to XML, and the Jettison driver for XStream adds in the JSON part. First, we create an instance of the XStream serializer with the Jettison driver ❽. Then we use our `classAlias` to set the alias for the object we're serializing ❾. If we didn't do this, our JSON would name the object with the fully qualified class name—`manning.utils.User`. It'd be much nicer to have this just show up with a name that's more suitable for our JavaScript code, such as user or artist. We've parameterized this value so the user can choose his own alias. Finally, we serialize the `jsonModel` to the response output stream ❿.

For the curious, here's what our JSON response looks like:

```
{"artist":{"username":"Mary","password":"max","portfolioName":"Mary's
Portfolio","firstName":"Mary","lastName":"Greene",
"receiveJunkMail":"false"}}
```

Even without a short course in JSON, you should be able to see that this notation defines an associative-array–based object. An *associative array* is something like a normal array, but with values mapped to string keys instead of numerical indexes. In this case, the JSON defines an object named `artist`. The `artist` object is an associative array containing name-value pairs equivalent to the properties of our Struts 2 Portfolio's user object. Our JavaScript client code can make quick work of instantiating an object from this bit of JSON, as you'll soon see.

And, believe it or not, that's all there is to our custom `JSONResult`. We could make many refinements to this result, but this one works and has remained simple enough to give you a good idea of how results get their hands on the `ValueStack` and other objects they want. With a result that can return JSON to our client, we're now ready to implement some Ajax functionality in our application. The next sections show how we implement our Ajax artist browser that uses this `JSONResult`.

AN AJAX CLIENT

On the client, we use JavaScript Ajax techniques to submit an asynchronous request to our Struts 2 application. Since Ajax is beyond the scope of this book, we'll be brief here. We'd like to point out that our Ajax techniques come directly from another Manning title, *Ajax in Action*. If you'd like to learn more about Ajax, we highly recommend that acclaimed book.

The artist browser client code is defined in the ajaxUserBrowser.jsp page. That page sets up the select box and the information window, as seen in figure 8.3. The select box registers an Ajax JavaScript function, `fetchUser()`, for its onchange event. This function, defined in ajaxUserBrowser.js, submits the request. It gets the selected username from the select box, then submits an asynchronous request to the server. All of this can be seen in the following snippet:

```
function fetchUser(){
  console=document.getElementById('console');
  var selectBox = document.getElementById('AjaxRetrieveUser_username');
  var selectedIndex = selectBox.selectedIndex;
  var selectedValue = selectBox.options[selectedIndex].value
  sendRequest("AjaxRetrieveUser.action",
              "username=" + selectedValue , "POST");
}
```

Note that we no longer use the form to submit the request; we use programmatic access to send our request. Nonetheless, we still use a normal Struts 2 action as our target URL. You can dig deeper into the `sendRequest` function if you want to see the specifics of the Ajax stuff, but suffice it to say that it just gets an `XMLHttpRequest` object and uses that object to submit our request. It also, notably, registers a callback function that handles the JSON response when it arrives. Such callback functions are at the core of any Ajax application; they make the dynamic changes to the page when the response returns with the new data. Let's take a look at how our callback handles our JSON response. Here's the `onReadyState` function that handles our server's response:

```
function onReadyState() {
  var ready=req.readyState;
  var jsonObject=null;

  if ( ready == READY_STATE_COMPLETE ){      ❶
```

```
        jsonObject=eval( "("+ req.responseText +")" );         ❷
        toFinalConsole ( jsonObject );         ❸
    }
}
```

The XMLHttpRequest object actually calls this function at several intermediate stages of completion before the response has completely returned. In this case, we're not going to do anything until the response is fully cooked. With this in mind, we test for completion ❶ before starting to process the response. If the response is complete, we retrieve the JSON response text and directly instantiate it as a JavaScript object, the jsonObject, by using the built-in JavaScript eval() function ❷. With that one line, we now have a JavaScript version of the same object that our action prepared on the Java side. That's undeniably cool. Next, we send this object off to a function that dynamically modifies our blue window to show the new artist's information ❸. Again, if you're interested in the details of our dynamic HTML techniques, you can look at the source code to see how we update the artist info on the fly, but it's off topic for us to explore in this book.

Now that we have an Ajax client in place, it's time to build the action that processes the request. As you'll see, it's no different from the other actions we've been working with throughout the book.

THE ACTION

How hard is it to write an Ajax action? There's nothing to it. In fact, it's no different than a normal action. One of the good things about the clean MVC of Struts 2 is that our action won't have to know anything about what's happening in the result. Our actions continue to function in the same old mode of receiving data from request parameters, executing some business logic, preparing the final data objects, and then handing everything over to the result. In this case, our action receives a username from the Ajax artist browser's select box, retrieves a full user object, and puts it on a JavaBeans property where the result can find it. For our Ajax example, we wire this action to a result of the JSONResult type so that the user object gets serialized to JSON. But we could just as easily use this same action in non-Ajax settings if we like; we'd just have to wire it to a JSP or something. The action doesn't care whether the result serializes the user object to JSON or reads properties off of it with JSP-based Struts 2 tags.

Just to prove we've got nothing up our sleeves, we look at the RetrieveUser action class to confirm that we're still working with a standard Struts 2 action. Listing 8.2 shows the full code from RetrieveUser.java.

Listing 8.2   RetrieveUser retrieves a user and sets the jsonModel property

```
public class RetrieveUser extends ActionSupport {

  public String execute(){

    User user = getPortfolioService().getUser( getUsername() );     ❶
    setJsonModel(user);         ❷

    return SUCCESS;
  }
```

```
    private String username;        ❸
    private Object jsonModel;

    . . .

    JavaBeans Property Implementations Omitted for Brevity

    . . .

}
```

Again, this looks just like any other action we've been working with. It doesn't matter that the request came from a JavaScript XMLHttpRequest object or that the response is going to be a JSON serialization. Incoming and outgoing data is still carried on JavaBeans properties ❸. The execute() method still conducts our business logic, consisting of a call to our service object's getUser() method ❶, and then exposes the resulting data object, the user, by setting it on a local JavaBeans property ❷. We then return the result string to indicate which result we want to fire. If that result is of type JSONResult, it pulls the user off of the ValueStack, serializes it in JSON, and sends it back to the client.

The cool thing is that this action could be reused with a normal full-page JSP result without modifying a line of code. Let's say we had a JSP page that would rerender the entire page with the updated User information. We could just wire it to this same action and it would read the User information off of the ValueStack, with Struts 2 tags, as it built the page. Both the JSON result and the JSP result can easily work with the User object on the ValueStack. When the action prepares the User, it doesn't care who does what with that data. Any result could be wired to this action. This can be helpful if you're, say, migrating an existing Struts 2 web application from classic full-page HTTP cycles to a more Ajax-based application.

DECLARING AND USING THE JSONRESULT TYPE

Now that you've seen all the parts, let's look at how we wire it all together for the Struts 2 Portfolio. We've already been through the process of declaring actions and their results, but in this case we've created a whole new result type, and that requires more work. Previously, we've only worked with results that come predeclared as a part of the struts-default package. Obviously, our JSONResult hasn't been declared in that default package. So, we need to declare our JSONResult as an available result type in our package. We do this with the following declaration from our chapterEight.xml document:

```
<result-types>
  <result-type name="customJSON" class="manning.chapterEight.JSONResult" />
</result-types>
```

This is simple. We use the result-type element, which must be contained in the result-types element, to map a logical name to our implementation class. With this in place, we can use this result type anywhere in our package or in any package that extends our package. We do just that in the declaration of our AjaxRetrieveUser action, which is the action that responds to our Ajax request. Here's the declaration of that action:

```
<action name="AjaxRetrieveUser"
    class="manning.chapterEight.RetrieveUser">
  <result type="customJSON">artist</result>
</action>
```

Since the custom JSON result type is not the default result type for this package, we must specify it with the `type` attribute. If we were going to do a lot of Ajax work, we'd probably make a separate package for those requests and declare the JSON result as our default type. Next, see that we've passed in `artist` as our default parameter, which is set to our result's `classAlias` property. Earlier, we saw how this was used as the name of the JSON serialization of our object.

That covers all the pieces of our Ajax artist browser. With this mapping in place, our Ajax request, submitted by our JavaScript client-side application, will come into the framework and hit the `AjaxRetrieveUser` action. Looking back to figures 8.1 and 8.2, you can see that the framework handles this Ajax submission no differently from normal requests. The `AjaxRetrieveUser` action prepares the `User` data, puts it on the `ValueStack`, and hands processing of the response over to the `customJSON` result. That result serializes our user object into JSON and sends it back to the client. On the client, a callback method receives the JSON, makes a JavaScript object out of it, and passes that object to a method that dynamically updates the page to show the new user information. That's one way to do Ajax with Struts 2.

Ajax Tips

As you might suspect from a newly minted web application framework, there's a bit of attention being paid to Ajax. Using a custom result to return an Ajax-suitable re-sponse is one good way to build a Struts 2 Ajax application. JSON is definitely not the only option for implementing Ajax. If you wanted to use something else, such as XML, you could easily roll your own result type for returning just about anything.

We should point out that there's already a plug-in to the framework that provides a more robust version of a JSON result type. You can find this and other plug-ins in the Struts 2 plug-in repository at http://cwiki.apache.org/S2PLUGINS/home.html. We recommend you test-drive that plug-in if you want to do something along the lines we've demonstrated in this chapter to integrate Ajax into your Struts 2 application.

Additionally, there's an Ajax theme for the Struts 2 tag API. At the time of writing, this tag library is too beta for us to document. However, we highly recommend visiting the Struts 2 website to check on the status of this exciting project.

By now, you can probably see the flexibility the result component adds to the Struts 2 framework. The separation is so clean that the same set of actions can be wired to many different kinds of result types. Additionally, the result type itself is flexible enough to support any kind of result that you could dream up. It has all of the resources of the framework, such as the all-important `ValueStack`, at its disposal.

Now that you have a feel for what results can do, it's time to peruse the various types that come with the framework. The offering is rich; we'll start by looking at the most commonly used types.

8.2 *Commonly used result types*

In this section, we cover the usage of the most common result types. The framework comes with quite a few built-in result types, and we invite you to peruse the whole set of them on the Struts 2 website: http://struts.apache.org/2.x/docs/result-types.html. In this section, we show you how to use the ones we think will cover 90 percent of your development needs. The results shown in table 8.1 cover the most common use cases of a classic web application. We cover each of these thoroughly in this section.

Table 8.1   The most commonly used built-in result types

Result type	Use case	Parameters
dispatcher	JSPs, other web application resources such as servlets	location (default), parse
redirect	Tell browser to redirect to another URL	location (default), parse
redirectAction	Tell browser to redirect to another Struts action	actionName (default), namespace, arbitrary parameters that will become querystring params

Note that all these built-in result types are defined in struts-default.xml. They're only built in if you extend the struts-default package. We assume that you'll do this. A result-type declaration maps a logical name to a class implementation. The following snippet shows the declaration of the FreemarkerResult from struts-default.xml:

```
<result-type name="freemarker"
  class="org.apache.struts2.views.freemarker.FreemarkerResult"/>
```

In all packages that extend the struts-default package, we can simply refer to the FreemarkerResult by the more convenient name freemarker. Throughout our following coverage of the various built-in result types, we'll indicate both the formal class name and the logical name to which that class is mapped: for example, the FreemarkerResult, a.k.a. freemarker. You'll see what we mean. Incidentally, we cover the Freemarker-Result in section 8.3.

8.2.1 *The RequestDispatcher, a.k.a. dispatcher*

The short story is that you use this result when you want to render a JSP page as the result of your action. For the normal Struts 2 workflow, this understanding of the dispatcher result type will serve you well enough. By normal Struts 2 workflow, we mean that a request comes in to an action, that action processes the request and hands off to a result that writes the response back to the client. In this routine use case, using the RequestDispatcher result is easy.

The fact that we've been using this result type in all of our sample code, without mentioning it, speaks to the ease with which you can use it. So far, we haven't even had to specify this type when declaring our results. This is because when you extend the `struts-default` package, you inherit the `DispatcherResult` as the default type. One result type per package is allowed to claim itself as the default type. Here's the snippet from struts-default.xml that specifies the `dispatcher` as the default type of the `struts-default` package:

```
<result-type name="dispatcher"
  class=" . . . ServletDispatcherResult" default="true"/>
```

First, note that we've omitted the full package name of this class due to space concerns. With this declaration in place, we can write simple result elements like the following if we are using JSPs:

```
<action name="PortfolioHomePage" class=". . . chapEight.PortfolioHomePage">
  <result>/chapterEight/PortfolioHomePage.jsp</result>
</action>
```

Using JSPs in the common use case is a no-brainer; for the most part, we can keep our gray matter out of this. However, there's a fair chunk of logic occurring, or potentially occurring, within this innocent-looking result. At the least, you might be wondering why it's called the `DispatcherResult`. And, eventually, you'll probably need to know how to use this result in a nonstandard Struts 2 workflow. With that in mind, we present the following account of what a dispatcher result does. Warning: it helps to understand the Servlet API. If you need a primer, we still recommend reading the Servlet Specification; it's the shortest path to enlightenment.

THE SERVLET HEART OF THE DISPATCHER RESULT

At the core of the `DispatcherResult` result type is a `javax.servlet.Request-Dispatcher`. This object, from the Servlet API, provides the functionality that allows one servlet to hand processing over to another resource of the web application. Usually this is a servlet, and this servlet is commonly a JSP page. The handoff must be to another servlet in the same web application as the first servlet. The `Request-Dispatcher` exposes two methods for handing execution over to the other servlet: `include()` and `forward()`. These two methods determine how much control over the response will be given to the secondary resource.

A temporary handoff is done via a call to the `include()` method. This means that the first servlet has already started writing its own response to the client but wants to include the output from the second servlet in that response. A permanent handoff is done via a call to the `forward()` method. In this case, the first servlet must not have sent any response to the client before the call is made. In a forward, the servlet is delegating the complete response rendering to the second servlet.

These two dispatch methods are quite different from each other, but they do share some things in common. Most importantly, they're both distinguished from an HTTP redirection. Whereas a redirection sends the browser a redirect response telling it to make another request to a different URL, the dispatcher methods don't send the browser any response at all. The transfer of control, from one resource to another, is completely within the server. In fact, it's even in the same thread of execution. Another important detail is that the include() and forward() methods both pass the original request and response objects to the new servlet. This important detail allows the second servlet to essentially process the same request.

NORMAL WORKFLOW: DISPATCHING AS A FORWARD()

Now let's get back to Struts 2. Let's consider the normal Struts 2 workflow from a Servlet perspective. By normal workflow, we mean the simple case where an action receives the request, processes the business logic, prepares the data, then asks a result to render the response. This case has no indirection, no slight of hand, just an action and a result. We start by examining the case with which we're already familiar, the JSP result.

First of all, note that the framework is itself actually just a servlet. Well, a servlet filter, but that's a fine point not worth quibbling over for the moment. When the framework first processes a request, we can consider it as the work of the *primary* servlet. Thus, when your initial action is executing, it's executing as the primary servlet. When it's finished, the action selects a JSP result to render the view. Since JSP pages are actually servlets, this transfer of execution from the action to the JSP page is a transfer of control from the first servlet to a second. This normal case is done with the Request-Dispatcher's forward() method.

This implies that the Struts 2 action, processing under the control of the first servlet, obviously can't have written anything to the response yet. If it had, we'd be limited to an include() call. By forwarding to the result JSP servlet, the action gives full control over writing the response to that JSP. This is the low-level expression of the framework's MVC separation of concerns, in case you're interested in that sort of thing. Note that the JSP has access to all of the data from the action via the ThreadLocal ActionContext, and its most important citizen, the ValueStack; this access to the ActionContext depends on the fact that the dispatching of requests, with forward() or include(), always occurs on the same thread of execution.

FORWARDING TO ANOTHER SERVLET

But you don't have to limit yourself to JSPs. You can point a RequestDispatcher result at any resource of a web application. By web application, we're talking about the Servlet API concept. In addition to a JSP, it could be another servlet or even a static resource of some kind that can be served by your web application. In the chapter 8 version of the Struts 2 Portfolio, we've built a demonstration of handing off to another servlet in the web application. On the chapter 8 home page, enter your favorite color in the field shown in figure 8.4.

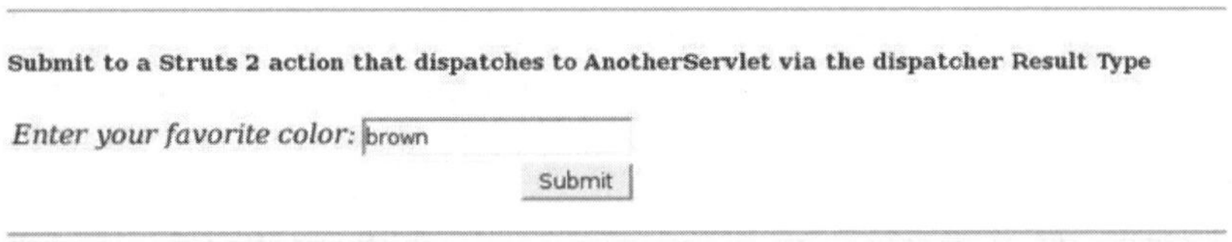

Submit to a Struts 2 action that dispatches to AnotherServlet via the dispatcher Result Type

Enter your favorite color: brown

Submit

Figure 8.4 A simple form that submits to a Struts 2 action that uses another servlet to render the result.

When you submit your form, the `ForwardToAnotherServlet` Struts 2 action does some simple processing and then turns over the rendering of the result, a.k.a. the servlet response, to another servlet in our web application. Listing 8.3 shows our `AnotherServlet` class, the servlet that renders the response for our action.

Listing 8.3   `AnotherServlet` renders a response, pulling data from various locations

```
public class AnotherServlet extends HttpServlet {          ❶

  protected void doPost(HttpServletRequest request, HttpServletResponse
      response) throws ServletException, IOException {
    response.setContentType( "text/html");
    response.getOutputStream().println( "<html>");
    response.getOutputStream().println( "<head>");          ❷
    response.getOutputStream().println( "</head>");
    response.getOutputStream().println( "<body>");
    response.getOutputStream().println("<p>Hello from
      anotherServlet's doPost()</p>");
    response.getOutputStream().println("<p>Attribute set in the
      struts 2 action = " +
      request.getAttribute("attributeSetInS2Action" ) + "</p>");   ❸
    response.getOutputStream().println("<p>Favorite color from
      request parameters = " + request.getParameter("favoriteColor")
      + "</p>");          ❹
    String propertyFromAction = (String)

  ActionContext.getContext().getValueStack().findValue("testProperty");  ⟵
    response.getOutputStream().println("<p>Value retrieved from action    ❺
      property on ValueStack = " + propertyFromAction + "</p>");   ⟵
    response.getOutputStream().println( "</body>");
    response.getOutputStream().println( "</html>");
  }
}
```

`AnotherServlet` extends `HttpServlet` ❶ to become a servlet. Then it overrides the `doPost()` method. As you can see, the `AnotherServlet` servlet writes a fully structured HTML page ❷ to the response's output stream. It even sets the content-type header for the HTTP response. This is what we mean when we say that a forward gives full control of the response rendering over to the other servlet. Next, the servlet begins writing to the response stream.

AnotherServlet pulls data from several sources while rendering the response just to demonstrate the various methods for passing data. First, we pull a named `request` attribute ❸ into the rendering. This attribute will have been set in our Struts 2 action. This demonstrates passing data via the Servlet API objects, the request map in this case. Next, we pull the request parameter ❹, the favorite color that we entered in the form that was submitted. This also comes to us via the Servlet API's request object.

But what about the Struts 2 data? Next, just to prove that the `ActionContext`'s `ThreadLocal` nature does indeed make all of the Struts 2 stuff available to our dispatched servlet, we pull some values, programmatically, from the `ValueStack` itself ❺. As it turns out, this value from the `ValueStack` was a property we set on our action during its execution. This method of retrieving values from the ValueStack, from the secondary servlet, approximates the details of how our Struts 2 JSP tags have been accessing our ValueStack values. In this case, we had to go with programmatic access, but that's what the tag implementations do themselves.

Now let's take a look at the ForwardToAnotherServlet action to see how all of this data was put in place prior to the dispatch. Listing 8.4 shows the complete code from FrowardToAnotherServlet.java.

Listing 8.4 Putting data on a property and in the request map

```
public class ForwardToAnotherServlet extends ActionSupport implements
  RequestAware{

  public String execute(){
    getRequest().put( "attributeSetInS2Action", "Hello from       ❶
    a request attribute set in the S2 Action");
      return SUCCESS;
    }

  private Map request;

  public void setRequest(Map request) {
    this.request = request;
  }
  public Map getRequest (){
    return request;
  }

  public String getTestProperty(){                        ❷
    return "myValueFromActionProperty";
  }
}
```

Not too much new here. We just want to follow the data flow to demonstrate how two servlets, linked by the RequestDispatcher, share in the processing of a single request. First, we see that our action uses the RequestAware interface to have the request map injected. It then uses the request map to set the attributeSetInS2Action attribute ❶, which AnotherServlet will retrieve, as we saw in listing 8.3. We also see that this action exposes the testProperty JavaBeans property ❷, which AnotherServlet pulls off the ValueStack with programmatic access.

As for wiring our action to our result rendering servlet, it works just like a JSP:

```
<action name="ForwardToAnotherServlet"
    class="manning.chapterEight.ForwardToAnotherServlet">
  <result>/anotherServlet</result>
</action>
```

We put the path to the servlet, relative to our web application, just as we've been putting the paths to our JSPs. Note that this all assumes we've declared AnotherServlet with a servlet mapping in our web application's web.xml file. Take a look at that file, in the source code, if you want to see how that's done.

We should sum up the point of this example. The AnotherServlet example renders an HTML page result. If you have the choice, you should never do this. This is what JSPs are for. However, this example will prove useful as a demonstration of accessing data from another servlet if you ever find yourself called to integrate Struts 2 with an external servlet. This is something that happens fairly often. As this example demonstrates, it's easy to pass data from the framework to external web application resources, such as AnotherServlet.

Now we've seen two normal workflow examples of an initial action passing control over to a servlet, or JSP, for rendering its response. In these normal cases, we're still in the realm of the forward() method of the RequestDispatcher. Let's now look at some cases where the include() method is used.

DISPATCHING AS AN INCLUDE()

It's quite important to know when the dispatcher will use a forward() and when it'll use an include(). The main reason is because included material must make sense as a fragment, since it's dumped midstream into the primary response. Our previous servlet example, which wrote its own <html>, <head>, and <body> tags, would most likely not be a suitable target for inclusion, as the initial servlet might already have written these elements. So when will we see an include?

The most common case is the use of the Struts 2 action tag. This tag, which we've already seen in chapter 6, invokes the execution of another action from the execution of a JSP page. All actions invoked via the action tag will be includes. This means the result of the action, if it renders, must be a valid fragment of the first result. If you want more details on this case, please refer back to our action tag examples in chapter 6.

SETTING UP A REQUESTDISPATCHER RESULT

Configuring a dispatcher result is simple. First, the dispatcher result must be defined as a result type. As with all of the built-in result types, this is already done in the struts-default package, which your packages will typically extend. In the case of the dispatcher result type, it was configured as the default result type. The following snippet shows the configuration of the dispatcher result type from the struts-default.xml file:

```
<result-type name="dispatcher"
    class="org.apache.struts2.dispatcher.ServletDispatcherResult"
    default="true"/>
```

The result-type element maps a logical name to a Java class that provides an implementation of the Result interface. These declarations are made on the package level and can be inherited. This is just as we've seen with interceptors. Since our Struts 2 Portfolio packages extend the struts-default package, we can use this result type in our applications. We just need to reference it by its name, as follows:

```
<action name="SelectPortfolio"
  class="manning.chapterSeven.SelectPortfolio">
    <result type="dispatcher" >
      /chapterSeven/SelectPortfolio.jsp
    </result>
</action>
```

This `action` declaration, from our chapterSeven.xml file, doesn't actually specify the `type` attribute of the result element like this. We've added it only for this listing. We can omit it in the actual application because the declaration of the `dispatcher` result type sets its default attribute to `true`.

Like many of the result types, it's possible to parameterize the `dispatcher` result type in a given instance. The `dispatcher` has two parameters, but they're seldom used, as they both provide strong default values. The first parameter is the `location` parameter. This parameter gives the location of the servlet resource to which we should dispatch the request. The second parameter is the `parse` parameter. This parameter determines whether the location string will be parsed for OGNL expressions. Here's the previously seen action declaration rewritten to explicitly use these parameters:

```
<action name="SelectPortfolio"
    class="manning.chapterSeven.SelectPortfolio">
  <result type="dispatcher" >
    <param name="location">/chapterSeven/SelectPortfolio.jsp</param>
    <param name="parse">true</param>
  </result>
</action>
```

You probably won't use these parameters too often because the default settings are so sensible. We show them here to demonstrate how to parameterize your results. In this case, the `location` parameter is what's known as the default parameter of the `result` element. Since `location` is the default parameter, you can omit the `param` tag, as we usually do, and pass the path to your JSP in as the text content of your `result` element. As for the `parse` parameter, it's true by default. If you ever feel the need to squelch parsing of OGNL in your location string, you can use this parameter.

Why would you want to put OGNL in your location string? The short answer is to make it dynamic. For instance, you could dynamically build querystring parameters. In the case of the dispatcher result, dynamically inserting data doesn't make a lot of sense. All the data that you might insert into the querystring will be available to your result page anyway, via OGNL, tags, and so on. We demonstrate how to take advantage of OGNL parsing in the location string in the next section, which covers redirect results.

Rather than returning a page to the client yourself, you'll sometimes want to redirect the client to another web resource. The next two results, from table 8.1, provide ways of redirecting to other resources. We start with the standard redirect result.

8.2.2 *The ServletRedirectResult, a.k.a. redirect*

Though the `RequestDispatcher` result can hand over processing to another resource, and is commonly the right tool for the job, you'll sometimes want to use a redirect to hand control to that other resource. What's the difference? The defining characteristic of the `RequestDispatcher` is that the handoff is completely on the server side. Everything happens within the Servlet API and on the same thread. This means that all the data from the first resource is available to the second resource via both the Servlet API and the Struts 2 `ActionContext`. We saw this clearly in our examples from the `RequestDispatcher` section. This is critical if your second servlet expects to have full access to all the data.

A redirect, on the other hand, considers the current request finished and issues an HTTP redirect response that tells the browser to point to a new location. This act officially closes the current request from both the Struts 2 `ActionContext` perspective and the Servlet request perspective. In other words, all server-side request- and action-related state is gone. While it's still possible to persist some of the current request's data over to the second resource, the techniques for doing so are inefficient. We'll show how to do this, but if you really need to carry much data over to the second resource, you should probably just use the `RequestDispatcher`.

NOTE If you need to persist data from the initial request to the resource that's the target of your redirect, you have two choices. The first choice is to persist the data in querystring parameters that are dynamically populated with values from the `ValueStack`. You can embed OGNL in the `location` parameter to do this. We'll demonstrate this technique when we discuss the `ActionRedirect` result, a special redirect result to be used when redirecting to other Struts 2 actions.

The second option is to persist data to a session-scoped map. This has a couple of drawbacks. First, it only works when the secondary resource belongs to the same web application. Second, best practices warn against unnecessary use of the session scope as a data storage.

The most common reason for using a redirect arises from the need to change the URL shown in the browser. When a redirect is issued, the browser handles the response by making a new request to the URL given in the redirect. The URL to which the redirect is issued replaces the previous URL in the browser. The fact that the new URL replaces the old URL in the browser makes the redirect particularly useful when you don't want the user to resubmit the previous URL by clicking the Reload button. Or, for that matter, any time you just want to change the URL in the browser.

SETTING UP A REDIRECT RESULT

As with all Struts 2 components, the `redirect` result must be declared and mapped to a logical name. And as with all built-in components, this occurs in the struts-default.xml document. The following snippet shows the declaration of this result type from that file:

```
<result-type name="redirect"
class="org.apache.struts2.dispatcher.ServletRedirectResult"/>
```

Nothing unusual here. Note that this result isn't set to default as the `Request-Dispatcher` declaration was. This just means that we need to explicitly specify our `type` attribute when we use this result type. The following snippet shows how we might configure a redirect result that would tell the browser to go to another URL:

```
<action name="SendUserToSearchEngineAction" class="myActionClass">
    <result type='redirect'>http://www.google.com</result>
</action>
```

To redirect to another resource, we just need to specify a full URL, or a relative one if the redirect is to another resource in our web application, and name the redirect type explicitly. Here we redirect to the omnipotent Google search engine. Note again that the name given to the `type` attribute matches the `name` attribute of the `result-type` element from the `struts-default` package.

The redirect result supports two parameters: `location` and `parse`. These are the same parameters supported by the `RequestDispatcher`. As you can guess, the `location` parameter is the default parameter, so we don't have to specify it by name when we give the URL for the location in the body of the `result` element. And `parse` is `true` by default, so unless you have reason to turn off the framework's parsing of the location value for OGNL expressions, you won't be handling that parameter much either. Since the use of embedded OGNL to pass along querystring params to the secondary resource is particularly helpful with redirect results, we'll explore this technique now. But keep in mind that you can use embedded OGNL with any of the result types that support it.

EMBEDDING OGNL TO CREATE DYNAMIC LOCATIONS

We should now look at an example of how to embed an OGNL expression in the `location` parameter value in order to pass some data forward to the second action. Note that this method of embedding OGNL to create dynamic parameter values can be used in any of the previous result types that support the `parse` parameter. The following example shows how we could pull a value from the `ValueStack`, at runtime, and pass that value as a querystring parameter to the same URL we used in the previous example:

```
<action name="SendUserToSearchEngineAction" class="myActionClass">
  <result type='redirect' >
    http://www.google.com/?myParam=${defaultUsername}
  </result>
</action>
```

First of all, take careful notice of the fine point of the dollar sign. We've been using the percent sign throughout the book for our OGNL escape sequence, but in the context of our struts.xml, and other XML documents used for the declarative architecture, we must use a $ instead. Other than this inconsistency, the OGNL access still works the same. The OGNL looks up the property on the `ValueStack`. Provided that the imaginary `myActionClass` did something to make the `defaultUsername` property appear on the `ValueStack`, such as exposing it as a JavaBeans property, this result would render into a redirect response that'd point the browser to the following URL (assuming that the `defaultUsername` property, on the `ValueStack`, held the value of Mary): http://www.google.com/?myParam=Mary

Of course, this URL will get you nowhere. We show a real example of using this kind of embedded OGNL when we discuss the `redirectAction` result in the next section. For now, just note that you can use OGNL to build dynamic parameter values by pulling values from the `ValueStack`. You can do this to all the parameters that a result takes, as long as the result type itself supports the parsing of OGNL.

8.2.3 *The ServletActionRedirectResult, a.k.a. redirectAction*

The `redirectAction` result does the same thing as the plain redirect result, with one important difference. This version of `redirect` can understand the logical names of the Struts 2 actions as defined in your declarative architecture. This means that you don't have to embed real URLs in your result declarations. Instead you can feed the `redirectAction` names and namespaces from your action and package declarations. This makes your declarations more robust in the face of changes to URL patterns. As an example of such a URL pattern change, let's say you wanted to change the action extension from .action to .go. If you'd used the plain redirect result extensively to target Struts 2 actions, then you'd have a lot of hard-coded URLs to adjust.

As an example, let's look at the `Login` action mapping from our earlier versions of the Struts 2 Portfolio application. This mapping, as seen in the following snippet, uses the plain `redirect` result:

```
<action name="Login" class="manning.chapterSeven.Login">
  <result type="redirect">
    /chapterSeven/secure/AdminPortfolio.action
  </result>
  <result name="input">/chapterSeven/Login.jsp</result>
</action>
```

As you can see, we have a real URL embedded in our declarative architecture. This would have to be manually corrected in the face of our hypothetical action extension change. The following snippet, from the chapter 8 version of the application, shows how we can do the same thing with the `redirectAction` instead:

```
<action name="Login" class="manning.chapterEight.Login">
  <result type="redirectAction">
    <param name="actionName">AdminPortfolio</param>
    <param name="namespace">/chapterEight/secure</param>
  </result>
  <result name="input">/chapterEight/Login.jsp</result>
</action>
```

Functionally, this is no different than the previous version. They both create a redirect response that points to the following URL: http://localhost:8080/manningSample App/chapterEight/secure/AdminPortfolio.action

The difference is that the `redirectAction` result would stand up to a variety of changes in the URL pattern handling, such as the action extension we mentioned earlier.

There is one other goodie supported by the `redirectAction` result. We can easily configure request parameters to be passed on to the target action. With the plain redirect, we had to write the querystring parameter out by hand. Now we can use the `param` tag. In this case, we give the parameter whatever name and value we like. These arbitrary name-value pairs are appended as querystring parameters to the generated URL. Take the following real example from our chapter 8 version of the Struts 2 Portfolio's `Login` action:

```
<action name="Login" class="manning.chapterEight.Login">
  <result type="redirectAction">
    <param name="actionName">AdminPortfolio</param>
    <param name="namespace">/chapterEight/secure</param>
    <param name="param1">hardCodedValue</param>        ❶
    <param name="param2">${testProperty}</param>       ❷
  </result>
  <result name="input">/chapterEight/Login.jsp</result>
</action>
```

This result configuration is no different than the previous except for the addition of two request parameters. First, we hard-code a value for param1 ❶. Then, we use our previously learned OGNL embedding skills to dynamically pass a second parameter ❷. Here's the new URL to which our result will redirect the browser, complete with our querystring parameters: http://localhost:8080/manningSampleApp/chapterEight/secure/AdminPortfolio.action?param1=hardCodedValue&param2=777

As you can see, our Login action must have done something to make the testProperty property exist on the ValueStack and hold the value of 777. As it turns out, our AdminPortfolio action won't do anything with these values except write them to the result page to prove they went through. But this should be adequate to demonstrate how one goes about passing dynamic values into result parameter values with embedded OGNL. Again, any result that supports a parse parameter supports these kinds of techniques.

With that, we're finished with the most commonly used result types. Some developers will rarely need anything more. But while JSPs still retain their preeminence, many teams are choosing Velocity or FreeMarker to render their response pages. In the next section, we look at the results that support using Velocity or FreeMarker templates instead of JSPs.

8.3   JSP alternatives

In this section, we a look at two result types that support alternative view-layer technologies: FreeMarker and Velocity. While using these is as straightforward as using the dispatcher result for JSPs, we do want to give clear demonstrations of using each. For each of these alternative technologies, we'll rewrite one of the pages that we've already done with JSPs and the dispatcher result.

In the past, some energy has been spent debating whether templating engines provide better performance than JSPs. At this point, any performance difference doesn't seem quite large enough to warrant making a view-layer technology decision on that basis alone. For mission-critical performance, you might want to investigate the performance issues in the context of the most recent versions of the common web application servers. The most obvious performance issues center around the fact that both Velocity and FreeMarker results write directly to the original response stream of the original request. In other words, the RequestDispatcher and all of the Servlet overhead implied therein aren't involved. This and other performance issues are well documented on the

Web, and we suggest you consult the most recent e-opinions if you need to hit maximum levels of performance.

8.3.1   *VelocityResult, a.k.a. velocity*

Velocity templates are a lightweight and well-proven technology for mixing dynamic data into the rendering of view-layer pages. Using the Struts 2 tag API in Velocity templates, even for the Velocity novice, poses a gentle learning curve. Besides the quick bit about learning the syntactical differences of how the tags are written, the most sophisticated portion is still the OGNL used by the tags to reference the data in the `ActionContext` and the `ValueStack`. But, as we've indicated, the OGNL works the same as in all the JSP-based examples we've given throughout the book.

In passing, we note that the `velocity` result type also exposes the Struts 2 data to the native Velocity expression language capabilities. This means that you could forgo using the Struts 2 tag API and still access values on the `ValueStack` or in the `Action-Context`. We won't cover the details of this access for a couple of reasons. First of all, we really believe that the Struts 2 tag API represents the best way to render your pages. Second, the manner in which the data objects are exposed to the Velocity EL is not tightly synchronized with the exposure to the OGNL used in the Struts 2 tags. This can be confusing when trying to learn the OGNL. If you find that you want to use the native expression language capabilities of Velocity to access the data exposed by the Velocity result, please consult the Struts 2 website at http://struts.apache.org/2.x/docs/velocity.html.

Now let's see how to get set up and start using Velocity templates as your view-layer technology. To demonstrate this, we'll reimplement the Struts 2 Portfolio's `ViewPortfolio` action.

USING VELOCITY RESULTS

The first thing you need to do is make sure that you have the Velocity JAR files in your application. At the time of writing, the Struts 2 distribution doesn't come with the Velocity JAR files. It does come with a built-in `velocity` result type, defined in the following snippet from struts-default.xml:

```
<result-type name="velocity"
  class="org.apache.struts2.dispatcher.VelocityResult"/>
```

This is just like all declarations we've seen. With this in place, we can use the logical name to specify Velocity as the type for our results. Note that many applications that choose to use Velocity templates as their view-layer technology will want to go ahead and declare the `velocity` result type as the default result for their packages. We aren't doing this for the Struts 2 Portfolio application, but if you want to do so you can. Just add a redeclaration of the `velocity` result to your package's `result-types` element with the `default` attribute set to `true`, as in the following snippet:

```
<result-types>
  <result-type name="velocity"
    class="org.apache.struts2.dispatcher.VelocityResult" default="true"/>
</result-types>
```

Now let's take a look at our Velocity version of the `ViewPortfolio` action. If you go to the visitor's page of the chapter 8 version of the application, you'll find three versions of the `ViewPortfolio` page, one each for JSPs, Velocity, and FreeMarker templates. If you test them out, you'll see that they all work exactly the same. Even the XML declarations themselves look very similar. Here's how we declare our `velocity` result version of the `ViewPortfolio` action:

```
<action name="ViewPortfolioVM" class="...ViewPortfolio" >
  <result type="velocity">/chapterEight/ViewPortfolio.vm</result>
</action>
```

The only difference here is that the type of the result is specified as the `velocity` result type defined in the `struts-default` package. The default parameter is still the `location` parameter. Listing 8.5 shows the Velocity template that renders the result.

> **Listing 8.5** Using Velocity templates to reimplement the `ViewPortfolio` page

```
<html>
  <head>
    <title>Viewing Portfolio</title>
  </head>
  <body>

    <h5>
      This is the #sproperty ("value=portfolioName") portfolio of the
      artist currently known as #sproperty ("value=username")
    </h5>
    <a href='#surl ("action=PortfolioHomePage")'>Home</a>
  </body>
</html>
```

We've already covered the syntax differences of the Struts 2 tags as applied across the various view-layer technologies. As you can see, we're using the Struts 2 property tags and, while the syntax is a bit different, the OGNL in them is the same. It still pulls data from the `ValueStack` just as when using the `property` tag from a JSP. You might also note some fundamental differences between JSP and Velocity, such as the lack of directives at the top of the page. As we said, Velocity is simpler than JSP in some ways. If you want to learn more about Velocity, check out their excellent documentation on the Web at http://velocity.apache.org.

That's about all there is to using the `velocity` result type. As we indicated at the start of this section, the `velocity` result also exposes all of the Struts 2 data to the native Velocity expression language. In some cases, such as in the reuse of existing Velocity templates, that might prove useful. Note also that the `velocity` result type supports the same embedded OGNL, and `parse` parameter, that we saw used with the earlier `dispatcher` and `redirect` result types.

Now, let's see how to use FreeMarker results.

8.3.2 *FreemarkerResult, a.k.a. freemarker*

Another built-in result type makes it possible to easily transition to FreeMarker as your choice of page-rendering technology. When compared to JSPs, FreeMarker templates feature the same potential performance benefits as Velocity templates. Again, this mainly arises from the fact that the FreeMarker templates are written directly to the original request's response stream. Many developers wax poetic over the rich features of FreeMarker. And, as we've learned, Struts 2 uses it internally to render the UI components. It's clearly a hot technology for the view layer.

As with Velocity, we don't have the space to give a tutorial on FreeMarker templates, but you don't really need to know too much about FreeMarker to get started. In particular, using the Struts 2 tags from FreeMarker should be a snap. If you need to know more about FreeMarker in general, check out the excellent documentation on the FreeMarker website: http://www.freemarker.org. Again, like the `velocity` result, this result exposes much of the Struts 2 data to the native FreeMarker expression language. And again, we won't cover those details here because we think it can needlessly confuse our coverage of the Struts 2 tag API. However, all the details can be found on the Struts 2 site: http://struts.apache.org/2.x/docs/freemarker.html.

We now reimplement the same `ViewPortfolio` action, this time using a FreeMarker result to render the view.

USING FREEMARKER RESULTS

You won't have to add any JAR files to use FreeMarker. Since the framework uses FreeMarker itself, those resources are already included in the distribution. And the result itself is already declared in struts-default.xml with the following line:

```
<result-type name="freemarker"
    class="org.apache.struts2.views.freemarker.FreemarkerResult"/>
```

As long as you extend the `struts-default` package, this result type is available for your use. All you have to do is specify the logical name `freemarker` in your result's `type` attribute. Again, if you plan to make FreeMarker your primary view-layer technology, you might as well make it the default result type for your packages by adding a line to your package's `result-type` element, as in the following snippet:

```
<result-types>
  <result-type name="freemarker"
    class="org.apache.struts2.views.freemarker.FreemarkerResult"
    default="true"/>
</result-types>
```

Now, let's take a look at how we set up the `ViewPortfolio` action to use the freemarker result. The following snippet, from our chapterEight.xml, shows the declaration of the FreeMarker version of the `ViewPortfolio` action:

```
<action name="ViewPortfolioFM"
    class="manning.chapterEight.ViewPortfolio" >
  <result type="freemarker">/chapterEight/ViewPortfolio.ftl</result>
</action>
```

Again, we point the result's `type` attribute to FreeMarker, and the `location` parameter at the FreeMarker template itself. As with the Velocity result, you can use OGNL embedding to pass dynamic values into your parameter values. Or you can turn this parsing off with the parse parameter. Listing 8.6 shows the `ViewPortfolio` template in full.

Listing 8.6 Using FreeMarker templates to reimplement the `ViewPortfolio` action

```html
<html>
  <head>
    <title>Viewing Portfolio</title>
  </head>
  <body>
    <h5>
      This is the <@s.property value="portfolioName" /> portfolio of
      the artist currently known as <@s.property value="username" />
    </h5>
    <a href="<@s.url action='PortfolioHomePage'/>">Home</a>
  </body>
</html>
```

As you can see, it's quite intuitive. The syntax for the Struts 2 tag API is a bit different, as documented earlier in this book, but it still uses the same OGNL to access data on the same `ValueStack`. As promised, the Struts 2 tag API makes switching between view-layer technologies a snap.

That completes our tour of the most commonly used built-in result types. We have one more topic to hit before wrapping up our coverage of results. Up until now, we've just shown how to declare a result locally to a single action. Sometimes, however, you might want to reuse a single result across many actions. In the next section, we show how to declare results that can be used with all the actions in a package.

8.4 Global results

As an alternative to configuring results locally to specific actions, you can also configure results globally. This means that a result can be used from any action in the entire package. When an action returns a result control string, such as `"error"`, the framework first consults the set of results as defined locally to the action. If no `error` result is found, it then consults the set of globally defined results for an `error` result. In this fashion, your actions can utilize any globally defined result just by returning the appropriate string. Note that a locally defined result will override a globally defined result during this lookup process.

This is particularly useful for such results as errors. It's common to display all error states via a standard error page. This page can be reused throughout the application. We've already discussed this in chapter 4, in the context of the `Exception` interceptor. For that example, we declared a global error result. Declarations of global results go inside your package's `global-results` element, as seen in the following snippet from our chapter 4 example:

```xml
<global-results>
  <result name="error">/chapterFour/Error.jsp</result>
</global-results>
```

The result declaration is no different. The only difference is the location of the declaration; it's inside the global-results element rather than in an action element. With this declaration in your package, any of your package's actions can return a result string of error and the rendering of the result page will be handled by this JSP result. Please refer back to chapter 4 if you want to check out the implementation.

8.5   *Summary*

In this chapter, we saw the last of the framework's core MVC components, the result. Results provide an encapsulation of whatever work should occur after the action has fired. As we've seen, this is most frequently the generation of an HTTP response that's sent back to the client browser as an answer to its original request. For many developers, the JSP-based generation of an HTML page will serve most of the needs of their applications. We've seen that the framework also provides support for using a couple of other technologies to render these pages: Velocity and FreeMarker.

One of the most important things that we covered in this chapter was implementing a custom result that can return a JSON response suitable for Ajax requests. This custom result serves a couple of purposes. First, it helps demonstrate how to integrate Ajax applications into the Struts 2 framework. Ajax techniques are still somewhat of a moving target, and integrating with them will be a focal point for many development teams in the near to immediate future. The flexibility of the Struts 2 framework was intended for just such cases.

We hope that the JSON custom result also demonstrates the internal details of results in general, so that you can confidently come up with custom result types as solutions to the unforeseen integration problems you'll assuredly be faced with. Custom results can provide powerful solutions. They can access all the important data from the request, including the ValueStack, ActionContext, and even the action itself. Furthermore, the result component has been designed to keep the action completely oblivious to the details of the result. This can provide powerful reuse of both results and actions. As we noted when implementing the Ajax artist browser for the Struts 2 portfolio, our action that looks up an artist by username could just as easily be used in a non-Ajax context.

With the completion of this chapter, we've completed not only our tour of the view layer of Struts 2 but our tour of the core components themselves. The next part of the book addresses finer points of web application polish, such as integration with Spring for IOC resource management, data persistence with Hibernate, the framework's XML-based validation framework, and support for internationalization.

Part 4

Improving your application

At this point, you can build a Struts 2 application. But what about building that application to the highest standards of industry practice? The next three chapters start you on your way to refining your application. We will, of course, be making these refinements to our Struts 2 Portfolio sample application as we go.

In chapter 9, we'll introduce Spring resource management to our application. Many developers agree that dependency injection is a nonnegotiable component of a well-implemented Java application. We'll learn to use the Struts 2 Spring plug-in to start letting Spring manage our dependencies. We'll also bump our persistence layer up a notch or two by introducing the Java Persistence API to our modest application. By the time we get these two things in place, we'll have a respectable, enterprise-class application in our hands.

Chapter 10 continues the process of improving our applications by showing us how to take advantage of Struts 2's validation framework to get a metadata-driven validation mechanism in place, one that will prove much more flexible and reusable than the simple validation mechanism we've been using thus far. Finally, chapter 11 will expose all the details of the framework's support for internationalization.

Integrating with Spring and Hibernate/JPA

This chapter covers

- Managing objects with Spring
- Knowing when to use dependency injection
- Adding Spring to Struts 2
- Integrating Struts 2 and the Java Persistence API

Now that we've finished the core chapters, we know how to build a basic Struts 2 application. We've even done so with our Struts 2 Portfolio. This chapter starts the part of the book dealing with how to finish the application with a variety of refinements that many developers consider best practices. The refinements that we introduce in this chapter are specifically related to integrating a Struts 2 application with a pair of popular third-party technologies, Spring and the Java Persistence API (JPA).

First, we learn how to use a Spring container to provide a more sophisticated means of managing our application resources. While Spring provides many different services to the application developer, we focus here on the use of Spring as a means of dependency injection. In short, we use Spring to intervene in the creation of both framework and application objects for the purpose of injecting dependencies into those objects. We both explain what this means and demonstrate the details by upgrading our Struts 2 Portfolio to use Spring for such purposes as injecting our service object into the actions that require it.

After we get Spring in place, we move into a discussion of using JPA/Hibernate to handle our data persistence needs. Hibernate is a popular object-relational mapping (ORM) technology, and the Java Persistence API is a new standardized interface for working with persistence technologies. We'll be coding to the standard JPA, but we'll be using Hibernate beneath the covers. Though Struts 2 doesn't do anything specifically to support integration with the JPA, the framework has generally been designed to ease such tasks. We demonstrate the commonly accepted best practices for using JPA with a Struts 2 application. We also upgrade our Struts 2 Portfolio application to use a JPA `PortfolioService` object. To top it all off, we use the Spring techniques learned in the first half of the chapter to manage our JPA service.

Where to start? Since Spring serves as the foundation for integrating JPA into the application, we get started in the next section by clearing up what we mean by *dependency injection*. Right after that, we show you how to introduce Spring into the framework's object-creation and management mechanisms.

9.1   *Why use Spring with Struts 2?*

Good question. Many people ask this question when first confronted with the Spring + Struts 2 equation. (Other people might note that this is not actually an "equation," mathematically speaking.) The confusion here is that Spring is a large framework that contains solutions to many different aspects of a J2EE application. Spring even has its own MVC web application framework, but that's not the part we're going to learn how to use in this chapter. In fact, we won't learn much about Spring at all, at least in the big sense. We'll be focusing on the part of Spring that provides dependency injection. Many Struts 2 developers consider this resource management service to be an essential part of a well-built web application.

In this section, we start by introducing the concept of dependency injection and cover the fundamentals of how Spring handles this. If you're familiar with Spring, you'll probably be comfortable skipping past this introductory material and proceeding straight to section 9.2, where we describe the details of integrating Spring with Struts 2.

9.1.1   *What can dependency injection do for me?*

We start by describing the problem that we'll use Spring to solve. In a nutshell, a Java application consists of a set of objects. These objects cooperate to solve the problems facing the application. In a Struts 2 application, these objects include application objects like our `PortfolioService` object, as well as core framework components such as actions and interceptors. It's now time to think about how all these objects get instantiated, and how they come to have references to one another.

Some objects are created by the framework. For instance, when a request comes into the framework, Struts 2 must decide which action class maps to that request.

Once it determines the correct action class, it creates an instance of that class to handle the processing of that request. As a developer, you write the action class and map it to the appropriate URL with XML or Java annotations. You never create an action yourself. Creation of actions and other objects is one of the main jobs of the framework internals. In fact, one of the most important internal components of the framework is the ObjectFactory, wherein all framework objects come to life.

But other objects, such as our PortfolioService object, aren't automatically created by the framework. At least not yet! Many of our actions depend on this service object to do their work. One way or another, these actions must obtain a reference to a service object. So far, we've been manually creating these objects with a low-tech strategy: the new operator. This unsophisticated strategy has created a tight bond between our actions and this PortfolioService. It's time to make some improvements in the way we manage our objects and their dependencies upon one another.

One of the most popular technologies for managing the creation of objects in a Java application is Spring. What does Spring add to the management of object creation? As we've been suggesting throughout this book, a well-designed application minimizes the coupling between its objects. The Struts 2 framework itself follows this design imperative quite well. A Struts 2 action, for instance, doesn't contain any references to the Servlet API even though it runs on top of that API when it executes inside the framework. We should strive to continue this level of decoupling as we build our applications on the framework. Spring can help in our decoupling.

But before we look at how Spring does this, let's take a brief look at what it means for objects to be tightly coupled in the first place.

TIGHTLY COUPLED OBJECTS

We can't get around the fact that our objects depend upon each other to do their work. In the code, this means they must acquire references to each other at some point in time. If the acquisition of references is done in the wrong way, the objects become tightly coupled, introducing a variety of issues from complicated testing to nightmarish maintenance. In order to make this issue more clear, we'll explore the shortcomings of the current version of the Struts 2 Portfolio.

The main resource upon which all of our actions are dependent is the Portfolio-Service object. This object provides all the data persistence and business logic needs of our application. It's great that we've been wise enough to extract all of that into a tidy service class. Thanks to our foresight, the action code is clean. However, we've allowed a tight binding to sneak in. Consider our chapter 8 version of the Register action, seen in listing 9.1. In particular, take note of the method by which we acquire our reference to the service object.

> **Listing 9.1 Using the new operator to construct the PortfolioService object**

```
public class Register extends ActionSupport implements SessionAware {

    public String execute(){

        //Prepare the new user object
```

```
        .   .   .
    getPortfolioService().createAccount( user );          ❶
    session.put( Struts2PortfolioConstants.USER, user );

    return SUCCESS;
}

private String username;                    Properties to
private String password;                    receive data
private String portfolioName;               transfer
private boolean receiveJunkMail;

 // getters and setters omitted

public PortfolioService getPortfolioService( ) {

    return new PortfolioService();                        ❷
}
}
```

In case you've forgotten, this action simply collects the data from the registration form, creates a new User object with that data, then uses the PortfolioService object ❶ to persist that new user. But the real point of interest here is how we acquire our PortfolioService object. Our Register action clearly has a dependency upon the PortfolioService object. It must obtain a reference to a service object so that it can do its work. This service object is obtained with direct instantiation via the new operator ❷. While this works, it presents two major problems:

1 We're bound to a specific type, the old memory-based PortfolioService object.
2 We're bound to a specific means of acquisition, the new operator.

We now discuss each of these briefly.

The first problem is that we're bound, or coupled, to this implementation of the PortfolioService object because our code has a specific and naked type in it. To see how this is a problem, consider the task that we'll be faced with later in this chapter when we create a new portfolio service object that uses JPA for its data persistence. Let's say the new service class is called JPAPortfolioService. In order to integrate that back into the application, we'll have to go into every class that creates a specific instance of the PortfolioService object ❷ and change the code by hand to something like the following:

```
public JPAPortfolioService getJPAPortfolioService( )
    return new JPAPortfolioService();
}
```

The second problem is that we're bound to the new operator as a means of acquiring our object references. In some ways, this is the worst possible way to acquire your references. There are many other methods of acquisition that make various improvements upon the vulgar new operator, ranging from factories to service locators. But even these still suffer from the tight coupling inherent in any code-level means of acquisition. Basically, this means that we still have to touch code in order to change the object being used, such as our service object. The most obvious headaches caused by this are maintenance and testing. Consider testing. If we wanted to plug in a mock service object to test our action, we'd be forced to intervene at the code level in every occurrence of the acquisition code. It'd be nice to make the change with a single line of declarative metadata, wouldn't it?

We'll now show a best-practice solution to these two problems, tight coupling to a specific implementation and tight coupling to an acquisition method. This solution utilizes a Spring container to inject dependencies into our objects, thus escaping the coupling to a specific acquisition method. Simultaneously, we'll also introduce an interface to provide a layer of separation from our specific service object implementation and our code that handles it. While the interface separation isn't required by Spring, many folks believe it to be a very powerful one-two punch of software design.

First, let's look at how Spring can resolve the issue of resource acquisition.

9.1.2 *How Spring manages objects and injects dependencies*

As we said, Spring is many things, but one of its most popular uses is the management of object creation and the injection of dependencies into those objects as they're created. Rather than using code to acquire our resources, we use metadata to declare what dependencies a given object requires. Spring reads this metadata, commonly located in an applicationContext.xml file, to learn about the dependencies of the objects it manages. Spring offers several means of injecting dependencies into managed objects, but one common method is via setter methods exposed by the managed object.

> **FYI**   Struts 2 itself uses a form of setter injection to acquire decoupled access to things such as the Servlet API attribute maps. Actions that want access to the session map, for instance, can implement the `SessionAware` interface, which exposes the `setSession(Map session)` method. The `servletConfig` interceptor, part of the `defaultStack`, will inject the session map into this setter for all actions that implement the `Session-Aware` interface. Note that, like the Spring injection we're introducing, this interface allows the action to have decoupled access to the Servlet API session map. The action itself doesn't touch the Servlet API, and the type of the setter is the `Map` interface, thus keeping the action free of binding to a particular map. We could now easily inject a mock session map for testing.

Let's see how our `Register` action would look if we used Spring to inject our service object, rather than directly acquiring it in our code:

```
private PortfolioService portfolioService;

public PortfolioService getPortfolioService( ) {
  return portfolioService;
}

public void setPortfolioService(PortfolioService portfolioService) {
  this.portfolioService = portfolioService;
}
```

Instead of worrying about how to create our service object, we just let Spring create and inject it into a setter method. We completely get rid of the acquisition code and are left with only a simple JavaBeans property. This is all it takes, in the code, to have your resources injected. It doesn't look like much, but that's because everything's been removed to the Spring metadata layer, most likely applicationContext.xml. It is in that file where we tell Spring the details of the object's creation. We learn about that metadata in section 9.2, when we cover the details of integrating and using Spring.

First, though, we need to talk about the second part of that one-two punch. Remember the interface we're also going to introduce, the one that will solve the problem of being bound to a specific implementation of the service object? We look at that next.

9.1.3 *Using interfaces to hide implementations*

While the code snippet in the previous section has completely removed the resource acquisition code by allowing the service object to be externally injected by Spring, we still have a tight binding to the type of the object being injected, a memory-based `PortfolioService` class in this case. As you can see, our `Register` action's JavaBeans property is specifically typed to that class. When we want to upgrade to another implementation of our service object that uses JPA, we'll be forced to refactor all these properties across all the objects that depend on a service object. After that, we'll be just as bound to that JPA version of the service. To solve this binding problem, we'll introduce an interface for service objects that both the memory-based and the JPA-based versions can implement. Then, we'll change the property to that interfaced type.

We've done just this for the chapter 9 version of the Struts 2 Portfolio. Listing 9.2 shows the full source code of our new interface `manning.chapterNine.utils.Port-folioServiceInterface`.

> **Listing 9.2   The `PortfolioServiceInterface` provides a layer of separation.**

```
public interface PortfolioServiceInterface {
  public boolean userExists ( String username );

  public void updateUser( User user ) ;

  public void addImage ( File file ) ;

  public User authenticateUser(String username, String password) ;

  public Collection getUsers();

  public Collection getAllPortfolios() ;

  public User getUser( String username );

  public User getUser( Long id );

  public Portfolio getPortfolio ( Long id );

  public String getDefaultUser() ;

  public void persistUser ( User user );
```

```
  public boolean contains ( User user );

  public void updatePortfolio( Portfolio port );

}
```

There shouldn't be any surprises here. This interface simply defines the core business methods that our application uses. We could implement this interface with native Hibernate, JPA, XML files, raw JDBC, or anything else you like. You could even implement a mock service object for testing. For this chapter, we've implemented a JPA version of the service.

Now, our actions that depend upon a service object provide setters typed to this interface, rather than a specific implementation, to receive the Spring injections. With this done, changing the service object used by the actions is as simple as flipping a switch in the Spring metadata. Listing 9.3 shows the full source of our chapter 9 Login action, in which we've changed the setter to use the interface.

Listing 9.3   Login exposes a setter into which Spring injects the service object

```
public class Login extends ActionSupport implements SessionAware {      ❶
  public String execute(){
    User user = getPortfolioService().authenticateUser( getUsername(),
            getPassword() );          ❷

    if ( user == null )
    {
      return INPUT;
    }
    else{
      session.put( Struts2PortfolioConstants.USER, user );             ❸
    }
    return SUCCESS;
  }

  private String username;
  private String password;

  //getters and setters omitted

  PortfolioServiceInterface portfolioService;

  public PortfolioServiceInterface getPortfolioService( ) {
    return portfolioService;
  }

  public void setPortfolioService(PortfolioServiceInterface          ❹
                                  portfolioService) {
    this.portfolioService = portfolioService;
  }

  private Map session;

  public void setSession(Map session) {            ❺
    this.session = session;
  }
}
```

Not much to look at. The service setter now takes an object of type `PortfolioService-Interface` ❹. We've worked with this action before, but let's revisit a couple of points in light of our new understanding of dependency injection. To recap this action's business logic, it checks whether or not the login credentials returned a valid user ❸. If valid, the user is stored in the session scope. But if the credentials don't map to a valid user, we return the user back to the input page, a.k.a. the login page. As we mentioned earlier, the `Login` action needs to access the session-scoped map because a `User` object will be placed in that map when a user successfully logs in. We know that Struts 2 is probably running on the Servlet API, so this map is actually the Servlet session map. But the framework has a strong commitment to loose coupling. In order to get a reference to this map in a loosely coupled manner, `Login` implements the `SessionAware` interface ❶. The contract of this interface is fully satisfied by the exposure of a single setter method ❺ into which the framework will inject a session map. At runtime, this map is most likely going to be the Servlet API map. Thanks, however, to the loose coupling of the `SessionAware` interface, you could easily set a mock map for testing purposes. In general, the `Aware` interfaces offered by the framework provide a good form of dependency injection. Unfortunately, they mostly just handle servlet-related things.

Thankfully, we can use Spring for injecting stuff like our service object. With Spring, the dependent object doesn't need to implement any specific interface, like the `Aware` interfaces, in order to receive the injection. Spring tries hard to keep your code independent of Spring. When it's time to conduct the business, the service object is just there. In this case, the `Login` action uses the service object to authenticate the user ❷. It could be a mock service object that returns `true` every time, or it could be our JPA service object that makes a live check against our database. This is what Spring dependency injection is all about.

Now it's time to see the details of adding Spring to our Struts 2 application.

9.2   *Adding Spring to Struts 2*

In this section, we see how to add Spring to a Struts 2 application. It's quite easy. There are a couple of strategies for the actual injection of dependencies into your objects. We cover those in this section. But first we need to show you how to get Spring set up. The basic idea is that we need to give Spring a chance to handle the objects that are created by Struts 2. One way to let Spring do this is to provide a Spring extension of the Struts 2 `ObjectFactory`, the class that creates each of the objects used in the framework. We do just this in this section.

First, we need to download and add the Spring plug-in to our application. As you'll see in chapter 12, plug-ins can modify or enhance the core structure of the framework. One such example is the Spring plug-in. This plug-in provides a Spring extension of the core `ObjectFactory`. With this plug-in in place, Spring has the opportunity to manage the creation of any objects that the framework creates. Note that while the Spring `ObjectFactory` adds the opportunity for Spring to manage the creation of objects, it's not necessary for Spring to be involved in all object creation. Basically, the Spring `ObjectFactory` only intervenes when you tell it to; all other objects get created in the normal fashion.

You can find the Spring plug-in in the Struts 2 plug-in registry at http://cwiki.apache.org/S2PLUGINS/home.html. The plug-in comes as a JAR file, struts2-spring-plugin-2.0.9.jar. You also need to get the Spring JAR, spring.jar, found at www.springframework.org. With these two added to your lib directory, you just need a way to create the Spring container itself. Since we're building web applications, we can use a Spring application-context listener. This comes with the Spring JAR and is set up with the following snippet from our web.xml file:

```
<listener>
  <listener-class>org.springframework.web.context.ContextLoaderListener
  </listener-class>
</listener>
```

At this point, you're completely ready to start managing your objects with Spring. But, as we indicated earlier, Spring won't just start handling all of your objects. You must tell Spring to intervene. To have Spring manage your objects, you need to declare these objects as Spring beans in a Spring configuration file. By default, the Spring container created by the `ContextLoaderListener` looks for metadata in an XML file at /WEB-INF/applicationContext.xml. You can pass in a parameter to the listener to specify different locations, and even multiple files, if you like. Consult the Spring documentation for this listener if you'd like to know more. As for the structure and usage of the XML metadata, we'll start to explore that in the next two sections as we explore some basic strategies for managing dependencies with Spring.

9.2.1 Letting Spring manage the creation of actions, interceptors, and results

With the Spring plug-in set up, it's time to put it to use. We start by showing how to let Spring directly manage the creation of framework objects such as actions, interceptors, and results. First, we'll let Spring handle the creation of our `Login` action. As we've seen, this action depends on our `PortfolioService` object. In the last couple of sections, we've already prepared the `Login` class for Spring injection by adding the setter into which we can inject a `PortfolioServiceInterface`-typed object. To put that setter to use, we need to tell Spring how to manage the creation of our `Login` action.

As we've hinted, one common way to tell Spring about the objects it should manage is with metadata contained in XML files. In our case, we use a file called applicationContext.xml. Listing 9.4 shows what to put in applicationContext.xml to have Spring manage the creation of a `Login` action, complete with the injection of a portfolio service object.

Listing 9.4   Telling Spring how to inject our service bean into our `Login` action

```
<?xml version="1.0" encoding="UTF-8"?>
<beans xmlns="http://www.springframework.org/schema/beans"
    xmlns:xsi="http://www.w3.org/2001/XMLSchema-instance"
    xsi:schemaLocation="http://www.springframework.org/schema/beans
http://www.springframework.org/schema/beans/spring-beans-2.0.xsd">
```

```
<bean id="portfolioService"                                          ❷
    class="manning.chapterNine.utils.PortfolioServiceJPAImpl"/>

<bean id="springManagedLoginAction" class="manning.chapterNine.Login"
    scope="prototype">
  <property name="portfolioService" ref="portfolioService"/>    ❹    ❸
</bean>
</beans>
```

At first glance, this might be an eyeful. But it's actually simple. The critical chunks are the declaration of two Spring beans, objects that Spring should manage for us. Before we get to those, let's look at that messiness at the start. We've got a huge bunch of namespace and schema stuff at the top ❶. Spring uses a lot of namespaces, so sometimes this stuff differs from one file to another depending upon the Spring functionality in play. You'll get by fine by copying ours unless you want to do something special with Spring. After that, we get to the good stuff, the declaration of two Spring beans. Notice that the root element of the applicationContext.xml file is the <beans> element ❶. All of the objects that Spring manages are known as *Spring beans*. We declare two.

The first of our beans is our JPA implementation of our PortfolioServiceInterface ❷. It's pretty accurate to just imagine this bean declaration as an instantiation of the object, or the definition of how to instantiate the object. In this case, we simply give the bean tag our fully qualified class name and an ID. The ID is used to identify the bean, much like a reference is used to identify an object in Java code. Next, we've told Spring to manage the creation of instances of our Login action. We've done this with another bean tag, giving it the class name and an ID ❸. We've also set the scope attribute to prototype. Why did we do this? By default, Spring beans are created as singletons. This won't work for Struts 2 actions, because they carry data related to each individual request. In order to make Spring create a new Login action bean each time one is needed, we must set the scope attribute to prototype. Our service object, like many application resources, works well as a singleton.

WARNING   Make sure that your Spring-managed actions are configured to be created as new instances each time they're needed. By default, Spring creates singletons and reissues them when that bean is requested. You can force Spring to create a unique instance for each request if you set the scope attribute to prototype. Very important!

Now we get down to the business of wiring the portfolio service bean that we declared in the first bean tag into our Login action. We use Spring's property tag to do this ❹. The property tag looks for a setter for a property with the same name as the property tag's name attribute. The value to inject into this setter is then specified with the ref attribute, which takes a reference that points, in our case, to the ID we gave to our service object in the first bean tag.

Okay. We've told Spring how to create a couple of our objects for us. Whenever someone asks for the portfolioService or springManagedLoginAction bean, Spring serves up a bean matching those IDs managed just as we've asked. If someone asks for a `springManagedLoginAction`, Spring creates a unique instance of our `manning.chapterNine.Login` class and injects a `portfolioService` Spring bean into it. But this doesn't mean that Spring will intervene any time a `Login` action is created. It won't do anything until someone asks, by ID, for one of the beans it manages. Every instance of a `Login` action in the system is not inherently the `springManagedLoginAction` Spring bean. So how do we make the framework ask Spring for this bean when it needs a `Login` action? Good question.

Normally, Struts 2 creates its action objects by instantiating the class defined in the declarative architecture metadata. If a request comes in with a URL that maps to the `Login` action, as defined in our declarative architecture XML or annotations, the framework consults the declaration of that action to find out which class should be instantiated. Here's how we've been declaring our `Login` action up until now:

```
<action name="Login" class="manning.chapterNine.Login">
  <result type="redirectAction">
    <param name="actionName">AdminPortfolio</param>
    <param name="namespace">/chapterEight/secure</param>
  </result>
  <result name="input">/chapterEight/Login.jsp</result>
</action>
```

This mapping tells the framework to create an instance of the `manning.chapterNine.Login` class to use as its action object for this request. As we've indicated, the framework has an `ObjectFactory` that normally handles all of this. Even with the `SpringObjectFactory` in place, via the Spring plug-in, this mapping is still handled in that standard fashion. If we want the framework to ask Spring to create one of its beans for us, we need to refer to that Spring bean's ID from within our Struts 2 action mapping, as follows:

```
<action name="Login" class="springManagedLoginAction">
  <result type="redirectAction">
    <param name="actionName">AdminPortfolio</param>
    <param name="namespace">/chapterEight/secure</param>
  </result>
  <result name="input">/chapterEight/Login.jsp</result>
</action>
```

Now, the framework asks Spring for a bean going by the name of `springManagedLoginAction` and Spring gladly returns that bean with the `PortfolioService` injected and ready to go.

That's about all you need to know to have Spring directly manage the creation of framework objects such as our `Login` action. You can do the same thing with interceptors or any other framework components. Oddly enough, we don't recommend using Spring in this manner for most situations. We showed this technique first because it's the most straightforward way of understanding what Spring does. But it's not always the best way to use Spring for dependency injections. If you want to take advantage of some other Spring-fu, like some of its aspect-oriented features, then you'll need to use this heavy-handed, direct object management technique. But if all you want to do is inject dependencies, such as the `PortfolioService` object, there's a much easier method: autowiring! Let's have a look.

9.2.2 *Leveraging autowiring to inject dependencies into actions, interceptors, and results*

The direct management of your actions, interceptors, and results by Spring is a perfectly good way to do things, but it's verbose. To make things super easy, you'll want to take advantage of Spring's ability to autowire dependencies. Autowiring is a way to inject dependencies without explicitly declaring the wiring in your application-Context.xml. In other words, we can have the `PortfolioService` object automatically injected into all the actions that need it without actually having to generate any metadata regarding those actions. You don't have to do anything to enable autowiring; it's on by default. There are several flavors of autowiring. You can autowire by `name`, `type`, `constructor`, or something called `auto`. We cover each of them in this section.

AUTOWIRING BY NAME

The default behavior of the Spring plug-in autowiring is by `name`. Autowiring by name works by matching the ID of a managed Spring bean with setter method names exposed on potential target objects. As it turns out, every object created by the framework is a potential target object. Since all of our actions are clearly created by the framework, they're all potential targets of autowiring without any explicit intervention on the behalf of the developer. Listing 9.5 shows what our applicationContext.xml would look like if we rely on name-based autowiring instead of direct Spring management of our dependencies.

> **Listing 9.5   Autowiring requires less metadata in our applicationContext.xml.**

```xml
<?xml version="1.0" encoding="UTF-8"?>
<beans xmlns="http://www.springframework.org/schema/beans"
   xmlns:xsi="http://www.w3.org/2001/XMLSchema-instance"
   xsi:schemaLocation="http://www.springframework.org/schema/beans
http://www.springframework.org/schema/beans/spring-beans-2.0.xsd">

  <bean id="portfolioService"
class="manning.chapterNine.utils.PortfolioServiceJPAImpl"/>

</beans>
```

As you can see, we now do nothing more than declare the bean that we need to inject, our `portfolioService` bean, and give it an ID. There are no bean tags telling Spring how to manage our action objects. In fact, Spring won't handle the creation of our action objects in this case. Nonetheless, the framework lets Spring do a postcreation inspection of all objects that it creates, such as actions and interceptors, and try to autowire them with beans that it knows about. In our case, we've told Spring about our `portfolioService` bean. Spring tries to automatically inject this bean into any framework object that exposes a setter with a name that matches the ID of the service bean. To receive the automatic injection of this `portfolioService` bean, a framework object just needs to expose a setter like the following:

```
PortfolioServiceInterface portfolioService;
public void setPortfolioService(PortfolioServiceInterface portfolioService)
  this.portfolioService = portfolioService;
}
```

The key here is that the setter naming convention matches the Spring bean ID. All objects created by the framework are subject to this injection. This isn't just actions. Our `manning.chapterNine.utils.AuthenticationInterceptor` also receives this injection. Due to the ease and elegance of autowiring by name, this'll probably be your preferred Spring usage as long as your need for Spring doesn't extend past dependency injection.

Before moving on to the next method of autowiring, we should make one point. In the previous section, where we had Spring actually create our action objects for us, we had to write our declarative architecture to point to Spring IDs rather than the normal class names. Since Spring is no longer creating our action objects, we can revert our declarative architecture back to the previous form. In other words, we no longer map our `action` element to a Spring ID name; we map it to the class name again, as seen in the following snippet:

```
<action name="Login" class="manning.chapterNine.Login">
  <result type="redirectAction">
    <param name="actionName">AdminPortfolio</param>
    <param name="namespace">/chapterNine/secure</param>
  </result>
  <result name="input">/chapterNine/Login.jsp</result>
</action>
```

The `class` attribute now points to an actual Java class rather than the ID of a Spring bean. With autowiring, the framework creates the action, then Spring inspects to see whether it can inject anything. This is a subtle but different mechanism than we discussed in the previous section.

Autowiring comes in several other varieties. Let's consider our options.

AUTOWIRING BY TYPE, CONSTRUCTOR, AND AUTO

Spring provides several other means of autowiring that are also available to us in the context of Struts 2. In the interest of space, we won't demonstrate these other strategies, but we'll give brief explanations of what they do. They're quite simple. The first step to using an alternative method of autowiring is configuration. If you want to change the method of autowiring, you need to set a Struts 2 configuration property. You need to add something like the following to your struts.properties file:

```
struts.objectFactory.spring.autoWire=type
```

Or, as with all Struts 2 configuration settings, you can set this property via a `constant` element in one of your XML files, such as struts.xml, or chapterNine.xml if you like. Here's what the `constant` element would look like:

```
<constant name="struts.objectFactory.spring.autoWire" value="type"/>
```

It doesn't matter which way you do it. Now, let's talk a bit about what each of these alternative autowiring methods means.

Essentially, they all do the same thing. They tell Spring to inspect the objects created by the framework for places where it can inject the beans that it knows about. If you choose to do autowiring by type, rather than the default name, Spring will try to match the type of the beans it knows about to the types of setter methods it finds on the objects created by the framework. The secret here is that you should only tell Spring about one bean per type; otherwise it can't figure out which bean to inject and it complains. The only thing faintly subtle about autowiring by type is that interfaces count. In other words, since the manning.chapterNine.utils.PortfolioServiceJPAImpl bean that we told Spring about implements manning.chapterNine.utils.PortfolioService-Interface, it's autowired to setters of the interface type. Since the setter on our Login action takes type PortfolioServiceInterface, this injection will occur automatically if we change the autoWire property to type. This is another sign that interfaces are the right thing to do!

The next two alternative methods of autowiring are constructor and auto. If you choose constructor, your objects must have a constructor that takes its dependencies as parameters. Beans known to Spring will be injected into the constructor parameters as they match up by type. This has the same limitations as the type-based method discussed in the previous paragraph. If more than one Spring bean of the matching type is available, Spring will throw an exception rather than try to decide which one to inject. The last method of autowiring is auto. This method simply tries to inject by constructor first and then by type.

And that's it. Spring's not such a big deal, huh? Well, this is a small part of Spring. Moreover, it's a tribute to the power of Spring that the end result can look so effortless. Nonetheless, this simple use of Spring can make your code much more maintainable and testable, the twin joys of loose coupling. Keep in mind that we've only shown you how to use the dependency injection features of Spring, but it offers a lot more than just DI. Many of you will want to take advantage of some of that other stuff in your Struts 2 applications. With limited book space, we can only point the way. One thing to keep in mind is this. If you want to add further Spring management to your beans, such as Spring's aspect-oriented programming features, you need to let Spring directly manage your actions, interceptors, and results. We showed how to do this in section 9.2.1. Spring has a lot to offer and the Spring plug-in makes it easy to leverage these offerings from a Struts 2 application. Enjoy.

Now it's time to see how we can make another drastic improvement to your Struts 2 Portfolio. In the next section, we're going to introduce the powerful Java Persistence API (JPA) and show how to let it manage your application's data persistence needs.

9.3   *Why use the Java Persistence API with Struts 2?*

In this section, we show you how to integrate the Java Persistence API (JPA) into your application. This technology, wrapped around Hibernate, represents the bleeding edge of enterprise Java data persistence. Coding to the JPA works a lot like coding to native Hibernate, but its interface-based architecture gives you the ability to switch out the vendor supplying the underlying implementation. In our examples, we use Hibernate. Still, the techniques we demonstrate are applicable regardless of which underlying engine you choose.

The topics of JPA and Hibernate go beyond the scope of this book. This section doesn't intend to teach you anything specific about JPA and Hibernate. The purpose of this section is to demonstrate a best practice of integration with those technologies. If you don't know anything about JPA and Hibernate, you'll need to seek basic instruction elsewhere. We recommend the Manning title *Java Persistence with Hibernate*. If you're already familiar with these topics, we build on that by walking you through one of the most successful solutions to integrating JPA into a Struts 2 web application. This solution solves two of the most immediate issues a developer faces when integrating JPA with a web application. First, we show how to use a servlet filter to solve the infamous Open Session In View problem. Second, we show how to use the well-respected Spring support for JPA to make management of the JPA all that much easier.

Before we get to the integration, we should start with the mundane, but essential, details of setting your project up to use JPA with Hibernate.

9.3.1 *Setting your project up for JPA with Hibernate*

First, there's no plug-in or anything for integrating JPA with your Struts 2 application. Setup includes adding a few JAR files, a configuration file or two, getting a database, and some other odd bits or two. We'll sail right through these in no time, starting with the issue of JAR files.

COLLECTING THE APPROPRIATE JAR FILES

There's quite a list here. Some of these resources belong to Hibernate and some belong to the JPA. There's also the issue of a driver for your choice of database. Some libraries are already in the project; some we need to add just for this chapter. As always, these kinds of things change over time; a trip to the Hibernate, JPA, or the MySQL website will yield the most accurate and up-to-date word on dependencies.

At the time of writing, here's what we're using:

- antlr.jar *
- asm.jar
- asm-attrs.jar
- c3po.jar
- cglib.jar
- commons-logging.jar *
- commons-collection.jar *
- dom4j.jar
- hibernate3.jar
- jta.jar
- hibernate-annotations.jar
- hibernate-commons-annotations.jar
- ejb3-persistence.jar
- hibernate-entity-manager.jar
- mysql-connector-java-5.1.5-bin.jar
- jboss-archive-browsing.jar
- javassist.jar

The ones with asterisks are the ones that would already be in a Struts 2 project. The rest are all specific requirements of our current persistence work.

CHOOSING A DATABASE

You can use just about any database you like. We use MySQL because it's familiar to many, including ourselves. If you opt to use another database, then you should switch out the MySQL driver in our list of resource dependencies. In addition, you'll need to change a couple of settings in the data source and Hibernate configuration found in the applicationContext.xml. We'll cover that file in a moment.

After you install a database, you just need to do the prerequisite admin stuff to set up the account by which you'll connect to the database. While you can change the settings, our current configuration expects to find a database account with `username/ password` equal to `manning/action`. This database user must, of course, have the appropriate rights to create, update, alter, and so forth.

With the database and resources all in place, it's time to configure JPA. As we said, we're going to leverage Spring's built-in support for JPA to do this. Since we've taken the time to integrate the Spring container, we should take the opportunity to really benefit from it.

USING SPRING TO MANAGE OUR JPA DEPENDENCIES

After all the trouble of setting up the Spring plug-in, we might as well make the most of it. Actually, using Spring to manage JPA is a nice thing. Spring comes with packages dedicated to making the management of JPA easy and powerful. By the end of this chapter, we think you'll have to admit that the combination is elegant. Let's jump right in by examining our new applicationContext.xml to see just exactly what we're asking Spring to do for us. Listing 9.6 shows that Spring configuration file in full glory.

Listing 9.6   Letting Spring manage our JPA dependencies and transactions

```
<?xml version="1.0" encoding="UTF-8"?>
<beans xmlns="http://www.springframework.org/schema/beans"
   xmlns:xsi="http://www.w3.org/2001/XMLSchema-instance"
   xmlns:tx="http://www.springframework.org/schema/tx"
   xsi:schemaLocation="                                                    ❶
   http://www.springframework.org/schema/beans
  http://www.springframework.org/schema/beans/spring-beans-2.0.xsd
    http://www.springframework.org/schema/tx
 http://www.springframework.org/schema/tx/spring-tx-2.0.xsd


   <bean class="org.springframework.orm.jpa.support.
                    PersistenceAnnotationBeanPostProcessor" />        ❷

   <bean id="portfolioService" class="manning.chapterNine.utils.
                       PortfolioServiceJPAImpl"/>                     ❸


   <bean id="entityManagerFactory"
   class="org.springframework.orm.jpa.LocalContainerEntityManagerFactoryBea
   n">|#4
     <property name="dataSource" ref="dataSource" />
     <property name="jpaVendorAdapter">                              ❹
       <bean class="org.springframework.orm.jpa.vendor.
                       HibernateJpaVendorAdapter">
```

```
            <property name="database" value="MYSQL" />
            <property name="showSql" value="true" />
        </bean>
    </property>
</bean>
```
④

```
<bean id="dataSource"
class="org.springframework.jdbc.datasource.DriverManagerDataSource">
    <property name="driverClassName" value="org.gjt.mm.mysql.Driver" />
    <property name="url" value="jdbc:mysql://127.0.0.1:3306/manning" />
    <property name="username" value="manning" />
    <property name="password" value="action" />
</bean>
```
⑤

```
<bean id="transactionManager"
class="org.springframework.orm.jpa.JpaTransactionManager">
    <property name="entityManagerFactory" ref="entityManagerFactory" />
</bean>
```
⑥

```
<tx:annotation-driven transaction-manager="transactionManager" />
```
⑦

```
</beans>
```

This might look like a lot at first, especially if you're unfamiliar with the JPA. But we can remedy all that quickly. Here's a nutshell version of what's happening. All we're really doing is having Spring create our JPA EntityManager and inject it into our service object. That's it. And, of course, we're still having the service object autowired into our actions. But everything here is all about creating the EntityManager and injecting it into our service object. Now, let's pick it apart line by line to take the sting out of it.

First, we've got a gigantic wad of namespace and schema stuff ❶. Too bad the printed word doesn't do code folding yet. Next, we declare a bean postprocessor that checks all the beans managed by Spring for persistence-related annotations ❷, such as the annotations that mark which setter methods should be injected with the EntityManager. We put one of these annotations in our PortfolioServiceJPAImpl class. Next, we have the familiar declaration of our service object ❸ as a Spring bean. As we've seen, this is autowired by name into our actions and interceptors. This hasn't changed in the slightest.

All of the rest of this mess sets up our JPA stuff. And it's not really messy at all. The main entry point into the JPA is something called the EntityManager. This object manages all of your persistent entities—our users and portfolio objects. Our PortfolioServiceJPAImpl uses an EntityManager to read, write, and update our objects. If you're familiar with Hibernate, the EntityManager is equivalent to the Session. Rather than telling Spring how to create an EntityManager, we need to tell Spring how to create an EntityManagerFactory ❹. This is also where we configure our JPA persistence unit. As you can see, we tell Spring which JPA vendor we're going to use as well as which data source we're going to use. The data source that we wire to the factory is another Spring bean ❺, which we've configured to work with our MySQL database and the database account we created.

Finally, since all JPA and Hibernate work must occur within transactional boundaries, we register a transaction manager with Spring ❻, which we also wire to the `EntityManagerFactory`. We then tell Spring that we'll use annotations to tell the transaction manager about our transactional boundaries ❼. You can also define transactional boundaries in the XML, but we're using transaction annotations in our `PortfolioServiceJPAImpl` class. Once you get familiar with it, it's fairly elegant.

That's the Spring part of it. Next, we look at how to handle the problem of lazy loading in the view layer.

HANDLING LAZY LOADING WITH SPRING'S OPENENTITYMANAGERINVIEW FILTER

If you've used Hibernate before, you're probably familiar with the view-layer lazy loading issue. To summarize the problem, when you retrieve Java objects from a persistence technology such as JPA, optimizations are made to reduce traffic with the database. One of the primary optimizations is the lazy loading of deeper elements in the data structure contained by the retrieved object. Let's say we retrieve a `User` from the JPA `EntityManager`. All of the `Portfolios`, for instance, might not be loaded when this `User` is first loaded. In fact, they might not be loaded until they're referenced. This is *lazy loading*.

In an MVC web application, the action classes generally load the data from the database, such as the `User` mentioned previously. Then they forward control over to the view layer, a JSP result, let's say. Many times, data such as a given `Portfolio` referenced within that `User` won't be read until a JSP tag iterates over that set of `Portfolios` while rendering the result page. If the persistence context, the `EntityManager` in the case of the JPA or the `Session` in the case of native Hibernate, has been closed, this attempt to read the unloaded `Portfolio` data will fail because lazy loading is no longer available.

A well-known fix to this has been around for some time. In Hibernate terms, the fix is known as the OpenSessionInView pattern. This fix typically uses a servlet filter or some kind of interceptor to wrap a Hibernate `Session` around the entire request-processing pipeline, including the view layer. You can find many examples of this on the Web. In JPA terms, we need a OpenEntityManagerInView fix. Fortunately, Spring provides a servlet filter implementation of this fix that's widely used: one of the key reasons for going with the Spring support for JPA. We don't need to do anything other than configure this filter in our web.xml file, as seen in Listing 9.7.

Listing 9.7   Configuring the `OpenEntityManagerInViewFilter`

```
<filter>
  <filter-name>struts2</filter-name>
  <filter-class>
    org.apache.struts2.dispatcher.FilterDispatcher
  </filter-class>
</filter>

<filter>
  <filter-name>SpringOpenEntityManagerInViewFilter</filter-name>
  <filter-class>
```

```
    org.springframework.orm.jpa.support.OpenEntityManagerInViewFilter
  </filter-class>
</filter>

<filter-mapping>
  <filter-name>SpringOpenEntityManagerInViewFilter</filter-name>
  <url-pattern>/*</url-pattern>
</filter-mapping>

<filter-mapping>
  <filter-name>struts2</filter-name>
  <url-pattern>/*</url-pattern>
</filter-mapping>
```

If you're familiar with web.xml files, there's nothing complicated here. There's one critical thing, though. The mapping of the Spring filter must come before the mapping of the `struts2` filter; otherwise nothing will work. Once in place, this filter creates and binds an `EntityManager` to the thread that's processing the request. It uses the factory declared in our Spring container to do this. This threadbound `Entity-Manager` will always be used by our other Spring-controlled JPA code. You don't have to do anything in your code. It's very convenient.

With all of that in place, we're now ready to look at how it all works. The next section walks us through the code that uses the JPA as we've configured here.

9.3.2 Coding Spring-managed JPA

In the previous section, we showed you how to set up your Struts 2 application to use JPA. In addition to adding the resources for JPA and Hibernate, we showed you how to leverage the Spring plug-in we added earlier in this chapter to manage your JPA resources. With all that in place, we're now ready to examine the code-level implementation of a JPA persistence layer. In our Struts 2 Portfolio, this takes place inside the `PortfolioServiceJPAImpl` class.

We start with a quick discussion of the JPA persistence unit.

THE PERSISTENCE UNIT

When you use the JPA, the entirety of your persistence-related pieces is known as a *persistence unit*. The `EntityManagerFactory` managed by Spring encapsulates most of the details of the persistence unit. These details include everything from the metadata that describes how your Java classes map to database tables to the database connection details. The main entry point into configuring your persistence unit is the persistence.xml file. Just as a web application must have a web.xml file, a JPA project must have a persistence.xml file. Listing 9.8 shows the full details of this important file, which can be found in the project at /WEB-INF/classes/META-INF/persistence.xml.

> **Listing 9.8 The mandatory configuration entry point for a JPA persistence unit**

```
<persistence xmlns="http://java.sun.com/xml/ns/persistence"
  xmlns:xsi="http://www.w3.org/2001/XMLSchema-instance"
  xsi:schemaLocation="http://java.sun.com/xml/ns/persistence http://
  java.sun.com/xml/ns/persistence/persistence_1_0.xsd" version="1.0">
```

```
<persistence-unit name="struts2InAction">
  <properties>
    <property name="hibernate.hbm2ddl.auto" value="create"/>
  </properties>
</persistence-unit>

</persistence>
```

It's of interest that such an important file contains so little. Mostly, this is because we're deferring the management of our JPA details to Spring. The important thing here is the name of the persistence unit and the fact that we pass in a Hibernate property to control the autocreation of our database schema. We're using the development-friendly create setting. Every time the application is started, the database schema will be created anew. This means that your data won't persist over multiple application startups. If you want to preserve the database from a preceding state, just take this out before restarting the application.

The next critical element of a JPA project is the metadata that maps your Java classes to database tables. The next section covers this important topic.

USING ANNOTATIONS TO MAP OUR JAVA CLASSES TO DATABASE TABLES

One of the great things about using JPA is that we can use Java annotations to map our Java classes to the database. Though people, including myself, can debate whether annotations are fluff or stuff, it's hard to deny some of the benefits of using them. A few of the benefits of using the JPA annotations in this context include IDE support, less verbosity, automatic scanning for annotated classes, and type checking—annotations are actual Java types after all.

We're going to keep it simple, so let's start by cracking the source code to our persistent entities, a.k.a. our `User` and `Portfolio` classes. Listing 9.9 shows the source for our `manning.chapterNine.utils.User` class.

> **Listing 9.9   This version of the `User` class is a JPA persistent entity.**

```
@Entity         ❶
public class User {

    private String username;
    private String password;
    private String firstName;
    private String lastName;

    @OneToMany ( cascade={CascadeType.ALL }, mappedBy="owner")    ❷
    private Set<Portfolio> portfolios = new HashSet<Portfolio>();

    @Id @GeneratedValue        ❸
    private Long id;

    //getters and setters omitted

    public Set getPortfolios()
    {
        return portfolios;
    }
    public void setPortfolios( Set portfolios ) {
        this.portfolios = portfolios;
```

```
  }

  public void addPortfolio ( Portfolio portfolio ){
     portfolio.setOwner( this );                          4
     portfolios.add( portfolio );
  }

}
```

This class uses annotations to tell JPA how to map its properties to the database. The entity annotation ❶ marks this class as one that should be scanned by the JPA and mapped to the database. This is required. Next, note the absence of any metadata describing mappings between the properties and the database. We could annotate these, but we can also sit back and let JPA generate sensible database column names for each of these properties. They will each be columns in our User table. We then map an association to our collection of Portfolio objects that belong to this user ❷, and annotate our id property ❸. This id property is the only actual change we have to make to our class to make it work as a persistent entity managed by the JPA Entity-Manager. As a final point of interest, we'd also like to point out that while we can rely on the JPA to manage our persistence, we still have to manage our Java relationships. In the interest of this, we have an addPortfolio method that manages the directional references between a Portfolio and the owning User ❹. This is required so that we can track the User from the Portfolio, if need be.

If you check out the manning.chapterNine.utils.Portfolio class, you'll find similar annotations. Again, these annotations are automatically located and scanned by JPA when it fires up. You don't have to register the annotated classes anywhere.

At this point, we've done everything we need to do. We have annotation metadata that describes how we want to map our Java classes to the database. We have a database. We've configured the Spring container to create our JPA EntityManagerFactory with all the necessary settings. When the EntityManagerFactory starts up, it scans our annotated classes and automatically creates the schema in the database. The only thing left is to get our hands on an EntityManager and start writing the JPA persistence code in the PortfolioServiceJPAImpl class. So that's what we'll do now.

USING THE JPA ENTITYMANAGER TO IMPLEMENT OUR SERVICE OBJECT

We're finally ready to look at the PortfolioServiceJPAImpl class itself and see what the actual JPA code looks like. Be forewarned, it doesn't look like much. As we indicated earlier, the actual work of JPA code will mostly involve an instance of the EntityManager class. This is why we've asked Spring to set up an EntityManagerFactory for us. Somewhere along the line, we need to get a reference to an real EntityManager in our code. As you might've guessed, we're planning to have Spring inject it. But how? Autowiring? Not quite, but close.

You might've noticed that we didn't actually declare an EntityManager bean in our Spring applicationContext.xml file. So we can't use autowiring to inject one into our service object. But we can take advantage of the Spring support for JPA. We can use annotations to tell Spring where to inject an EntityManager. The following snippet shows the annotation on our PortfolioServiceJPAImpl's entityManager setter:

```
@PersistenceContext
public void setEntityManager(EntityManager entityManager) {
  this.entityManager = entityManager;
}
```

The PersistenceContext annotation indicates that Spring should inject an entity-Manager at this setter. The naming of the setter is unimportant. It's not autowiring by name. This works because of two things. First, we declared the following bean postprocessor in our applicationContext.xml:

```
<bean class="org.springframework.orm.jpa.support.
              PersistenceAnnotationBeanPostProcessor" />
```

This postprocessor looks for the PersistenceContext annotations. Second, we declared an EntityManagerFactory in our applicationContext.xml. Without this factory, Spring wouldn't know where to get the EntityManager to inject in the annotated setters.

Now we have the EntityManager in hand and we're ready to write code. Listing 9.10 shows how we get down to the business of using the EntityManager in our PortfolioServiceJPAImpl class.

Listing 9.10   Using the JPA to manage the persistence of our Users and Portfolios

```
@Transactional          ①
public class PortfolioServiceJPAImpl
  implements PortfolioServiceInterface {

  public boolean userExists ( String username ) {

    Query query = entityManager.createQuery ( "from User where
      username = :username" ).setParameter("username", username);    ②
    List result = query.getResultList();

    return !result.isEmpty();

  }

  public void updateUser( User user ){
    entityManager.merge( user );                                     ③
  }

  public Collection getUsers(){

    Query query = entityManager.createQuery ( "from User" );
    return query.getResultList();
  }

  public Portfolio getPortfolio ( Long id ){
    Portfolio port = entityManager.find(Portfolio.class, id);        ④
    return port;
  }

  public void persistUser ( User user ){
    entityManager.persist(user);                                     ⑤
  }

  private EntityManager entityManager;
```

```
    @PersistenceContext
    public void setEntityManager(EntityManager entityManager) {
      this.entityManager = entityManager;
    }
  }
```

As we've indicated, we don't want to present a primer on JPA. We'll just point out the highlights of how we're using the injected `EntityManager`. First, we take advantage of Spring transaction management and the accompanying annotations to declare that this class is transactional ❶. This means that every method in the class will be transactional. Typically, you'd want to pursue a more fine-grained approach to the description of your transactions, but this works for us. In JPA, as in native Hibernate, all data access has to occur within the bounds of a transaction. You can open and commit these transactions programmatically, but you can also let Spring do it by configuring a transaction manager as we did in our applicationContext.xml. We also chose to use annotations to describe our transactions.

With transactional control out of the way, we can start persisting, loading, and updating data. The JPA offers a full API to make this work easy and clean. We can write queries against the database with a high-level query language that allows us to use our Java names instead of the database names that'd be required by native SQL ❷. We can update the database by merging new data objects with the persistence context ❸. We can, of course, retrieve an object ❹ and persist a new object ❺. While this can't teach you JPA, it does serve as a clean demonstration of a full set of CRUD functionality implemented in JPA.

This object, injected with the `EntityManager`, is then injected via autowiring into all of our actions that need to use it. They simply call these methods to persist their objects. Furthermore, the actions only handle an interface. You could easily switch this JPA implementation out for any other implementation, including test mockups.

Oh my, that was a fast run through a rather sophisticated technology. Again, our point here is not to teach JPA, but to demonstrate a best-practice integration technique. Based on our experience and our conversations with others doing Struts 2 web applications, this combination of JPA with Spring support is hard to beat. We hope you enjoy it.

9.4   *Summary*

In this chapter, we've seen how to integrate a Struts 2 application with two of the more commonly used third-party technologies. Both of these technologies, Spring and JPA, offer much more than we could've shown you in this brief chapter. Some JPA books are 800 pages long. Rather than try to tell you about those technologies, we've focused instead on showing you some best practices concerning the integration itself. Let's review what we've seen.

First, we saw how to use the Spring plug-in to extend the framework's `Object-Factory` with a `SpringObjectFactory` that gives you the opportunity to manage framework objects in a Spring container. While we hinted that this management could offer you more bonuses than we have the time to discuss, such as AOP, we did show you what many people consider to be the bottom-line in Spring usage for a Struts 2 application: dependency injection. We saw how to inject dependencies into managed beans and how to use several varieties of autowiring to inject dependencies into objects that the framework creates in the normal fashion. Dependency injection is great, hence all the hoopla. But we encourage you to check out all the other stuff that Spring has to offer its managed beans.

Finally, we took on the large task of upgrading our service object to use JPA. We went on a whirlwind tour of using Spring's support for JPA to make management of the JPA...well...manageable. Our fast coverage of JPA covered the critical issues of integrating with a persistence technology such as JPA. We showed you how to set up the OpenEntityManagerInView filter. We also showed you how to use Spring to inject the `PortfolioService` into the actions that depend on it. Somewhere in the midst of all that, we gave you a peek at using JPA annotations to map Java classes to the database, as well as Spring-managed transactions.

With all of this dense information crammed into a single chapter, we have no doubt that some of you are breathless. We fully expect that you might need to consult a Hibernate or JPA resource. They are complex topics that offer a lot to those willing to come to grips with their full breadth and depth. However, once you have the persistence technology background, we think this chapter will provide you with a good case study for getting that technology into your Struts 2 application.

With our core application shaping up, we can pick off a couple more points of refinement before moving into the advanced topics section of the book. Next up, we look at improving our validation code in chapter 10.

Exploring the
validation framework

This chapter covers

- Introducing the validation framework
- Wiring your actions for validation
- Building a custom validator
- Adapting the validation framework to your needs

Building on the refinements we saw in the previous chapter, where we added Hibernate-based persistence and Spring resource management to our sample application, this chapter introduces another advanced mechanism of the Struts 2 Framework, the validation framework. We've had robust data validation in our Struts 2 Portfolio since chapter 3, where we learned how to implement an action-local form of validation with the `Validateable` interface's `validate()` method. While this method works fine, it has some limitations that eventually become burdensome. We revisit the details of this basic form of validation in the first section of this chapter, and then quickly move on to explore the higher-level validation framework that comes with Struts 2.

The validation framework provides a more versatile and maintainable solution to validation than the `Validateable` interface. Throughout this chapter, we explore the components of the validation framework and learn how easy it is to work with this robust validation mechanism. We demonstrate this in code by migrating the Struts 2 Portfolio to use the validation framework instead of the `Validateable` interface mechanism. This example shows you how to wire up your actions for validation as well as demonstrates the use cases of the more common built-in validators. During this process, you'll learn all you need to leverage this advanced validation tool in your own projects.

One of the stronger points of the validation framework is the `Validator`, a reusable component in which the logic of specific types of validations are implemented. Some of the built-in validators handle such validations as checking whether a given string represents a valid email address or whether a date falls within a given range. We also demonstrate the extensible nature of the `Validators` by implementing a custom `Validator` for use in the Struts 2 Portfolio. We even point out some advanced nuances and techniques before we wind things up.

But let's get started by exploring the basic architecture of the validation framework. As you'll soon see, the learning curve is gentle.

10.1   Getting familiar with the validation framework

As with most aspects of Struts 2, the validation framework is well engineered. As we've indicated, Struts 2 is a second-generation web application framework. As with most of its components, validation has been a part of web application frameworks for a while, but Struts 2 takes it to a new level of refinement, modularity, and clean integration. Due to this, we can benefit greatly from a high-level study before kicking off into our code examples. We'll take the first section of this chapter to examine the architecture of the validation framework as well as how it fits into the workflow of Struts 2 itself. First, we'll look at the architecture.

10.1.1   The validation framework architecture

While it may make some people groan to learn that even validation has its own framework and architecture in Struts 2, we think a clean architecture just means it's easier to learn. Figure 10.1 shows the main components of the validation framework.

As you can see in figure 10.1, there are three main components at play in the validation framework: the *domain data*, *validation metadata*, and the *validators*. Each plays a vital role in the work of validation, which we explain in the next sections.

DOMAIN DATA

First, we must have some data to validate. We can see that the domain data depicted in figure 10.1 resides as properties on a Struts 2 action: `username`, `password`, and `age`. These properties are assumed to hold the data our action will work with when it begins execution. This is a common scenario we've become familiar with throughout the course of the book. However, we also know that such domain data could also be implemented in a couple of other ways, via a `ModelDriven` action for instance. All such

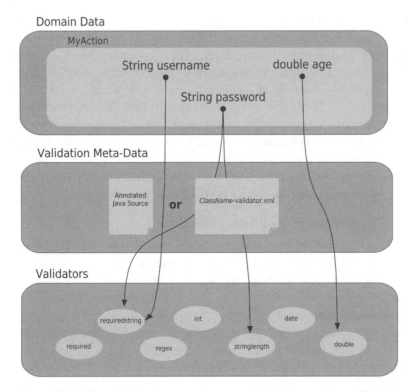

Figure 10.1   The validation framework uses metadata to associate validators with data properties.

variations on domain data handling can use this method of validation, but we'll start with this simplest case of simple JavaBeans properties on the action while we first explore the validation framework behavior. Later in the chapter, we'll demonstrate using `ModelDriven` actions.

VALIDATION METADATA

In figure 10.1, we see that a middle component lies between the validators and the data properties themselves. This middle component is the metadata that associates individual data properties with the validators that should be used to verify the correctness of the values in those properties at runtime. You can associate as many validators with each property as you like, including zero if that makes sense for your requirements.

When it comes to the details of implementation, the metadata layer offers a choice. The developer can map data properties to validators with XML files or with Java annotations. During this chapter, we'll focus our energies on the XML versions. We'll show how the annotations work at the end of the chapter. Ultimately it doesn't matter which one you use, as they're both just interfaces to the underlying validation mechanisms.

VALIDATORS

The actual work in all of this is done by the validators themselves. A validator is a reusable component that contains the logic for performing some fine-grained act of validation.

For instance, in figure 10.1 our `username` property is mapped to the `requiredstring` validator. This validator verifies that the value of the `username` property, or whatever property it validates, is a nonempty `String` value. The `password` property is mapped to `requiredstring` and `stringlength`. The `stringlength` validator checks that the string is of a desired length. The framework comes with a rich set of built-in validators, and you can even write your own. To have your data validated by these validators, you simply wire up your properties to the desired validators via some XML or Java annotations. When the validation executes, each property is validated by the set of validators with which it's been associated by the metadata layer.

But how does the validation framework actually get executed? Good question. In the next section, we examine how it fits into the Struts 2 workflow.

10.1.2 *The validation framework in the Struts 2 workflow*

Now let's look at how all of this validation actually gets done. As you might guess, there's an interceptor involved. Before we get into the details of that interceptor, let's take a moment to review how the basic version of validation, which we've already been using, works.

REVIEWING BASIC VALIDATION

Up until now, we've been putting our validation in the `validate()` method on our actions. We'll now provide a quick summary of how that validation works. If you want all of the details, you can go back to chapter 3 and review them, but a quick refresher should work fine.

The actions of our Struts 2 Portfolio all extend `ActionSupport`, which implements a couple of interfaces that play an important role in validation. These interfaces are `com.opensymphony.xwork2.Validateable` and `com.opensymphony.xwork2.Validation-Aware`. `Validateable` exposes the `validate()` method, in which we've been stuffing our validation code, and `ValidationAware` exposes methods for storing error messages generated when validation finds invalid data. As we learned before, these interfaces work in tandem with an important interceptor known as the `workflow` interceptor.

When the `workflow` interceptor fires, it first checks to see whether the action implements `Validateable`. If it does, the `workflow` interceptor invokes the `validate()` method. If our validation code finds that some piece of data isn't valid, an error message is created and added to one of the `ValidationAware` methods that store error messages. When the `validate()` method returns, the `workflow` interceptor still has another task. It calls `ValidationAware`'s `hasErrors()` method to see if there were any problems with validation. If errors exist, the `workflow` interceptor intervenes by stopping further execution of the action by returning the input result, which returns the user back to the form that was submitted.

With that quick recap out of the way, let's see how the validation framework works.

INTRODUCING THE VALIDATION FRAMEWORK WORKFLOW

As you'll see, the validation framework actually shares quite a bit of the same functionality we've previously outlined for basic validation; it uses the `ValidationAware` interface to store errors and the `workflow` interceptor to route back to the input page if necessary. In fact, the only thing that changes is the validation itself. But this is a significant change.

We start by noting that both the basic validation examples and the validation framework examples all work in the context of the `defaultStack` of interceptors that come with Struts 2. The `workflow`, as dictated by this stack of interceptors, remains constant regardless of which type of validation you choose to use. In particular, note the following sequence of interceptors from the `defaultStack`, as defined in struts-default.xml:

```
<interceptor-ref name="params"/>
<interceptor-ref name="conversionError"/>
<interceptor-ref name="validation"/>
<interceptor-ref name="workflow"/>
```

In this snippet, we've excerpted only the portion of the `defaultStack` that pertains to our current discussion. As you can see, the `params` interceptor and the `conversionError` interceptor both fire before we get to the validation-related interceptors. These two interceptors finish up the work of transferring the data from the request and converting it to the correct Java types of the target properties. If you recall from our discussion of basic validation in chapter 3, the `validation` interceptor has nothing to do with that form of validation. Recall that the `workflow` interceptor invokes the `validate()` method to conduct basic validation. Now we need to take note of the `validation` interceptor because it's the entry into the validation framework. When this interceptor fires, it conducts all the validation that's been defined via the validation metadata we mentioned in the previous section.

Figure 10.2 illustrates the workflow of the validation framework.

As we've said, all Struts 2 workflow, such as shown in figure 10.2, is ultimately determined by interceptors. This figure assumes the `defaultStack`. As you can see, the first functional unit in the pipeline is the data transfer and type conversion process. This process, conducted by the `params` and `conversionError` interceptors, moves the data from the request parameters onto the properties exposed on the `ValueStack`. In this

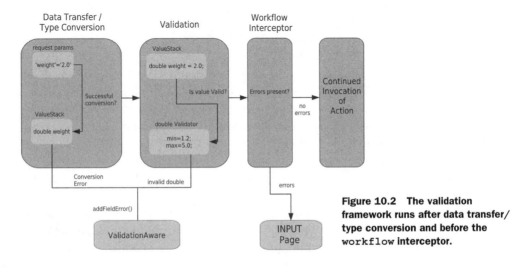

Figure 10.2 The validation framework runs after data transfer/ type conversion and before the `workflow` interceptor.

case, we're moving the string value 2.0 onto the type-double property weight. In figure 10.2, this conversion is successful. If it weren't, note that an error would be added to the ValidationAware methods exposed on our action.

After type conversion, we proceed to the validation phase. In the figure, we're talking about the validation framework. The validation interceptor, which follows the conversionError interceptor in the defaultStack, provides the entry point into this validation process. Looking at figure 10.2 shows that the weight property, which was just populated by the params interceptor, is validated against a double validator that's been configured to verify that the double value falls in the range of 1.2 and 5.0. If this weren't true, then an error would be added to the ValidationAware methods. Note that both conversion errors and validation errors are collected by Validation-Aware. In our case, 2.0 passes this validation and no errors are added. Whether errors are added or not, we still proceed to the next interceptor, the workflow interceptor.

We've discussed the workflow interceptor several times in this book. We know that it has two phases. The first phase is to invoke the validate() method, if exposed by the current action. This is the entry point into basic validation. Let's assume, since we're using the validation framework, that we didn't implement this method. Fine. We quickly proceed to phase two of the workflow interceptor: checking for errors. At this point, the workflow interceptor checks the ValidationAware method hasErrors(). If there are none, it passes control on to the rest of the action invocation process. If errors are found, workflow is diverted and we return to the input page and present the user with error messages so she can correct the form data.

Before wrapping this overview up, we should make one fine but important point about the relationship between the basic validation methods and the validation framework. You can use them both at the same time. As you've seen, due to the clean lines of Struts 2, everything except the actual validation logic itself is shared between the two methods. When you use the defaultStack, both the validation and workflow interceptors fire every time. Ultimately, this means that you could use both forms of validation at the same time, if you like. First, the validation interceptor runs all validations that you define with the validation framework metadata. Then, when the workflow interceptor runs, it still checks to see if your action implements the validate() method. Even if you've already run some validators via the validation interceptor, you can still provide some additional validation code in a validate() method. When the second phase of the workflow interceptor checks for errors, it doesn't care or know who created them. The effect is the same.

But why use both validation mechanisms at once? One reason is common. Perhaps the strongest point of the validation framework is that the validation code is contained in reusable validators. As long as your validation needs are satisfied by the built-in validators, why write code to do that stuff? Just wire the validators to your properties and let them go.

Eventually, you'll have some validation logic that isn't handled by the built-in validators. At that point, you'll have two choices. If your validation logic is something that you can foresee reusing in the future, it probably makes sense to implement a custom validator. However, if your validation logic truly appears to be a quirky requirement that will most likely only be applied in this one case, it makes more sense to put it in the validate() method. In a one-off case like this, it's much more efficient to take the quick and local fix.

That's about it. Now that you understand the architecture of the validation framework and how it fits into the interceptor-controlled Struts 2 workflow, we're ready to get back to our Struts 2 Portfolio sample application and convert it to use the validation framework.

10.2 *Wiring your actions for validation*

Staying true to our *in Action* name, we'll dive right in with a live example. To demonstrate the details of using the validation framework, we'll migrate our existing Struts 2 Portfolio application from the basic validation it currently uses. We'll migrate the entire thing in the sample code, which you can peruse at your convenience, but here we'll focus on the Register action as our case study.

The Register action, if you've forgotten, registers a new user of the Struts 2 Portfolio. As such, this action receives data from a registration form that collects a few pieces of information such as username and password. If you consult the older versions of this action, such as the chapter 8 version shown in listing 10.1, you can see how we'd previously implemented our validation in the validate() method.

> **Listing 10.1 An earlier version of the Register action that uses basic validation**

```
public class Register extends ActionSupport implements SessionAware {      ❶

    public String execute(){

        //Make user and persist it.      ❷

        return SUCCESS;
    }

    private String username;
    private String password;                        ❸
    private String portfolioName;
    private boolean receiveJunkMail;

    // Getters and setters omitted

    public void validate(){

        PortfolioService ps = getPortfolioService();

        if ( getPassword().length() == 0 ){
            addFieldError( "password", getText("password.required") );      ❹
        }
        if ( getUsername().length() == 0 ){
            addFieldError( "username", getText("username.required") );
        }
        . . .

    }
}
```

First, we note that the basic validation relies upon the `ValidationAware` implementation provided by `ActionSupport` ❶. We aren't required to extend `ActionSupport`, but, if we didn't, we'd need to implement `ValidationAware` ourselves to provide a place to store errors. Usually, we just extend `ActionSupport` to use the built-in implementation it provides. We do this regardless of which validation method we use. The `execute()` method of the `Register` action just creates the user object with the submitted data and persists that object ❷; we don't need to rehash that at this point, but you can look at the source code of the sample application if you like. Our main interest, at this time, is the use of the `validate()` method ❹ to programmatically validate the data contained in the JavaBeans properties ❸ this action exposes to hold the request data. Glancing at this code, you'll see that it programmatically tests the values in the JavaBeans properties. If it finds some validation problems, it programmatically sets a field error using the `ValidationAware` method implemented by `ActionSupport`.

10.2.1 *Declaring your validation metadata with ActionClass-validations.xml*

Now let's rewrite the `Register` action to use the validation framework instead of the `validate()` method. As we saw in the overview sections of this chapter, the `default-Stack` has everything in place to handle both kinds of validation. To make the switch, we just need to change the way the validation logic is invoked. We replace the programmatic validations of the `validate()` method with some metadata that creates associations between our data properties and the validators that contain the desired logic. For now, we do this with an XML file. Listing 10.2 shows the complete listing of our `Register` action's validation metadata file, Register-validation.xml.

Listing 10.2   Declares the validators that validate each exposed property

```
<!DOCTYPE validators PUBLIC "-//OpenSymphony Group//XWork Validator 1.0.2//
    EN" "http://www.opensymphony.com/xwork/xwork-validator-1.0.2.dtd">        ❶
<validators>                                     ❷
  <field name="password">                                              ❸
    <field-validator type="requiredstring">
      <message>You must enter a value for password.</message>          ❺
    </field-validator>
  </field>                                                             ❹
  <field name="username">
    <field-validator type="stringlength">
      <param name="maxLength">8</param>
      <param name="minLength">5</param>
      <message>While ${username} is a nice name, a valid username must
            be between ${minLength} and ${maxLength} characters long.
      </message>
    </field-validator>
  </field>
  <field name="portfolioName">
    <field-validator type="requiredstring">
      <message key="portfolioName.required"/>
    </field-validator>
  </field>
```

```
    <field name="email">
      <field-validator type="requiredstring">
        <message>You must enter a value for email.</message>
      </field-validator>
      <field-validator type="email">
        <message key="email.invalid"/>
      </field-validator>
    </field>
    <validator type="expression">
      <param name="expression">username != password</param>
      <message>Username and password can't be the same.</message>
    </validator>
  </validators>
```

❻

❼

Listing 10.2 shows the Register-validation.xml file from our chapter 10 version of the Struts 2 Portfolio. The name of this file is derived from the name of the class that implements the action for which the validation rules apply. In this case, we're validating our `Register` action. The naming convention of the XML validation metadata file is *ActionClass*-validations.xml. This file is then placed in the package directory structure next to the action class itself. If you look back to figure 10.1, which shows the architecture of the validation framework, this XML file is the metadata component. This metadata associates sets of validators with each of the pieces of data you'd like to validate.

At the top of our Register-validations.xml file, we have a `doctype` element ❶ that you must include in all of your validation xml files. Next, we have a `validators` element ❷ that contains all of the declarations of individual validators that should be run when this action is invoked. There are two types of validators you can declare: field and nonfield.

FIELD VALIDATORS

Field validators are validators that operate on an individual field. By *field* we mean the same thing as when we say *data property*. The validators use the word field in the sense that they're coming from fields on the HTML form that submitted the request. This makes sense because, until the validator approves, the data hasn't been formally accepted into the Java side of things.

The first field declared in listing 10.2 is the `password` field ❸. Once we declare a `field` element for our data, we just need to put `field-validator` elements inside that `field` element to declare which validators should validate this piece of data. In the case of the `password`, we declare only one validator, the `requiredstring` validator ❹. This validator verifies that the string has been submitted and isn't an empty string. If the `password` string doesn't pass this verification, then a message is displayed to the user when the `workflow` interceptor sends him back to the input form. The `message` element ❺ contains the text of this message. To see how this works, go to the chapter 10 version of the sample application, navigate to the user homepage, and register for an account. If you omit the password, you'll receive this message.

A `field` element isn't limited to declaring just one the validator. It can declare as many as it likes. As an example, our `email` field ❻ in listing 10.2 declares both the `requiredstring` validator and the `email` validator.

NONFIELD VALIDATORS

You can also declare validators that don't apply logic targeted at a specific field. These validators apply to the whole action and often contain checks that involve more than one of the field values. The built-in validators only offer one instance of a nonfield validator: the `expression` validator. This useful validator allows you to embed an OGNL expression that contains the logic of the validation you wish to perform. As you've seen earlier, OGNL provides a rich expression language. You can easily write sophisticated validation logic into the expression validator.

Listing 10.2 declares a single nonfield validator ❼. This validator uses OGNL to compare two of the other fields. It's important to understand that this OGNL, like all OGNL, resolves against the `ValueStack`. Since we're in the middle of processing our action, that action and the properties it exposes are on the `ValueStack`. Thus, we can easily write a concise OGNL expression that says that the `username` and the `password` shouldn't be equal. If they're not equal, then our expression returns `true` and validation passes. If they're the same, validation will fail and the user will be returned to the input page, where he'll see the message specified in this validator's `message` element.

MESSAGE ELEMENT OPTIONS

The `message` element is used to specify the message that the user should see in the event of a validation error. In the simplest form, as seen in listing 10.2, we simply embed the message text itself in the `message` element ❺. However, several more options present themselves. First, we can use OGNL to make the message dynamic. An example of this can be seen in Register-validation.xml's declaration of the `username` field. The following snippet shows the code:

```
<field name="username">
  <field-validator type="stringlength">
    <param name="maxLength">8</param>
    <param name="minLength">5</param>
    <message>While ${username} is a nice name, a valid username
          must be between ${minLength} and ${maxLength}
          characters long.
    </message>
  </field-validator>
</field>
```

First of all, those `param` elements are as simple as they seem. Many of the validators, such as the `stringlength`, take parameters that configure their behavior. In this case, the `maxLength` and `minLength` parameters specify the length requirements that are imposed on the `username` string when this `stringlength` validator runs. When we list all the built-in validators shortly, we'll show all the parameters that each supports.

In the `message` element in the snippet, we see three embedded OGNL expressions. These resolve at runtime against the `ValueStack`. In this case, the `username` is pulled from the stack to customize the message that the user sees when he returns to the input page. Next, we pull the `minLength` and `maxLength` values themselves from the `ValueStack`. As it turns out, the `Validator` itself has been placed on the `ValueStack`, thus its properties are also exposed. So, you can access pretty much any data you'd want to inject into a message. Before we move on, we should point out that the OGNL in these XML files uses the $ rather than the % sign that's normally used in OGNL.

The next thing you can do with `message` elements is externalize the message itself in a resource bundle. By default, Struts 2 works with properties file–backed resource bundles. As you might recall from chapter 3, `ActionSupport` implements the `TextProvider` interface to provide access to localized messages. As you can see if you refer back to listing 10.1, the basic validation in the `validate()` method calls the `TextProvider`'s `getText()` method to retrieve localized messages. This method takes a key and retrieves a locale-sensitive message from the properties file resources. The validation framework provides even easier access to our localized messages. The following snippet from Register-validation.xml shows how this works:

```
<field name="portfolioName">
  <field-validator type="requiredstring">
    <message key="portfolioName.required"/>
  </field-validator>
</field>
```

The `message` element in this snippet doesn't have a text body. Rather, it sets the key attribute to a value to be used to look up the message via the `TextProvider` implementation provided by ActionSupport. In other words, this key is used to find a locale-sensitive message in your properties files. The contents of the Register.properties file follow:

```
user.exists=This user ${username} already exists.
portfolioName.required=You must enter a name for your initial portfolio.
email.invalid=Your email address was not a valid email address.
```

If the previous `requiredstring` validator finds that the `portfolioName` doesn't hold a value, then it pulls the error message from this properties file when it adds the error. Of course, since the `ResourceBundle` is locale-sensitive, the message might come from Register_es.properties if that locale is specified in the information submitted by the browser and returned by the `LocaleProvider` interface, which `ActionSupport` also implements. Change the locale in your browser and run through the registration process a few times to see this in action. If you need a refresher course on that process, please refer back to chapter 3.

Now that we've seen how validators are declared, we'll take the time to cover all the validators that come bundled with the validation framework.

10.2.2 *Surveying the built-in validators*

We've referred to the built-in validators more than once. The framework comes with a rich set of validators to handle most validation needs. They mostly perform such straightforward tasks that little has to be said about them. You've seen some of them already in the previous section, when we migrated the `Register` action from basic validation to the validation framework. In this section, we give a full summary of the built-in validators. Table 10.1 lists them all.

Table 10.1   Built-in validators that come with Struts 2

Validator name	Params	Function	Type
`required`	None	Verifies that value is non-null.	field
`requiredstring`	`trim` (default = true, trims white space)	Verifies that value is non-null, and not an empty string.	field
`stringlength`	`trim` (default=true, trims prior to length check), `minLength, maxLength`	Verifies that the string length falls within the specified parameters. No checks are made for unspecified length params—if you give no minimum, then an empty string would pass validation.	field
`int`	`Min, max`	Verifies that the integer value falls between the specified minimum and maximum.	field
`double`	`minInclusive, maxInclusive, minExclusive, maxExclusive`	Verifies that the double value falls between the inclusively or exclusively specified parameters.	field
`date`	`Min, max`	Verifies that the date value falls between the specified minimum and maximum. Date should be specified as `MM/DD/YYYY`.	field
`email`	None	Verifies email address format.	field
`url`	None	Verifies URL format.	field
`fieldexpression`	`expression` (required)	Evaluates an OGNL expression against current `ValueStack`. Expression must return either `true` or `false` to determine whether validation is successful.	field
`expression`	`expression` (required)	Same as `fieldexpression`, but used at action level.	action
`visitor`	`Context, appendPrefix`	Defers validation of a domain object property, such as `User`, to validation declarations made local to that domain object.	field
`regex`	`expression` (required), `caseSensitive, trim`	Verifies that a `String` conforms to the given regular expression.	field

As you can see, the table provides a brief description of the functionality of each validator, a summary of the parameters supported by the validator, and the type: field or nonfield. The functionality of most of these is simple. We've already shown how to use parameters and OGNL in the messages. The only validator that requires further discussion is the `visitor`, which allows you to define validation metadata for each domain model class, such as our Struts 2 Portfolio User object. We'll show how to do this in the Advanced Topics section at the end of this chapter.

The only other thing you need to know about the built-in validators is the location of their declarations. The validation framework is actually a part of a low-level framework, upon which Struts 2 has been built, called *Xwork*. You don't need to know much about Xwork to use Struts 2, but if you like you can visit the project home page at http://www.opensymphony.com/xwork. The only reason we mention it now is to show you where the validators of the validation framework are defined. If you look in the XWork JAR file, something like xwork-2.0.4.jar, you can find an XML file that declares all these built-in validators, located at /com/opensymphony/xwork2/validator/validators/default.xml. When we build a custom validator in the next section, we see how to properly add new validators to this declaration.

10.3   *Writing a custom validator*

Writing your own custom validator is little different than writing any of the other custom Struts 2 components. We've already seen how to write custom interceptors, results, and type converters. In this section, we follow a familiar path of extending a convenience class, declaring our new component with XML, then wiring it in to a working code example. For our example, we write a custom validator that checks for a certain level of password integrity. After we implement it, we add it to the Struts 2 Portfolio Register action to make sure that people are using strong passwords for their accounts.

10.3.1 *A custom validator to check password strength*

As with other custom components, a custom validator must implement a certain interface. In this case, all validators are obligated to implement the Validator or Field-Validator interface. The two interfaces, found in the com.opensymphony.xwork2.validator package, represent the two types of Validators as described earlier, field and nonfield. As you might expect, the framework also provides some convenience classes to make the task of writing custom validators all the more agreeable. Typically, you'll extend either ValidatorSupport or FieldValidatorSupport, both from the com.opensymphony.xwork2.validator.validators package.

In our case, we extend the FieldValidatorSupport class because our validator, like most, operates on a given field. We design our password validator to make three checks:

  1 The password must contain a letter, uppercase or lower.
  2 The password must contain a digit, 0–9.
  3 The password must contain at least one of a set of "special characters."

The special characters have a default value but can be configured with a parameter, similar to the stringlength parameters that we used earlier. Note that we won't ask our password validator to check for password length, because that would be duplicating functionality already provided by the stringlength validator. If we want to also enforce a length requirement on the password, we can use both validators.

Without further delay, listing 10.3 shows the full code of our `manning.utils.` `PasswordIntegrityValidator`.

Listing 10.3   Verifying that a password contains the required characters

```
public class PasswordIntegrityValidator extends FieldValidatorSupport {   ❶

    static Pattern digitPattern = Pattern.compile( "[0-9]");            ❷
    static Pattern letterPattern = Pattern.compile( "[a-zA-Z]");
    static Pattern specialCharsDefaultPattern = Pattern.compile( "!@#$");

    public void validate(Object object) throws ValidationException {   ❸

      String fieldName = getFieldName();                               ❹
      String fieldValue = (String) getFieldValue(fieldName, object );

      fieldValue = fieldValue.trim();
      Matcher digitMatcher = digitPattern.matcher(fieldValue);
      Matcher letterMatcher = letterPattern.matcher(fieldValue);
      Matcher specialCharacterMatcher;

      if ( getSpecialCharacters() != null ){                           ❺
        Pattern specialPattern =
               Pattern.compile("[" + getSpecialCharacters() + "]" );
        specialCharacterMatcher = specialPattern.matcher( fieldValue );
      } else{
        specialCharacterMatcher =
               specialCharsDefaultPattern.matcher( fieldValue );
      }

      if ( !digitMatcher.find() ) {
        addFieldError( fieldName, object );
      }else if ( !letterMatcher.find() ) {                             ❻
        addFieldError( fieldName, object );
      }else if ( !specialCharacterMatcher.find() ) {
        addFieldError( fieldName, object );
      }
    }

    private String specialCharacters;        ❼

    //Getter and setter omitted

}
```

The first thing we need to do is extend the convenience class `FieldValidator-Support` ❶. Most custom validators do this. If we were writing a nonfield validator, such as one that performed a validation check involving more than one field, we'd extend `ValidatorSupport`. Extending these convenience classes provides implementations of several helper methods that we use in this example. As a developer, you're left to focus on the details of your own logic. This logic is placed in the `validate()` method ❸, the entry method defined by the `Validator` interface and left unimplemented by the abstract support classes that you extend. Another preliminary duty of the developer is creating JavaBeans properties ❼ to match all parameters that should be exposed to the user. In this case, we want to allow the user to set the list of `specialCharacters`; a valid password must have at least one of these characters. The following snippet shows how a parameter is passed in from the XML file to this property:

```
<field-validator type="passwordintegrity">
    <param name="specialCharacters">$!@#?</param>
    <message>Your password must contain one letter, one number, and one
            of the following "${specialCharacters}".
    </message>
</field-validator>
```

Now, let's look at how this validator works. It's mostly a matter of Java regular expressions and string handling, but we want to make sure you see where the code is calling on the helper methods provided by the convenience classes. Most of these helper methods are actually defined in `ValidatorSupport`, which is extended by `FieldValidatorSupport`. First, note that we define some regular expression patterns as static members of our class ❷. There's even a default set of special characters defined here in case the user doesn't specify a set herself.

Next we retrieve the value of the field via a couple of calls to our helper methods ❹. Note that the `validate()` method receives the object that's being validated. Since we've defined our validations at the action level, via Register-validation.xml, the object passed into the `validate()` method is our action. Later we'll learn how to have validation run on a domain object itself. In the case of field validators, we usually want to get our hands on the actual field value as soon as possible.

Obtaining the password value is a two-step process. First, we call the `getField-Name()` method, then the `getFieldValue()` method. Again, these helper methods are defined by the support classes.

With the password in hand, we quickly move on to build our `Matchers` ❺ and then search the password for the required characters. If a password doesn't have a required character, we generate an error and add it to the set of stored errors ❻, again with helper methods inherited from the support classes. That's it. If errors are stored, the workflow interceptor will find them and divert the user back to the input page with the appropriate error messages.

Next, we wire this validator into our Struts 2 Portfolio application to help our users start making better passwords.

10.3.2 *Using our custom validator*

First things first. As we mentioned at the start of this chapter, all validators must first be declared so that they can be referenced when we write our validation metadata that maps fields to validators. As we said, the built-in validators are already declared in the XWork JAR file at /com/opensymphony/xwork2/validator/validators/default.xml. We declare our own custom validators in an application-local validators.xml file, which we put at the root of our `classpath`—directly under our src folder, which will be moved to WEB-INF/classes/ during the build. Listing 10.4 shows the complete source of this important file.

Listing 10.4 Using validators.xml to declare our custom validator

```
<?xml version="1.0" encoding="UTF-8"?>
<!DOCTYPE validators PUBLIC
    "-//OpenSymphony Group//XWork Validator Config 1.0//EN"
    "http://www.opensymphony.com/xwork/xwork-validator-config-1.0.dtd">

<validators>
  <validator name="passwordintegrity"
        class="manning.utils.PasswordIntegrityValidator"/>
</validators>
```

The brief validators.xml file, shown in listing 10.4, simply declares our `Password-IntegrityValidator` as an available validator that can be referenced under the logical name `passwordintegrity`. To declare your own custom validators, simply copy this page and insert your own validator declarations. With this in place, we can use our new validator just as easily as the built-in validators.

As promised, we'll now use the password integrity validator to ensure that our aspiring artists create good passwords. I don't want to point any fingers, but I suspect this group of users sports an alarmingly poor average strength of password. To do this, we just need to add this validator to the validators mapped to the `password` field in our Register-validation.xml file. Listing 10.5 shows the new `password field` element from that file.

Listing 10.5 The `password` element that uses our `PasswordIntegrityValidator`

```
<field name="password">
  <field-validator type="stringlength">
    <param name="maxLength">10</param>
    <param name="minLength">6</param>
    <message>Your password should be 6-10 characters.</message>
  </field-validator>
  <field-validator type="passwordintegrity">        ❶
    <param name="specialCharacters">$!@#?</param>        ❷
    <message>Your password must contain one letter, one number, and one
        of the following "${specialCharacters}".
    </message>        ❸
  </field-validator>
</field>
```

This `field` element maps two validators to our `password` field. The first one is the `stringlength` validator, which we've already seen in action. Next, we map the `passwordintegrity` validator to the `password` field. This works just like using the built-in validators; we simply use a `field-validator` element to declare the type ❶, using our logical name as specified in the validators.xml file. Next, we pass in the `special-Characters` parameter ❷ to indicate the set of required characters, one of which all good passwords must include. Remember, this is received by the JavaBeans property, of matching name, that we exposed on the `PasswordIntegrityValidator`. Finally, we specify the message that the user will see if his password doesn't pass the integrity check ❸. This message pulls the special characters off of the validator, which sits on the `ValueStack` at runtime, to inform the user exactly what characters are needed.

We already have this implemented in our chapter 10 version of the Struts 2 Portfolio, so feel free to check out this action by playing around with the Create an Account page found on the User Home Page section of the application.

We've now covered the fundamentals of using the validation framework. We hope you're convinced that it's a powerful, yet user-friendly way of validating your data. The final section of this chapter addresses some advanced topics and nuances.

10.4 Validation framework advanced topics

In this section, we address some advanced topics of using the validation framework. Some of these advanced topics merely explore the nuances of the validation mechanism, but others demonstrate adapting the validation framework to some of the more specialized development patterns of Struts 2, such as `ModelDriven` actions and alias-mapped actions. (Using alias mappings to wire action mappings to alternative methods exposed on the action implementation class is demonstrated in full in chapter 15.) The validation topics covered in this section include inheritance of validators, mapping validation to domain model objects instead of actions, and short-circuiting out of validation when one validator fails.

10.4.1 Validating at the domain object level

In our earlier demonstrations of the validation framework, we defined our validation metadata in an XML file on a per-action basis. This is a convenient method for wiring into the validation framework. On the other hand, if you're exposing domain objects directly to the Struts 2 data transfer, then you might find it more convenient to declare your validation metadata on a per-domain object basis. We'll do just this when we continue our migration of the Struts 2 Portfolio application to the validation framework.

The `UpdateAccount` action allows a user to modify her account information. The form that submits to this action contains exactly the same set of data as the registration form with which we've been working. For the registration action, we received our data on a JavaBeans properties–exposed action, and we defined the validation metadata in an action-local XML file that mapped validators to each field of the incoming form. This time, we define our metadata in an XML file local to our domain object, `manning.utils.User`. The corresponding change in the `UpdateAccount` action itself, as opposed to the `Register` action we just worked with, is that the entire `User` object is exposed directly on a JavaBeans property. If you need to know more about exposing domain objects, refer back to chapter 3.

The first thing we need to do is define our metadata. Listing 10.6 shows the full source of our User-validation.xml.

Listing 10.6   Declaring the validators that validate each property of the user object

```
<!DOCTYPE validators PUBLIC "-//OpenSymphony Group//XWork Validator 1.0.2//
   EN" "http://www.opensymphony.com/xwork/xwork-validator-1.0.2.dtd">
<validators>
```

```
<field name="password">
  <field-validator type="stringlength">
    <param name="maxLength">10</param>
    <param name="minLength">6</param>
    <message>Your password should be 6-10 characters.</message>
  </field-validator>
  <field-validator type="passwordintegrity">
    <param name="specialCharacters">$!@#?</param>
    <message>Your password must contain one letter, one number, and
             one of the following "${specialCharacters}".
    </message>
  </field-validator>
</field>
<field name="username">
  <field-validator type="stringlength">
    <param name="maxLength">8</param>
    <param name="minLength">5</param>
    <message>While ${username} is a nice name, a valid username must
             be between ${minLength} and ${maxLength} characters long.
    </message>
  </field-validator>
</field>
<field name="portfolioName">
  <field-validator type="requiredstring">
    <message key="portfolioName.required"/>
  </field-validator>
</field>
<field name="email">
  <field-validator type="requiredstring">
    <message>You must enter a value for email.</message>
  </field-validator>
  <field-validator type="email">
    <message key="email.invalid"/>
  </field-validator>
</field>
<validator type="expression">
  <param name="expression">username != password</param>
  <message>Username and password can't be the same.</message>
</validator>
</validators>
```

As you can see, this file is exactly the same as the XML file we used to define our validators for the Register action. This is because we're validating the same User data. The only difference is that, in the case of the Register action, the data was being exposed directly on the action itself as individual properties. Now we expose our entire User object on an action-local property. We can now raise the validation metadata to the level of the User class itself, which allows us to reuse it across all actions that work with User. Once we've created our User-validation.xml file, we place it next to the User class itself at /manning/utils/.

With our User validations in place, we now need to make a connection between the action that uses a User and these validations. This is done by the visitor validator. But this validator doesn't go in the User-validation.xml file. It goes in an action-local validation file. The following snippet shows the brief contents of the UpdateAccount-validation.xml file:

```
<!DOCTYPE validators PUBLIC "-//OpenSymphony Group//XWork Validator 1.0.2//
    EN" "http://www.opensymphony.com/xwork/xwork-validator-1.0.2.dtd">
<validators>
  <field name="user">
    <field-validator type="visitor">
       <message>User: </message>
    </field-validator>
  </field>
</validators>
```

While much shorter, the UpdateAccount-validation.xml file still serves the same purpose as all ClassName-validation.xml files. But where those files usually define many fine-grained mappings of validators to fields, this one simply uses the `visitor` validator to make a wholesale deferral of validation details to the validation metadata made on the class of the specified field name. In this case, we've specified the user field. We know that our `UpdateAccount` action's user property is of type `manning.utils.User`. The `visitor` validator uses this information to locate User-validation.xml and uses the validation logic described in that file to validate all the properties on the user. At this point, it all works exactly the same as our earlier examples. The only item worth noting is the body of the `message` element. The content of the message body is used as a prefix that's attached to the error messages generated by the validations defined at the `User` level. Again, if you want to see this in action, check out the update account page on the chapter 10 version of the Struts 2 Portfolio.

USING THE VALIDATION FRAMEWORK WITH MODELDRIVEN ACTIONS

You can also use the preceding technique when your actions implement the `Model-Driven` interface. As we learned in chapter 3, `ModelDriven` actions expose domain objects via a `getModel()` method rather than exposing them directly on a JavaBeans property. The `ModelDriven` magic is such that you can now access the properties of your domain model object with top-level OGNL syntax. Instead of having fields such as `user.username` and `user.password`, we would now have, simply, `username` and `password`. Since this is almost exactly like the previous `visitor` example, we'll gallop through at a quick pace.

First of all, everything is the same unless we note a difference. For instance, the User-validation.xml file doesn't change. The main changes are to the actions and to the JSP pages. In the actions, we must implement the `ModelDriven` interface. If we were working with the update account page, we'd need to convert two actions, `UpdateAccountForm` and `UpdateAccount`. The first action prepopulates the form and the second one processes the update. Changing these to `ModelDriven` amounts to little more than adding the `ModelDriven` interface and implementing its one method, `getModel()`. If you need to see how to do this, check chapter 3 for the details.

The next step is to change your JSP page form elements to contain the simpler OGNL references. The following snippet shows what the UpdateAccountForm.jsp page would look like:

```
<s:form action="UpdateAccount">
  <s:label key="username" />
  <s:hidden name="username" />
  <s:password name="password" label="Password" showPassword="true"/>
  <s:textfield name="portfolioName" label="Initial Portfolio"/>
  <s:textfield name="email" label="Email Address"/>
  <s:checkbox name="receiveJunkMail"  label="Do you want to receive junk
                                        mail?" />
  <s:submit/>
</s:form>
```

This differs only slightly from the current page. Here we've omitted the user level of the OGNL and are left with top-level references such as username and password. Based on this change of reference namespace, we now need to make a single, slight change to the visitor validator mapping in UpdateAccount-validation.xml. Here's the new content of that file:

```
<validators>
  <field name="model">
    <field-validator type="visitor">
      <param name="appendPrefix">false</param>
      <message>User:  </message>
    </field-validator>
  </field>
</validators>
```

Two changes have been made. First of all, since our ModelDriven domain object is exposed with the getModel() getter method, we now need to change the field name to model. Second, we need to use the appendPrefix parameter to tell the visitor validator that we no longer need the user prepended to the field names. Setting this parameter to false allows the validator to find the top-level field names. That's it. Combining the validation framework with ModelDriven actions is approaching a pretty efficient level of development.

In the next section, we investigate another high-level development technique and explore how it fits in with the validation framework.

10.4.2 Using validation context to refine your validations

We've already seen how to define your validation metadata on a per-action and per-domain class level. As it turns out, you might find you need a more fine-grained level of control over what validations run when. In order to control this, the validation framework introduces the notion of *context*. Context is pretty straightforward. Validation context provides a simple means of identifying the specific location in the application that's using the data that we want to validate.

The first use case for validation context arises when you use the framework's ability to define more than one entry point method for action execution. Thus far, we've stuck to the default execute() method as our single point of entry into an action. In chapter 15, we'll show you how to use multiple entry point methods on a single action class. These multiple entry point methods can then be mapped to multiple Struts 2 actions that have different names, or aliases. Note the difference between a Struts 2 action component, one of the action mappings from your declarative architecture, and an action class, the Java class that can be used to back a Struts 2 action component.

Imagine we have a Java action class that provides a sorting capability. Now, suppose that we want to have several sort algorithms exposed by this action class. We could have put each one in its own class, but it makes sense to gather them together into a single class, both from a logical and design point of view. So, we have something like `manning.sort.SortAction` and it exposes two entry point methods named `bubbleSort()` and `heapSort()`. And let's assume we don't even use the `execute()` method, since Struts 2 doesn't require us to.

Here's a snippet of XML that declares two Struts 2 action components that both use this one action class:

```
<action name="BubbleSort" class="manning.sort.SortAction"
                       method="bubbleSort">
  <result>/sort/SortResults.jsp</result>
</action>
<action name="HeapSort" class="manning.sort.SortAction" method="heapSort">
  <result>/sort/SortResults.jsp</result>
</action>
```

Now let's assume that we have our validations defined in a single file for the `SortAction` named, appropriately, SortAction-validation.xml. This is what we did earlier in this chapter. This works great, but what happens if we decide that one of the sort entry points, or contexts, requires a different set of validations? Obviously, we need a finer granularity for our validation definitions. The notion of validation context solves this problem ASAP. If we need a different set of validations for each entry point method, we just replace the single SortAction-validation.xml with two new files, SortAction-BubbleSort-validation.xml and SortAction-HeapSort-validation.xml. Just to be clear, the naming convention is ActionClassName-aliasName-validation.xml. When one of the aliases from the preceding snippet is invoked, the validation framework automatically picks up the corresponding alias-named validation file. Note that if you still have a general SortAction-validation.xml defined, the validations defined in it will also be loaded. The aliased validations do not prevent the general ones from being used. This allows you to define common validations separate from the ones specific to the various contexts. Now, let's look at another use case where validation context can be helpful.

USING VALIDATION CONTEXT WITH THE VISITOR VALIDATOR AND DOMAIN OBJECTS

Earlier in this chapter, we learned how to use the `visitor` validator to point to validations declared at the level of the domain object itself. Validation context can be used in these situations as well. There are a couple of ways you can use validation context with the `visitor` validator. The first method follows the alias patterns described in our earlier `SortAction` example. In the `SortAction` example, we defined our validations at the action class level. Now imagine that we've defined the validations at the domain object level instead. If our domain object is the `User`, we end up with validations in a file next to the `User` class with a name of User-validation.xml.

Again, assume we need to have different validation rules for the User class depending upon the context in which it's being used. One option follows the previous pattern to define separate files for the different contexts that arise from different action aliases. The solution here is to create, again, a file for each alias such as ClassName-aliasName-validation.xml. If our User was being used from the two contexts of the SortAction defined previously, we could break the validations into the two files User-BubbleSort-validation.xml and User-HeapSort-validation.xml. Again, the validation framework is aware of the alias/context under which the action is being invoked and automatically use the correct validations.

The final variation on context usage aims to check the proliferation of validation definitions in the face of numerous alias-based contexts. A domain object such as User will most likely be used from dozens of locations throughout the application. If we define our validations at the User level, and we require context-based variations in those validations, then we could easily end up with a mess of User-thisAlias-validation.xml and User-thatAlias-validation.xml. To solve this problem, the visitor validator provides the context attribute to allow the developer to introduce a user-defined context. Let's say that the User object is used from 15 different action aliases. If we can identify special validation needs shared by 7 of these and another set of needs shared by the other 8, then we really only have 2 contexts, not 15. But obviously we can use the alias names of these 15 with the alias-naming scheme for our XML.

The solution is to invent two logical names for the two sets of validation needs. Let's say the two needs can be described as admin and public. With this determination made, we simply divide our validations into two files named for these contexts, User-admin-validation.xml and User-public-validation.xml. Since these context names don't match the alias names of our various action mappings, we need to somehow link the various action mappings to these contextual validations. To do this, we use the context attribute of the visitor validator. Recall that this validator is placed in the action-local validations file. Let's say we have an action, UpdateUserAction, that allows us to update the user, and that it exposes two aliased entry points, one for users to update themselves—UpdateUser—and one for administrators to update user data—UpdateUserAdmin. The second one obviously requires that the User be validated under the admin context. Here's how it works.

We've already defined our two contextual validations files at the User level. Now we just need to configure the visitor validator for the alias. The validations file for the UpdateUserAdmin alias would be UpdateUserAction-UpdateUserAdmin-validation.xml and it would contain the following visitor definition:

```
<field name="user">
  <field-validator type="visitor">
    <param name="context">admin</param>
    <message>User: </message>
  </field-validator>
</field>
```

This visitor now seeks out the admin validations defined at the domain object level in the file User-admin-validation.xml. Again, note that any validations defined generally for the User in User-validation.xml will also be used with the contextual validations.

10.4.3 *Validation inheritance*

Now that we've seen that validations can be declared at various levels and under various contexts, we need to briefly describe inheritance of validation declarations. This is simple, and we've already mentioned it indirectly. Recall that we said that general validations still run when contextual validations are also defined. This is part of the inheritance chain, but it's actually more complex. The following list shows the locations from which validations are collected when the framework begins its processing:

- *SuperClass*-validation.xml
- *SuperClass-aliasName*-validation.xml
- *Interface*-validation.xml
- *Interface-aliasName*-validation.xml
- *ActionClass*-validation.xml
- *ActionClass-aliasName*-validation.xml

When defining your validations, you should take advantage of this structure to define common validations at higher levels in the search list, thus allowing you to reuse definitions.

In the next section, we see how to forgo unnecessary validations by short-circuiting when one validation fails.

10.4.4 *Short-circuiting validations*

A useful feature of the validation framework is the ability to short-circuit further validation when a given validation fails. Let's say you have a series of validations defined for a given field. Take our password field for example. Listing 10.7 shows the declaration of our password field validators from User-validation.xml.

> **Listing 10.7 Using the `short-circuit` attribute to cancel unnecessary validations**

```
<field name="password">
  <field-validator type="stringlength" short-circuit="true">
    <param name="maxLength">10</param>
    <param name="minLength">6</param>
    <message>Your password should be 6-10 characters.</message>
  </field-validator>
  <field-validator type="passwordintegrity">
    <param name="specialCharacters">$!@#?</param>
    <message>Your password must contain one letter, one number, and
             one of the following "${specialCharacters}".
    </message>
  </field-validator>
</field>
```

The only thing we've added here is the short-circuit attribute, which we've set to true. We've done this because we don't want the passwordintegrity check to run if the stringlength check fails. There's no point in wasting processing resources and there's no point in adding another error message to the user interface. Note that since this short-circuit is defined on a field validator, the rest of the validations for that field are short-circuited. If you define a short circuit at the action level, all validations are short-circuited.

With this, you've seen all the features offered by the validation framework. Before closing the chapter, we'll take the next section to tell you how you could set up your validations with annotations rather than XML-based metadata. All of the same features are available; it's just a different interface to the metadata.

10.4.5 *Using annotations to declare your validations*

At all levels of Struts 2, you generally have a choice between using XML or Java annotations for your various configuration and metadata needs. The validation framework is no different. In this section, we show you how to use annotations to declare your validations. Warning: this section makes no attempt at thoroughness. The idea here is to merely show you how it's done, roughly, and refer you to the proper resources if you feel like you want to use annotations.

First of all, the validation framework is the validation framework no matter how you declare your metadata. With that in mind, we just write a version of the Register action that uses annotations to declare its validations. Our new version of the Register action is manning.chapterTen.RegisterValidationAnnotated. Listing 10.8 shows the source.

Listing 10.8   Using annotations to describe the required metadata

```
@Validation          ❶

public class RegisterValidationAnnotated extends ActionSupport
                          implements SessionAware {
  @ExpressionValidator(expression = "username != password",
          message = "Username and password can't be the same.")     ❷
  public String execute(){

    User user = new User();
    user.setPassword( getPassword() );
    Portfolio newPort = new Portfolio();
    newPort.setName( getPortfolioName() );
    user.getPortfolios().put ( newPort.getName(), newPort );
    user.setUsername( getUsername() );
    user.setReceiveJunkMail( isReceiveJunkMail() );
    user.setEmail( getEmail() );

    getPortfolioService().createAccount( user );
    session.put( Struts2PortfolioConstants.USER, user );

    return SUCCESS;
  }
```

```
private String username;
private String password;
private String portfolioName;
private boolean receiveJunkMail;
private String email;

@RequiredStringValidator(type = ValidatorType.FIELD,
                message="Email is required.")
@EmailValidator(type = ValidatorType.FIELD, key="email.invalid",
                        message="Email no good.")    ❹
public void setEmail(String email) {
   this.email = email;
}
public String getEmail() {
   return email;
}

@RequiredStringValidator(type = ValidatorType.FIELD,
               message = "Portfolio name is required.")
public String getPortfolioName() {
   return portfolioName;
}
public void setPortfolioName(String portfolioName) {
   this.portfolioName = portfolioName;
}

@StringLengthFieldValidator(type = ValidatorType.FIELD, minLength="5" ,
        maxLength = "8",  message = "Password must be between
        ${minLength}  and ${maxLength} characters.")
 @RequiredStringValidator(type = ValidatorType.FIELD,
                message = "Password is required.")
public String getPassword() {
   return password;
}
public void setPassword(String password) {
   this.password = password;
}

@RequiredStringValidator(type = ValidatorType.FIELD,
                    message = "Username is required.")
@StringLengthFieldValidator(type = ValidatorType.FIELD, minLength="5" ,
            maxLength = "8",  message = "Username must be between
            ${minLength} and ${maxLength} characters.")
public String getUsername() {
   return username;
}
public void setUsername(String username) {
   this.username = username;
}

}
```

❸

These annotations work with the same built-in validators that we've been working with throughout this chapter. We still map field validators to JavaBeans properties and map nonfield validators to the action as a whole. Let's see how it works. First, we must include a class-level annotation ❶ to mark the entire class as something that should be scanned by the validation framework. Next, we define a nonfield annotation, the same expression validator ❷ that checks to make sure that the username and password aren't identical.

Next, we define all of our field validators. These must come right before the getter and setter of the corresponding property. We can see many of these throughout this class. For instance, we associate both the requiredstring and email validators with the email property by placing annotations just before the getter and setter for the email property ❸. Note that the annotations set the same parameters that we set in our XML-based validation metadata.

One slight difference is in the way the message is handled. The message attribute is a required attribute of the annotations. If you want to use a message from your properties file resource bundle, you don't write the key in as the message value. Rather, you add the key attribute to the annotation, as we've done for the email field's email validator ❹. Contrary to what you might expect, you still have to put a message value in the message attribute. It's considered the default message, in case the key lookup fails. While it may never reach the light of day, it's required.

If you want to see this annotated version in action, simply switch it out for the regular one in the chapterTen.xml file. Here's what the Register action element from that file would look like if you use the annotated version:

```
<action name="Register"
        class="manning.chapterTen.RegisterValidationAnnotated">
  <result>/chapterTen/RegistrationSuccess.jsp</result>
  <result name="input">/chapterTen/Registration.jsp</result>
</action>
```

As we've mentioned in respect to some of the other Struts 2 annotations, the annotations mechanisms are being improved daily. They're all part of a movement toward a zero-configuration development pattern that seeks to eliminate all of the XML artifacts. If you're keen on annotations, it would pay to keep an eye on the Struts 2 website and mailing lists. Completing the annotations is one of the priority milestones of the Struts 2 project. You may be able to say goodbye to those XML files sooner than you think.

10.5   Summary

We've now covered the validation framework in substantial detail. Before we move on, we should recap what we've learned in this chapter. First of all, the validation framework extends the work of the previous chapter to show yet another way to refine your Struts 2 development practices. With the validation framework, we can add a more sophisticated level of validation to our applications. While earlier chapters introduced a strong form of basic validation that uses the Validateable interface and its validate() method, the validation framework provides many enterprise-strength benefits not found with the validate() method strategy.

The most obvious benefit of using the validation framework arises from the reusable nature of the Validator component. This component contains the logic for a given validation type and makes that validation available to any data that wants to be verified against that logic. We saw that Struts 2 comes with a set of 13 built-in validators that developers can immediately take advantage of to start validating their own data. Associating these with your data, both at the action level and the domain object level, can be done quickly with convenient XML or annotations-based metadata.

We also learned how to write custom validators that allow developers to add their own validation logic to the framework, thus allowing them to reuse their own efforts as easily as they use the built-in components. We hope that you'll be able to create many powerful validators, and we hope that you'll contribute them back to the Struts 2 community. But you don't have to, of course ;)

In the next chapter, we'll cover another topic of application refinement, internationalization.

Understanding
internationalization

This chapter covers

- Internationalizing your applications
- Reading messages from properties files
- Localizing your messages
- Setting and overriding the locale

In the previous chapter, we learned how to refine our Struts 2 applications by upgrading their validation to the validation framework. Now we'll learn how to refine our application even further. Internationalization represents, in some aspects, the finest finishing touches that you can put on a web application. Many people like to separate the topic of this chapter into two concepts, *internationalization* and *localization*. Many people also like to shorten these cumbersome words to the numeronyms *i18n* and *l10n*.

While the semantic differences between i18n and l10n can be meaningfully expounded upon, we find the practical aspects of developing multilingual web applications don't call for all the verbiage. Rather than spend too much time trying to pin down exactly where i18n ends and l10n begins, we're going to gloss over the semantics and skip straight to the practical aspects of making an application speak different languages for different users in an elegant fashion. Throughout the remainder of this chapter, we'll refer to the entire undifferentiated mass of this process as *i18n*.

Nomenclature

Internationalization and *localization*: The literature makes a point of differentiating between these two terms, though the distinguishing marks between the two seem to waver a bit depending on the writer. In the interest of clarity, we provide two quick definitions that clearly overdramatize the distinction between the two. *i18n* is the process of designing an application so that it has the functionality to change to a different language without resorting to programmatic change of the application; developers need not be involved, technically speaking. *l10n* is the process of creating the actual language-specific texts and formatting; it's the nonprogrammatic adaptation of the application to another language. Sometimes people expect you to know the difference; other times these terms seem to be used completely interchangeably, and, in the end, we think it doesn't matter. In other words, we're recommending that you don't spend too much time limning the border between i18n and l10n. We'll show you what you really need to know.

ICYDK (in case you didn't know): i18n is an abbreviation, of sorts, of internationalization. The *i* is the first letter, the *n* is the last letter, and the *18* means that there are 18 letters between the first and last letters of this unwieldy word. l10n is similarly derived from localization.

In practice, it's an easy process. First, you need to find someone on the team who can identify all of the culturally sensitive elements of your web application user interface, and then translate each of those items into all of your target languages and cultures. All right, that's not a simple task. Is that a job for the JavaScript guy, or maybe the DBA? Probably neither. Actually, there's nothing simple about this first phase at all. But, thankfully, it's not the phase that we Java developers are employed to solve.

The part that does fall to the developer, the technical aspects of introducing locale sensitivity to your application's user interface, is in fact straightforward in Struts 2. This chapter covers the technical details of preparing your application to "speak" different languages, not to mention different date and currency formats. Since the Struts 2 i18n support is a relatively thin wrapper over the native Java support, it's important to understand the Java basics. Toward this end, we'll start by giving a short primer on the Java platform's native support for i18n. We'll then move quickly on to show you how Struts 2 provides a higher-level wrapper over these native Java resources, and, as always, we'll provide implementation examples with the Struts 2 Portfolio sample application.

11.1 The Struts 2 framework and Java i18n

The Java platform has long provided built-in support for i18n. Most experienced Java developers are familiar with the process of externalizing messages to a properties file and retrieving those messages from a `ResourceBundle` via keys. Even if you're not familiar with this stuff, we'll provide a crash course to get you up to speed. The bottom line is that Struts 2 provides a higher-level, ultra-convenient wrapper around the native Java support for i18n. While Struts 2 won't make you handle the native Java platform classes yourself, you need to be familiar with the underlying mechanics. In this section, we provide a brief course in the general Java concepts and then explain how Struts 2 makes it all easier.

11.1.1 *Retrieving localized text with ResourceBundle and Locale*

The Java support for i18n centers around two classes from the `java.util` package, `ResourceBundle` and `Locale`. In this section, we explain the roles these two classes play in i18n. The first step in i18n-ing an application is identifying all locale-sensitive text on the application's pages. If you look at an unlocalized application, like our current Struts 2 Portfolio, you'll find these message texts hard-coded in our JSP pages. If we're to achieve any level of i18n, we have to move these texts out of the JSP page and into some sort of Java `ResourceBundle`. We'll be doing this in a few moments.

But the `ResourceBundle` isn't just a container for our texts. The `ResourceBundle` is a locale-sensitive object. Let's clarify this concept briefly. The resources that are most commonly found in these bundles are message texts. If your internationalized home-page has a greeting, you'd need to have a version of that greeting for each locale you want your application to support. If your application supports Turkish and English users, then your `ResourceBundle` needs to contain the English and Turkish equivalents of this greeting, "Hello" and "Merhaba." If these two greetings are contained by a locale-sensitive resource bundle, then that bundle will be aware of which locale is in play and will return the appropriate version of the "greeting" text when asked for it.

In theory, that's all there is to it. Let's look quickly at the Java classes and how they work together to bring this theory to life.

STORING RESOURCES IN A RESOURCEBUNDLE

Java's `ResourceBundle` is an abstract class. It's up to subclasses to provide an implementation that can manage the resources contained in the bundle, such as the greeting text we mentioned earlier. Subclasses of `ResourceBundle` can manage their resources in any way they like. Greetings could be stored in the database and retrieved with database code contained in the subclass. The Java platform provides a couple of convenient subclasses for your use. The most commonly used of these is the `PropertyResourceBundle`, which loads its resources from plaintext properties files. This properties file style of bundles is so ubiquitous that we'll use it throughout this chapter in all our examples. Along the way, we'll say a word or two about using alternative bundles, but we leave it to you to read the Java documentation if you find yourself going in that direction.

Let's quickly cover some Java `ResourceBundle` fundamentals, using properties files `ResourceBundle`s, of course. We'll walk through a brief example to show how these native Java classes, `ResourceBundle` and `Locale`, work together to provide i18n.

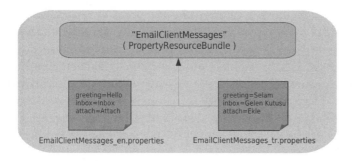

Figure 11.1 The `EmailClientMessages ResourceBundle` is backed by two properties files, one English and one Turkish.

Our example assumes that we're working on some sort of email client application. Let's create a properties file resource bundle for our email client. All bundles must have a name so that we can identify the one from which we'd like to retrieve messages. Figure 11.1 shows a `ResourceBundle` with the name `EmailClientMessages`, which is backed by a pair of properties files.

Since we're using properties files to store our resources, we don't have to write any Java code to implement our bundle. The bundle uses the built-in `PropertyResource-Bundle`. We just provide a set of properties files that follow a specific naming convention, as follows:

```
BundleName_languageCode.properties
```

You can observe this pattern in action in the names of the two properties files shown in figure 11.1. The bundle name shared by the properties files is `EmailClientMessages`. Thus, we refer to the entire bundle as the `EmailClientMessages` bundle. There's one file for each language-specific version of the text resources. If we wanted to support more locales, we could add dozens more properties files with different locale extensions. Regardless of the number of supported locales, all of the properties files that share the same root bundle name belong to a single bundle.

With our properties files in place, we're ready to work with our bundle. Let's see how we can create the bundle and then retrieve locale-sensitive messages for our fictitious email client software.

WORKING WITH NATIVE JAVA RESOURCEBUNDLES

If we want to retrieve a localized text, we must first obtain a reference to the bundle that contains that text. After we have a reference to the bundle, we can start to pull texts from it by key. The following code snippet demonstrates how this works:

```
Locale currentLocale = new Locale( "tr");           ❶
ResourceBundle myMessages = ResourceBundle.getBundle("EmailClientMessages",
                            currentLocale);         ❷
String greetingLabel = myMessages.getString( "greeting");     ❸
```

As we've said, `ResourceBundles` are locale-sensitive, so the first thing we need to do is create a `java.util.Locale` object that represents the locale for which we want to retrieve texts. Based on the two properties files that are backing this bundle, we know that both English and Turkish are supported. We need to use a `Locale` object to inform the `ResourceBundle` about which version of the resources to return. So we programmatically create a `Locale` to represent the Turkish language ❶. Note that we pass in the Turkish language code string, which matches precisely our properties file naming extension. We then pass this `Locale` object, along with the name of the bundle we want, to the static `ResourceBundle.getBundle()`. This method returns an instantiated `EmailClientMessages ResourceBundle` ❷ from which we can start to pull message texts by their key value. The `greetingLabel` retrieved with the `getString()` method ❸ would contain the string "Merhaba" since that's the correct message for the Turkish language locale.

How does the `getBundle()` method know that it should use our properties files to create a bundle? Good question. The answer is simple. This method has a two-phase search process. First, it searches for properties files that match the bundle name parameter that it receives. After that, it also searches for Java class implementations of the bundle. These would be implemented in Java classes named similarly to the properties files, such as EmailClientMessages_tr.java. Since we haven't provided a class-based `ResourceBundle`, none is found. Instead, our properties files are found and a `ResourceBundle` is made from them.

In summary, we can describe the native Java support for i18n as containing the following steps:

1 Create the `ResourceBundles`, most commonly by providing a set of properties files following the naming convention of the bundle and containing the localized message values for each of the message keys in the bundle.

2 Programmatically create a `Locale` object to match the locale for which you want to retrieve message texts.

3 Programmatically instantiate a `ResourceBundle` with the static `ResourceBundle.getBundle ( bundleName, currentLocale )`.

4 Retrieve locale-sensitive resources, such as message texts, with that bundle's `getString( key )` method.

As you can see, the native Java stuff is simple, but tedious. Every time you want to retrieve a message, you need to create the bundle by hand. Another particularly unwieldy aspect of the native Java stuff is the way we have view-layer code—code that's knowledgeable about the text of the UI—embedded in the Java layer. As you've seen, Struts 2 developers aren't accustomed to such things as the vulgar handling of UI labels in direct Java code.

With the foundation poured, let's see how Struts 2 builds on these native Java classes. In the next section, we give an overview of how Struts 2 adds a higher-level interface to these i18n services.

11.1.2 *How Struts 2 can ease the pain of i18n*

Struts 2 takes a lot of the effort out of i18n. The framework still uses the Java classes we just saw, but it makes things easier. For one thing, you don't have to instantiate your `ResourceBundles`. Struts 2 automatically creates the `ResourceBundles` for you, handling the whole mess of determining which bundle you need. Additionally, the framework also handles determining the correct locale. The framework automatically determines the Locale by examining the HTTP headers from the browser. If you like, you can also override this behavior and use other means to determine the locale, such as letting the user manually select a locale through a user-interface–based choice.

If the framework is going to automatically create the bundles, you obviously need to know where to put your properties files and how to name them. As with most automated features, the Struts 2 bundle-creation process uses a mixture of convention and configuration to locate your properties files. It's a two-way street. Struts 2 tells you where it'll look for properties files, but you can also tell Struts 2 where to look for properties files. Of course, you can also do both of these at the same time. We'll learn all the details and variations in the coming pages of this chapter; section 11.3.1 describes in detail all of the places that Struts 2 will look for properties files.

In addition to handling the creation of the ResourceBundles, the framework also handles retrieving the messages from the bundles. You don't have to do this programmatically. The framework provides several high-level mechanisms for retrieving the messages from the bundles for you. Among the options are Struts 2 tags made especially to retrieve messages from the bundles, OGNL access (did you guess that the bundles would be on the ValueStack?), as well as via the framework's validation framework and type-conversion facilities.

In short, using i18n with Struts 2 comes down to two things. First, you learn where to put your properties files. Second, you learn how to pull text from the bundles the framework creates from your properties files. In the next section, we run through a demonstration of this easy process.

11.2 A Struts 2 i18n demo

Internationalization lends itself particularly well to the tutorial style of explanation. With that in mind, we're going to cut directly to the heart with a quick example of how Struts 2 does things. In section 11.3 we go through all the detailed nooks and crannies of the framework's i18n facilities, but we'll start with a practical demonstration. For many, the material covered in this demo might even be enough to fulfill the i18n needs of their own applications.

11.2.1 A quick demo of Struts 2 i18n

We're going to jump right in and start upgrading our Struts 2 Portfolio sample application to support a robust level of i18n. First, we add the properties files. Struts 2 provides many options for where and how you make your properties files available. One of the options is to associate the properties file, by name, with the action class. In this example, we'll work with the home page of the Struts 2 Portfolio, shown in figure 11.2.

To add i18n to our home page, we have to provide ResourceBundles that have localized message texts for all of the text on the page for each locale we want to support. In our case, we're going to provide text for two locales, English and Spanish.

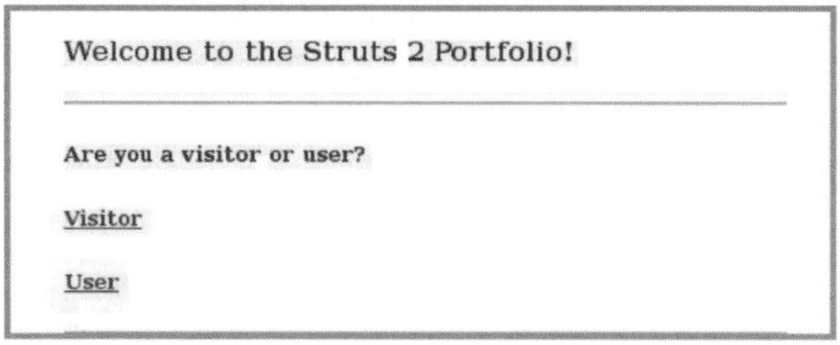

Welcome to the Struts 2 Portfolio!

Are you a visitor or user?

Visitor

User

Figure 11.2   The Struts 2 Portfolio home page presents a greeting and a navigational choice.

When Struts 2 creates the `ResourceBundles` that it makes available to a given request, one of the first bundles it attempts to instantiate is a bundle with a name that matches the current action. In the case of our home page, the current action is the `manning.chapterEleven.PortfolioHomePage` class. Based on this, we know that one of the bundles the framework will attempt to create is `PortfolioHomePage`, located in the `manning.chapterEleven` package. We implement this, for reasons already discussed, as a properties-file–backed bundle. To this end, we create two properties files with the correct root bundle name and the correct locale endings, one for English and one for Spanish. Listing 11.1 shows the English-language version of the properties file.

Listing 11.1   The default resources for the `PortfolioHomePage` bundle

```
artistHomePage.greeting=Welcome to the Artist HomePage!
chooseLanguage=Select a different language.
visitor=Visitor
user=User
site.entrance.text=Are you a visitor or user?
visitorHomePage.viewPortfolio=View a portfolio
visitorHomePage.greeting=Welcome to the Visitor HomePage!
artistHomePage.accountManagement=Account Management
artistHomePage.register=Register for an account.
artistHomePage.login=Login to an existing account.
visitorHomePage.submit=View
visitorHomePage.selectPortfolio=Select an artist and a portfolio.
```

Note that our English-language resources are in the default properties file rather than in an English-specific file, such as PortfolioHomePage_en.properties. There's a good reason for this. We're assuming that English is the default language for the application. If you want to make another language the default language, then it should go into the default properties file. If a request comes in that specifies an unsupported locale, then the default locale will be used. If we had put the English language resources in a PortfolioHomePage_en.properties file and left the default properties file empty, then requests for unsupported languages would have nothing to fall back on. Thus, it's always important to use the default properties file for your default language. Listing 11.2 shows the Spanish language version of the properties file.

Listing 11.2   The Spanish language resources for the `PortfolioHomePage` bundle

```
homepage.greeting=Beinvenido a el Struts 2 Portfolio
artistHomePage.greeting=Beinvenido a la página de inicio de artista.
chooseLanguage=Cambiar idioma.
visitor=Visitante
user=Usuario
site.entrance.text=Es usted un visitante o usuario?
visitorHomePage.viewPortfolio=Buscar una cartera
visitorHomePage.greeting=Beinvenido a la Página de inicio de Visitantes
artistHomePage.accountManagement= Administrar el perfil de su cuenta
artistHomePage.register= Regístrarse una cuenta
artistHomePage.login=Acceder a su cuenta.
visitorHomePage.submit=Ver
visitorHomePage.selectPortfolio= Seleccioner una artista y una cartera.
```

No surprises here. It's just the same, but with Spanish! Once we've created these files, we just need to put them into the package directory structure next to the action class itself. With these two files in place, the framework automatically instantiates the `PortfolioHomePage` `ResourceBundle` every time a request comes in for the `PortfolioHomePage` action. Furthermore, the framework will have automatically determined the user's locale based upon information sent from the browser, and created the `ResourceBundle` accordingly. Now, let's see how we can pull messages out of those bundles. The following snippet from the PortfolioHomePage.jsp page shows the most common way of retrieving localized text, the Struts 2 `text` tag:

```
<h4><s:text name="homepage.greeting"/></h4>
<hr>
<h5><s:text name="site.entrance.text"/></h5>
<h5><a href="<s:url action='VisitorHomePage'/>">
    <s:text name="visitor"/>
  </a></h5>
<h5><a href="<s:url action='ArtistHomePage'/>"><s:text name="user"/></a>
</h5>
<hr>
```

As you can see, the Struts 2 `text` tag is simple. It's similar to the Struts 2 `property` tag, but it takes a `ResourceBundle` key instead of an OGNL expression. Let's analyze what's happening in this front-end markup. First of all, this JSP snippet is the same code that created the screen capture shown in figure 11.2. In the previous versions of the Struts 2 Portfolio, we've simply hard-coded the welcome message directly into the JSP. Now, we've replaced that locale-sensitive message with a Struts 2 `text` tag that retrieves a `ResourceBundle` message based on the key passed in to the name attribute. If we're executing in the presence of a Spanish locale, this key resolves to the corresponding message from the PortfolioHomePage_es.properties file. Otherwise, it resolves to the default English message. And that's about all there is to it.

Now, let's revisit what's happening in this simple demo from a Struts 2 internals point of view.

11.2.2   *A quick look behind the scenes*

In the previous demonstration, we saw how easy it can be to take advantage of the i18n features of Struts 2 to provide localized message text in your pages. We now take a look at the framework mechanics that drive this. As you might've guessed, it's going to involve a couple of interfaces and the `ValueStack`. First, we introduce the main character in this mystery, a shady guy known as the `TextProvider`.

The `com.opensymphony.xwork2.TextProvider` interface exposes an overloaded method `getText()`. The many versions of this method have at their heart the retrieval of a message value based on a key. In other words, the `TextProvider` is the guy who takes your key and tracks down an associated message text from the `ResourceBundles` that it knows about. This guy pretty much handles all of the i18n duties of the framework. While you can always implement your own `TextProvider`, a default implementation is provided by the framework. The helper class `ActionSupport`, which we've been using throughout the book, provides this default implementation. Thus, as long as you have your action classes extend `ActionSupport`, you automatically get the built-in i18n support we discuss in this chapter.

As you already know, when the framework begins processing a request, one of the first things that it does is create the action object and push it onto the `ValueStack`. If your action extends `ActionSupport`, as ours do, you've automatically pushed a `TextProvider` onto the `ValueStack` as well. Very convenient. The default implementation of the `TextProvider` loads the `ResourceBundles` that have names matching the current action, as well as several others; we'll explore the full process by which all the resource bundles are located in the next section. Figure 11.3 shows our `TextProvider` sitting on the `ValueStack` ready to serve messages from our `PortfolioHomePage` `ResourceBundle`.

With our `TextProvider` on the `ValueStack`, our `ResourceBundle` messages are available to every part of the framework. The Struts 2 text tag, as seen in the following snippet, looks for a `TextProvider` on the `ValueStack` and asks that provider to retrieve the message based on the key you provide it:

```
<s:text name="homepage.greeting"/>
```

Since the `TextProvider` is on the `ValueStack`, we can also access its `getText()` method with OGNL. This allows us to pull `ResourceBundle` messages into many places, including other Struts 2 tags. In order to do this, we take advantage of OGNL's ability to call methods on objects. The following use of the Struts 2 property tag is absolutely equivalent to the previous Struts 2 text tag:

Figure 11.3   Our `PortfolioHomePage` action extends `ActionSupport` and thus carries a default implementation of the `TextProvider` onto the `ValueStack`.

```
<s:property value="getText('homepage.greeting')"/>
```

Note that the value attribute of the property tag is a nonstring attribute, thus we don't have to force OGNL evaluation with the %{*expression*} syntax.

Now, you pretty much know how Struts 2 i18n and l10n work. It's as easy as 1-2-3.

1 Make your actions extend ActionSupport, so that they inherit the default Text-Provider implementation.

2 Put some properties files somewhere they can be found by the default Text-Provider, such as in a properties file with a name mirroring the action.

3 Start pulling messages into your pages with the Struts 2 text tag or by hitting the getText() method with direct OGNL.

That's it. But we still have a lot of details to track down. For instance, where else can we put properties files and expect the framework to find them? And, in what other ways does the framework provide access to the resources contained in the bundles? These questions and more are answered in the next section.

11.3   *Struts 2 i18n: the details*

In the previous section, we ran through a quick demo of how Struts 2 uses Text-Providers to load ResourceBundles and make their messages available with the help of the ValueStack. In that quick demo, we went through a use case that featured the path of least resistance, but, actually, you've already seen the real deal. And, as promised, it wasn't rocket science. In this section, we sort out the details.

This section is going to be a hodgepodge. We start by going through the entire process by which the default TextProvider locates the bundles that it makes available and retrieves texts from that set of bundles. After that, we'll show you the other ways, beyond the Struts 2 text tag, that you can pull texts from those bundles. Finally, we'll see how you can parameterize your texts and leverage the data and currency-formatting power of the Java MessageFormat class.

But first things first. Let's start by exploring all the different places you can put your properties files.

11.3.1   *Struts 2 default TextProvider ResourceBundle location algorithm*

This isn't that complicated, but it's the kind of thing you need to know if you want to find the best solution for your own project. Some of it may not seem obvious at first glance, but we'll try to provide a clear outline of the process that the framework's default TextProvider goes through when locating ResourceBundles. It's a rich model. Essentially, Struts 2 leaves the door wide open for you to distribute the localized text of your application in about any way you see fit. We've already seen that the framework looks for bundles that match the name of your current action class. But this is just the tip of the iceberg.

In addition to the action-class–named ResourceBundles, the default implementation of TextProvider searches in several other "well-known" locations for bundles that might've been created by the developer. Many of these locations follow a similar naming pattern based on the names of superclasses and implemented interfaces. The following sequence shows the name and derivation of the ResourceBundles that Struts 2 attempts to load:

1 *ActionClass*—Is there a ResourceBundle with the same name as the current action class? In other words, is there a set of properties files like Action-Class.properties, ActionClass_es.properties, and so forth?

2 *MyInterface*—If your action implements any interfaces, are there Resource-Bundles associated with those interfaces? In other words, if the current class implements MyInterface, is there a set of properties files like MyInter-face.properties, MyInterface_es.properties, and so forth? Superinterfaces of each interface will also be searched accordingly, with more specific interfaces taking precedence over superinterfaces.

3 *MySuperClass*—If your action extends a superclass, is there a ResourceBundle associated with that superclass? In other words, if the superclass is MySuper-Class, is there a set of properties files like MySuperClass.properties, MySuperClass_es.properties, and so forth? Note that the search continues up the superclass chain all the way to Object, looking for ResourceBundles all the way. Again, the ResourceBundles of classes lower on the chain take precedence over the higher ones. In other words, Object.properties comes last, if it exists.

4 If the action implements ModelDriven, the class of the model object itself will be used to look up ResourceBundles. In other words, if our model object is our User class, then User.properties, and so on, will be loaded if they exist. Further-more, the entire process of searching up the interface and class hierarchy, as outlined, will be repeated in the context of the model object class.

5 *package.properties*—Next, the search tries to load a package ResourceBundle for the package of the current action class, and every superpackage back up the chain. In other words, if our current action is manning.chapterEleven. PortfolioHomepage, the framework will attempt to find a package.properties file located in the manning.chapterEleven package, then in the manning pack-age. Note that these properties files are all named *package.properties*, and are located in the directory structure of the package to which they belong.

6 *Domain model object exposed on the ValueStack referenced by key*—This is similar to #4, ModelDriven. Given a key such as user.username, if the ValueStack has a prop-erty exposed on it named user, then the class of that property will be used to load ResourceBundles, again following the same process we've outlined. How-ever, when resolving the key against those bundles, the first element of the key is stripped away. In other words, given the key user.username, and a user prop-erty on the ValueStack (of type User), the ResourceBundles associated with User, beginning with the User.properties, will be searched for a message with the key username, not user.username.

7 *Default ResourceBundles*—Struts 2 allows you to specify global bundles that will always be available.

All bundles that are found are added to the stock of messages that the TextProvider will make available. The various ResourceBundles that are loaded into the TextProvider form a lookup hierarchy for resolving message keys. Figure 11.4 demonstrates how the TextProvider retrieves texts from the bundles that it has found.

Figure 11.4 shows a scenario in which the default TextProvider has found three ResourceBundles while searching according to the algorithm given earlier in this section. This figure assumes that the current request resolved to the PortfolioHomePage action. This TextProvider has located properties files for an action-associated bundle, an interface-associated bundle (our action must have implemented the MyInterface interface), and, finally, a default global-messages bundle. We'll show how to tell the framework about your default bundles in a page or two. These bundles are ordered just as they are in the bundle search order algorithm. The highest is the bundle associated directly with the action class, and the lowest is the default bundle. Let's look at what happens when the default TextProvider attempts to retrieve texts from this set of bundles.

Figure 11.4 shows two hypothetical calls to the TextProvider's getText() method. Let's look at what happens when the provider is asked to return a text for the key submit. The process is simple. The TextProvider starts at the top of the bundle stack and works its way down. The first bundle, from the top, that can return a value for the key

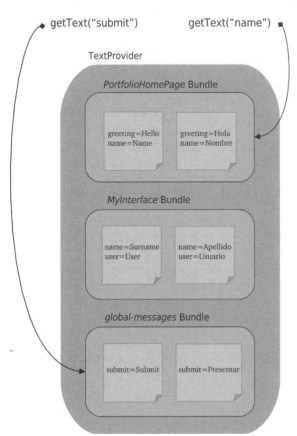

Figure 11.4 The framework's default TextProvider retrieves text by resolving the key against all of its bundles in a hierarchical fashion.

wins. In the case of the submit key, no bundle except the default bundle has a value, so the default bundle is the one that returns the value. In the case of the name key, the bundle associated with the class name has a value. In this case, the interface bundle also has a value for the key, but that value is masked by a higher bundle.

One complication to this tidy process is locale specificity. We explore this complexity next.

LOCALE SPECIFICITY AND MESSAGE RETRIEVAL

When working your way through the bundle search and the text retrieval hierarchy, you might've asked yourself how locale influences the retrieval of messages. Of course, if the current locale matches one of the properties files locale extensions, we expect that the text comes from that file's set of values. If that file doesn't exist, or if the request key isn't defined in that file, we must fall through to the next most specific locale match. A quick example: assume that we're retrieving a message for the key homepage.greeting. Also, assume the current locale is American English, en_US. According to Java's ResourceBundle specifications, a given bundle, such as Portfolio-Homepage, should return the most locale-specific message that it can find. Assuming this bundle is backed by properties files, the key should be first attempted against PortfolioHomepage_en_US.properties, then against PortfolioHomepage_en.properties, and finally against PortfolioHomepage.properties.

This locale specificity hierarchy is always used when Struts 2 attempts to locate your message text. However, this algorithm is isolated within a given bundle from the bundle hierarchy outlined previously. Consider that a ResourceBundle associated with an interface takes precedence over a ResourceBundle associated with a superclass. Here's a quick scenario explaining how locale specificity factors into this. Assume the locale of en_US again. Also, assume that our action implements an interface, MyInterface, and also has a superclass, MySuperClass. Assume too that both the interface and the superclass have properties files associated with them so the framework will create both the MyInterface and the MySuperClass bundles. Now let's see what happens if we try to resolve the homepage.greeting key.

As we know, this key will first be tried against the interface bundle, according to the search order we've outlined. Here's the question regarding locale specificity. What happens if MyInterface only has a MyInterface.properties file, a default set of resources, but MySuperClass has a specific MySuperClass_en_US.properties file? You might think that the more specific locale should win, but it doesn't. The default message is retrieved from the MyInterface.properties file ahead of the more locale-specific superclass file. This is because locale specificity only matters within the bounds of a given resource bundle, in this case MyInterface. Being higher in the bundle search order trumps locale specificity.

Now let's look at how to define those default bundles referenced by step 7 of the bundle search order.

DEFINING DEFAULT BUNDLES

The first six steps of the bundle search order outline convention-based locations where Struts 2 will search for properties files. In order to have Struts 2 find your properties files, you must put them where it wants them. The framework, however, does provide you with a way to locate your properties files according to your own whim. This is the role of default bundles.

Default bundles are great. If none of the convention-oriented bundles exist, such as the action class–associated bundle, there's always the default bundles. These are the last place where the framework will look when trying to resolve a key. For some projects, it might suffice to use default bundles exclusively, filling them with all of the text resources required by your entire application. This is a common practice. Other applications might want to organize their text resources according to application region and package space. Within this more hierarchical organization of text resources, you still might find it useful to define globally useful text in a default bundle. Default bundles can, in fact, be thought of as global bundles.

Whatever your use case, defining default bundles is as simple as telling the framework the name of your bundles. To do this, you just need to set the value for the Struts 2 property `struts.custom.i18n.resources`. You can set this, and all Struts 2 properties, either in the struts.properties file or with a `constant` element in one of your XML configuration files, for example struts.xml or one of the files it sources, such as our chapterEleven.xml. Either way, it doesn't matter. The following shows the `constant` element, which can be placed in struts.xml or any other XML sourced by that file:

```
<constant name="struts.custom.i18n.resources" value="global-messages" />
```

Here's the same bit of configuration as done in the struts.properties file:

```
struts.custom.i18n.resources=global-messages
```

You can specify a comma-separated list of bundles, to be searched in the given order. You can also specify package space for the location of the bundles. Here's what this would look like:

```
struts.custom.i18n.resources=global-messages,manning.utils.otherBundle
```

This would look for a properties file otherBundle.properties in the manning.util directory space. If for some reason you mix configuration patterns, bear in mind that the struts.properties file trumps the `constant` element from the XML.

Now that we've shown you a gazillion places to incorporate your properties files, let's start exploring all the ways you can retrieve texts from those bundles.

11.3.2 *Retrieving message texts from your bundles*

There are several ways that the framework can pull messages from your `ResourceBundles`. We've already shown the most common method when we demoed the Struts 2 `text` tag in section 11.2.2. In fact, we also saw how to invoke the `getText()` method of the `TextProvider` by using OGNL in the attribute values of other tags. In this section, we cover a couple of other ways that the framework allows you to pull messages out of your `ResourceBundles`.

But first we say a word or two about how the framework knows which locale to use when creating the `ResourceBundles`.

RETRIEVING THE RIGHT LANGUAGE

Of course, the whole point of i18n and l10n is to make applications that can detect the user's locale and automatically use messages in the right language and format. Luckily, this is all built into the framework. There's nothing for a developer to do. Well, we'll give you some work along those lines later in the chapter when we show how to allow the user to interactively choose a locale in section 11.4. But out of the box, the framework comes with a decent mechanism for autodetecting the locale and choosing messages accordingly. Here's how it works.

When a browser submits a request, it sends along some information in HTTP headers that indicates the default locale settings from the user end. Typically, a user can set his locale preference by configuring his browser settings. The framework takes this and makes it the locale under which the request will be served. For instance, if the user sets his browser to specify the `es_SP` locale—Spanish language and Spain as the country— the default implementation of `TextProvider` attempts to locate the appropriate version of the `ResourceBundles` for which it searches. The first choice would be a bundle such as `MyResources_es_SP.properties`. The second choice would be a bundle such as `MyResources_es.properties`. And the default choice, if nothing more specific can be located, would be `MyResources.properties`. This is the reason to always provide your default language in the default bundle. For us, this means putting our English language resources in `MyResources.properties` rather than `MyResources_en.properties`. There must be a default bundle to fall back on if the requested locale isn't supported.

Once we're confident that the right locale is set, we can start to pull text from our bundles. In addition to the `text` tag and the `getText()` method, the framework provides several other convenient means of pulling localized text from our bundles.

USING THE KEY ATTRIBUTE OF UI COMPONENT TAGS

One of the most elegant ways to use the localized message texts from your `Resource-Bundles` is with the `key` attribute found on all of the UI component tags. Listing 11.3 shows the form from the manning/chapterEleven/UpdateAccountForm.jsp page, which has been modified to use the powerful `key` attribute.

Listing 11.3   The `key` attribute can use your bundles to make your markup simple.

```
<s:form action="UpdateAccount">
  <s:label key="user.username" />
  <s:hidden name="user.username" />
  <s:hidden name="id" />
  <s:textfield key="user.firstName"/>          ①
  <s:textfield key="user.lastName"  />
  <s:password key="user.password"  showPassword="true"/>
  <s:textfield key="user.email" />
  <s:checkbox key="user.receiveJunkMail"  />
  <s:submit key="submit"/>
</s:form>
```

These tags have a single attribute. Our previous versions specified a `name` attribute as well as a `label` attribute. Now we can create a `textfield` for the user's first name with the specification of a single attribute ❶. As we'll explain shortly, the `key` attribute can be used to completely configure the UI component, from binding it to `ValueStack` properties for data transfer purposes to pulling a localized text from a ResourceBundle to create a locale-sensitive label for the UI. We'll explain all this in a moment, but first let's consider where the bundles are coming from for this particular example.

This JSP is the result of the `UpdateAccountForm` action. This action has an associated `UpdateAccountForm` ResourceBundle, backed by a pair of properties files, UpdateAccountForm.properties and UpdateAccountForm_es.properties. These files are right next to the Java class in the directory structure. They contain the keys referenced by the tags in listing 11.3. Listing 11.4 shows the full contents of Update-Account.properties.

> **Listing 11.4 A `ResourceBundle` for the `UpdateAccountForm` action**

```
user.username=Username
user.password=Password
user.firstName=First Name
user.lastName=Last Name
user.email=Email
user.receiveJunkMail=Send Junk Mail
account.update.greeting=Edit your account information
```

As you can see, each of the keys named in the tags of listing 11.3 is contained in this file. When this page renders, the key is used to retrieve a localized message text from the ResourceBundle. This localized text is used for the form field's `label`. Next, if your tag doesn't specify a `name` attribute, the key itself is used as a `name` attribute. If you recall from chapter 7, the `name` attribute is what binds the form field to a property on your action or domain model to enable such things as automatic data transfer. If you check out the source for our `UpdateAccountForm` action class, you'll see that it exposes a user JavaBeans property to match these keys.

As an additional bonus, this key propagates from the `name` attribute to the `value` attribute of the UI component tag to bind the property for form prepopulation. If you need a refresher on all of that, revisit chapter 7. Even if you need a refresher on the details, it's easy to see how simple your JSP markup can become by using Resource-Bundles and the `key` attribute. Also note that you don't have to let the `key` attribute propagate onto your `name` and `value` attributes. If you need, you can specify the `key` attribute and the `name` attribute both explicitly. The `key` is used to do the label, and the `name` value is used for binding the component to the data transfer, and so on.

In addition to pulling localized messages into UI components with the `key` attribute, you can also use your localized messages in your validation work.

LOCALIZING YOUR VALIDATION ERROR MESSAGES

In chapter 10, we learned how to employ the validation framework to validate our incoming data against validation rules defined in XML- or annotation-based metadata.

When a validation fails, an error message is automatically provided when the user is taken back to the input form. As we saw in chapter 10, this message can be hard-coded into the metadata or it can be referenced with a `key` attribute. The following snippet, which defines the `email` field validators for the `manning.chapterEleven.Register` action, shows both styles:

```
<field name="email">
  <field-validator type="requiredstring">
    <message>You must enter a value for email.</message>    ❶
  </field-validator>
  <field-validator type="email">
    <message key="email.invalid"/>    ❷
  </field-validator>
</field>
```

As you can see, you can specify a hard-coded message in the body of the `message` element ❶, or you can use the `key` attribute of the `message` element to specify a key ❷ that's used to look up a localized message in your bundles. In this case, the Struts 2 Portfolio has messages for this key stored in the `Register` bundle, backed by Register.properties and Register_es.properties. Note that you can also specify a key and a hard-coded message. If you do, the hard-coded message will be the default in case the key lookup fails.

In addition to validation error messages, you can also pull type conversion error messages from your localized bundles.

LOCALIZING YOUR TYPE CONVERSION ERROR MESSAGES

In chapter 5, we learned all about the automatic type conversion mechanism employed by the framework to convert your incoming request parameters from `String` values to the native Java types of their target properties. Sometimes this doesn't work out and we must kick the user back to the input page and give him an error message letting him know about the problem with his data. By default the user sees a generic message as shown in figure 11.5.

The problem with the data in this screen shot is that the property on the back end expects a valid `double` from the `Age` field. It looks like our man Lando has been the vic-

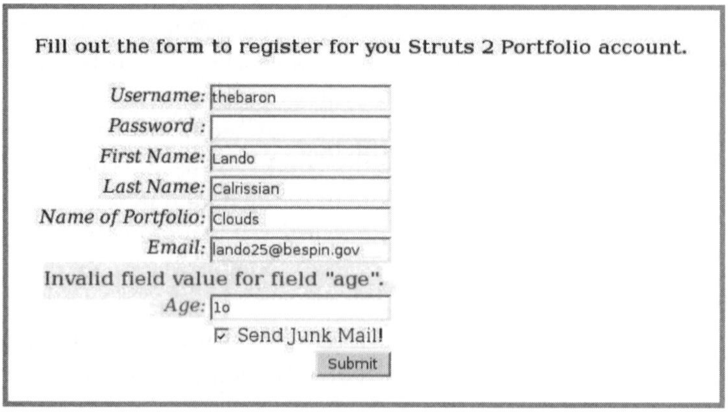

Figure 11.5 By default, the type conversion mechanisms of the framework display a generic message complaining about bad data.

tim of a typo. He's entered the letter *o* instead of a zero. You can easily add custom and localized messages via the ResourceBundle system. To add a custom type conversion error message for this `Age` field, you just need to add a property to one of your accessible bundles following the naming convention of `invalid.fieldvalue.fieldname`. The following property defines an error message for the `Age` field:

```
invalid.fieldvalue.age=Please enter a numerical value for your age.
```

Just add this to a bundle accessible to the `Register` action, such as the Register.properties file, and you're good to go. Another thing you might want to do is to change and/or localize the default type conversion message. You can do this by adding the following property to our default `global-messages` bundle.

```
xwork.default.invalid.fieldvalue=We can not convert that to a Java type.
```

While this message isn't that user-friendly, it does demonstrate how to change the default type conversion error message. Note that if we also put a Spanish language version in our global-messages_es.properties file, we've also localized our type conversion error. The framework's default message isn't localized.

During all of our examples thus far, we've assumed that the messages were being retrieved from the `ResourceBundles` loaded by the framework's default `TextProvider` implementation—via the bundle location algorithm of section 11.3.1. In the next section, we see how to specify the bundle manually.

11.3.3 *Using the i18n tag to specify a bundle*

While it's nice to let the framework handle the details of bundle location, sometimes you just want to slap a given ResourceBundle in place and pull your messages. This functionality is provided by the Struts 2 `i18n` tag. This tag takes the specified `Resource-Bundle`, creates it, wraps it in a `TextProvider`, and puts it on the `ValueStack`. During the body of the tag, all attempts to retrieve messages resolve against the specified bundle. The following snippet shows the usage:

```
<s:i18n name="manning.chapterEleven.SpecialMessages">
  <s:text name="greeting"/>
</s:i18n>
```

Provided that a `SpecialMessages` bundle exists, such as in the form of a SpecialMessages.properties file or two in the manning/chapterEleven package directory, this code will use the `greeting` key to look up a message in that bundle. The `SpecialMessages` bundle will only be on the `ValueStack` for the body of this tag. Note that all forms of message access we've discussed in this chapter will work in this context as long as they occur within the body of the `i18n` tag.

We've now covered all of the ways to make bundles available and to pull messages from them. Next, we look at how you can parameterize your message texts.

11.3.4 *Parameterizing your localized texts*

Sometimes you want to pull dynamic runtime values into the texts of your `Resource-Bundles`. There are two ways to add dynamic values into your message texts. The first method uses embedded OGNL expressions to pull values from the ValueStack or ActionContext. The second method uses the native Java mechanisms for adding parameters to resource bundle message texts. We start by looking at the use of embedded OGNL.

PARAMETERIZING YOUR MESSAGE TEXTS WITH OGNL EXPRESSIONS

By now you should be familiar with the use of OGNL to pull values from the Value-Stack or ActionContext. This technique is the backbone of the Struts 2 tags. The use of OGNL in the context of ResourceBundles is no different. Consider the following property defined in the global-messages.properties file, which we've defined as the default bundle for our Struts 2 Portfolio sample application:

```
portfolio.view.greeting=Welcome to the ${portfolio.name} Portfolio
```

This text is the greeting the users see when viewing a given portfolio. Since we want to blend the name of the actual portfolio being shown, we need to blend in some run-time values. We can do this by pointing the current portfolio's name with a bit of OGNL. As you can see in the preceding snippet, the text contains an OGNL expression escaped with the ${*expression*} sequence. As with the OGNL embedded into the validation framework XML files, this embedded OGNL varies from the typical % syntax and uses the $ syntax. Keep an eye on this quirk.

Despite the syntactical variance, the OGNL works the same as usual. When this message is resolved at runtime, the OGNL will be replaced with the appropriate value from the ValueStack. In this case, we can see that the property on the ValueStack will most likely hold the name of the portfolio, thus customizing this portfolio page greeting. If you want to see this in action, check out the ViewPortfolio action, which exposes the portfolio property, and check out the ViewPortfolio.jsp page that pulls this message from the ResourceBundles with a Struts 2 text tag.

PARAMETERIZING YOUR MESSAGE TEXTS WITH NATIVE JAVA CAPABILITIES

Java also provides a means for parameterizing message texts as they're pulled from ResourceBundles. Here's a message from the global-messages.properties file that uses this style of parameterization:

```
portfolio.view.tagline=Created by {0} {1}
```

The Java version of parameters uses placeholders. You can have up to 10 of these place-holders in a given message. When the text is retrieved, you must pass in the appropriate parameters. Doing this from the Struts 2 text tag makes use of the Struts 2 param tag. The following demonstration is from our ViewPortfolio.jsp page:

```
<s:text name="portfolio.view.tagline">
  <s:param value="portfolio.owner.firstName"/>
  <s:param value="portfolio.owner.lastName"/>
</s:text>
```

The parameters are inserted into the placeholders according to the sequence in which they're defined inside the body of the text tag. The value attributes are OGNL expressions pointing to values on the `ValueStack`, exposed by our `ViewPortfolio` action in this case. You could also specify literal values in the body of the `param` tag:

```
<s:param>Lando</s:param>
```

That wouldn't be all that dynamic, but this isn't intended as a use case; it's just a hint at what you can do. Instead of putting the simple string inside the body of the `param` tag, you could actually nest all sorts of tags and JSP fragments. This could be used to solve large issues of dynamic and localized pages.

Before wrapping up our coverage of parameterizing messages, we should show you how to use them from the other most common means of message retrieval, the `getText()` method exposed by `TextProvider`. If you're retrieving your parameterized messages with the `getText()` method, perhaps from the attribute of another Struts 2 tag as we described earlier, you can easily pass in the required parameters. As we mentioned before, the `TextProvider` `getText()` method is overloaded. Note the following two signatures:

```
String getText(String key, List args);
String getText(String key, String[] args);
```

The values in the `List` or in the `String []` are used to fill the parameters in the returned message text.

Another critical aspect of localization in which Java provides some strong native support is formatting dates and numbers. We show you how to leverage that from your Struts 2 application next.

11.3.5 *Formatting dates and numbers*

Just as Java provides a native means for parameterizing messages, it also provides a native means for formatting dates and numbers in a locale-sensitive fashion. Using this support, we can easily pull in runtime values for dates and other numerical values, and these values will automatically be formatted according to the current locale. Consider the following message from our global-messages.properties file:

```
timestamp=Today is {0,date,long}
```

We use this to put a nice timestamp message on our pages. Basically, this is another version of the placeholder parameter we saw in the previous section. The difference here is that the parameter that comes into the placeholder is going to be a date. We specify the parameter index as `0`, the type as `date`, and the format as `long`. The magic is that Java automatically handles the localization formatting of this date, whatever the current locale. The following snippet from our ViewPortfolio.jsp page shows how to use this:

```
<s:text name="timestamp">
  <s:param value="currentDate"/>
</s:text>
```

The date we're passing into the message comes from the property on the `ValueStack` at which our value attribute's OGNL points. In this case, we've implemented a simple getter on our `ViewPortfolio` action to feed this value. The getter simply creates a `java.util.Date` object and returns it. All of this is live in the sample application if you want to check it out.

Java also makes it easy to format currency and other numbers. Java's built-in support for currency works much like the date. A message text in a `ResourceBundle` might look something like this:

```
item.price={0,number,currency}
```

Again, you just need to pump in a numerical parameter when you retrieve this text. We could go on about this but it's a bit beyond our scope. If you need to exploit the fuller powers of date and number formatting, consult the documentation for the Java platform. The central figure in the native Java support for this stuff is the `java.text.MessageFormat` class.

We've now covered the basics of building `ResourceBundles` and retrieving texts from them. This should get you pretty far. Before calling it quits, we'll show how to override the framework's default locale detection by letting the user set the locale interactively, or by setting it programmatically in the back-end code.

11.4   Overriding the framework's default locale determination

As we've already seen, the framework automatically determines the user's locale when starting to process a request. This determination is made from the HTTP headers in the request. Typically, this works well as a determination of which locale the user wishes to use to view the pages. But sometimes you might want to override this default locale determination. For instance, you might want to let the user make an active locale choice from a UI component such as a select list. Or you might want to allow registered users to store their locale preferences as part of their account information. You could then set the locale for that user at login by pulling the value from the database. However you want to set the locale, the techniques described in this section will help you do it.

First, let's see how we can modify the Struts 2 Portfolio to allow the user to select their own preferred locale via a UI component such as a radio box.

11.4.1 Letting the user interactively set the locale

Under normal usage, the framework determines the locale from the HTTP headers that come in with the request. Determining the locale is just part of setting up the request processing. As we've learned, when the framework starts to process a request, it creates several important objects that play important roles in serving the request. One of the more important of these objects is the `ActionContext`.

As you might recall, an `ActionContext` object contains all of the important data elements related to the request. One of the most important data objects that it contains is the weighty `ValueStack`. The `ActionContext` also contains such data elements as the parameters from the request and a map of session-scoped objects. So it should come as no surprise to find that the `ActionContext` also holds the locale under which the request will be processed. When the framework is setting up the `ActionContext` at the start of request processing, it sets the locale based on the HTTP headers of the request. This can be overridden with an interceptor from the `defaultStack`, the `i18n` interceptor.

THE I18N INTERCEPTOR

The `i18n` interceptor provides a simple service. It checks to see whether the request contains a parameter named `request_locale`. If a `request_locale` parameter exists in the request, then this value is set on the `ActionContext`, thus overriding the default locale choice made by the framework. Better still, the `i18n` interceptor is already in the `defaultStack`. All you need to do is provide the user with a form by which he can submit his preferred locale choices. As you can see from figure 11.6, we've added just such a form on the Struts 2 Portfolio home page.

Now the user can override the default locale determination with an interactive selection of locales. If you check out the chapter 11 version of the Struts 2 Portfolio, you'll also notice that the form automatically prepopulates with the current locale. Let's take a look at the source of chapterEleven/PortfolioHomePage.jsp to see how this works. The following snippet shows the code that creates the locale selection form:

```
<s:form>
  <s:radio name="request_locale" list="locales" value="locale"/>
  <s:submit key="chooseLanguage"/>
</s:form>
```

Ultimately, it's pretty simple. The most important thing is the radio component's `name` attribute. As we've just seen, the `i18n` interceptor looks for a request parameter named `request_locale`. If the user submits this form, rather than following one of the links on the page, then the `i18n` interceptor will take that parameter and set it as the locale on the `ActionContext`. Easy enough.

You might've noticed, however, that we left a couple of details out. First of all, where does the collection of locale options come from? This is up to you. For this example, we've provided them in a statically defined `java.util.Map`, exposed as a JavaBeans property on our `PortfolioHomePage` action, shown in listing 11.5.

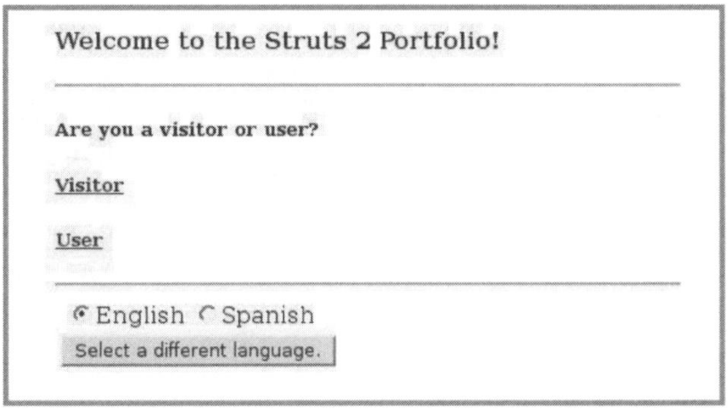

Figure 11.6 Presenting the user with an interactive choice of locales

Listing 11.5 Exposing our supported locales via a JavaBeans property

```
static public final Map locales = new HashMap();      ❶

static {
  locales.put("en_US", "English");
  locales.put("es_SP", "Spanish");                     ❷
}

public Map getLocales (){
  return locales;                                      ❸
}
```

It wouldn't matter where the locales come from, as long as you can get to them with an OGNL expression from your Struts 2 form element tags. You could store them in the database, or you could even hard-code them directly into JSP with an OGNL map literal. This choice depends largely on your requirements. We've defined them in a static map ❶ just to make things simple. Due to the semantics of the collection-backed Struts 2 UI components, such as this radio box, it's convenient to use a map pairing the locale string, such as en_US, with a real language label, such as "English" ❷. Finally, we provide a getter ❸ so that the map can be retrieved off of the `ValueStack` with a simple OGNL expression, as seen in our JSP snippet.

Next, you might be wondering how the prepopulation works. As you can see, the value attribute of our radio box points to an OGNL expression `locale`. What's this? Good question. As it turns out, in addition to `TextProvider`, `ActionSupport` also implements the `LocaleProvider` interface. `TextProvider` doesn't check the `Action-Context` directly when discovering the current locale. Rather, it gets this information from the `LocaleProvider`. The most important part of this for our current business is the fact that `LocaleProvider` exposes a single method, `getLocale()`. Since our action is on the `ValueStack`, and it extends `ActionSupport`, we can hit this getter with a simple OGNL–like locale. Thus, our radio box pulls this value to preselect one of the locale options.

Finally, you might also be wondering how the user-selected locale persists across all the other requests that don't submit the `request_locale` parameter. Once the user chooses a locale, she doesn't need to choose again. The answer is that the i18n interceptor, when it finds a `request_locale` parameter, does a bit more than just set that locale on the current `ActionContext`. That wouldn't be enough to persist the locale, since the `ActionContext` exists only for one request. When the i18n interceptor finds a `request_locale` parameter, it sets that locale on the current `ActionContext` *and* it caches that locale value as a session-scoped attribute, under a well-known key, WW_TRANS_I18N_LOCALE.

And this leads us to something else the i18n interceptor does. When it processes each request, it does more than just check for the presence of the incoming `request_locale` parameter. It also checks for a value in the session map under the key WW_TRANS_I18N_LOCALE. If there isn't a `request_locale` parameter, but there's a locale value cached in the session map, the one from the session map will be set on the current `ActionContext`. Thus, once a user interactively selects a locale, it'll persist for the duration of his current session, or until he submits another `request_locale` parameter to override the one in session scope.

As you can see, the i18n interceptor giving the user the power to select her locale is easy in Struts 2 applications. Before closing this chapter down, we'll look at a closely related topic: setting the locale programmatically with back-end logic.

11.4.2 *Programmatically setting the locale*

Now that you know the secrets of the i18n interceptor, you might've already realized that you could set the locale entirely from back-end logic. Who needs the user anyway? Let's say you want to store user preferences for locale in the database and set the locale for that user automatically each time he logs in. Or imagine whatever method of locale determination you want; the process is going to be the same.

As we saw earlier, the i18n interceptor checks for the existence of a request parameter containing a user-chosen locale preference. The i18n interceptor then sets this value automatically on the `ActionContext`, and into the session. Once the locale is in the session map, the i18n interceptor takes care of persisting that value onto the `ActionContext` of each new request associated with that session. You can easily take advantage of this. If we stored user locale preferences in the database, we could add some logic to our `Login` action to retrieve that locale preference and store it in the session map under the key `WW_TRANS_I18N_LOCALE`. Now the i18n interceptor will take care of the rest of the work for us, propagating that value onto each new request's `ActionContext`.

Another solution you might choose, depending upon your needs, would be to provide your own implementation of `LocaleProvider` on your action. The `LocaleProvider` exposes just one method, `getLocale()`. The default implementation provided by `ActionSupport` simply retrieves the value from the `ActionContext`, as you can see.

```
public Locale getLocale() {
   return ActionContext.getContext().getLocale();
}
```

Your action can easily override this method so it inherits from `ActionContext` to provide whatever means of determining the locale you might need. This solution differs significantly from the previous one, but both serve certain requirements quite well.

The ability to elegantly add programmatic determination of the locale gives a more robust quality to the i18n structure of Struts 2. We hope these flexible techniques will help you solve your complex internationalization problems.

11.5 *Summary*

In this chapter, we added another level of refinement to our Struts 2 Portfolio application. With the i18n support provided by the framework, we've given our application the ability to render its pages with text pulled from locale-sensitive `ResourceBundles`. Let's take a moment to recap the highlights of Struts 2's support for i18n.

As a Java-based framework, Struts 2 makes heavy use of Java's built-in i18n support. The central figures from this native Java functionality are the classes `ResourceBundle`,

Locale, and MessageFormat. Java ResourceBundles hold collections of resources, commonly String messages texts, mapped to String keys. A common way of handling ResourceBundles in a J2EE application is through the use of properties files. We've demonstrated this approach thoroughly in our Struts 2 Portfolio sample application.

You can also implement Java classes that provide the resources. While we didn't show this in this chapter, it's well documented in the Java documentation. If you provide class-based ResourceBundles for your Struts 2 application, the framework will work just as well with them. One point of warning, however. The class and interface name–oriented portions of the framework's default bundle lookup process will be problematic when used with class-backed ResourceBundles. This is because the action class itself will have a name conflict with the class-based ResourceBundle that the lookup would attempt to locate.

You might also want to further investigate the MessageFormat class of the Java platform. We saw its fundamentals in this chapter when we learned of the native Java support for parameterization of message texts and the autoformatting of date and numbers. As we indicated earlier, the MessageFormat class is much richer than we've had the time to demonstrate. We recommend consulting the Java documentation if you have further formatting needs as well.

Finally, we saw that one can easily override the locale determination made by the framework. The Locale class determines which version of a ResourceBundle's resources will be used (English or Spanish in the case of our Struts 2 Portfolio application). While the framework can automatically determine the locale from headers in the HTTP request, you can also let the user choose her own locale interactively, or you can set it programmatically. This flexibility is thanks to another powerful interceptor from the defaultStack, the i18n interceptor.

With i18n out of the way, we're ready to head on into deeper waters. With the close of this chapter, we've finished part 4. With the next chapter, we embark on the final part, part 5.

Part 5

Advanced topics and best practices

You should now have a firm grasp of Struts 2 and its architecture. From actions to interceptors and ultimately the result, the pieces interact like parts in a well-oiled machine. In fact, you've learned enough now to run off and start building your website. But hold your horses! In part 5, we cover material that can help you work smarter.

Chapter 12 explains the plug-in architecture and how the framework can be extended by simply dropping a plug-in JAR on your classpath. You might never need to write one yourself, but once you discover the bounty of plug-ins already available, you may quickly incorporate their features into your site. Modern software adheres to the open-closed principle, which means it's open for extension but closed to modification. Simply stated, we no longer check out code and monkey around with it to get extended behavior. The plug-in architecture in Struts 2 is similar to that found in Firefox and Eclipse.

In chapter 13, you'll learn best practices from the trenches. Topics shared here are those that you can easily begin using right away to provide immediate benefit to you and your project. We discuss setting up your IDE, unit-testing code, validation, and maximizing reuse.

Chapter 14 covers migrating an existing Struts 1.x application to Struts 2. It also compares and contrasts what you already know about Struts Classic with concepts found in the new framework. You might be surprised to learn that you can leverage existing Struts 1.x artifacts in your Struts 2 application.

We wrap up with chapter 15, which covers advanced topics that are largely appreciated only after writing applications without this knowledge. The information discussed here can save you oodles of time by doing things the right way to begin with. From web page look and feel to optimized feature mappings, this is a must-read before building your website.

Extending
Struts 2 with plug-ins

This chapter covers

- Extending the functionality of Struts 2
- Integrating with SiteMesh, Tiles, and JFreeChart
- Injecting constants and beans
- Writing a breadcrumb plug-in

At this point, you've looked at all the essential artifacts that make up Struts 2. You've seen how all the parts fit together and could go off and write some amazing code. However, you probably wouldn't get the best return on your investment. This section begins our review of the advanced features that tie all the basics together in exciting and useful ways.

Like any well-designed software, you should be able to extend the functionality without modifying existing code. Struts 2 leverages the plug-in architecture for this very purpose. If you use Firefox or Eclipse, you already know how this works. When you need to use a feature that wasn't included in the "baseline," you simply install a plug-in that provides the new capability you seek. A plug-in includes the software ingredients to enable features that weren't considered in the design of the original code base. Think of them as strategic points in the framework where you can plug in your own features and behaviors. In fact, you can write your own plug-in with relative ease. Perhaps one day you'll contribute your custom plug-in and it'll become the most downloaded of them all. In this chapter, we crack open a plug-in and study what's inside, and also learn how they're packaged and made ready for deployment.

We review several plug-ins included with Struts 2 and demonstrate ways to extend the framework by using them. Finally, we create a breadcrumb plug-in from scratch to demonstrate how the elegant plug-in architecture can change the way you think about adding features. Where we might've once changed existing code to get a custom behavior, we can now simply drop in a plug-in to accomplish the goal.

12.1   Plug-in overview

The Struts 2 plug-in architecture allows developers to extend the framework by simply adding a JAR file to their application classpath. These extensions can support the framework itself or be used to extend the web user experience. You must be excited to get started, so let's see what a plug-in can do.

Plug-ins can be written to do essentially anything you like. In a nutshell, they're typically designed to add custom interceptors and results to the framework. For example, if you want to replace the way URLs are digested by the framework, you can drop your custom plug-in on the classpath to supersede the original processing. Of course, you can do other imaginative things with them too, as we'll soon discover. Struts 2 was designed so any piece of the framework can be replaced, extended, or removed in a standard, consistent way. Several plug-ins that ship with the framework leverage this capability to extend the framework by providing support for third-party packages such as Spring, Guice, and SiteMesh. A plug-in is basically a miniature S2 context that can be snapped into a larger S2 application to modify the runtime configuration of the larger environment. This allows us to affect the overall behavior without changing existing code. These modifications can either add or override features. Struts 2 has a single runtime configuration that's built up in the following order:

1   struts-default.xml (bundled in the struts2-core-x.y.z.jar)
2   struts-plugin.xml (as many as can be found in plug-in JARs)
3   struts.xml (provided by your application)

Since the struts.xml file is always loaded last, it can use any resources provided by the plug-ins bundled with the distribution, or any other plug-ins you've added to your application. In fact, when Struts 2 is started, it searches for configuration files by snooping inside all the JARs on your classpath. In this way, you can customize the behavior of your runtime configuration by merely dropping a JAR on your classpath that contains a configuration file. This gives you flexibility unparalleled in Struts 1.

Some plug-ins are designed to package new capabilities that you can leverage in your declarations, while others silently replace default behaviors. This plug-in architecture is explained more fully in section 12.3. Plug-ins can provide a variety of configuration options. The runtime plug-in elements that can be modified are

- Bean
- Constant
- Package/namespace
- Interceptor/result
- Exception

We explore combinations of assembling these elements inside plug-ins throughout the remainder of this chapter. Since plug-ins can be designed to do just about anything, you'll have to use some imagination until we get to the specifics later in the chapter. All right, this is starting to sound cool, but does Struts 2 have a marketplace for plug-ins like Firefox and others do? We discuss this next.

12.1.1 How to find plug-ins

Of course you can write your own plug-ins, but what if one of your brother or sister developers already has this functionality built? We're already starting to see vendors writing Struts 2 plug-ins to provide easy access to their packaged software. The Struts 2 website contains a plug-in registry that's already starting to grow. In fact, if you Google Struts 2 plug-ins, you'll see interest emerging from many sources. The last check of the registry revealed several new entries, and I expect plug-ins to become quite plentiful in the coming months.

12.2 Common plug-ins

Struts 2 ships with several plug-ins to allow out-of-the-box compatibility with mainstream frameworks considered necessary to supplement a rich web application. These plug-ins range from connecting to dependency-injection frameworks to providing hooks into look-and-feel libraries. In an attempt to introduce these integrated plug-ins, we provide an overview of a few. These introductions won't go into details of third-party frameworks, but we provide links to their respective websites. Once we've studied several of these integrated plug-ins, we then create a breadcrumb plug-in so you can see how easy it is to change the overall Struts 2 request life cycle. If you're ready, let's review the SiteMesh, Tiles, and JFreeChart plug-ins.

12.2.1 SiteMesh

SiteMesh is a web page look-and-feel, layout, and navigation framework. If you're using SiteMesh to decorate your web pages, Struts 2 provides a SiteMesh plug-in to expose the framework's `ValueStack` to your SiteMesh page decorators. This plug-in provides filters for both FreeMarker and Velocity templates, and incorporating either framework requires a few entries in web.xml. The standard filter chain optionally starts with the `ActionContextCleanUp` filter, followed by other desired filters. Lastly, the `Filter-Dispatcher` handles the request, usually passing it on to the `ActionMapper`. The primary purpose of `ActionContextCleanUp` is to provide SiteMesh integration. The cleanup filter tells the dispatcher filter exactly when to remove obsolete objects from the request. Otherwise, the `ActionContext` may be removed before the decorator has had a chance to access it. The plug-in combined with this sequence of filters is uniquely

designed to merge the `ValueStack` with either Velocity or FreeMarker templates. Listing 12.1 illustrates how we'd configure our web.xml to use the plug-in with FreeMarker.

Listing 12.1   web.xml with SiteMesh-relevant entries

```
<filter>                                              ❶ Context
  <filter-name>struts-cleanup</filter-name>      ◄┐    cleanup filter
  <filter-class>
      org.apache.struts2.dispatcher.ActionContextCleanUp
  </filter-class>
</filter>
<filter>                                              ❷ SiteMesh
  <filter-name>sitemesh</filter-name>            ◄┐    filter
  <filter-class>
      org.apache.struts2.sitemesh.FreeMarkerPageFilter
  </filter-class>
</filter>
<filter>
 <filter-name>struts</filter-name>
 <filter-class>
  org.apache.struts2.dispatcher.FilterDispatcher
 </filter-class>
</filter>

<filter-mapping>
  <filter-name>struts-cleanup</filter-name>
  <url-pattern>/*</url-pattern>
</filter-mapping>
<filter-mapping>
  <filter-name>sitemesh</filter-name>
  <url-pattern>/*</url-pattern>
</filter-mapping>
<filter-mapping>
  <filter-name>struts</filter-name>
  <url-pattern>/*</url-pattern>
</filter-mapping>
```

The `ActionContextCleanUp` filter ❶ is designed to dereference objects following a
successful request life cycle. We have to be concerned with memory management
when processing requests using the `ThreadLocal` model, and `ActionContextCleanUp`
handles this task wonderfully. The timing of this cleanup becomes more interesting
when we incorporate a package such as SiteMesh ❷. Consider figure 12.1.

The `ActionContextCleanUp` filter precedes SiteMesh in the list of filters. In this
case, `ActionContextCleanUp` determines the appropriate time to clear the resources,
thereby allowing SiteMesh a pass at the value stack containing the dynamic data for
this request. This is all there is to it. Of course, the sitemesh-2.x.jar must be on your
classpath and you need to provide your preferred decorator templates that specify the
"extra content" for your pages. If this sounds cool but you don't have much experience with SiteMesh, you can find all the details at http://www.opensymphony.com/
sitemesh/. For those who use Tiles instead of SiteMesh, the next section discusses how
to integrate Struts 2 with Tiles.

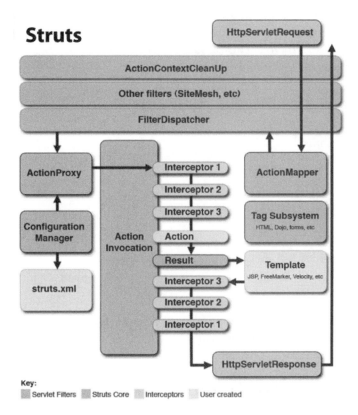

Figure 12.1   Struts 2 Request life cycle

12.2.2 *Tiles*

Apache Tiles is a framework that allows developers to build templates that simplify the development of web application user interfaces. If you're using Tiles to manage your site layout, the Struts 2 Tiles plug-in provides a new result type that utilizes your tile definitions for rendering pages. Listing 12.2 illustrates how we would configure our web.xml to use this plug-in.

Listing 12.2   web.xml with Tiles-relevant entries

```
<context-param>
  <param-name>
    org.apache.tiles.impl.BasicTilesContainer.DEFINITIONS_CONFIG
  </param-name>
  <param-value>/tiles/myTiles.xml</param-value>          ◁───┐  Our Tiles definitions
</context-param>                                             ❶  files are here
...
<listener>                                                  ❷  Tiles
  <listener-class>                                             listener
    org.apache.struts2.tiles.StrutsTilesListener      ◁───┘
  </listener-class>
</listener>
```

The context parameter ❶ is where we specify the location of our Tiles definitions file, and the listener ❷ is how we bootstrap the integration. The plug-in creates a new result type that you can use to specify that Tiles should render the result. Listing 12.3 reveals the declarative elements for this plug-in.

Listing 12.3   struts-plugin.xml file inside struts2-tiles-plugin-2.x.jar

```
<?xml version="1.0" encoding="UTF-8" ?>

<!DOCTYPE struts PUBLIC
"-//Apache Software Foundation//DTD Struts Configuration 2.0//EN"
"http://struts.apache.org/dtds/struts-2.0.dtd">

<struts>
  <package name="tiles-default" extends="struts-default">      ❶ New
    <result-types>                                                  package
      <result-type
        name="tiles"                                           New Tiles
        class="org.apache.struts2.views.tiles.TilesResult"/>   result
    </result-types>
  </package>
</struts>
```

The first thing to notice is that the new `tiles-default` package ❶ extends the `struts-default` package. This means we can extend `tiles-default` in our package and inherit the new result type plus all the support provided by `struts-default`. Once we have these entries in place, Tiles is active and ready to render responses. Listing 12.4 contains the configuration for an action mapping that uses the Tiles page rendering framework.

Listing 12.4   Our application's members.xml file

```
<?xml version="1.0" encoding="UTF-8" ?>
<!DOCTYPE struts PUBLIC
"-//Apache Software Foundation//DTD Struts Configuration 2.0//EN"
"http://struts.apache.org/dtds/struts-2.0.dtd">                Extends the Tiles ❶
                                                               plug-in package
<struts>
  <package name="members" namespace="/members" extends="tiles-default">
  <result-types>                            ❷ Sets default
    <result-type                               result to tiles
            name="tiles"
            class="org.apache.struts2.views.tiles.TilesResult"
            default="true"/>
  </result-types>

    <action name="list">                    ❸ Tiles definition
      <result>membersPage</result>             name
    </action>
  </package>
</struts>
```

The application package extends ❶ the plug-in package and thereby inherits the new Tiles result type. If the package uses Tiles exclusively, we can even set the default result type to use `tiles` ❷ and not have to specify the `type` attribute on each result mapping. Lastly, we see our Tiles definition ❸ being specified as the page to render for the response. As Tiles is a respectable alternative to SiteMesh, you might want to review it at http://tiles.apache.org/.

In the next section, we turn our attention to a plug-in designed for those who believe a picture is worth a thousand words.

12.2.3 JFreeChart

The JFreeChart plug-in allows an action to return generated charts and graphs to be included in your web page. Like the Tiles plug-in, it adds a new result type that we can use in our declarative mappings. Listing 12.5 reveals the declarative elements for this plug-in.

Listing 12.5 struts-plugin.xml file inside struts2-jfreechart-plugin-2.x.jar

```xml
<?xml version="1.0" encoding="UTF-8" ?>

<!DOCTYPE struts PUBLIC
"-//Apache Software Foundation//DTD Struts Configuration 2.0//EN"
"http://struts.apache.org/dtds/struts-2.0.dtd">

<struts>
  <package name="jfreechart-default">             ❶
    <result-types>
      <result-type
        name="chart"
        class="org.apache.struts2.dispatcher.ChartResult">    ❷
        <param name="height">150</param>        ❸
        <param name="width">200</param>
      </result-type>
    </result-types>
  </package>
</struts>
```

The first thing to notice is the new `jfreechart-default` package ❶. The consequence of inheriting this package in your application allows you access to the new `chart` result ❷. Lastly, we see the declaration contains a default chart size ❸ to be rendered and returned to your page.

So now we use the plug-in to generate a neat graph to be displayed on our web page. Listing 12.6 shows one of our declarative configuration files in the application.

Listing 12.6 Our application's chart.xml file

```xml
<?xml version="1.0" encoding="UTF-8" ?>
<!DOCTYPE struts PUBLIC
"-//Apache Software Foundation//DTD Struts Configuration 2.0//EN"
"http://struts.apache.org/dtds/struts-2.0.dtd">

<struts>
  <package name="charts"
        namespace="/charts"
```

```
                extends="struts-default , jfreechart-default">        ❶

      <action name="chartScreen">        ❷
        <result>/jsp/chart.jsp</result>
      </action>

    <action name="chart" class="com.strutsschool.action.CreateChart">     ❸
      <result type="chart">        ❹
        <param name="width">400</param>         ❺
        <param name="height">300</param>
      </result>
    </action>

    </package>
  </struts>
```

Our application package extends both the struts-default and the plug-in parent packages ❶. This allows us to inherit all the standard intelligent defaults plus the new chart ❹ result type. This file includes a declarative mapping ❷ for a web page that contains the request for chart ❸ action where we're specifying a graph sized to 400 by 300 ❺.

It looks like everything is in place, so we issue the request .../chartScreen.action to see the beautiful chart appear on the page. Figure 12.2 shows an example of the capabilities of JFreeChart.

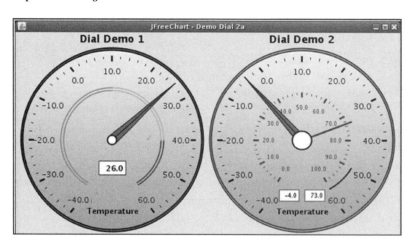

Figure 12.2
Sample
JFreeChart

In this example, our package inherits the configuration elements from a couple of parent packages. You may extend as many parent packages as necessary by listing them on the package extends clause. In the next section, we discuss the internals that build the runtime configuration.

12.3 *Internal component system*

At the heart of the framework, Struts has an internal component system that builds and configures the framework. It works like a specialized dependency injection framework that manages the life cycle of the components and wires them together with other components and configuration. In fact, the first version of the `inject` package, as it's termed internally, was a fork of an early version of the popular dependency injection library, Google Guice, which incidentally was created by Bob Lee, also a Struts committer. To complete the circle, Bob developed Guice based on ideas he had while working with the internals of Struts.

There are two types of objects that can be registered with the inject framework: constants and beans.

12.3.1 Beans

Beans can be any Java object, sometimes termed a *Plain Old Java Object* or *POJO*, that doesn't have to extend any class, implement any interface, or contain any annotations. When declaring a bean in the XML configuration, the attributes shown in table 12.1 are available.

Table 12.1 Bean attributes

Name	Description	Required
name	The class name of the bean	Yes
type	The primary interface the bean implements, defaults to the name value	No
alias	The alias of the bean, necessary if more than one bean is registered for a given type	No
scope	The scope of the bean, could be default, singleton, thread, request, session, or wizard	No

The primary way beans are defined is by declaring them in the XML configuration: struts-plugin.xml for plug-ins and struts.xml for applications. If we were writing a plug-in and wanted the plug-in to define its own `ObjectFactory` (more on that in section 12.3.4), our XML would look like listing 12.7.

Listing 12.7 Bean definition example

```
<bean    type="com.opensymphony.xwork2.ObjectFactory"
         alias="myFactory"
         class="com.mycompany.MyObjectFactory" />
```

Alternatively, you can register beans directly with the container by implementing the `com.opensympony.xwork2.config.ConfigurationProvider` interface and specifying your class in web.xml as the `configProviders` init parameter for the Struts filter. Listing 12.8 shows the code.

Listing 12.8 Registering a `ContainerProvider` in web.xml

```
<init-param>
   <param-name>configProviders</param-name>
   <param-value>com.mycompany.MyContainerProvider</param-value>
</init-param>
```

This technique is only recommended for application developers and not plug-in developers. as it requires manual configuration steps on the part of the user.

12.3.2 *Constants*

Constants are simply configuration settings that can be injected into beans, and are as simple as a name/value pair. During initialization, constants defined by the framework can be overridden by plug-ins, and further overridden by application configuration. There are many more ways to declare constants than beans, and constants are loaded in the following order:

1. web.xml init parameters for the Struts filter
2. default.properties in the Struts JAR
3. struts.properties in WEB-INF/classes (deprecated in Struts 2.1)
4. struts-plugin.xml in each plug-in JAR
5. struts.xml in WEB-INF/classes

Constants can also be used to select an alias of the desired implementation of a defined framework or plug-in extension point, as we talk about more in section 12.3.4.

12.3.3 *Injection*

After all the configuration has been loaded, the injection framework is initialized with the defined beans and constants. Then, as each internal Struts component is needed at runtime, the framework creates the object and provides it with its bean and constant dependencies. A bean can tell the framework that it needs an instance of another bean or constant by using the @Inject annotation on a constructor argument, private field, or setter method. The class type of the dependency to be injected comes from the class defined for the constructor argument, private field, or setter method. How does the framework know to inject a constant or bean? Constants are simply a subset of beans, where their class type is java.lang.String.

The @Inject annotation takes the parameters shown in table 12.2.

Table 12.2 @Inject **annotation parameters**

Parameter name	Description	Required
value	The alias of the desired bean or name of the desired constant	False
required	Whether the dependency is required or not	False

While injection is primarily meant for internal Struts components, you can also use the @Inject annotation in your actions, interceptors, and results.

Let's look at an example. Say we wanted to write a new plug-in that needed its own ObjectFactory. In writing our new SpecialObjectFactory, we realize we need the Struts configuration information. We also want to allow our users to customize the behavior of the plug-in, so we want to support a new constant named struts. specialFeature. Our code would look something like listing 12.9.

Listing 12.9 Injection example

```
public class SpecialObjectFactory extends ObjectFactory {

    private ConfigurationManager configurationManager;
    private String specialFeature;

    @Inject
    public void setConfigurationManager(ConfigurationManager mgr) {
        this.configurationManager = mgr;
    }

    @Inject("struts.specialFeature")
    public void setSpecialFeature(String value) {
        this.specialFeature  = value;
    }

    // the rest of the class
}
```

Alternatively, we could've used constructor injection, by placing an `@Inject` annotation on the constructor, or even private field injection, by putting an `@Inject` annotation before the declaration, although private field injection isn't generally recommended.

12.3.4 *Struts internal extension points*

The last step of the initialization of the injection framework is to select which implementations of key Struts components are chosen. Between built-in components and the various plug-ins that are loaded, there may be multiple implementations of a component, each with its own bean alias. The `BeanSelectionProvider`, an implementation of `ContainerProvider`, is responsible for determining and loading the selected implementations.

To determine which alias to choose for a given Struts component, there generally exists a respective constant, whose value could be

- The alias of the desired bean implementation
- The class name of a new bean

The default implementation, provided by the Struts framework in struts-default.xml, has the alias of `struts`, so this is the default value of the respective constant. Plug-ins that replace framework components such as the Spring plug-in, which among other things provides an alternative implementation of `ObjectFactory`, generally set the respective constant to their implementation alias. Since struts.xml is loaded last, it has the final say on which framework component implementations are used. In some cases, there's no selection constant, as all implementations are loaded and used.

Table 12.3 shows the available framework extension points and their constant selector available in Struts 2.

As you can see, many of the extension points are only available in Struts 2.1 and later, so take note as you plan your plug-in.

Table 12.3 Framework extension points

---

com.opensympony.ObjectFactory

Constant selector	`struts.objectFactory`
Description	Builds important objects such as actions, interceptors, and results. Extended by several plug-ins to integrate with dependency injection frameworks such as Spring and Guice.

---

com.opensympony.ActionProxyFactory

Constant selector	`struts.actionProxyFactory`
Description	Builds the `ActionProxy` and `ActionInocation` objects, which manage the action-interceptor-result process. Override to have full control over how actions, interceptors, and results are executed.

---

com.opensympony.conversion.ObjectTypeDeterminer

Constant selector	`Struts.objectTypeDeterminer`
Description	Determines the type of objects in a `Collection` or `Map`.

---

org.apache.struts2.dispatcher.mapper.ActionMapper

Constant selector	`struts.mapper.class`
Description	Maps the incoming request URI to an action name and namespace. Override if you want to change the URI pattern for your application.

---

org.apache.struts2.dispatcher.multipart.MultiPartRequest

Constant selector	`struts.multipart.parser`
Description	Parses multipart requests in the case of a file upload.

---

org.apache.struts2.views.freemarker.FreemarkerManager

Constant selector	`struts.freemarker.manager.classname`
Description	Loads and processes FreeMarker templates.

---

org.apache.struts2.views.velocity.VelocityManager

Constant selector	`struts.velocity.manager.classname`

---

com.opensymphony.xwork2.util.PatternMatcher

Constant selector	`struts.patternMatcher`
Description	Processes wildcard patterns in action names and namespaces. Only available in Struts 2.1 or later.

---

com.opensymphony.xwork2.validator.ActionValidatorManager

Constant selector	`struts.actionValidatorManager`
Description	Handles the loading of validators and validator configuration. Only available in Struts 2.1 or later.

Table 12.3   Framework extension points (*continued*)

com.opensymphony.xwork2.util.ValueStackFactory	
Constant selector	`struts.valueStackFactory`
Description	Creates `ValueStack` instances for each request. A key component to replace if you want to change the expression language, as value stacks apply expressions to your actions. Only available in Struts 2.1 or later.
com.opensymphony.xwork2.reflection.ReflectionProvider	
Constant selector	`struts.reflectionProvider`
Description	Provides reflection services to the framework. Also important to override if defining your own expression language. Only available in Struts 2.1 or later.
com.opensymphony.xwork2.reflection.ReflectionContextFactory	
Constant selector	`struts.reflectionContextFactory`
Description	Creates the reflection context object that's passed to the reflection methods. Allows per-call reflection configuration values to be passed to the reflection methods. Only available in Struts 2.1 or later.
com.opensymphony.xwork2.config.PackageProvider	
Constant selector	N/A—all implementations are automatically loaded.
Description	Provides package configuration objects that contain actions, interceptors, and results. Only available in Struts 2.1 or later.

12.4   *Writing a breadcrumb plug-in*

As promised, we now discuss the details of creating a plug-in from scratch. This plug-in will capture user requests and create a breadcrumb trail. This trail will contain recent user web requests, allowing them to click back to anywhere they've been. Of course, before writing it, we search the plug-in registry to see if one already exists. Since plug-ins are designed to be plug-and-play, we want to design it to have smart defaults out of the box. In addition, we want to allow developers to configure it to their liking. As we consider the breadcrumb plug-in, the following points seem worth considering:

1 Developers should be able to set a limit for the number of breadcrumbs to be managed.
2 Should the crumbs be unique in the list?
3 Do we want to filter which requests drop a crumb?
4 What if we only want to include requests that were HTTP GET types?
5 We need to support the Struts 2 wildcard request type.
6 Some packages may not want to participate in crumb tracking.

This suggests what aspects will need to be variable in our design. Developers like to be able to set preferences, and these usually vary according to context. We take advantage of several core framework components to assemble this plug-in. This is where we start to see the elegance in the Struts 2 architecture. Most of the request life cycle is processed by a clever assembly of interceptors. In chapter 4, we saw how these interceptors are sandwiched into named stacks that play a pivotal role in the declarative architecture. We're implementing the breadcrumb plug-in as an interceptor. Writing an interceptor is a simple matter of implementing the interceptor interface, as shown in listing 12.10.

Listing 12.10   Interceptor interface

```java
public interface Interceptor extends Serializable {
    void destroy();
    void init();
    String intercept(ActionInvocation invocation) throws Exception;
}
```

In looking around Struts 2, you'll discover several ready-built implementations of this interface that provide prebuilt solutions to common interceptor needs. One such implementation is the `MethodFilterInterceptor`, which allows you to configure lists of method names to filter from the interception. This satisfies the requirement that we might want to filter which requests drop breadcrumbs. Listing 12.11 reveals this implementation.

Listing 12.11   `MethodFilterInterceptor` interface

```java
public abstract class MethodFilterInterceptor extends AbstractInterceptor {
    protected transient Log log = LogFactory.getLog(getClass());

    protected Set excludeMethods = Collections.EMPTY_SET;
    protected Set includeMethods = Collections.EMPTY_SET;

    public void setExcludeMethods(String excludeMethods) {
        this.excludeMethods =
        TextParseUtil.commaDelimitedStringToSet(excludeMethods);
    }

    public Set getExcludeMethodsSet() {
        return excludeMethods;
    }

    public void setIncludeMethods(String includeMethods) {
        this.includeMethods =
        TextParseUtil.commaDelimitedStringToSet(includeMethods);
    }

    public Set getIncludeMethodsSet() {
        return includeMethods;
    }

    public String intercept(ActionInvocation invocation) throws Exception {
        if (applyInterceptor(invocation)) {
            return doIntercept(invocation);      // ❶ Invoke intercept
        }
        return invocation.invoke();              // ❷ Skip intercept
    }

    protected boolean applyInterceptor(ActionInvocation invocation) {   // ❸ Should method be intercepted?
```

❶ Invoke intercept

❷ Skip intercept

❸ Should method be intercepted?

```
        String method = invocation.getProxy().getMethod();
        // ValidationInterceptor
        boolean applyMethod = MethodFilterInterceptorUtil.applyMethod(
                    excludeMethods,includeMethods, method);
        if (log.isDebugEnabled()) {
          if (!applyMethod) {
         log.debug(
                "Skipping Interceptor... Method [" + method + "]
                found in exclude list.");
          }
        }
        return applyMethod;
    }

    /**
     * Subclasses must override to implement the interceptor logic.
     *
     * @param invocation the action invocation
     * @return the result of invocation
     * @throws Exception
     */
    protected abstract String doIntercept(ActionInvocation invocation)
                                    throws Exception;

}
```

The applyInterceptor ❸ method compares our interceptor configuration against the current method being executed on the Struts action class. If this method is determined to be excluded, the interceptor is not invoked ❷. Otherwise, the interceptor is called ❶ to do its part.

The remaining requirements from our list can be met with a little code in our plug-in class. Listing 12.12 reveals the abbreviated source code for our plug-in. The complete source listing is included with the plug-in, which can be downloaded from the Struts 2 plug-in registry.

Listing 12.12 Breadcrumb interceptor

```
public class BreadCrumbInterceptor extends MethodFilterInterceptor {      ❶

    private static final String timerKey =
      "BreadCrumbInterceptor_doIntercept:";        ❷ Crumbs
                                                      stack
    private Stack<Crumb> crumbs;          ◄─────┘

    private int crumbMax;                       ❸ Attributes for
    private boolean uniqueCrumbsOnly;             configurable
    private boolean getRequestsOnly;              elements
    private String wildCardSeparator = "!";


    @Override
    protected String doIntercept(ActionInvocation invocation) throws Exception {    ❹
      try {
        UtilTimerStack.push(timerKey);
        dropCrumb(invocation);              ❺
```

```
      return invocation.invoke();               ❻
    } catch (RuntimeException e) {
      String msg = (new StringBuilder()).append("Error in intercept: ")
                                 .append(e.getMessage()).toString();
      LOG.error(msg, e);
      throw new Exception(msg, e);
    } finally {
      UtilTimerStack.pop(timerKey);
    }
  }
```

Our interceptor extends MethodFilterInterceptor ❶, enabling us to configure method names to be intercepted. It contains a stack ❷ for the breadcrumbs and attributes ❸ to hold all the other configurable aspects of the plug-in. The doInter-cept ❹ method overrides the abstract version from the parent and is where the action happens. The dropCrumb method ❺ is where we determine how to process the request and maintain the stack of crumb objects. Remember, if this request were a result of an action method we wanted to omit from the interception, this would have been bypassed by our parent and would never be invoked! Lastly, we invoke the next interceptor ❻ on the list.

The final piece we need to include is the struts-plugin.xml file that serves to register this plug-in when Struts 2 is started. Listing 12.13 shows the code.

Listing 12.13   Breadcrumb struts-plugin.xml

```
<!DOCTYPE struts PUBLIC
  "-//Apache Software Foundation//DTD Struts Configuration 2.0//EN"
  "http://struts.apache.org/dtds/struts-2.0.dtd">
<struts>
<package name="com.strutsschool.interceptors.breadcrumbs"
        extends="struts-default">             ❶
   <interceptors>
     <interceptor name="breadCrumbs"           ❷

   class="com.strutsschool.interceptors.breadcrumbs.BreadCrumbInterceptor">
       <param name="wildCardSeparator">!</param>
       <param name="uniqueCrumbsOnly">true</param>
       <param name="getRequestsOnly">true</param>   ❸
       <param name="crumbMax">4</param>

     </interceptor>
   </interceptors>
  </package>
</struts>
```

Our package extends struts-default ❶ and adds a new interceptor ❷ to the mix. The parameters for the interceptor allow developers to configure the breadcrumb plug-in for their Struts 2 application according to their preferences. If you compare these parameters ❸ to the interceptor in listing 12.11, you'll see how the pieces go together.

The last thing we have to do is jar up the pieces and drop it on our application classpath. The Struts 2 startup will detect the new JAR and extract struts-plugin.xml for inclusion in the runtime configuration. Of course, if you believe the plug-in serves a utilitarian purpose, why not promote it to the registry for others to enjoy?

12.5 Summary

This chapter covered the plug-in architecture and how the internal component system builds the runtime configuration from the JARs on your application classpath. We looked at how the request life cycle could be modified by simply adding a JAR to the application. The plug-in architecture allowed us to easily incorporate third-party frameworks into our application without modifying existing code. We discussed the Struts 2 plug-in registry and how to search for the latest plug-ins that might provide our application with new features. Lastly, we described the recipe for this new architecture by designing a breadcrumb utility from scratch that we packed as a plug-in. In the next chapter, we explore best practices by sharing tips and techniques from the trenches.

Best practices

The book has now covered the essential ingredients you need to start using Struts 2. You might be wondering how to optimally leverage all the capabilities within such a flexible framework, and this chapter is where we set out to answer these questions and more. This chapter contains an assortment of techniques and tips from the trenches. While it isn't required that you understand this material before writing your first Struts 2 site, it's strongly encouraged. We liken this chapter to those tips your parents shared with you as a youngster. You didn't have to apply them right away, but life was simpler when you did. This chapter presents topics ranging from how to optimize your development environment to registering your web features using a wild technique known as wildcard mappings. Of course, there's also a mish-mash of useful tips in between. We present the practices in an easily consumable fashion, so you can take advantage of them right away. Using these practices will minimize the refactoring you might need to do after the application is built.

This chapter expands your vocabulary and coding style, so you'll be the confident one making suggestions during the next code review. If at any time you feel overwhelmed during your reading, realize that this is new material and it's a fresh approach to things. Learning to tie your shoes wasn't easy, but it sure helped with all the scraped knees. Take a deep breath and realize we were overwhelmed too, and we're no smarter than you!

13.1 Setting up your environment

Unless you're getting paid by the keystroke, I assume you're using an IDE as your development workbench. Since the IDE wars are as hotly contested as religion and politics, I'm not going to discuss which one is better. Instead, I'm going to present the Eclipse IDE available at http://www.eclipse.org/, which has become the de facto standard among developers. The fact that this IDE is available at no charge makes it particularly attractive, and when you add the feature richness Eclipse provides, it starts to make sense why so many developers have chosen it. To get started with Struts 2, all you need is a project that contains the Struts 2 libraries required for your website. Adding these libraries to an Eclipse project is a fancy way of having Eclipse add them to your classpath! Let's face it, setting the classpath is a nuisance and nobody wants to continuously mess around with it.

13.1.1 Setting up your IDE

The following describes the setup required to start a Struts 2 project. Depending on the version, figure 13.1 reveals the minimum set of libraries currently required for a Struts 2 application. If you find yourself wanting to expand your site by adding third-party features, you'll need to add those JARs and likely the corresponding Struts 2 plug-in JAR file as well. As we've been keeping up with the Struts 2 evolution, we find

Figure 13.1   Struts 2 libraries

ourselves referring to the struts2-blank-2.0.x.war file that's included in the download. This is a bare-bones Struts 2 web application and can be used to establish the minimum requirements for your Struts 2 project.

To download the latest version of Struts 2, visit http://struts.apache.org/download and select Full Distribution. This provides you with everything you need to use the framework. At this point, you can unzip <drive>:\struts-2.0.x\app\struts2-blank-2.0.x.war and you'll have a working Struts 2 web application shell.

13.1.2 *Reloading resources*

We're going to make this easy for you. There's an Eclipse plug-in available to make reloading resources during development a piece of cake. This is available from www.myeclipseide.com for less cash than a pan pizza and a couple of beers. This plug-in takes care of reloading resources as you make source code changes, and even reloads classes in your server of choice. This way, clicking Refresh in your browser reveals your latest code changes. Compare this to bailing out of the IDE to run Ant scripts and then bouncing the server, and you'll quickly decide it's worth the meager purchase price.

There are configuration settings that you need to be aware of as you transition your Struts 2 site from development to production that affect the application's performance. These settings are useful during your development with the framework, but are intended to be turned off before moving your product to production. These settings can be made in either your struts.xml or struts.properties files, although it's a good practice to keep these in properties files for easy transition between environments. This way, you don't need to remember to make changes to the struts.xml as your application moves from development to production. These properties are listed in table 13.1.

Table 13.1 Struts 2 runtime properties that control resource reloading

Property	Value
struts.devMode	True if DEV; false if PROD
struts.i18n.reload	True if DEV; false if PROD
struts.configuration.xml.reload	True if DEV; false if PROD

Now that we've downloaded Struts 2 and configured our desktop using Eclipse, we're ready to a look at writing test cases for our actions. The next section explains how to write unit tests around your Struts 2 actions.

13.2 *Unit-testing your actions*

Test-driven development is sweeping the nation. Testing code is no longer considered something we might do at the end of the project. Your work is expected to perform correctly as it interacts with all the other objects that make up an object-oriented application. As we pointed out in chapter 1, a great thing about Struts 2 is that action classes are Plain Old Java Objects (POJOs) and can be tested independently of all the complicated plumbing that comes with web and/or application servers. Actions in Struts 1 were tangled up with the Servlet API and were difficult to test outside of the server environment. This often led to either no testing at all or complicated tests involving funky mock objects configured to "trick" your actions into thinking they were interacting with the Servlet API code they so desperately relied upon. Struts 2 avoids tangling its actions up with the Servlet API so you can easily test them. Another tenet of modern software design is to minimize dependency. Rather than have your code dependent on other code, it's based loosely on interfaces or roles. This allows different concrete implementations to be injected into your code according to the context or environment in which it's running. The next section reveals how this can be useful in the context of testing.

13.2.1 *The advantage of IoC for testing*

When it comes to testing your action objects, the objects they interact with will likely need to be "test" versions of the objects your action would otherwise encounter running in the "real" mode. Back in chapter 9, we discussed the affinity Struts 2 has with Spring when it comes to specifying these dependencies. This is where IoC (inversion of control, a.k.a. dependency injection) saves the day. When using this design philosophy, dependent target objects are "injected" into the source object and the target object adaptation can be swapped out without touching your Java source code. Struts 2 has built-in support for dependency injection and even lets you plug in your favorite IoC implementation. Since the Spring framework is so wildly popular, we demonstrate using Spring.

Actions need to be injected with their dependent objects while the tests are being executed in much the same way they are when running in production, the likely difference being certain injected objects will be unique while testing. For instance, you'll probably inject a data source while testing that behaves differently than your production data source. One additional consideration is the fact that Struts 2 never calls your action directly. Instead, it wraps an `ActionProxy` around your action so registered interceptors can be called before and after consulting with your action. So do we test an action with all the pomp and circumstance of the `ActionProxy` and interceptors, or simply as a naked POJO? The answer is that you get to decide; both ways are clearly valid. If the interception of your action is necessary in order to run a valid test, test your action through the `ActionProxy`. Otherwise, test the action directly as a naked POJO.

If you choose to test your action independently of the interceptors, it's drop-dead simple. Just create an instance of your action class and set whatever properties you like. At this point, you can start making assertions against this action object the same way you would any other POJO. If you need to test your action in the context of running inside your Struts 2 application, you'll need a handle to the `ActionProxy` that wraps around your action. We explain this process in the next section.

13.2.2 *JUnit and the tests*

We want to get something out of the way before writing the tests. You're probably asking yourself, "How am I going to access the `HttpServletRequest` object?" The short answer is, "Why do you need to?" Is this just a bad habit from years of doing it this way? Remember, Struts 2 avoids tangling its actions up with the Servlet API so you can easily test them. The Struts 2 action is expected to have properties that hold the user inputs. The framework even populates these properties so you don't have to mess around with fishing them out of the HttpServletRequest yourself. If you have a genuine desire to manhandle the HttpServletRequest attributes inside an action, you can implement the RequestAware interface. This is how an action asks the framework to populate a Map property with the objects associated with the HttpServletRequest. Now all your unit tests need to do is read and write to this Map in order to accomplish the old request.setAttribute(k,v) and request.getAttribute(k);.

We start off testing an action in the wild and then consider the action in the context of the framework. Listing 13.1 demonstrates a CustomerSearchAction class.

Listing 13.1   A typical action class

```
public class CustomerSearchAction {
  private String nextStep ="List";            ◁——  Populated by
  private Customer model;                            web page
  public void setModel(Customer customer) {   ◁——  Used to inject
    this.customer=customer;                          the model
  }
  public String execute(){                    ◁——  Default method the
    if(model.getZip().equalsIgnoreCase(ALL))         framework calls
      nextStep = "PagedList"                  ◁——  Breadcrumb
    return nextStep;                                to determine
  }                                                 next step
}
```

Listing 13.1 is a typical Struts 2 action class with an execute() method that returns a String, which determines the next step in the workflow. As you can see, if the user chooses to search across all ZIP codes, the action will guide the workflow such that a pageable list is displayed rather than potentially loading up hundreds of customers all at once. Listing 13.2 reveals the simplicity involved in testing this action.

Listing 13.2   The simple JUnit test of our action as a naked POJO

```
public class CustomerSearchActionTest extends TestCase {   ◁——  Normal JUnit
  CustomerSearchAction action;                                    TestCase
  public void testSearchByAllZips() {
    action=new CustomerSearchAction();        ◁——  Create the action
    Customer customer = new Customer();       Create/configure model
    Customer.setZip(ALL);                     and inject action
    action.setModel(customer);
    assertEquals("PagedList", action.execute());   ◁——  Test response
  }
}
```

Simple, huh? Now let's consider a more comprehensive test where our action is injected by Spring and requires the interceptor stack to be involved as well. In this case, we can't simply instantiate the action ourselves. Rather, we need to have the action (and its `ActionProxy`) created for us by a helper factory. Since the interceptors are registered in struts.xml, this file needs to be consulted. Also, the fact that an action's symbolic name can be repeated across different package namespaces necessitates that we provide this information to the helper factory as well. If you're new to Java generics, what you're about to see might amaze you. Before we get into the helper factory, let's use it to create a full-blown reference to an action context:

```
searchAction = helper.createAction(CustomerSearchAction.class,
    "/searchNameSpace", "/search"))
```

This is considered a polymorphic factory method. Try saying that five times fast! The first argument is the type of object you'd like created. The factory method uses Java generics to return a type compatible with your request. The next two arguments are the namespace and symbolic name you specified in your declarative architecture for this web feature. This does all the heavy lifting of combing the interceptors from struts.xml. After writing several versions of this helper class ourselves, we decided to use the example found at www.arsenalist.com to do this creation. Why recreate the wheel, right? Listing 13.3 shows a more comprehensive test that takes advantage of this `ActionProxy`.

> **Listing 13.3 The JUnit test with a proxy**

```
public class CustomerSearchActionTest extends BaseStrutsTestCase {    ❶
  CustomerSearchAction action;
  public void testSearchByAllZips() {
    String ns ="/searchNameSpace";       ❷
    String mapping = "/search";       ❸
    action=createAction(CustomerSearchAction.class,ns, mapping);      ❹
    Map p = new HashMap();
    p.put("customer.id", "bogus123");                              ❺
    proxy.getInvocation().getInvocationContext().setParameters(p);
    String result = proxy.execute();      ❻
    assertEquals(result, "input");
  }
}
```

Our test extends the `BaseStrutsTestCase` helper class ❶. This base class provides the magic ❹ `createAction` behavior. The magic method takes the namespace ❷ and the symbolic name ❸ chosen for our mapping and creates a configured action object. At this point, we inject request parameters into the map ❺ that test the search behavior, and finally ❻ execute and verify results.

Note that in this example we didn't create a `Customer` object; Spring did. Also, we didn't inject the customer into the action. It was injected into the action by the framework. All we did was simulate some user inputs followed by the `proxy.execute()`. The interceptors took care of populating the domain value with the request parameters, so all we had to deal with was testing the results of the `execute()` method. This should indicate just how easy it is to comprehensively test your action classes outside of the server environment. No more excuses! Let's see the tested code coverage hit 90.9%.

13.2.3 *Testing validation.xml files*

Before we leave the topic of unit testing, let's see how we can test our declarative validations to make sure bad input doesn't make its way into our system. If you need a refresher on the validator framework, you can flip back to chapter 10. Validations can be specified external to the Java code. We simply specify the rules in an XML file named corresponding to the action class it's protecting. Listing 13.4 demonstrates testing our XML validation.

Listing 13.4   The validation testing with JUnit

```
public class CustomerSearchActionTest extends BaseStrutsTestCase {      ❶
  CustomerSearchAction action;
  public void testSearchByAllZips() {
    String ns ="/searchNameSpace"        ❷
    String mapping = "/search"        ❸
    action=createAction(CustomerSearchAction.class,ns, mapping);      ❹
    Map p = new HashMap();
    p.put("customer.id", "bogus123");                                  ❺
    proxy.getInvocation().getInvocationContext().setParameters(p);
    String result = proxy.execute();      ❻
    assertEquals(result, "input");      ❼
    int errorCount=action.getFieldErrors().size();                    ❽
    assertTrue("Should contain errors", errorCount>0);

  }
}
```

Our test extends the `BaseStrutsTestCase` helper class ❶. This base class provides the magic ❹ `createAction` behavior. The magic method takes the namespace ❷ and the symbolic name ❸ chosen for our mapping and creates a configured action object. At this point, we inject request parameters into the map ❺ that test the search behavior, and ❻ execute the proxy. In this test we validate the return type ❼, and assert that field errors were added to the collection ❽.

It should also be noted that you can pull many different references from the proxy for making assertions. For example, you could pull the collection of interceptors out to test for the existence of a required interceptor.

You should now have a good understanding of how to test Struts 2 action classes using JUnit. In the next section, we shift gears and look at how the data is getting into your actions. Struts 2 uses a clever approach to building web pages that interact with your users. We now explore this UI toolkit and the underlying FreeMarker scripting that makes it work.

13.3 *Maximizing reuse*

In a world where users expect new website features with instant access, we must reach for more prebuilt software. The fact that you're using Struts 2 suggests you chose a ready-made framework to manage your website. In this section, we look into ways that Struts 2 allows us to build unique UI widgets by extending prebuilt components. The widgets have full access to the OGNL and value stacks within the framework, so their access to data is automatic.

For those of you who've written your own custom tags using the JSP specification, this'll seem unbelievable to you. I remember writing a few custom tags before JSTL came on the scene, and it was always a horror. Instead of writing Java classes to support the UI widgets, we now have the ability to use a scripting language to generate the markup. This scripting language is FreeMarker and internally the JSP, FTL, and Velocity tags are all rendered using it. Simply put, FreeMarker combines static and dynamic content to generate real-time output. In case you jumped over here without exploring the chapter covering UI components, you'd be well advised to slip a bookmark into this page and circle back to chapter 7.

Now then, a few definitions might be in order before jumping in. A *tag* is a small piece of code executed from within JSP, FreeMarker, or Velocity. A *template* is code, usually written in FreeMarker, that can be rendered by certain tags. A *theme* is a collection of templates packaged together to provide common functionality.

In the next section, we see how to combine these ideas to create a custom tag that adds to our UI toolbox.

13.3.1 *Componentization with the component tag*

The `component` tag renders a UI widget using a specified template. Beyond the full complement of the OGNL and `ValueStack` variables, additional objects can be passed into the template using the `param` tag. These make up the dynamic data that's merged into the template. The component hierarchy for UI tags is illustrated in figure 13.2.

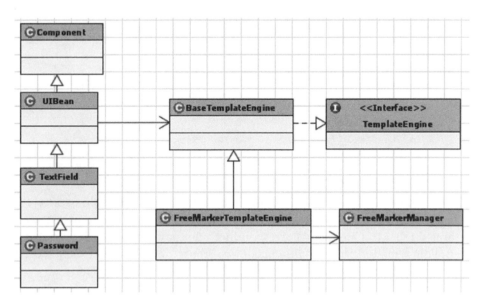

Figure 13.2 Component hierarchy for UI tags

There are other template engines as well, but we'll concentrate on FreeMarker for now. The real power of this architecture is that you get the feature richness of object inheritance for data access and the ease of UI widget scripting with FreeMarker. FreeMarker is an integral piece of Struts 2, so we should understand what it's designed to do. It's intended to dynamically generate output by combining static and dynamic content. This output can correspond to the grammar of any syntax you like. Our example generates HTML output. The component tag renders a UI widget using the specified FreeMarker template. Each subclass in the Struts 2 UI toolkit has its own stylistic FreeMarker template that weaves its static and dynamic content together to produce a cohesive HTML widget. However, we can write our own FreeMarker template and pass it into the component custom tag to be rendered.

Let's write a FreeMarker template that outputs the current date and time in a div tag. Figure 13.3 illustrates how we'd like the widget to look.

Figure 13.3   The current date/time widget

Now let's look at the web page that included this widget. We begin by showing the single line of code that generated the HTML output:

```
<s:component template="now.ftl"/>
```

So the interesting code must be in the now.ftl file, but where is it? By default. the templates you write (or override) go in a folder <web-root>/template/{*theme*} where {*theme*} is either a theme that's included with Struts 2 or a custom theme you design yourself. That takes care of where it goes, so let's look inside it. Listing 13.5 illustrates the template.

Listing 13.5   The now.ftl file

```
<#include ".../controlheader.ftl" />
  <div>
    <fieldset>
      <legend>
        Current date/time
      </legend>
    <@s.textfield theme="simple" value="${now?datetime}"/>
    </fieldset>
  </div>
<#include ".../controlfooter.ftl" />
```

The variable now is retrieved from the ValueStack just like you'd expect. The component tag will also allow you to parametrically pass in name/value pairs to control generated DOM ID names and corresponding values to be looked up on the ValueStack. Building up widgets like this maximizes reuse and guarantees standard look and behavior. Think of these as the HTML tags the W3C forgot to include.

13.3.2   *Leveraging the templated tags*

In the previous section, we discovered how FreeMarker templates are the heart and soul of the UI tags included in Struts 2. Moreover, we saw how we could write our own

FreeMarker templates that the component tag would process to generate meaningful HTML widgets. In this section, we extend the discussion of templates and tags by presenting the UI library and the corresponding templates. The UI tags are divided into form and nonform groups. The following are the form tags:

- autocomplete
- checkbox
- checkboxlist
- combobox
- datetimepicker
- doubleselect
- file
- form
- head
- hidden
- label
- optiontransferselect
- optgroup
- password
- radio
- reset
- select
- submit
- textarea
- textfield
- token
- updownselect

The following are the nonform tags:

- actionerror
- actionmesssage
- component
- div
- fielderror
- table
- tabbedPanel
- tree
- treenode

The templates that support these tags are located in the struts2-core-2.0.x.jar. As mentioned earlier, they're grouped into themes and located in folders named template.{*theme*}. We wrap up this exploration by discussing the mechanics of the Struts 2 UI textfield tag more closely. Once you see how we connect the data dots, you can apply the same knowledge to any other tag.

Struts UI tags are designed to use the data from your action and ValueStack or from Struts data tags. The action/value stack is the comprehensive tree of nodes that contains, among other objects, your action. It's straightforward to link object data to your tag by simply providing an accessor method in your web-page-related action class. In the advanced topics chapter, we'll look at an additional technique for making data available to UI tags. The following are the Struts data tags:

- action
- bean
- date
- debug
- i18n
- include
- param
- property
- push
- set
- url

Now that we've looked at all the individual pieces that make this baby work, let's take a crack at connecting the dots in order to see the entire puzzle assembled.

13.3.3 *Connecting the UI-to-object dots*

If it's true that a picture's worth a thousand words, this section may overflow my page quota. Figure 13.4 illustrates what the browser output looks like with our new custom

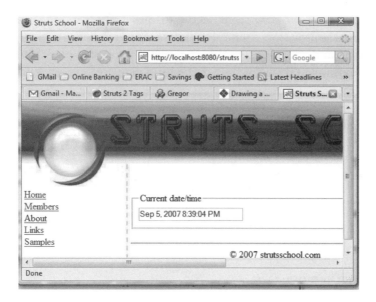

Figure 13.4   The browser output

tag. The concentration here is on our new widget and not the overall web page. We'll discuss comprehensive web pages using Tile in the advanced topics chapter.

The web page in figure 13.4 contains a bevy of Struts 2 custom tags. In fact, it's constructed entirely of Struts 2 tags. Notice the current date/time widget that we built in section 13.3.1. This widget searches the ValueStack to find a getNow() behavior whose return value will be substituted into the ${now} placeholder of the now.ftl template. This template merely wraps this value returned from the ValueStack in a fieldset tag and writes the chunk of HTML to the enclosing page. While this was a simple example, the only limitation relating to FreeMarker and custom UI widgets is your imagination. If the Struts UI game is your bag, the next section discusses ways to take the templates to another strata.

13.4   Advanced UI tag usage

If you're reading this, extending the Struts UI tags must be of interest to you. There are plenty of UI tags included in Struts 2 to build commercial applications. However, if you wish to personalize the appearance beyond cascading style sheets, you have options here too. Struts 2 is designed to allow you the freedom to enhance the tags to your heart's content. Remember, they're generated using simple FreeMarker scripting templates. In fact, you can create an entirely new theme that shows the world your individual creativity. Let's review the options.

13.4.1   Overriding existing templates

As we saw earlier in this chapter, you can tweak tags and have the rendering framework select your modified template. This allows you to reuse the guts of the existing templates and simply make minor tweaks. This is accomplished by copying the FreeMarker template you'd like to change into the folder <web-root>/template/{*theme*}. At this point, you can make any changes you like to the template and the rendering framework will select your template as opposed to its own. The rules for selecting templates are as follows. Templates are loaded based on the template directory and theme name. The template directory is defined by the `struts.ui.templateDir` property in struts. properties and defaults to `template`. This directory is first searched for within the application; if not found, the search proceeds to the classpath. The default templates provided in struts-core.jar should suit the needs of many applications. But if a template needs to be modified, it's easy to override with a new version. Extract the template you need to change from struts-core.jar, make the modifications, and save the updated copy to /template/$theme/$template.ftl. If you're using the `xhmtl` theme and need to change how the select tags render, edit that template and save it to /template/xhtml/ select.ftl. Now we will look at the steps involved in writing your own custom themes.

13.4.2 *Writing custom templates*

In the previous section, we looked at overriding existing templates. We now explore the steps involved in creating custom templates for your web pages. If you're duplicating chunks of HTML all over the place, you need to read this closely. Writing custom templates is analogous to creating custom tag libraries, only without all the pain. Struts 2 provides the UI component tag `<s:component template='customTemplate.ftl'/>`, which expects a custom template that it merges with dynamic data located on the action/value stack. Writing the custom FreeMarker template is all there is to it. If you're surprised, you're not alone. It almost seems too easy. For a refresher on how your custom FreeMarker template interacts with the other pieces, please review section 13.3.3.

13.4.3 *Writing custom themes*

Most often, an application just needs to override a template so that a certain UI widget renders differently. Or maybe you need to add a new template to an existing theme for a custom UI widget. However, if you want to create an entirely new theme, perhaps because you're building a rich set of unique and reusable templates for your organization, there are three ways to do it.

CREATE A NEW THEME FROM SCRATCH (HARD!)

It's probably never a good idea to create a new theme from scratch. Instead, use the `simple` theme as a starting point. The `simple` theme provides just enough foundation to make it easy to create new controls by extending or wrapping the basic controls. Before starting a new theme, be sure to review the source templates for all of the provided themes. These templates can be found in struts-core.jar. The existing themes are your best guide to creating new themes.

WRAP AN EXISTING THEME

Wrapping is a great way to augment the basic HTML elements provided by the simple theme. In fact, if you look at the `xhtml` theme, you'll find this is what it's doing. It wraps the `simple` theme by adding unique FreeMarker header and footer templates to automatically render elements such as error messages, internationalized labels, and hover help for a control.

EXTEND AN EXISTING THEME

One benefit of object-oriented programming is that it lets us "design by difference." We can extend an object and code only the behavior that's different. UI themes provide a similar capability. The subdirectory that hosts a theme can contain a theme.properties file. A `parent` entry can be added to the property file to designate a theme to extend. The `ajax` theme extends the `xhtml` theme using this technique. An extended theme doesn't need to override every template from the parent theme. It only needs to override the templates it wants to behave or appear different than the parent version.

13.5   *Summary*

This chapter has covered many practices that you can begin using on your first Struts 2 project. You learned about testing your code so that pesky and embarrassing bugs don't make it into your production release, and speeding the development of custom UI widgets through the use of templates and themes. We also saw how the FreeMarker template engine makes writing dynamic web components a breeze. In the next chapter, we discuss migration strategies to get your existing Struts 1 sites converted to Struts 2.

Migration from Struts Classic

14

This chapter covers

- Migrating from Struts 1 to Struts 2
- Switching to the new tag library
- Breaking up message resources
- Migrating one piece at a time

So you're convinced Struts 2 is worth the effort to learn, but you also have all this knowledge and experience with Struts 1, also called Struts Classic. And what about all those Struts 1 websites in production? This chapter compares and contrasts the similarities and differences between the two Struts versions and provides useful migration strategies for you. The good news is you don't have to relearn everything. In fact, some of the esoteric things you had to remember to do in Struts Classic have been eliminated. Also, many features we always wished for in Struts 1 have finally arrived in Struts 2. So grab a lovely beverage and let's get started. I am going to trust you are familiar with a version of Struts Classic.

14.1 *Translating Struts Classic knowledge*

You come to work on Monday morning to learn that your company is adopting this new version of Struts. At first you're excited to learn a modern web framework, but you've also heard it's quite different from Struts Classic. What does this mean for your career? What if you're no longer the person everyone calls the Struts guru? How do you quickly become the Struts 2 expert you know you can be? Luckily, you've already taken the first step by purchasing this fine book. In fact, chapter 1 showed you how the two Struts flavors aren't really that different. You should've walked away from chapter 1 realizing Struts Classic and Struts 2 are both MVC-patterned, but Struts 2 provides a much cleaner implementation. This chapter will transition your expert status to the new Struts before anyone realizes your confidence was shaken. Our first stop will be the Struts action.

14.1.1 *Actions*

You'll be happy to know the action is still the workhorse in Struts 2 that it was in Struts Classic. In fact, it's now a thoroughbred! The first change to grasp is that an action is no longer a singleton. Each request gets its own action instance that is thread-safe. This means you can have first-class instance variables of complex types! The next change is that the action has divorced the Servlet API. Listing 14.1 reveals a typical Struts 1 action. Note how the Servlet API and Struts 1 framework objects are bound into your code. Not only does this make the action hard to test, it also blurs the division of responsibility between the action and the server plumbing. A couple more things to recognize before we look at the Struts 2 action are the name of the method and the action class that our `SamplesAction` is extending. Listing 14.1 shows the requirements of the Struts Classic actions.

Listing 14.1 Struts Classic Action

```
public class SamplesAction extends Action {          ❶
  public ActionForward execute(           ❷
                    ActionMapping mapping,          ❸
                    ActionForm form,
                    HttpServletRequest request,          ❹
                    HttpServletResponse response)
  {
    SamplesWebForm webForm=(SamplesWebForm) form;          ❺
    // business logic here…
    return mapping.findForward("success");          ❻
  }
}
```

First, our `SamplesAction` was required to extend the Struts Classic `Action` class ❶. Next, we were required to receive the framework mapping and form references ❸ in the `execute()` method ❷. The framework form passed to the `execute()` method was always quirky. It had to be cast ❺ to a subclass, which could easily throw an exception and was chock full of strings representing user input that we had to wrestle into "real" data types. You can also see that we had to receive Servlet API references ❹ for the request and response. Lastly, we had to determine the `ActionForward` object ❻ and return it to the framework. If you were reading closely, we were expected to do many things the framework should've been doing itself! Now let's look at the corresponding Struts 2 Action in listing 14.2.

Listing 14.2   Struts 2 Action

```
public class SamplesAction{            ❶
  private SamplesBean model;           ❷

  public String execute(){             ❸
        // business logic here ...
    return "success";                  ❹
  }
  public SamplesBean getModel(){
    return model;
  }                                              ❺
  public void setModel(SamplesBean model){
    this.model = model;
  }
}
```

First, our Struts 2 `SamplesAction` is a simple POJO ❶. Now that action classes aren't singletons, we have an instance variable ❷ that preserves the user input. The method requires us to receive no arguments ❸ and can be named whatever we like. The return value is a simple string that serves as a symbolic name ❹ the framework digests to determine what should happen next. Lastly, the `get/setModel()` ❺ behaviors are accessed by the framework to keep its internal value stack synchronized with user inputs.

Pretty slick, huh? This JavaBeans action contains no Servlet API dependencies, so testing it is a breeze. The fact that the `execute()` method can be called anything you like turns out to be an extremely cool feature that we'll explore in more detail later when we discuss wildcard mappings. Now let's take a closer look at how the data flows between the Web and Struts 2.

14.1.2   What happened to ActionForms?

Can we have a moment of silence in memory of the `ActionForm`? The `ActionForm` has been booted out of the framework and we're better off because of it. It never measured up and at one point in the evolution of Struts Classic, we were even allowed to pretend it didn't exist by using the infamous `DynaForm`. Of course the `DynaForm` was just an `ActionForm` in disguise. The `ActionForm` was weak at best and only existed as a bridge to shuttle user inputs between the action and web page. It did little more than hold the `String` request parameters from the `HttpServletRequest` so we didn't have to fish them out ourselves. But once we received the form, we were left to convert it into a business-savvy domain model before we could do anything useful with the user inputs.

Struts 2 has removed the `ActionForm` and now serves the action a business-savvy domain model freshly adapted from the user inputs. Struts 2 translates and converts all the `String` request parameters to their complex data types found in the action. If you've written adapters to map web pages to domain objects, you can already see this automation will save many hours of manual work. Struts 2 also takes care of translation in the other direction to satisfy the `String` requirements of the HTML.

The translation between `Strings` and your business-savvy domain model is performed by the OGNL `DefaultTypeConverter`. It understands many data types, dates, arrays, maps, and collections. Of course, as you discovered in chapter 5, if you have requirements beyond the scope of the framework and would like to create your own type converters for your custom data types, here's the recipe:

1 Create your converter extending `StrutsTypeConverter`.
2 Register your new converter for either an individual class in *ClassName-*conversion.properties or globally in xwork-conversion.properties.

In case you jumped to this migration section before reading the earlier chapters, it's worth mentioning that Struts 2 populates your objects with the user input via an interceptor. Recall that interceptors do most of the heavy lifting in this new framework (see chapter 4), so this makes sense. This interceptor uses the web page input control name to find a setter method on your action class. Once the set method is located, it determines the actual data type the method is expecting and has the `String` converted to this anticipated type (see chapter 5). Lastly, the converted data type is passed to the setter method and the object is injected with the user input. Figure 14.1 illustrates this parameter-setting flow.

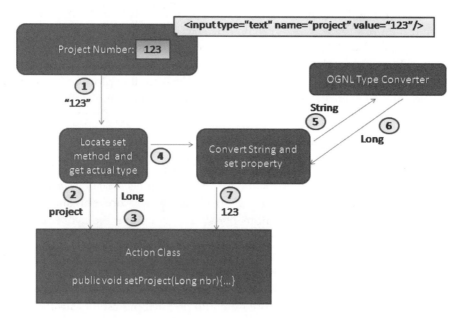

Figure 14.1 Parameter interception and conversion

Of course, if our HTML control had been named `department.project`, then our action would contain a set/getDepartment method that returns a `Department`. The `Department` would contain a `getProject()` method that would ultimately contain the `setProject(...)` operation. This powerful Struts 2 capability will accommodate shuttling user inputs between the web page and a rich domain model without human intervention.

Now that we've explained how Struts 2 has effectively eliminated the `ActionForm`, let's discuss web pages and their custom tags that operate as the opposite end of this data exchange.

14.1.3 Switching tag libraries

Struts has always had an affinity for tag libraries. In fact, the Struts tag libraries work closely with the Struts framework itself to handle data movement and workflow navigation. They're doing many "Struts" things behind the scenes. Struts Classic had several different tag libraries with an occasional overlap among them. Struts 2 has cleaned this up by combining its tags into one library. This simplifies figuring out which `taglib` directive to include in your web pages.

The biggest difference between the two versions of Struts is that Struts 1 tags were dependent on the old `ActionForm` whereas Struts 2 utilizes the OGNL `ValueStack`. For the sake of comparison, these two schemes are about as similar as a Ford Escort and a Chevrolet Corvette! Whereas the Struts 1 scheme merely shuttled string data types between the web page and `ActionForm`, the Struts 2 approach is amazingly different.

Unless you've jumped right to this chapter in the book, you should have a clear understanding of the `ValueStack` and the Object-Graph Navigation Language that form the core of Struts 2. This `ValueStack` is an ordered list of real-time objects. This means objects are being pushed on and popped off the stack as the framework executes requests. The tags are one such agent allowed to push and pop the stack. As properties are requested, the stack is searched from the top down. This flexibility allows us to reference properties without needing to first know which object contains the property. Consider figure 14.2.

As you can see from this illustration, the OGNL searches for your expression starting at the top of the stack and proceeds downward until either it's located or the list is exhausted. Learning this powerful navigation language will be a valuable tool in your toolkit. Visit the

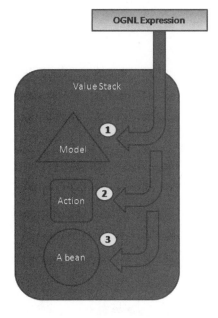

Figure 14.2 `ValueStack` **and expression navigation**

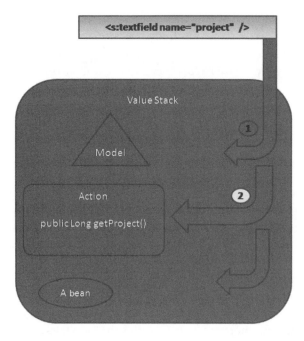

Figure 14.3   **Custom tag interplay with** `ValueStack`

website http://www.ognl.org for more information. Now, let's take a look at an example of our web page interacting with dynamic objects on this stack. Figure 14.3 reveals how a Struts 2 custom tag would find the `project` property.

In this case, the first object where the `project` property could be accessed was in the `Action` object.

Migrating your Struts 1 web pages to Struts 2 will require replacing the Struts 1 tag directives with the single `<%@ taglib prefix="s" uri="/struts-tags"%>`. Details of this conversion are included later in this section. The Struts 2 tags automatically include support for internationalization and field-level messages without much fuss. This allows you to remove much of the HTML you had to write to get this support with the Struts Classic tags.

Before leaving this section, we need to comment on JSTL. Struts Classic contained several tag libraries, each of which contained a related grouping of tags. Once JSTL came onto the scene, you were encouraged to select the JSTL version where there was a corresponding tag in a Struts Classic library. This was because of the JSTL support for the new Expression Language that enabled objects to be interwoven with the tag itself to produce the desired markup.

The JSTL `${someObject.someMethod}` expression language is rich and can be used to reach deep into an object graph. Plus there's also support for working with `Maps` and `Lists`. Struts 2 has full access to JSTL in the same way Struts Classic does. Where we see the real difference is that Struts 2 has its own tag libraries that interact with the OGNL and the `ValueStack` where Struts Classic knows nothing about these new capabilities.

Next we look at how to organize all those internationalized resource files.

14.1.4 *Breaking up message resources*

Java has always provided native support to allow us to easily access locale-sensitive text and formatting. The hardest part is having all the text translated into other dialects, which has nothing to do with Struts. Struts Classic leveraged this native support through the use of the `java.util.PropertyResourceBundle` and the `java.util.ListResourceBundle`, and so does Struts 2. Where Struts 2 differs is in the flexibility you have in selecting a language bundle. This is covered in greater detail in chapter 11. So that we don't confuse what's meant by the bundle selection, let me first identify what we mean about this selection. Suppose our website has been designed to accommodate English, German, Spanish, and French. This would require us to have the following files on our classpath:

- MyWebBundle.properties
- MyWebBundle_en.properties
- MyWebBundle_de.properties
- MyWebBundle_es.properties
- MyWebBundle_fr.properties

The file selected would depend on the language the requester passed in on the HTTP header. For sake of illustration, let's suppose it was a French requester. Judging from what we know so far, MyWebBundle_fr.properties would be selected. In Struts 1, all your keys were expected to be in this file. Since it's never a good idea to put all the text for your entire website in a single file, Struts 1 allowed you to have French text in multiple French files. However, it was a messy technique that was clearly added as an afterthought. It required a custom Java class and you had to prefix your message keys with a file designator so the custom class could determine which file it should select your text from. It was clumsy and error-prone.

Struts 2 makes it easy to set up language files for your entire application, sections of the site, or even down to the action and property level. At the application level, it works the same as Struts Classic. Simply provide the default bundle in the struts.properties as follows:

```
struts.custom.i18n.resources=resources.package
```

Where things get more interesting in Struts 2 is how you can deal with special cases. Let's suppose you have special needs for an action named `MemberAction`. If you create a bundle called `MemberAction.properties` and place it alongside this action class, Struts 2 will retrieve values from this locale bundle. There are many variations between choosing the scope of the entire application or an individual Action. This following is the search order:

1 A `ResourceBundle` is selected with the same name and package as the class of the object on the stack, including the interfaces and superclasses of that class. The search hierarchy is as follows:
   - Look for the message in a `ResourceBundle` for the class.

- If not found, look for the message in a `ResourceBundle` for each implemented interface.
- If not found, traverse up the class's hierarchy to the parent class, and repeat from step 1.

2 If the message text isn't found in the class hierarchy search and the object implements `ModelDriven`, call `getModel()` and do a class hierarchy search for the class of the model object. There was no concept in Struts Classic for scoping messages to a particular bean.

3 If the message text still is not found, search the class hierarchy for default package texts. For the package of the original class or object, you look for a `Resource-Bundle` named `package.properties` in that package. For instance, if the class is `com.strutsschool.enrollment.MemberAction`, look for a `ResourceBundle` named `com.strutsschool.enrollment.package.properties`. You continue along this line for each superclass in turn.

4 If Struts 2 hasn't found the text at this point, it checks whether the message key refers to a property of an object on the `ValueStack`. If a search for members on the `ValueStack` returns a nonnull object and the text key you're looking for is `member.course.description`, use the member's class to look for the text key course.description, searching up its class hierarchy, and so on, as in previous steps.

5 The last resort is to search for the text in the default `ResourceBundles` that have been registered in struts.properties.

As you look at this flexibility, it's clear that Struts 2 learned a valuable lesson from Struts 1. All these capabilities might at first seem ridiculous, but once you find yourself faced with that exceptional use case, you'll be happy to know the framework is prepared to provide an elegant solution to your problem.

A wise man once said you can't eat an elephant in one bite. I didn't understand what he meant until I was faced with migrating a large Struts Classic web application to Struts 2. In the next section, we begin discussing how we can do this in small increments.

14.2   *Converting by piecemeal*

We're going to extend a convention that's been followed throughout the book. We'd like to refer to Struts Classic as S1 and Struts 2 as S2. This makes it easier to discuss the two frameworks as we compare and contrast them. While S2 is a quantum leap forward, converting your S1 application is fairly mechanical. We'll soon begin to see tools that assist with the conversion, but for now, you can also find comfort in the fact that we don't need to convert everything at once. Much like eating an elephant in one bite, this just isn't practical. There are several possibilities when it comes to the S1 and S2 unity:

- Leave the S1 application unchanged.
- Convert the entire S1 application to S2.

- Merge S1 and S2 technologies and convert using a piecemeal approach:
  - Calls between the two are easy
  - The S1 plug-in allows you to use S1 actions in an S2 application

If you have a stable S1 website that doesn't require maintenance, you might as well leave it alone. If you have a relatively small S1 site that's evolving, you might consider a wholesale migration to S2. Lastly, since most S1 applications are large, we concentrate on the merge and piecemeal approach, with a sidebar on the Struts 1 plug-in. If you're the proud parent of an S1 website and would like to adapt it to S2, let's begin our conversion.

14.2.1 *Eating an elephant a piece at a time*

While it's true that S2 is easier to configure and provides many more features, the two frameworks can coexist, as they each

- Declaratively map a URL to a Java class
- Declaratively map a response to a web resource
- Contain custom tags to link requests to their respective framework

The first thing to consider is the declarative URL mapping that determines where the request should be routed. S1 is typically mapped to digest a URL matching /*.do and S2 /*.action. While these may be configured using different extensions, they need to be unique if you plan to combine the two frameworks into a single web application. Let's take the first bite of the elephant. The first step is to copy the S2 JARs to the WEB-INF/lib folder of our S1 application and add the S2 elements to the web.xml file. Listing 14.3 covers these elements in detail.

Listing 14.3   web.xml combining both S1 and S2 into the same web application

```xml
<?xml version="1.0" encoding="UTF-8"?>
<!DOCTYPE web-app PUBLIC
  "-//Sun Microsystems, Inc.//DTD Web Application 2.3//EN"
  "http://java.sun.com/dtd/web-app_2_3.dtd">

<web-app>
 <!-- Struts 2 -->
 <filter>
  <filter-name>struts2</filter-name>            ❶
  <filter-class>
   org.apache.struts2.dispatcher.FilterDispatcher
  </filter-class>

 </filter>
  <!-- extensions are included in the struts.properties -->
  <!-- struts.action.extension=action -->
 <filter-mapping>
  <filter-name>struts2</filter-name>            ❷
  <url-pattern>/*</url-pattern>
 </filter-mapping>
```

```
<listener>
 <listener-class>
   org.springframework.web.context.ContextLoaderListener    ❸
 </listener-class>
</listener>
<listener>
 <listener-class>
   org.apache.struts2.tiles.StrutsTilesListener    ❹
 </listener-class>
</listener>

<!-- Struts 1 -->
<servlet>
 <servlet-name>action</servlet-name>    ❺
 <servlet-class>
   org.apache.struts.action.ActionServlet
 </servlet-class>

 <init-param>
   <param-name>config</param-name>
   <param-value>/WEB-INF/classes/struts-config.xml</param-value>
 </init-param>
 <load-on-startup>2</load-on-startup>
</servlet>

<servlet-mapping>
 <servlet-name>action</servlet-name>    ❻
 <url-pattern>*.do</url-pattern>
</servlet-mapping>

<!-- Either version -->
<welcome-file-list>
 <welcome-file>index.html</welcome-file>
</welcome-file-list>
<web-app>
```

The S2 framework leverages a filter to intercept requests ❶ and the URL mapping is set to /* ❷. where the actual extensions are specified in the struts.properties file. This property is shipped to handle requests with the .action extension, but can be changed. S1 mappings ❺ ❻ are shown for unity. The listener ❸ fires up the Spring framework, which S2 uses to instantiate its objects. This listener expects the file application-Context.xml to exist in the WEB-INF folder even if it's empty. This file is shown in listing 14.4. The listener ❹ fires up the Tiles 2 framework, which S2 may interface with for common look and feel.

Listing 14.4   applicationContext.xml

```
<?xml version="1.0" encoding="UTF-8"?>
<!DOCTYPE beans PUBLIC
"-//SPRING//DTD BEAN//EN"
"http://www.springframework.org/dtd/spring-beans.dtd ">
 <beans>

 </beans>
```

Our S1 application is now capable of handling both S1 and S2 requests. The `*.do` requests will be handled by S1 and the `*.actions` by S2. We can now begin to add new S2 features and also migrate existing S1 artifacts to S2. Likewise, we may have action mappings in S1 that direct to S2 resources and vice versa. Infusing our existing S1 application with S2 capabilities is what we refer to as *merging technologies*. This allows us to systematically migrate S1 to S2 while immediately being allowed to share many resources between the two "sides" of the web application.

Next, we look at how the action mappings have changed.

14.2.2 *The action mappings*

One of the real advances in website design was the advent of symbolic mapping. This allowed us to modify website behavior without getting tangled up in the HTML. This declarative mapping has been the hallmark of S1 for years and has improved markedly in S2. Any seasoned S1 developer can tell you about the hours she's spent modifying struts-config.xml. This file is essentially a registry where the symbolic features of your website are matched with their concrete counterparts. Let's take a look at a typical S1 action mapping in listing 14.5.

Listing 14.5 Struts Classic action mapping

```
<struts-config>
  <form-beans>
    <form-bean name="reportForm" type="ReportForm"/>          ❶
  </form-beans>

  <action-mappings>
    <action
      path="/reportDateSelection"          ❷
      input="/reportDateSelection.page"          ❸
      name="reportForm"          ❹
      type="ReportDateSelection"          ❺
      scope="request">          ❻
        <forward name="success" path="reportByDate.page"/>
        <forward name="largeDateRange" path="reportWarning.page"/>          ❼
    </action>
  </action-mappings>
</struts-config>
```

It was easy to retire as a wealthy S1 developer if you were paid by the keystroke! As you can see, this single web feature was verbose and often led to a bloated struts-config.xml file. In order to capture the user inputs for this action, we first had to create a form bean ❶ that was separate from the action itself. This form bean was assigned a name and could be associated with many different actions. The type ReportDateSelection ❺ is the Struts action class associated with this mapping. The `path` attribute ❷ is where we specified the symbolic name of the web feature. In this case, we're prompting the user for a date range to be used in selecting data for a report. The `input` attribute ❸ is where we specify what page should be displayed if validation fails. The `name` attribute ❹ is what links this action to the form bean ❶, and the scope ❻ is where we specify where S1 should store the form bean. Lastly, the forward tags ❼ are where we specify the list of eligible targets from which the action may select.

A web request for someContext/reportDateSelection.do would invoke this S1 action mapping. S2 streamlines this mapping substantially by leveraging smart defaults and storing user inputs inside the action itself. Listing 14.6 shows what this action mapping looks like in Struts 2.

Listing 14.6   Struts 2 action mapping

```
<struts>
<package name="invoicing" namespace="/invoicing">        ❶

<action name="reportDateSelection" class="ReportDateSelection">    ❷
    <result name="input">reportDateSelection.page</result>
    <result name="largeDateRange">reportWarning.page</result>      ❸
    <result>reportByDate.page</result>
</action>

</package>
</struts>
```

The first thing to notice is the new package tag ❶ used in our mappings. This works in a way similar to packages in Java, where similar actions are grouped together in a common namespace. The web request someContext/invoicing/reportDateSelection.action would invoke this S2 action. Note how this allows us to use this same action name in another package namespace as in someContext/payables/reportDateSelection.action. The action mapping itself ❷ has been greatly simplified. First off, there's no form bean to mess with, as S2 encapsulates the user inputs inside the action itself. Lastly, the eligible targets or "next steps" resulting from this action are cleanly laid out in the form of result tags ❸. Note that the last result doesn't specify a name. This is because success is the default. Also, unlike the S1 ActionForward, results in S2 can actually help prepare the response.

We've now discussed how to infuse S2 capabilities into our S1 application and we've looked at S1 and S2 mappings side by side. Now we'll look at the steps to migrate S1 artifacts to S2.

14.2.3   *Where the action meets the form*

In S1, the user inputs were stored in a form bean that the framework passed into the action class. S2 combines the utility of the form within the action itself, thereby eliminating the form bean. So the first step in the migration is to modify the S1 action to accommodate the user inputs. This could be as simple as removing the S1 code from the form bean and including this POJO as a field inside the action class. Listings 14.7 and 14.8 show the before-and-after form beans.

Listing 14.7   Struts 1 action form

```
public class ReportForm extends ActionForm {        ◁───❶ Framework class

    private boolean average;
    private boolean totals;              ❷ Simple types
    private String fromDate;
    private String toDate;

    getters/setters...

}
```

This S1 form bean extends a framework class ❶ and is comprised largely of primitive data types ❷. Listing 14.8 shows the migrated S2 version of this bean, which is a simple POJO.

Listing 14.8   Struts 2 POJO

```
public class Report {      ◁─── POJO

    private boolean average;
    private boolean totals;         Actual data
    private Date fromDate;          types
    private Date toDate;

    getters/setters...

}
```

As you can see, this is a plain Java class with useful data types to contain user inputs. In listing 14.1, we looked at a typical S1 action class and saw that it expected a framework form bean. In listing 14.9, we peer into the S2 action class to see how the user data is made available.

Listing 14.9   Struts 2 action with model bean

```
public class ReportDateSelection extends ActionSupport{     ◁┐      Extends
    private Report model;           ◁─────────┐             └─❶ S2 class
                                          Web data
    public String execute(){          encapsulated
        // business logic here ...  ❷ in model bean
      return SUCCESS;
    }
    public Report getModel(){        ◁─────────┐
      return model;                            │  Accessors for
    }                                      ❸   ValueStack
    public void setModel(Report model){  ◁─────┘
      this.model = model;
    }
}
```

First, our S2 `ReportDateSelection` extends the S2 `ActionSupport` base class ❶. While it isn't necessary, it contains several handy behaviors and tokens that we would end up writing ourselves. In this case, we're only leveraging the SUCCESS token. Next, since action classes are no longer singletons, we can have an instance variable ❷ that is the model POJO that preserves the user input. Lastly, the `get/setModel()` ❸ behaviors are accessed by the framework to keep its internal `ValueStack` synchronized with user inputs.

Let's turn our attention to web pages and how we go about migrating them to S2. This is probably the most time-consuming part, as this is the dimension of a website that the user sees. Much care and concern goes into this layer of development to allow the system to be user-friendly. In the next section, we turn our S1 pages into their S2 counterparts.

14.2.4 *Turn the page*

In the previous section, we eliminated the S1 form bean and moved the user inputs into the action itself. Now that we've explained how Struts 2 has effectively eliminated the `ActionForm`, let's discuss the web pages and their custom tags that operate as the opposite end of this user data exchange. The first thing that changes is the tag library declaration. Rather than have several libraries, S2 has combined the tags into a single library. The next big difference is that S2 tags get and set objects on the `ValueStack` whereas S1 used a form bean. Lastly, the S2 tags do more than simply shuttle web page content; they assist in the presentation of the web page. This is a real time saver and results in web pages that are much more readable. The S1 custom tags helped separate the Java from the presentation code in your web pages. S2 custom tags not only eliminate Java from your web pages but also drastically reduce the HTML you're expected to write. Before we get into the nitty-gritty, take a look at the web page in figure 14.4. Admittedly, it isn't complex from the end-user's point of view, but designing a screen that's dynamically generated from static and dynamic portions can be a considerable challenge.

Listing 14.10 shows the source code behind this S1 web page. Note that much of this code has to do with positioning elements on the page and pulling language constants from internationalized resource bundles. Also, we placed the user messages next to each control that might fail validation.

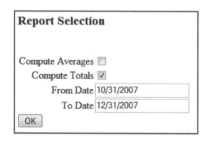

Figure 14.4   Report selection web page

Listing 14.10   Struts 1 web page

```
<%@taglib uri="/WEB-INF/struts-html.tld" prefix="html"%>
<%@taglib uri="/WEB-INF/struts-bean.tld" prefix="bean"%>
<H3> <bean:message key="promptTitle" /> </H3>
<BR>
<html:errors />
<html:form action="reportParameters">
<TABLE border="0" cellpadding="0">
<TBODY>
<tr>
```

```
<TD align="right">
<b><bean:message key="average" /></b>
</TD>
<TD>
<html:checkbox property="average"></html:checkbox>
</TD>
</tr>
<tr>
<TD align="right">
<b><bean:message key="totals" />
</b>
</TD>
<TD>
<html:checkbox property="totals"></html:checkbox>
</TD>
</tr>
<tr>
<TD align="right">
<b><bean:message key="fromDate" /></b>
</TD>
<TD>
<html:text property="fromDate"></html:text>
</TD>
<TD>
<html:errors property="fromDate" />
</TD>
</tr>
<tr>
<TD align="right">
<b><bean:message key="toDate" /></b>
</TD>
<TD>
<html:text property="toDate"></html:text>
</TD>
<TD>
<html:errors property="toDate" />
</TD>
</tr>
</TBODY>
</TABLE>
<html:submit property="submit">
<bean:message key="ok" />
</html:submit>
</html:form>
```

That's a bunch of code for such a compact web pagelet, and we haven't even discussed cascading style sheets. Listing 14.11 shows the source code for this same web page designed using S2 custom tags.

Listing 14.11   Struts 2 web page

```
<%@ taglib prefix="s" uri="/struts-tags"%>

<H3><s:label key="promptTitle" /></H3>

<s:form>
```

```
    <s:checkbox key="average" labelposition="left"/>
    <s:checkbox key="totals" labelposition="left"/>
    <s:textfield key="fromDate" />
    <s:textfield key="toDate"/>

    <s:submit key="ok" action="reportParameters" />
  </s:form>
```

What do you think about this? The same web page in S2 requires a fraction of the developer coding because the standard markup is generated by the tags. Actually, the markup is merely associated with the tags. S2 utilizes FreeMarker to generate the markup for the tags. In this case, the markup was HTML, but FreeMarker can generate any type of markup you like. Imagine being able to generate markup for HTML, WML, XSLT, and more, all from the same source. S2 has packaged these FreeMarker templates into themes to generate markup according to your preferred look and feel. Note that each tag contains a key property, which serves multiple roles. If you refer to listing 14.8, you'll find these keys are also the properties in our model object. What isn't as obvious is the fact that these keys are also located in our language Resource-Bundles, which is how the S2 tags retrieved the screen labels. These keys also become the DOM id and name properties for the page elements that are essential for validation and AJAX support.

14.2.5 *No speak English*

Chances are you have a rich set of localized messages that have been serving your S1 application. Since S1 and S2 both leverage the underlying Java i18n facilities, those same resources can also serve the S2 framework. In S1, we specified our resource files in the struts-config.xml with the following tag:

```
    <message-resources parameter="applicationResources" />
```

This existing ResourceBundle can be used in S2 by placing the following entry in your struts.properties configuration file:

```
    struts.custom.i18n.resources= applicationResources
```

This entry indicates that we have a ResourceBundle with the root name application-Resources and an alternate file named applicationResources_es.properties, where es is a standard locale code for Spanish. Both the ResourceBundle and the struts.properties file should be placed in the classes directory of a web application, so that they're accessible on the classpath. If you want to expand your migration to take full advantage of the flexibility S2 has to offer in this area, refer to section 14.1.4 for a review of the ways you can further break these message resources apart. Listing 14.12 reveals sample content for our reporting web page.

Listing 14.12   Localized language files

```
### applicationResources.properties
promptTitle=Report Selection
average=Compute Averages
```

```
totals=Compute Totals
type=Report Type
fromDate=From Date
toDate=To Date
ok=OK


### applicationResources_es.properties
promptTitle= Informe de selección
average= Promedios del cálculo
totals= Totales del cálculo
type= Tipo de informe
fromDate= A partir de fecha
toDate= Hasta la fecha
ok=OK
```

S1 action classes retrieved localized messages with

```
getResources(request).getMessage("promptTitle")
```

S2 is more succinct:

```
getText("promptTitle")
```

This is another contrast between S1 passing HTTP objects during method calls versus S2 dependency injection. The getText behavior in S2 can interrogate the request on its own. Lastly, you may recall that, in S1, if you asked for a message whose key couldn't be found in the resource file, you received a null in return. S2 will return the message key in this case, which indicates a missing message.

Now that we've discussed the changes in language support, let's turn our attention to validation. The language support we just looked at will play a big role in user messages as we construct meaningful dialog with the user interacting with our website.

14.2.6 *The data police*

How do your action classes handle invalid data entered by the user? We hope you never allow invalid data to make it into your action classes, at least not the kind that could be easily prevented. We now compare the S1 and S2 validation frameworks to see how they perform their traffic cop duties. These respective frameworks are layered between the web page and action class, and the validation rules for determining the data validity are configured independent of either one. In S1, the traffic cop was the Commons Validator, which leaned on the S1 ActionForm derivatives ValidatorForm and ValidatorActionForm. There was a great deal of stitching involved to get Commons Validator to cooperate with S1, and when one or the other API would evolve, you were back with a needle and thread to get it working again. In fact, as I was writing this chapter, my application started throwing heaps of stack trace data at the console that required a couple of hours to discover a mismatch in XML files. The funny thing is, while I was reading through the minutiae I had this vague reminiscence of researching the same problem a few years ago.

The validator engine in S2 is a core component of the framework that evolved from Open Symphony XWork. After working with it awhile, you'll discover how easily it performs all the tests the Commons Validator handled, even the complicated validations you once had to write Java code to authenticate. This section is intended to help you migrate your validations from S1 to S2. For a full tour guide of the S2 validation system, see chapter 10.

We compare the differences by validating the data keyed into the web page shown in figure 14.4. I'm assuming you already have Common Validator configured and plugged into S1, so we won't discuss that here. With S1, we added our rules to a validations.xml file as shown in listing 14.13.

Listing 14.13   Struts 1 validations.xml file

```
<?xml version="1.0" encoding="ISO-8859-1" ?>
<!DOCTYPE form-validation PUBLIC
"-//Apache Software Foundation//DTD Commons Validator Rules
Configuration 1.3.0//EN"
"http://jakarta.apache.org/commons/dtds/validator_1_3_0.dtd ">
<form-validation>                   ❶ Locale
  <formset>              ◁──────┘     section
                                          ❷ Sl form
                                             bean name          ❸ Validation
    <form name="S1ReportForm">      ◁────────────┘               rules to apply
      <field property="fromDate" depends="required,date">  ◁────────┘
        <arg0 key="fromDate"/>   ◁───────┐
      </field>                           ❹ Key from
                                           ResourceBundle       ❸ Validation
      <field property="toDate" depends="required,date">   ◁──────  rules to apply
        <arg0 key="toDate"/>   ◁────┐
      </field>                      ❹ Key from
    </form>                           ResourceBundle
  </formset>
</form-validation>
```

The `<formset>` ❶ tag defines a grouping of `<form>` ❷ tags according to a country and language code. The `<form>` ❸ section appeared many times in a typical S1 application, and each grouping addressed a particular form bean/web page scenario. As you can imagine, this file became large and was difficult to administer in a multiple-developers environment. The form bean property validity depends ❸ on the rules it's registered to pass. If a rule fails validity, the property name for this key ❹ is substituted into the respective error message that's displayed back to the web browser.

S2 takes a simpler approach to solving the validity problem. Rather than lump all the website validations in a single file, S2 allows you to manage the rules at the object level. This eases the burden of source file contention and allows you to focus on simpler units of work. There are many conventions you can use to achieve more or less granularity, and a common approach is the naming convention *{Action}*-validation.xml. However, if annotations are your deal, you can decorate your action classes instead of using the XML approach. In addition to base validation, S2 offers client-side validation with JavaScript and a new Ajax-based option. Let's take a look at the S2 validation for our report action shown in listing 14.9. The *{Action}*-validation.xml naming convention for this action yields ReportDateSelection-validation.xml, revealed in listing 14.14.

Listing 14.14   Struts 2 ReportDateSelection-validation.xml file

```
<!DOCTYPE validators PUBLIC
"-//OpenSymphony Group//XWork Validator 1.0.2//EN"
"http://www.opensymphony.com/xwork/xwork-validator-1.0.2.dtd">

<validators>
  <field name="model.fromDate">            ❶
    <field-validator type="required">           ❷
      <message key="required" />         ❸
    </field-validator>

    <field-validator type="date">       ❷
      <message key="date" />        ❸
    </field-validator>
  </field>
</validators>
```

The `<field>` ❶ tag defines a grouping of `<field-validator>` ❷ tags, each of which validates the field against specific rules. If a rule fails validity, the message key ❸ is constructed as the error message displayed in the web browser. The message in S2 can be constructed with variable data pulled directly from the `ValueStack` associated with this request. This allows you to build messages that make good sense to the user without having to jump through all the {0},{1},{2} hurdles to substitute dynamic bits into a message. If it's easy, chances are it'll get done. Please review the chapter on validation to get the big bang. This isn't just the Commons Validator warmed over!

This evening as I'm shopping the Web for better rates on HDTV service, I'm again reminded of how many Struts Classic applications are hosted on this planet. Most of the big players are using Struts Classic. As I gaze into those embedded .do web extensions, I start to think of ways I could offer you better returns on your S1 investments as you move to Struts 2. Before we wrap up, I want to discuss a plug-in that allows you to snap Struts Classic actions, forms, and validations into a Struts 2 application. I'm well aware that certain S1 artifacts are too "something" to refactor right away, so this might be a tool to allow you to continue receiving dividends on those works of art.

14.2.7   Can we just get along?

If you're a student of design patterns, chances are the open-closed principle is among your 10 commandments. Like any well-designed software, you should be able to extend the functionality without modifying existing code. Struts 2 leverages plug-ins for this very purpose. If you use Firefox or Eclipse, you already know how this works. When you need to use a feature that wasn't included in the "baseline," you install a plug-in that provides the capability you seek. Chapter 12 discussed plug-ins in detail, so here we simply discuss a plug-in that allows Struts Classic components to appear as if they were Struts 2 components. This plug-in is called struts2-struts1-plugin, appropriately enough, and to take advantage of it, you simply drop it in the WEB-INF/lib folder of your application and start using the new feature. This plug-in utilizes available S2 interceptors to adapt the request life cycle of an S1 action. Studying this will not only help you leverage your S1 actions, but may also reveal smarter design decisions.

All right, we know the action class was a singleton in S1 and that it interacted with a form bean in a scope you specified. S2 actions are thread-safe and have no concept of a form bean. So let's see how the S1 plug-in dresses up the old action/form pair to appear as an S2 action. If you aren't comfortable with interceptors, you might want to refer to the index for a refresher because you're about to see the interceptor magic performing a few tricks.

This plug-in creates a new S2 package called `struts1-default` that extends `struts-default`. The new `struts1-default` package includes new interceptors that are sandwiched into a default interceptor stack assembled to mimic the S1 request cycle logic. You simply create an S2 package that extends the `struts1-default` package and you're ready to roll. Listing 14.15 illustrates how we configure an S1 action to be executed in your S2 application.

Listing 14.15   Packaging Struts 1 actions in Struts 2 package

```xml
<?xml version="1.0" encoding="UTF-8" ?>
<!DOCTYPE struts PUBLIC
"-//Apache Software Foundation//DTD Struts Configuration 2.0//EN"
"http://struts.apache.org/dtds/struts-2.0.dtd">

<struts>

<package name="hybridActions"              ❶
       namespace="/old2new"                ❷
       extends="struts1-default">          ❸


<action name="enroll" class="org.apache.struts2.s1.Struts1Action" >     ❹
  <param name="className">com.strutsschool.s1.actions.EnrollAction</param>  ❺

  <interceptor-ref name="scopedModelDriven" >     ❻
    <param name="className">s1.webapp.forms.EnrollForm</param>     ❼
    <param name="name">enrollForm</param>     ❽
    <param name="scope">request</param>     ❾
  </interceptor-ref>

  <interceptor-ref name="struts1Stack"></interceptor-ref>     ❿

  <result name="success">enrollPage</result>
</action>

</package>
</struts>
```

The `<package>` ❶ is a typical configuration with a namespace ❷ and parent package to extend ❸. The action mapping is where things start to get interesting. The class you specify here is the S1 plug-in class ❹, and it expects a parameter ❺ which is the qualified name of the existing S1 action class. The next peculiar section is the configuration of the `scopedModelDriven` ❻ interceptor. This interceptor is an integral part of S2 and has a companion interface with the same name. The S1 class ❹ implements this interface so the parameters for `className` ❼, name ❽, and scope ❾ are where we specify our S1 action form. The last interceptor ❿ is actually defined in the S1 plug-in as the stack of interceptors that make the magic happen.

This plug-in also allows you other configurations according to what your S1 mapping looked like. For instance, you might not have used a form bean, or perhaps you were using the S1 Commons Validator. These use cases and more can be configured with the new plug-in.

14.3 Summary

This chapter has covered many practices that you can begin using to migrate S1 apps to S2. It shared a pragmatic approach to migrating your existing applications a piece at a time and wrapped up with a discussion about how the struts2-struts1-plugin allows you to bring your S1 artifacts into the S2 application without tampering with them at all. As you might imagine, this isn't exhaustive coverage of every migration technique possible, as that would be overwhelming. Regardless of the path you choose, this chapter will get you on your path to migration.

Advanced topics

This chapter covers

- Invoking messages
- Dealing with impatient users
- Working with CRUD operations
- Maintaining look and feel with Tiles

In the previous chapter, we discussed migration strategies for converting a Struts 1 website to Struts 2. We now discuss advanced topics that either didn't exist in Struts 1 or were cumbersome to implement. This is the feel-good chapter of the book, designed to assist both developers writing web pages and the infrastructure team tracking web hits and sizing machinery to handle the traffic. We show techniques to help keep users informed about why they're waiting and how much longer it's going to take. We also add a dash of Tiles pizzazz so you can change the look and feel of your entire site with a couple of keystrokes. Lastly, we look at ways to optimize your action mappings that take advantage of OGNL and the Value-Stack. Once you've completed this chapter, chances are you'll even look better!

15.1   Advanced action usage

By now you probably feel like you've seen every permutation of action mapping. It's true there are many ways to do things in Struts, and it was probably best that we waited until now to show these advanced features. Actions and their declarative mappings are at the heart of Struts 2, and it only makes sense that we should have freedom when it comes to wiring them together. Strap on your safety belt and let's look at the wild ways that we can optimize our action declarations.

15.1.1   Alternative method invocation

We've seen how you can easily write actions to respond to web requests and how your `execute()` method is called to begin the response processing. But suppose you have several closely-related web features. You wouldn't want to create a different action for each related feature, would you? Neither would we. Struts 2 offers support for wild-cards that allow you to have more than one method in your action class and have the correct method selected at request time. In addition to this mapping support, you can also specify the method that should be invoked as you configure the action mapping itself. Review the action mappings in listing 15.1.

> **Listing 15.1   Struts action mappings with method specified**

```
<action name="samples" class="Samples">        ┃  default execute()
  <result name="success">samplesPage</result>   ┃  method of Samples
</action>
                                                        ┃  head()
                                                        ┃  method of
                                                        ┃  Samples
<action name="samplesHead" method="head" class="Samples">  ◁──┘
  <result name="success">samplesPage</result>         ┃  tail()
</action>                                               ┃  method of
                                                        ┃  Samples
<action name="samplesTail" method="tail" class="Samples">  ◁──┘
  <result name="success">samplesPage</result>
</action>
```

Notice how we've specified the same action class for three distinct mappings. This is a straightforward way of specifying which method the framework should invoke without passing parameters that your `execute()` would have to turn around and switch on. Consider the following three requests:

1 http://www.strutsschool.com/samples/samples.action
2 http://www.strutsschool.com/samples/samplesHead.action
3 http://www.strutsschool.com/samples/samplesTail.action

Now look at the corresponding action class in listing 15.2. It contains the two methods, `head()` and `tail()`, that were specifically wired to action mappings `samplesHead` and `samplesTail` respectively. So what about the `execute()` method? When does it get called? The framework calls this method when you make request number one. It's the default method name that's expected to be there and doesn't need to be specifically mentioned in your action mapping.

Listing 15.2   Action class with multiple related methods

```
public class Samples {

  private String coinToss = "Not yet flipped";

  public String execute() {
    return SUCCESS;
  }

  public String head() {
    setCoinToss("Head");
    return SUCCESS;
  }

  public String tail() {
    setCoinToss("Tail");
    return SUCCESS;
  }

  public String getCoinToss() {
    return coinToss;
  }

}
```

As you can see, this makes it easy to use the same action in multiple action mappings. But do we really want so many action mappings at all? In the next section, we look at a powerful feature of Struts 2 called *dynamic method invocation*. This helps out by allowing us to remove the method name from the mapping altogether and simply pass the method name at runtime.

15.2   *Dynamic method invocation*

All right, the previous section described a declarative way to map web requests to methods in the same action. While this is useful in eliminating the need to create multiple related action classes and writing if/else spaghetti code in a single `execute()` method, this could get nuts if there were more than a couple of alternative methods in an action. Six related methods would require six action mappings, and you'd like to leave work today in time to take your friend out to dinner!

Dynamic method invocation takes the idea of alternative method selection to a higher level. Rather than code all the individual mappings yourself, we write a single mapping and turn the nitty-gritty details about which method to invoke over to the framework. After all, shouldn't the framework be doing the heavy lifting? In this section, we shift the Struts 2 declarative architecture into high gear.

15.2.1   *Wildcard method selection*

Let's take a look at a familiar requirement. We've been asked to design a new website feature that allows the user to maintain a coin collection. It's the same old routine: add, change, remove, list, print, yada-yada-yada...coins. In fact, didn't we write a new web feature last week that enabled the web users to add, change, remove, list, and print members? At this rate, your struts.xml action mappings are going to overflow the kernel.

As I started to write the code for the coins feature, déjà vu suggested I should stop what I was doing and take a step back. As I compared my coding last week to what I was about to write, the following pattern began to emerge. Table 15.1 identifies the methods that were common between these two web features.

Table 15.1   Recurring patterns found in `struts` mappings

Action method	Description	Next action method
add	Prepare web page for save	save
save	Commit INSERT	list
edit	Prepare web page for update	update
update	Commit UPDATE	list
destroy	Prepare web page for remove	remove
remove	Commit DELETE	list
show	Prepare web page for detail display	list
list	Prepare web page for list display	list
print	Prepare web page for print	list

I always try to factor out commonalities, and I never want to reinvent the wheel. I could see that specifying all these names in the struts.xml file was a bad habit from years gone by, so I decided to start searching the web to see how others had solved this problem with Struts 2. After looking at examples and sorting out their good and bad techniques, I ultimately crafted the approach that we explore over the next several pages. Since there are many moving parts, you need to study all the pieces to understand why any one puzzle piece works the way it does. This is the biggest problem in complex systems today; developers don't see the forest because they're too concentrated on a tree. Let's begin by looking at the action class for our coin collection feature in listing 15.3. Here we see an action class containing a common collection of behaviors found in many action classes, each of which differs only slightly.

Listing 15.3   The CoinAction class

```
public class CoinAction{          ❶
  public String show() {
    ...
    return SHOW;
  }
}
```

```
public String add() {
  ...
  return ADD;
}
public String edit() {
  ...
  return EDIT;
}
public String destroy() {
  ...
  return DESTROY;
}
public String list() {
  ...
  return LIST;
}
}
```

❷

❸

This action class is a simple POJO ❶. It contains a few methods, each of which returns a task-appropriate result. For instance, `add()` ❷ will prepare to add a page and return the resulting `add` to the Struts 2 framework. Likewise, the `destroy()` ❸ behavior will prepare to delete a page, where data is likely obtained for confirmation and the resulting `destroy` is returned to the framework.

In fact, this collection of standardized behaviors is so common that we extract them into their own class so similar actions can take advantage of the shared code. Now let's a look at the wildcard mappings for this action in listing 15.4. Note that it varies from the alternative method invocation in that it doesn't contain hard-coded methods to call in the action mapping declaration. Instead, it specifies the method to invoke as a substitution marker {1} that'll be interpreted at runtime by parsing the request URL. The asterisk at the end of the mapping name is where the method name is specified.

Listing 15.4   The CoinAction wildcard mapping

```
<action name="CoinAction_*" method="{1}" class="CoinAction">      ❶
  <result name="show">/pages/member/show.jsp</result>
  <result name="add">/pages/member/add.jsp</result>
  <result name="edit">/pages/member/edit.jsp</result>           ❷
  <result name="destroy">/pages/member/destroy.jsp</result>
  <result name="list">/pages/member/list.jsp</result>
</action>
```

This mapping is wired in such a way as to expect the desired method to immediately follow the underscored character ❶ on the request URL. This method name will be substituted in the `method="{1}"` attribute, as it's the first asterisk in the name. RESTful mappings might contain several such asterisks and their portions would be stripped from the URL and substituted into {1}, {2}, {3}, and so on. The resulting method execution will return the standard name `String` ❷, which Struts 2 matches on in order to present the appropriate web page.

Now that we've seen the `CoinAction` class and its declarative configuration, let's consider the following three web requests in terms of the wildcard substitution that results in the runtime requirements of the requests:

1   http://www.strutsschool.com/coins/*CoinAction_list*.action
2   http://www.strutsschool.com/coins/*CoinAction_add*.action
3   http://www.strutsschool.com/coins/*CoinAction_destroy*.action

These three requests would invoke the `list()`, `add()`, and `destroy()` methods respectively of the `CoinAction` class. This easily allows you to group your related behaviors together in a single action class, and also significantly reduces the required action mapping code.

One thing to be aware of is that the Struts 2 filter doesn't look for the best match; it looks for the first match. This means you have to make sure that less-specific wildcard mappings are coded after any more-specific mappings in your configuration. Struts 2 allows you to parameterize other elements of the action mapping, too. In the next section, we exploit an aspect of the mapping that allows us to determine in real-time what the next step should be in the workflow. I call this *dynamic workflow* for lack of a better name.

15.2.2 *Dynamic workflows*

In addition to the wildcard method selection that we studied in the previous section, Struts 2 also allows you to parameterize other aspects of your action mappings. This continues the theme of minimizing literal declarations in your configuration mappings. Any object on the OGNL `ValueStack` can be substituted into your declarative action mappings in real-time. Consider the requirement of dynamically figuring out the next step in workflow processing. Naturally, the next step can be a consequence of the previous step and the rules of the business. We can easily add a property to an action class to contain this "next step" instead of hard-coding all the use cases in an XML file. The magic is in the action mapping declaration and the way it retrieves the next step from the action at runtime. Say that certain advanced users are asking if you can turn off the "Are you sure?" pages included in your workflow. This requirement can be easily met with Struts 2 and is illustrated in listings 15.5 and 15.6.

Listing 15.5   More dynamic substitutions in our wildcard mapping

```
public class CoinAction{
  private String nextPage;          ◁──┐  Property to
                                        │  hold next step
  public String destroy() {
    if( user.dontConfirm() ){
    nextPage=LIST_PAGE;
    } else {
    nextPage=CONFIRM_PAGE;            Determine
    }                                 next step
    return REMOVE;
  }
}
```

```
public String getNextPage() {
  return nextPage;
} ...
```

**Method for action
mapping workflow**

Pay special attention to the getNextPage behavior in listing 15.5. The nextPage property is being determined based on user preferences, and the mapping in listing 15.6 is navigating the user accordingly.

Listing 15.6   More dynamic substitutions in our wildcard mapping

```
<action name="CoinAction_*" method="{1}" class="CoinAction">
  <result name="destroy">${nextPage}</result>
</action>
```

Now that we've seen how powerful the Struts 2 runtime can be, you should begin experimenting with ways to minimize the mappings in your declarative struts.xml file. If your file has hundreds of action mappings that look similar, chances are you could refactor them to take advantage of the Struts 2 runtime power by utilizing the wildcard-mapping support. In the next section, we discuss ways to prevent duplicate form submits, which happen when a web user becomes impatient and clicks the Submit button before the previous click finishes. We call this an impatient user.

15.3   *Using tokens to prevent duplicate form submits*

Users are an impatient lot. I've watched my mom load up a search screen and click the Go button three times in a matter of a few seconds. When I ask her what she's doing, she says "I must not have clicked in the middle of the button." Of course I love Mom to pieces, but when I hear this I'm convinced she's nuts! So how can we prevent my mom from killing the machinery in our server farm? The middleware is already reaching critical mass and the database server is glowing cherry-red. The last thing we need is transaction duplication. There are also times when processing a user request more than once could be a big mistake. Imagine a shopping cart checkout form. In this section, we take advantage of a Struts 2 feature that helps Mom with her impatience while easing the load on the server farm by allowing her first search to complete. We also discuss ways to prevent a form from being processed more than once.

15.3.1   *Using the <s:token/> form tag*

Suppose you're prompting the user to complete a banking transaction that involves a transfer of funds between her accounts. If she were allowed to accidentally submit the transfer more than once, she would likely be looking for a new bank. Struts 2 provides support for this conundrum by incorporating a custom tag in your web page and an interceptor to prevent duplicate requests. Struts 2 uses the following logic to make this work:

1 Prepare the web page with a unique token embedded as a hidden field.
2 Stash this unique token in the user session.
3 Return the page to user browser.

4 When the form is submitted, the two tokens are compared.

5 If the tokens do not match, `invalid.token` result is returned.

Now let's look at some code. This is illustrated in listing 15.7. The web page simply includes the `<s:/token/>` tag in the form that shouldn't be submitted more than once. The example is a coin toss and the request must be allowed to complete and never duplicate for a turn, or else it would be cheating.

Listing 15.7   Web page with token tag

```
<s:form>
  <s:token/>                           ← Token tag
    <s:textfield key="coinToss"/>
    <s:submit action="flipCoin"/>      ← Posts form to
</s:form>                                 the server
```

Now we'll look at the declaration that handles this request. This check is performed by combining the custom tag shown in listing 15.7 with the `tokenStack` interceptor stack. Remember, interceptors interrupt your action call so as to provide supporting behavior before your code is executed. It's precisely this stack of interceptors that checks to see whether the user has submitted a duplicate request. The mapping is found in listing 15.8. Once this technique is clear, we'll look at an alternative interceptor.

Listing 15.8   Declarative action mapping with token interceptor

```
<action name="flipCoin"  method="flipCoin" class="CoinAction">   tokenStack
  <interceptor-ref name="tokenStack"/>                       ← required
    <result name="success">samplesPage</result>
    <result name="invalid.token">duplicatePage</result>      ← Returned if
</action>                                                       duplicate submit
```

The `tokenStack` includes the `token` interceptor and is required for the duplicate checking to occur. The interceptor will return `invalid.token` when it determines the request was a duplicate. See Listing 15.9 for an example of this stack.

Listing 15.9   Interceptor stack for basic token support

```
<interceptor-stack name="myTokenStack">
  <interceptor-ref name="token"/>
  <interceptor-ref name="defaultStack"/>
</interceptor-stack>
```

The next interceptor we discuss is a more intelligent version of the `token` interceptor. It's called the `tokenSession` interceptor and it extends the `token` interceptor by adding sophisticated logic to the duplicate token-processing checks. Rather than return the `invalid.token` when it detects a duplicate request, it blocks the duplicate request and returns the result from the initial request. In this way, it's often called the "transparent" solution. The net effect is as though no duplicate submit were attempted. Listing 15.10 reveals the subtle difference in the interceptor stack configuration.

Listing 15.10 Interceptor stack for advanced token support

```
<interceptor-stack name="myTokenStack">
 <interceptor-ref name="tokenSession"/>
 <interceptor-ref name="defaultStack"/>
</interceptor-stack>
```

The Struts 2 support for eliminating duplicate transactions is powerful and easy to use. This support will protect your application against double-clicking and the pesky browser Back and Refresh buttons. In the next section, we discuss some finesse techniques to provide a finer level of configuration granularity. Perhaps you have methods in your class that you absolutely don't want the interceptors to intercept. We reveal how to make these exceptions known.

15.3.2 *Exceptions to the token interceptor rule*

The `token` and `tokenSession` interceptors we looked at in the previous section support an additional feature. In fact, this support we're about to discuss is available in many places across the framework. We know that interceptors and interceptor stacks can be applied to requests in Struts 2. We also know that wildcard support and the framework's flexibility allow us to have multiple methods in an action class. So now we're talking about the situation where interceptors might intercept different methods in your action class. But what if you need to specify methods that shouldn't be intercepted? This topic discusses how easily this is performed. If you have method(s) in your action mapping class that you *do not* want to be intercepted for participation in this token testing, you can exclude them from an include list (or include on an exclude list), so only those token-sensitive methods are included in the token interception. See listing 15.11.

Listing 15.11 Interceptor stack sensitive to method names to intercept

```
<interceptor-stack name="myTokenStack">
 <interceptor-ref name="tokenSession">
   <param name="includeMethods">save,proceed,whateverElse</param>
 </interceptor-ref>
 <interceptor-ref name="defaultStack"/>
</interceptor-stack>
```

This supported flexibility is provided by the `MethodFilterInterceptor`, which supports the notion of methods to include or exclude from an interceptor. Several interceptors allow you to specify methods to include or exclude according to your requirements. If you specify both `includeMethods` and `excludeMethods` parameters on your interceptor configuration and the same method name happens to appear in both lists, the method will be intercepted, which is to say included. The rules for this condition must be spelled out in advance, and include always trumps exclude. We saw in listing 15.11 one way to customize the configuration. Listing 15.12 reveals another technique.

Listing 15.12   Interceptor stack sensitive to method names to intercept

```
<interceptor-stack name="mySensitiveStack">          ❶
  <interceptor-ref name="myTokenStack">              ❷
    <param name="tokenSession.includeMethods">save</param>        ❸
    <param name="validation.excludeMethods">someMethod</param>    ❹
  </interceptor-ref>
</interceptor-stack>
```

The name we've chosen to give this stack of interceptors is mySensitiveStack ❶. If you look at listing 15.11, you'll see this custom stack is the defaultStack with the tokenSession ❷ added to the top. This interceptor will veto any attempt to process a request already received. The interesting thing to point out here is that we've chosen a few method names to include ❸ and yet another to exclude ❹. We can use include and/or exclude without lists.

Is Struts 2 flexible or what? Most questions about this new framework revolve around the best way to configure action mappings. As with any versatile framework, the right answer is usually "It depends!" You'll quickly discover which style has been adopted as a standard in your IT shop or for you personally. Now that you've seen the possible ways to architect the declarative mappings, maybe you'll be the one to make the decision for your company.

In the next section, we discuss a way to provide feedback to the impatient user. If a user has to wait much more than a couple of seconds for a response, statistics show that the user will make the request again. Perhaps he believes he didn't press the button hard enough or thinks this time it'll be faster. Admit it; you like it when a progress bar shows you why you're waiting and how much longer you're expected to wait before things complete. Let's see how to add this feature.

15.4   Displaying wait pages automatically

How long will your web users wait for a web page to be returned before they start clicking again? Do they not know you're running your best code back on the server or that some requests just take longer than others? Do they care? In this section, we provide a way for you to easily display a progress page that keeps your users informed about what's going on back on the server—while also ignoring their repeated clicks. The technique that Struts 2 uses is pretty clever and works well in the stateless HTTP world.

15.4.1   When users are impatient

Although the token and tokenSession interceptors can help prevent duplicate posts from being submitted and processed, the other common problem with web applications is users who click too frequently. Long-running pages are often resubmitted multiple times. The tokenSession interceptor can transparently address this issue, but sometimes having a simple Please Wait page while the action executes gives the user a better sense of confidence with your application. The execAndWait interceptor does that for you. We begin demonstrating this interceptor by looking at the action mapping in listing 15.13.

Listing 15.13   Declarative action mapping for long-running action

```
<action name="search" class="SearchAction">
  <interceptor-ref name="waitStack"/>
    <result name="success">resultsPage</result>
    <result name="wait">waitPage</result>
</action>
```

> Wait interceptor stack
> Result returned by interceptor

The interceptor stack definition is shown in listing 15.14. Note that the execAndWait interceptor is declared last. It's important that execAndWait be the last interceptor, because it stops the execution and no further interceptors will be called. In the thread created by the execAndWait interceptor, only the action is executed, so any interceptors after the execAndWait will never be run.

Listing 15.14   Interceptor stack for long-running action

```
<interceptor-stack name="waitStack">
  <interceptor-ref name="defaultStack" />
  <interceptor-ref name="execAndWait" />
</interceptor-stack>
```

The last part you need to configure is the page that's returned to the user while she waits for the action to complete. Listing 15.15 shows the waitPage returned by the search action. The most interesting element of the web page is the meta tag in the head section. This instructs the web browser to rerequest the URL that resulted in this wait page every two seconds. As long as the processing of the action is going on, the waitPage view is returned, which sets the browser timer to refresh again in two seconds. Eventually, the action finishes and a page refresh returns the result from the action by rendering the resultsPage in the browser.

Listing 15.15   waitPage to display during long-running action

```
<html>
  <head>
    <title>Please wait</title>
    <meta http-equiv="refresh" content="2;url=<s:url/>"/>
  </head>

  <body>
    Processing your request.  Please wait a moment...
  </body>
</html>
```

> Request same URL every 2 seconds
> Message displayed during wait

This rounds out tokens and wait pages. With a few lines of declaration, you can transform your website into a real jewel for the user and the server. The web pages keep users apprised of what's happening, and the fact that the original request finishes without all the duplicates coming in keeps the server running smoothly. In the next section, we change gears and discuss another powerful feature of Struts 2 that takes the pain out of creating your CRUD actions. The idea of augmenting a website to provide create, read, update, and delete behaviors is prevalent and deserves a streamlined facility to ease development. The next section discusses how Struts 2 allows you to easily add these capabilities.

15.5 *A single action for CRUD operations*

Let's first discuss what CRUD isn't. It's not that yucky code nobody wants, nor is it anything nasty at all. *CRUD* is an acronym that has come to mean create-read-update-delete and it typically has to do with persistent data stored someplace. For a new Struts 2 developer who's getting the hang of these Struts actions and their declarative mappings, it can be easy to get carried away with writing a mapping and action class for each type of request. Before you realize it, you have several hundred (or even thousand) mappings. So that you don't find yourself in this trap, we're going to explain a much better technique covered in the next several pages. This section discusses how easy it is to write beautiful code that's easily maintained without writing too many mappings.

15.5.1 *That CRUD*

Struts 2 provides several techniques for writing this sort of persistent storage update code. In the spirit of MVC, we won't be concerned about how the data is being stored or even where. Those responsibilities are outside the scope of Struts 2, and implementation details should be easily swapped out without regard for your Struts 2 code. Since this section involves several moving parts, let's first consider the players:

- Requests and parameters
- Action mapping and wildcards
- Action class and implemented interfaces
- Interceptor stack
- Custom tags and wildcards

This might be a great time to review table 15.1. We begin with a request to update a member. The request is invoked with a URL composed as follows: http://strutsschool.com/strutsschool/member/MemberAction_edit.action?id=11903950318411660

The anatomy of this URL is broken down in listing 15.16.

> **Listing 15.16 The anatomy of our wild URL**

```
http://strutsschool.com/strutsschool
.../member
.../MemberAction_edit.action
...?id=11903950318411660
```

The next thing to consider is how this request URL matches up with our declarative Struts 2 application. Listing 15.17 contains the declarations for this package. You'll recall that Struts 2 uses packages in a way similar to Java, allowing us to group related actions together within a single web application. This enables us to write as many list actions as we need without worrying about name collisions. So `strutsschool/members/list.action` can be easily identified as different from `strutsschool/companies/list.action`.

Listing 15.17   Package declaration

```
<package name="member" namespace="/member" extends="strutsSchool">

<default-interceptor-ref name="paramsPrepareParamsStack"/>

<action name="MemberAction_*" method="{1}"class="MemberAction">
  <result name="input">${destination}</result>
  <result name="success">${destination}</result>
  <result name="list">${destination}List</result>
</action>

</package>
```

The only thing that might appear a unusual here is the target destination ${destina-tion}. For now, just realize that our BaseAction class has a getDestination() method and Struts 2 is smart enough to call it using OGNL. The action mapping expects a runt-ime method to be specified, so Struts 2 extracts edit from the request URL and that's the method called on the action. But before looking at the action class, let's briefly dis-cuss interceptors again. Interceptors are invoked before your action class code is even considered. They're also invoked again in reverse order following your action's code execution. Our action class implements interfaces that'll be more easily understood if we first consider their related interceptors. In the next section, we describe the rela-tionship between the interceptors we use and their related interfaces.

15.5.2 *Interceptors and interfaces*

As we've mentioned many times in this book, interceptors are the heartbeat of Struts 2, and they determine workflow and even how much work should flow into a request. One of the essential interceptors is the params interceptor, which has the responsibility of grafting request parameters onto JavaBeans. Another interceptor we'll incorporate into our CRUD action is the prepare interceptor. Combining these interceptors in a clever way makes our code simpler and easy to understand. Lastly, we add the modelDriven interceptor to streamline our web page code that's responsible for reading and writing the model properties.

Struts 2 includes many interceptors and interceptor stacks that are predefined arrangements of interceptors. Our specified default paramsPrepareParamsStack is one such built-in interceptor stack. This stack allows our Preparable and ModelDriven action class implementations to do their magic. As the name paramsPrepare-ParamsStack suggests, the params interceptor is invoked at two strategic points in the interceptor stack workflow. Sandwiched in between these two params interceptors are the prepare and modelDriven interceptors. Let's look at listing 15.18 to see what behav-iors our two interfaces provide.

Listing 15.18   `Preparable` and `ModelDriven` roles

```
public interface Preparable {                    prepare
  void prepare() throws Exception;        ⤴     interceptor
}
```

```
public interface ModelDriven<T> {          modelDriven
  T getModel();                   ◄————┘   interceptor
}
```

Is this making sense so far? If not, you might want to back up and read from section 15.1.4 again. It is straightforward once you see it, but it took me several tries to get it all squared away. If you're doing okay, I believe it's time to look at our action class. This is where everything comes together. I view the action class as the hub in a spoked wheel. It interacts with the framework and is interacting with nonframework objects. Web page custom tags and back-end persistence objects are a couple that immediately come to mind. Listing 15.19 contains our action class.

Listing 15.19   The CRUD action class

```
package com.strutsschool.action;

import…

public class MemberAction extends BaseAction        Base class is
    implements ModelDriven,Preparable{              BaseAction

  private Member model;     ◄——— This is model of MVC

  public Member getModel() {   ◄──┐
    return model;                  ModelDriven
  }                                behavior
  public void prepare() throws Exception {   ◄──┐
    if (getRequestId()==0) {                     Preparable
      model = new Member();                      behavior
    } else {
      model = (Member) db.get(getRequestId());
    }
  }
}
```

Now this is what a Java class should look like! This code is simple, yet it does everything we need it to do. Part of what makes it so clean is the fact that we've factored out the common CRUD stuff into a base class, `BaseAction`. This base class has code that's leveraged polymorphically to support any action class needing to provide CRUD capabilities. There are also a few properties in this base class that coordinate with custom tags on the web pages via OGNL so we can minimize hard-coding in the HTML. As you recall from the chapter 4 discussion on workflow with interceptors, we sometimes need to "disengage" the validation interceptor from intervening during method execution. We showed you how to specify the `excludeMethods` parameter on your interceptor mapping as one way of switching this feature off. The CRUD technique takes a different approach to meeting the needs with annotations. You'll find the `@SkipValidation` annotation specified for those action methods that shouldn't be validated. This technique is functionally equivalent to specifying the methods in a comma-delimited string and passing it to the `excludeMethods` parameter. You can use the `excludesMethods` parameter to tell the `workflow` interceptor to ignore any validation problems on a per-method basis, or you can use annotations to mark the methods that should be excluded. We're going to use the annotations here.

We'll show you the code now and then discuss how a request flows through all the parts. Listing 15.20 reveals our BaseAction.

Listing 15.20   The Super class

```
package com.strutsschool.action;

public abstract class BaseAction extends ActionSupport {

  protected DB db;                                                    ← Injected persistence engine
  protected static Log log = LogFactory.getLog(BaseAction.class);
  private long requestId;                                             ← Unique request ID
  private boolean readOnly=false;           Used in concert with
  private String mappedRequest;             screen tags and mappings

  @SkipValidation
  public String show() {                    ←
    setReadOnly(true);
    setMappedRequest(Constants.LIST);
    return SUCCESS;
  }

  @SkipValidation
  public String add() {                     ←
    setMappedRequest(Constants.SAVE);
    return SUCCESS;
  }

  public String save() { // insert                    Web features
    db.save(getModel());                            accessed via URLs
    return list();
  }

  @SkipValidation
  public String edit() {                    ←
    setMappedRequest(Constants.UPDATE);
    return SUCCESS;
  }

  public String update() {// update
    db.save(getModel());
    return list();
  }

  @SkipValidation
  public String destroy() {                 ←
    setReadOnly(true);
    setMappedRequest(Constants.REMOVE);
    return Constants.SUCCESS;
  }

  public String remove() {// delete
    db.remove(getModel());
    return list();
  }

  @SkipValidation
  public String list() {                    ←
```

```
  // code to fetch list objects is in Tiles Controller
  setMappedRequest(Constants.LIST);
  return Constants.LIST;
}

public String getActionClass() {
  return getClass().getSimpleName();
}

public String getDestination() {
  return getClass().getSimpleName();
}

public String getActionMethod() {
  return mappedRequest;
}

// when invalid, the request parameter will restore command action
public void setActionMethod(String method) {
  this.mappedRequest = method;
}

// this prepares command for button on initial screen write
public void setMappedRequest(String actionMethod) {
  this.mappedRequest = getActionClass() + "_" + actionMethod;
  log.debug("setting mappedRequest to " + getActionClass() + "_"
  + actionMethod);
}

public void setReadOnly(boolean readOnly) {
  this.readOnly = readOnly;
  log.debug("setting readOnly to " + readOnly);
}

public long getRequestId() {
  return requestId;
}

public void setRequestId(long requestId) {
  this.requestId = requestId;
}


public void setDb(DB db) {
  this.db = db;
}

public boolean isReadOnly() {
  return readOnly;
}

public abstract Object getModel();
}
```

ModelDriven behavior

Unique request ID

Injected persistence engine

Used in concert with screen tags and mappings

Once you write a base class like this, it never needs to be tampered with. The illustration is here so you can see an example of how our CRUD stuff hooks together. The main thing to identify is that the getModel() method is abstract and therefore requires your specific CRUD actions to implement their behavior of this method. The real heavy lifting to read and write objects is encapsulated in this base class, and your subclasses get the richness for free. We're injecting the DB abstraction into this base class with Spring, so the underlying data store is independent of the web code. We should mention that the implementation we're writing uses the slick object database, DB4o.

The last element to consider before we step back and see how everything interoperates is the web pages. We've written just two pages to support all the CRUD. The first page is our membership listing and the other is the detail page. Figure 15.1 shows our list page.

ID	User Name	Email	Password	Created	Actions
1190076032294554000	stanlick	stanlick@gmail.com	fred	9/17/2007	Show Edit Destroy
1190413445659499000	barney	barney@bedrock.com	bambam	9/21/2007	Show Edit Destroy
1190413556786542000	fredFlintstone	betty@bedrock.edu	betty	9/21/2007	Show Edit Destroy
New					

© 2007 strutsschool.com

Figure 15.1   CRUD list page

This web page includes a dynamic table of rows from a persistent store and hyperlinks to do the CRUD. Let's suppose we clicked the hyperlink to edit fred-Flintstone. Figure 15.2 shows the detail page that would be presented.

Now let's change Fred's email address and click OK. Figure 15.3 returns us to the list page and the updated email for Fred is displayed.

Figure 15.2   CRUD detail page

These web pages were constructed using the Struts 2 custom tags so the interoperability with the action class and model is nearly automatic. We name the web fields and model properties the same, and the mapping between the two is performed by Struts 2. Listings 15.21 and 15.22 contain the model and detail pages respectively.

ID	User Name	Email	Password	Created	Actions
1190076032294554000	stanlick	stanlick@gmail.com	fred	9/17/2007	Show Edit Destroy
1190413445659499000	barney	barney@bedrock.com	bambam	9/21/2007	Show Edit Destroy
1190413556786542000	fredFlintstone	betty@strutsschool.com	betty	9/21/2007	Show Edit Destroy
New					

© 2007 strutsschool.com

Figure 15.3   CRUD list page after edit

Listing 15.21   The model

```
package com.strutsschool.beans;

public class Member {

  private long id = System.nanoTime();
  private Date created = new Date();
  private String email;
  private String userName;
  private String password;
  private String confirmPassword;
  ... get/set methods not shown

}
```

This Member bean is a simple POJO, and probably looks like one of the first Java classes you wrote when you were learning Java. Struts 2 follows the K.I.S.S. principle—we like to interpret the acronym to mean Keep It Simple, Strutter! These properties are made visible via Struts 2 custom web page tags, as we see in listing 15.22. Keep in mind that this POJO can have complex property types, and the powerful type conversion engine will easily convert between the web page string types and their corresponding types in the POJO. Of course, it converts in the opposite direction as well.

Listing 15.22   The web page

```
<%@ taglib prefix="s" uri="/struts-tags"%>      <——  Struts 2 tag library
<s:form>
  <s:hidden key="id" />                                      Retained for
  <s:hidden key="actionMethod" value="%{actionMethod}"/>  <┘ validation errors

  <s:textfield key="userName" readonly="%{readOnly}" />       readOnly set
  <s:textfield key="password" readonly="%{readOnly}" />       accordingly in
  <s:textfield key="confirmPassword" readonly="%{readOnly}" />  BaseAction
  <s:textfield key="email" readonly="%{readOnly}"/>

  <s:submit action="%{actionMethod}" key="label.ok"/>   <┐
</s:form>                                                    │ actionMethod
                                                            │ set accordingly
                                                            │ in BaseAction
```

Now we've looked at all the puzzle pieces and should be able to identify the parts and their function in the framework. In the next section, we put the puzzle together by following a web request from the browser through Struts 2 and finally back to the browser.

15.5.3   Connecting the parts

At this point, we need to stitch the parts together in our mind. My college professors called this "desk checking" the system, where I was expected to explain how and why things should work before asking for help. If we're not clear about how Struts 2 works, we aren't going to be clear about our expectations. Let's take the request URL that returned the list shown in figure 15.1 and follow it through the framework. This explains how Struts 2 works and may save you many hours of debugging. This might be a good time to run and get something to drink. In fact, we'll wait for you to return before we start the journey of a Struts 2 request. Wow, that was fast! All right, here we go:

1   Struts filter dispatcher receives the request and processes it: http://strutsschool. com//member/MemberAction_list.action.

2   A mapping (see listing 15.17) is found and the list() method is called on the action.

3   Members are retrieved and list is returned from the method.

4   Struts makes a move to the ${destination} that's determined by the base class.

5   The browser is loaded up with the list.

6   The user clicks an edit link to modify a member.

7   Struts filter dispatcher receives the request and processes it: http://strutsschool. com/member/MemberAction_edit.action?id=1190413556786542000.

8   A mapping (see listing 15.17) is found and the edit() method will be called on the action.

9   Any parameters received are set on the action and its beans. In this case. we know id was passed.

10 The prepare() method is called on the action, and if you look back you'll see that it either creates a new member or requests the existing member from the permanent store. In our case, it requests the existing member.

11 The parameter assignment is repeated as in step 9.

12 The edit() method is called on the action.

13 The mappedRequest (form action) is determined and success is returned from the method.

14 The detail page is dynamically built by accessing the getModel() on your action.

15 The browser is loaded up with the detail page.

16 User makes changes and clicks the OK button.

17 Struts filter dispatcher receives the request and processes it: http://strutsschool. com/member/MemberAction_update.action.

18 This is a form submit, so many web controls are passed along with request.

19 A mapping (see listing 15.17) is found and the update() method will be called on the action.

20 Any parameters received are set on the action and its beans. In this case, we know id was passed.

21 The prepare() method is called on the action, and if you look back, you'll see that it either creates a new member or requests the existing member from the permanent store. In our case, it requests the existing member.

22 The parameter assignment is repeated as in step 20.

23 The update() method is called on the action and list is returned from the method.

24 Struts makes a move to the ${destination} that the base class determined.

25 The browser is loaded up with the list with changes revealed.

It can't be overemphasized how important the interceptor stack is to Struts 2. With respect to processing a request, the interceptor stack determines what steps are executed and in what order. In fact, if we don't use the appropriate interceptors, it won't matter which interface our action classes implement, because unless the interceptor is included in the stack, the action class method(s) won't be called anyway.

Before we wrap up the chapter, let's talk about the look and feel of our website. You might've noticed in this section that we weren't specifying what the physical web page names were for the list and detail pages. This is because we've been utilizing Tiles the entire time, so UI concepts such as page arrangement and file names have been largely excluded from our discussion. In the next section, we demystify how to add the advanced features of Tiles to your website.

15.6 Tiles and Struts 2

Struts 2 and its declarative architecture allow you to develop web pages by specifying only symbolic links and actions instead of literal path names. This has enabled companies to easily upgrade and evolve their websites to meet architectural changes. However, Struts 2 does little to assist UI developers with page layout or site look and feel. This is where Tiles saves the day. Tiles and Struts have been companions for years, and Tiles has now emerged as Tiles 2, a Struts 2 plug-in. Without a disciplined approach to your website presentation, the user may become confused and lose confidence in your site. Maintaining a standard web appearance can be easy when you combine Tiles 2 with Struts 2. If you break out in a cold sweat when the marketing department asks you to change the website appearance, reading the following section might reduce your antiperspirant budget.

15.6.1 Taking care of the website look and feel

From 100 yards away, you can tell the difference between the layout of a professional website and one that was built without a plan. Every mouse click on a poorly designed site has you wondering if you have entered a different site! Consistent look and feel is considered the mark of a professional application, so how do many software developers maintain hundreds of web pages without deviating from the preferred layout? The next few sections describe how Tiles 2 allows you to sketch out your look and feel independent of the pages to be presented. In fact, since the layout is separate from the web pages, you can switch out the look and feel of your entire website in a few keystrokes. Figure 15.4 illustrates a typical website layout.

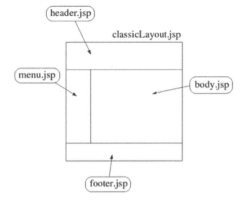

Figure 15.4   Classic layout

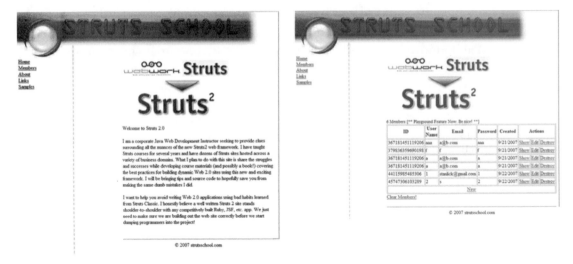

Figure 15.5   Example pages using Tiles layout

As you can see, the layout is not the content, but rather a placeholder for the content. A webpage in Tiles is actually made up of many small tiles that your miniature pages occupy. An individual tile can be further subdivided into tile regions, and on and on. Figure 15.5 shows a couple of pages that take advantage of this type of design.

As you can see, the pages share the same look and feel, and differ only by their body content. If we wanted to move the menu to the top and have it appear horizontally, this would be a change we could make in a single place that would affect the entire site. In the next section, we configure the interplay between Struts 2 and Tiles.

15.6.2   Configuring the interplay

In the previous section, we discussed the importance of a consistent website appearance overall and the need to be able to easily change the overall look and feel. In this section, we make it a reality. Figure 15.4 illustrated a typical layout; the Tiles declaration for this layout can be found in listing 15.23.

Listing 15.23   Tiles definitions

```
<tiles-definitions>
                                                    Base definition
 <definition name="baseLayout" template="/layouts/base.jsp">
  <put-attribute name="title" value="Struts School"/>
  <put-attribute name="bodyBackground" value="images/background.jpg"/>
  <put-attribute name="logo" value="images/logo.jpg" />
  <put-attribute name="menu" value="/tiles/menu.jsp" />
  <put-attribute name="body" value="/tiles/body.jsp" />
  <put-attribute name="footer" value="/tiles/footer.jsp" />
 </definition>

additional definitions here...

</tiles-definitions>
```

The name property of the put-attribute tag defines a tile region. Note that this definition has a few more regions than the classic illustration. Again, there's no limit to what you can do with these layouts. In listing 15.24, we explore file base.jsp, which determines the overall look and feel for the website.

Listing 15.24   Overall look and feel page

```
<%@ taglib uri="http://tiles.apache.org/tags-tiles" prefix="tiles"%>
<html>
<head>
<!---------------------- title zone ---------------->          ❶ title tile
<title><tiles:insertAttribute name="title" /></title>   ◁──┘      region
<!------------------------------------------------->
<link rel=stylesheet type="text/css" href="style/style.css">
</head>
<!---------------------- bodyBackground zone ---------------------->
<body bottommargin="0" leftmargin="0" marginheight="0" marginwidth="0"
rightmargin="0" topmargin="0"
background=<tiles:insertAttribute name="bodyBackground"/>>    ◁──
<!------------------------------------------------------------------->
<table width="780" height="143" cellpadding="0" cellspacing="0"
border="0">                                        bodyBackground
<tr valign="top">                                        tile region  ❷
<td width="780">
<!---------------------- Logo zone -------------------->
<img src="<tiles:insertAttribute name="logo"/>" width="780"    ◁──
height="143" border="0" alt="">
<!-------------------------------------------------------->
</td>
</tr>                                               logo tile region  ❸
</table>
<table width="100%" cellpadding="0" cellspacing="0" border="0">
<tr valign="top">
<td width="175">
<table width="175" cellpadding="4" cellspacing="0" border="0">
<tr valign="top">
<td width="175">
<!---------------------- Menu zone ->         ❹ menu tile
<tiles:insertAttribute name="menu" />    ◁──     region
<!--------------------------------
</td>
</tr>
</table>
</td>
<td width="510">
<table width="510" cellpadding="5" cellspacing="5" border="0">
<tr valign="top">
<td width="510">
<!---------------------- Body zone ->         ❺ body tile
<tiles:insertAttribute name="body" />    ◁──┘    region
<!-------------------------------->
</td>
</tr>
<tr valign="top">
```

```
<td width="510">
<!---------------------- Footer zone ->
<tiles:insertAttribute name="footer" />
<!------------------------------------->
</td>
</tr>
</table>
</td>
</tr>
</table>
</body>
</html>
```

6 footer tile region

This is the HTML for one of our overall layouts. You can see several places where we've included the `tiles:insertAttribute` tags. In **1**, we're going to insert the title from the particular Tiles page definition to be displayed. This keeps the title of the window in sync with the current request. A more interesting tile is the body **5**. This is the region that typically changes the most from page to page, and is often the center of the web page. Tiles **2**, **3**, **4**, and **6** are the other regions we chose when laying out this look and feel.

This page merely specifies what content will be presented and where it's to appear on the page. The Tiles magic happens where a `tiles:insertAttribute` in the layout page is matched up with the `put-attribute` from the tiles definition. In effect, the pages specified on the `put-attribute` are inserted into their respective tiles regions on the site layout master page. But we haven't discussed the coolest part yet. The definition in listing 15.23 is named `baseLayout` and it defines the overall look and feel. What about the two pages we looked at in figure 15.5? What did their definitions look like? For the sake of explanation, listing 15.25 includes the definitions for these two pages along with a repeat of the `baseLayout`.

Listing 15.25 Overall look and feel page

```
<tiles-definitions>                                              Base definition
  <definition name="baseLayout" template="/layouts/base.jsp">
   <put-attribute name="title" value="Struts School"/>
   <put-attribute name="bodyBackground" value="images/background.jpg"/>
   <put-attribute name="logo" value="images/logo.jpg" />
   <put-attribute name="menu" value="/tiles/menu.jsp" />
   <put-attribute name="body" value="/tiles/body.jsp" />
   <put-attribute name="footer" value="/tiles/footer.jsp" />
  </definition>
                                                         Home page
                                                         definition
  <definition name="HomePage" extends="baseLayout">
   <put-attribute name="body" value="/tiles/home/homeBody.jsp" />
  </definition>
                                                       Members list
                                                       definition
  <definition name="MemberActionList" extends="baseLayout"
      preparer="ListMembers">
   <put-attribute name="body" value="/tiles/member/membersBody.jsp" />
  </definition>
</tiles-definitions>
```

Note how these two definitions extend `baseLayout` and override only the tiles for which they provide unique content. Whatever regions (or tiles) they don't override will contain the content provided by the parent `baseLayout`. Is this awesome? You might be wondering what the preparer is for on the `MemberActionList` definition, and it's wonderful that you noticed. This is a Tiles controller and will be fully explained in section 15.6.4. It's now time to snap Tiles into the Struts 2 application and make things roar.

15.6.3 *Using the declarative architecture*

Struts 2 was designed with the notion of plug-ins, like Eclipse or Firefox. Plug-ins can override and extend the base Struts 2 architecture to provide custom and unique functionality. There are already many plug-ins written for Struts 2, and a new one will probably appear on the scene by the time we finish this chapter. Tiles is also a plug-in, and we'll describe how to introduce this extension to the framework now. A Struts 2 plug-in is a single JAR that contains classes and configuration code that extends, replaces, or adds to existing Struts framework behavior. A plug-in can be installed by adding the JAR file to the application's classpath. To configure the plug-in, the JAR should contain a struts-plugin.xml file, which follows the same format as an ordinary struts.xml file. The struts-plugin.xml file has the ability to

- Define new packages with results, interceptors, and/or actions
- Override framework constants
- Introduce new extension point implementation classes

The framework loads its default configuration first, then any plug-in configuration files found in other JARs on the classpath, and finally the bootstrap struts.xml:

1 struts-default.xml from struts core jar
2 struts-plugin.xml from each jar on classpath
3 struts.xml provided by your application

Now that we've discussed the basics of plug-ins, we add the Tiles plug-in to our web application classpath. As of this writing, several common plug-ins are included in the Struts 2 download, and Tiles is one. To plug Tiles into our Struts 2 application, we had to add struts2-tiles-plugin-2.0.9.jar and also the tiles API, core, and JSP JAR files to our classpath. Our hunch is that this'll be fixed in the next release of Struts 2, since the only JAR that's supposed to be added is struts2-tiles-plugin-2.0.9.jar. The next thing we do is add the required entries to our web.xml file. These entries are identified in listing 15.26.

Listing 15.26   Required additions to web.xml file

```
<context-param>
  <param-name>
    org.apache.tiles.impl.BasicTilesContainer.DEFINITIONS_CONFIG
  </param-name>
```

```
  <param-value>/tiles/tiles.xml</param-value>          ◁──┐  Tiles
</context-param>                                              definitions files

<listener>
  <listener-class>
    org.apache.tiles.web.startup.TilesListener      ◁──── Tiles listener
  </listener-class>
</listener>
```

The first thing to consider is the struts-plugin.xml file from the struts2-tiles-plugin-2.0.9. jar. Remember, this file is what adds the atypical behavior to the Struts 2 framework. Listing 15.27 contains this content.

Listing 15.27   struts-plugin.xml file

```
<struts>
  <package name="tiles-default" extends="struts-default">
  <result-types>                                              Plug-in adds a
    <result-type name="tiles"                      ◁───────┘  new result type
      class="org.apache.struts2.views.tiles.TilesResult"/>
  </result-types>
  </package>
</struts>
```

This new result type is what we add to our action mappings to arrange for Tiles to process our response and return those wonderfully consistent Tiles web pages. Listing 15.28 shows our application struts.xml file. Note how we've set `tiles` as the default result type.

Listing 15.28   struts.xml file

```
<struts>
 <package name="strutsSchool" extends="tiles-default">
  <result-types>
  <result-type name="tiles"
  class="org.apache.struts2.views.tiles.TilesResult"default="true"/>
  </result-types>
 </package>
                                                          tiles is default
                                                          result type
<include file="home.xml"/>
<include file="member.xml"/>
<include file="about.xml"/>
<include file="links.xml"/>
<include file="samples.xml"/>
</struts>
```

Listing 15.29 shows the action mappings for our tiles pages shown in figure 15.5.

Listing 15.29   Action mappings

```
<action name="home" class="com.strutsschool.action.Home">
  <result name="success">HomePage</result>      ◁──┐  Match HomePage
</action>                                              with listing 15.25

<action name="MemberAction_*" method="{1}"
    class="com.strutsschool.action.MemberAction">
```

```
<result name="input">MemberAction</result>
<result name="success">MemberAction </result>
<result name="list">MemberActionList</result>
</action>
```

Match MemberActionList with listing 15.25

If you look for these target names in listing 15.25, you'll see the only difference between the home page and member listing is the body content. The last thing we discuss is how the members were retrieved. You might recall from section 15.6.2 that we promised to explain the Tiles controller. The time has come to wrap up our journey of Tiles by talking about Tiles controllers. If you've used Tiles only to manage website look and feel, you might be surprised to know Tiles also assists you in fetching the data to be displayed. The next section shows you a slick way to fetch data just in time using Tiles controllers.

15.6.4 Preparing web page content with a tiles controller

When the request was made to display the members listing, Struts 2 received the following request: http://strutsschool.com//member/MemberAction_list.action.

If we follow this through the action mapping in listing 15.29, we determine the Tiles page MemberActionList is returned to the browser. Actually, Struts 2 refers to the MemberActionList Tiles definition in listing 15.25 to determine what pages to assemble. In addition to pages specified, we've also registered a Tiles *preparer* for this definition. This preparer is a Tiles controller that we can write to do prework before the tiles pages are assembled. The ListMembers class that we specified retrieves the members that are contained in membersBody.jsp The code for this controller can be found in listing 15.30.

Listing 15.30   Tiles controller (preparer)

```
public class ListMembers extends BaseController {

  public void execute(TilesRequestContext tilesContext,
            AttributeContext attributeContext) {
    tilesContext.getRequestScope().put("list", getMembers());
  }
}
```
Get member list and store in scope

Note how this list is consumed by the web page in listing 15.31.

Listing 15.31   membersBody snippet

```
<s:iterator value="#request.list">
  <tr>
    <td>
      <s:property value="id" />
    </td>
    <td>
      <s:property value="userName" />
    </td>
    <td>
      <s:property value="email" />
    </td>
```
Members list populated in Tiles controller

```
<td>
  <s:property value="password" />
</td>
<td>
  <s:date name="created" format="M/d/yyyy" />
</td>
<td>
  <s:url id="url" action="%{actionClass}_show">
  <s:param name="requestId" value="id"/>
  </s:url>
  <s:a href="%{url}">Show</s:a>
</td>
<td>
  <s:url id="url" action="%{actionClass}_edit">
  <s:param name="requestId" value="id"/>
  </s:url>
  <s:a href="%{url}">Edit</s:a>
</td>
<td>
  <s:url id="url" action="%{actionClass}_destroy">
  <s:param name="requestId" value="id"/>
  </s:url>
  <s:a href="%{url}">Destroy</s:a>
</td>
</tr>
</s:iterator>
```

This ties all the parts together. We hope this has answered every question you had about Tiles and Struts 2. There's nothing we didn't cover in this chapter as it relates to this plug-in. We encourage you to strongly consider this plug-in before you determine that your pages are inconsistent and you're knee-deep in alligators. This chapter can get your project look and feel tuned up before it gets hectic.

15.7 *Summary*

This chapter should have prepared you to make your website easy to maintain and easy to use. Our action mappings now incorporate the wildcard feature, and we saw a great demonstration of factoring all the common CRUD code into a base class. We've worked through issues where impatient users click too much by blocking the clicks and showing them progress pages. We wrapped up by looking at how to add the Tiles plug-in to Struts 2 so we can easily present a standard UI while modifying the look and feel as often as we like. If your copy of the book is like ours, this is the chapter with all the sticky notes marking topics. The techniques leverage the power of Struts 2 and often take a few reviews to master. All together, this book should have you prepared to build a world class Struts 2 website.

index